Financing Health Care

Edited by
Mingshan Lu and Egon Jonsson

Related Titles

D.D. Pointer, S.J. Williams, S.L. Isaacs,
J.R. Knickman

**Wiley Pathways Introduction
to US Healthcare System**

2006
ISBN 978-0-471-79075-4

D.N. Lombardi, J.R. Schermerhorn, B.E.
Kramer

**Wiley Pathways Healthcare
Management**

2006
ISBN 978-0-471-79078-5

X.S. Lin, Society of Actuaries

**Introductory Stochastic Analysis
for Finance and Insurance**

2006
ISBN 978-0-471-71642-6

T.E. Getzen

**Health Economics Fundamentals
and Flow of Funds**
International Edition

2003
ISBN 978-0-471-45176-1

A. Scott

Advances in Health Economics

2003
ISBN 978-0-470-84883-8

A.M. Jones, O. O'Donnell (Eds.)

**Econometric Analysis of Health
Data**

2002
ISBN 978-0-470-84145-7

A.B. Lawson, A. Biggeri, D. Böhning,
E. Lesaffre, J.-F. Viel, R. Bertollini (Eds.)

**Disease Mapping and Risk
Assessment for Public Health**

1999
ISBN 978-0-471-98634-8

Financing Health Care

New Ideas for a Changing Society

Edited by
Mingshan Lu and Egon Jonsson

WILEY-VCH

WILEY-VCH Verlag GmbH & Co. KGaA

Volume Editors:

Professor Mingshan Lu
University of Calgary
Department of Economics
2500 University Drive NW
Calgary AB T2N 1N4
Canada

Professor Egon Jonsson
University of Alberta
Department of Public Health Science
Institute of Health Economics
10405 Jasper Ave
Edmonton, AB T5J 3N4
Canada

Series Editor:

Professor Egon Jonsson
University of Alberta
Department of Public Health Science
Institute of Health Economics
10405 Jasper Ave
Edmonton, AB T5J 3N4
Canada

All books published by Wiley-VCH are
carefully produced. Nevertheless, authors,
editors, and publisher do not warrant the
information contained in these books,
including this book, to be free of errors.
Readers are advised to keep in mind that
statements, data, illustrations, procedural
details or other items may inadvertently be
inaccurate.

Library of Congress Card No.: applied for

British Library Cataloguing-in-Publication Data
A catalogue record for this book is available
from the British Library.

**Bibliographic information published by the
Deutsche Nationalbibliothek**
Die Deutsche Nationalbibliothek lists this
publication in the Deutsche Nationalbiblio-
grafie; detailed bibliographic data are available
in the Internet at http://dnb.d-nb.de

© 2008 WILEY-VCH Verlag GmbH & Co.
KGaA, Weinheim

Printed in the Federal Republic of Germany
Printed on acid-free paper

Cover Design   Anne Christine Keßler, Edenkoben

Typesetting   Aptara, New Delhi, India
Printing   Strauss GmbH, Mörlenbach
Binding   Litges & Dopf GmbH, Heppenheim

ISBN: 978-3-527-32027-1
ISSN: 1864-9947

Contents

Preface *IX*

List of Contributors *XI*

1   **Introduction**   *1*
Åke Blomqvist and Egon Jonsson
1.1   Health Systems Reform   *1*
1.2   Aging Populations and Advanced Medical Technology   *2*
1.3   Decentralization   *3*
1.4   The Content of this Book   *4*
     References   *15*

2   **Social Health Insurance: Government Funding of Health Care**   *17*
Åke Blomqvist
2.1   Introduction   *17*
2.2   Health Services, Health Insurance, and Market Failure   *18*
2.3   Different Models for Government Funding of Health Care   *28*
2.4   Conclusion: The Future of Social Health Insurance in Canada   *36*
     References   *37*

3   **Private Financing Outside the Publicly Funded System**   *49*
Mark Stabile
3.1   Introduction and the Evolution of Private Financing in Canada   *49*
3.2   Reviewing Economic Theory and Evidence on Parallel Public
     and Private Financing Structures   *51*
3.3   OECD Evidence on Private Financing   *65*
3.4   Overall Conclusions and Directions for Further Study   *75*
     References   *78*

4   **Prescription Drug Financing**   *81*
Steve Morgan
4.1   Introduction   *81*
4.2   Drug Expenditures and Financing in Canada and Abroad   *82*

Financing Health Care: New Ideas for a Changing Society. Edited by Mingshan Lu and Egon Jonsson
Copyright © 2008 WILEY-VCH Verlag GmbH & Co. KGaA, Weinheim
ISBN: 978-3-527-32027-1

4.3   Unique Aspects of Pharmaceuticals and the Pharmaceutical Sector   *88*
4.4   Considerations for Pharmaceutical Financing Reform   *96*
4.5   Conclusion   *100*
        References   *100*

5   The Economics of Consumer-Directed Health Care   *105*
        Ching-To Albert Ma
5.1   Introduction   *105*
5.2   Consumer-Preventive Care Decisions   *107*
5.3   Selection and Cross-Subsidization   *111*
5.4   Health Care Demand and Non-Linear Prices   *114*
5.5   Empirical Studies of Consumer-Directed Health Care   *118*
5.6   Conclusion   *120*
        References   *121*

6   Medical Savings Accounts: Promises and Pitfalls   *125*
        Jeremiah E. Hurley and G. Emmanuel Guindon
6.1   Introduction   *125*
6.2   MSA Financing Internationally   *127*
6.3   MSA Financing and System Performance   *133*
6.4   Conclusions   *143*
        References   *144*

7   Physician Payment Mechanisms   *149*
        Pierre Thomas Léger
7.1   Introduction   *149*
7.2   A Basic Model of Health-Care Provision and Consumption   *150*
7.3   Traditional Fee-For-Service (FFS)   *155*
7.4   Capitation and Fully Prospective Payments   *159*
7.5   Mixed-Payment Systems   *165*
7.6   Concluding Remarks   *171*
        References   *172*

8   Risk Adjustment in Health Care Markets: Concepts and Applications   *177*
        Randall P. Ellis
8.1   Overview   *177*
8.2   Introduction   *177*
8.3   Theory   *181*
8.4   Estimation Issues   *194*
8.5   Country Experience with Risk Adjustment   *205*
8.6   Conclusions   *218*
        References   *218*

9 **Inducing Quality from Health Care Providers in the Presence of Adverse Selection** *223*
Jacob Glazer and Thomas G. McGuire
9.1 Introduction *223*
9.2 The Basic Adverse Selection Problem *224*
9.3 Dealing with Adverse Selection *228*
9.4 The Regulator Can Observe Quality, but Consumers Cannot: Choosing What to Report *232*
9.5 Consumers Can Observe Quality and the Regulator Can Observe "Signals" about Consumers' Types: Risk Adjustment *237*
9.6 Concluding Remarks *241*
References *242*

10 **Equity in Health and Health Care in Canada in International Perspective** *245*
Eddy van Doorslaer
10.1 Overview *245*
10.2 Introduction: Canada's Health Care System and Equity *245*
10.3 Income-Related Inequity in Access to, and Delivery of, Care *246*
10.4 Inequalities in Health and Health Outcomes *257*
10.5 Conclusion and Discussion *264*
References *266*

Index *273*

Preface

Although this book about health care financing is focused largely on Canada, several of the issues discussed are also relevant to many other countries with a universal health care system.

Today, as most countries are experiencing rapidly rising costs of health care, the health policy makers seek continually to review their options for the funding of health services. The theories developed in health economics, and the empirical evidence in the field, along with the experience of various financing and payment models in different countries, represent important contributions in the search for funding models. The aim of this book is to provide insights to some of the questions that arise when approaching the subject of health care financing.

In this respect, the book deals with several issues of relevance for such debate not only in many provinces of Canada but also in other countries. For example; how are different countries dealing with government funding for health care? What strategies are available to finance pharmaceuticals and other medical technologies? Which mechanisms are available for payments to physicians? Could so-called "medical savings accounts" be a solution? What are the implications for equity of different models of health care financing?

Each of the chapters in this book may be used for the teaching health economics. Moreover, some of the findings may also contribute to the debate on how to approach funding problems as populations grow older and medical technologies become increasingly sophisticated – and expensive.

On behalf of the Institute of Health Economics in Alberta, Canada, we are indebted to all of the authors for their contributions which have made the publication of this book possible.

Calgary and Edmonton   *Mingshan Lu*
September 2007   *Egon Jonsson*

List of Contributors

Prof. Åke Blomqvist
National University of Singapore
Department of Economics
Faculty of Arts & Social Science
Singapore 117570
Singapore

Prof. Randall P. Ellis
Boston University
Department of Economics
270 Bay State Road
Boston, MA 02215
USA

Prof. Jacob Glazer
Boston University
Department of Economics
270 Bay State Road
Boston, MA 02215
USA

G. Emmanuel Guindon
McMaster University
Centre for Health Economics
and Policy Analysis
1200 Main Street West
Hamilton, Ontario L8Z 3N5
Canada

Prof. Jeremiah E. Hurley
McMaster University
Department of Economics
Center for Health Economics
and Policy Analysis
1280 Main Street West
Hamilton, Ontario L8S 4M4
Canada

Prof. Egon Jonsson
University of Alberta
Department of Public Health Science
10405 Jasper Ave
Edmonton, Alberta T5J 3N4
Canada

Prof. Pierre Thomas Léger
Institute of Applied Economics
HEC Montréal, CIRANO and CIRPÉE
3000, Chemin de la
Côte-Sainte-Catherine
Montreal, Quebec H3T 2A7
Canada

Prof. Ching-To Albert Ma
Boston University
Department of Economics
270 Bay State Road
Boston, MA 02215
USA

Financing Health Care: New Ideas for a Changing Society. Edited by Mingshan Lu and Egon Jonsson
Copyright © 2008 WILEY-VCH Verlag GmbH & Co. KGaA, Weinheim
ISBN: 978-3-527-32027-1

Prof. Thomas G. McGuire
Harvard Medical School
Department of Health Care Policy
180 Longwood Ave.
Boston, MA 02115
USA

Prof. Steve Morgan
University of British Columbia
Centre for Health Services and
Policy Research
201-2206 East Mall
Vancouver, BC, V6T 1Z3
Canada

Prof. Mark Stabile
University of Toronto
School of Public Policy and Governance
Canadiana Building, 3rd Floor
14 Queen's Park Cresent West
Toronto, Ontario M5S 3K9
Canada

Eddy van Doorslaer
Department of Health Policy
and Management
Erasmus School of Economics
Erasmus University Rotterdam
PO Box 1738 3000
DR Rotterdam
The Netherlands

1
Introduction
Åke Blomqvist and Egon Jonsson

The question of how society should pay for the health care of its citizens is one that countries have answered in very different ways. Indeed, it is difficult to think of any other large economic sector where the institutional design is as varied as it is in health care – the arrangements whereby countries mix private and public funding of health care, and the methods they use for paying for drugs and the services of doctors and hospitals, are strikingly different.

In Canada, the debate about health policy has focused much on comparisons with the United States. In such comparisons, Canada typically comes out well, as it seems to have put in place a much more equitable and efficient health care system. Likewise, in comparison with, for example, the United Kingdom, Canada's decentralized system of producing physician and hospital services seemed to function more smoothly than that in the UK National Health Service.

While the Canadian health care system continues to be much less expensive than its American counterpart, in comparison with a number of European countries it is more costly, even though the Canadian population is younger than most of those in Europe. Waiting lists for certain types of medical examination and treatment, and the difficulty in many provinces of finding a regular family doctor, has – over time – become problematic in Canada, as in most European countries. In addition, whilst the health care systems of many countries have been restructured substantially over the past few decades, the Canadian system is changing more slowly.

1.1
Health Systems Reform

In the history of health policy development it seems possible to identify a few stages through which many industrialized countries have passed over time in their approaches to health system organization [1, 2].

During the first "wave" of reform – from the late 1940s to the early 1970s – the emphasis was on creating guaranteed access to modern health care for broad segments of the population, in many cases through universal programs; that is, programs covering the entire population. This was part of the movement by which

Financing Health Care: New Ideas for a Changing Society. Edited by Mingshan Lu and Egon Jonsson
Copyright © 2008 WILEY-VCH Verlag GmbH & Co. KGaA, Weinheim
ISBN: 978-3-527-32027-1

industrialized societies strengthened the social safety nets designed to take care of those who otherwise would not be able to share in the growing prosperity that the expanding economies were creating for the citizenry during the 1950s and 1960s.

During this first wave, the emphasis thus was on reducing the extent to which the increasing private cost of health care created a barrier against access to modern health care for many people. Less attention was paid to the aggregate cost of health care for the population as a whole. Over time, however, all industrialized countries saw the per capita cost of health care grow at rates substantially in excess of those for the economy as a whole, so that the share of total economic resources devoted to health rose steadily.

The emphasis in health policy in many countries shifted toward attempts at controlling aggregate costs during the 1980s and early 1990s. A variety of approaches were tried, including increased charges to patients in some countries, the imposition of firmer expenditure ceilings for hospitals and controls on the establishment of new hospitals in others, and (in Canada) modified forms of federal-provincial cost-sharing to give provinces an incentive to reduce health care spending. In the US, the Medicare program experimented with new methods for paying hospitals (the DRG system) and doctors. In Germany, budget ceilings applicable to the medical profession as a whole were introduced.

These efforts in different countries to control aggregate health care costs have had mixed success. In most countries, health care spending has continued to grow at a faster rate than the economy as a whole, in spite of the spending restraints. At the same time, there has been increasing dissatisfaction with perceived health care "rationing" and waiting lists for certain types of examination and treatment.

1.2
Aging Populations and Advanced Medical Technology

There are some fairly obvious reasons why controlling aggregate expenditure in health care is proving difficult. One reason is population aging: in every society, the average spending on health care for people aged over 65 years is much larger than for those below that age, so when the share of the population aged over 65 increases, a larger share of the GDP will go to health care. Even more important, however, are advances in medical technology. As progress in biomedical research makes it possible to provide early diagnosis, to prolong life, to reduce suffering and to maintain or improve quality of life of many patients, the pressure becomes strong to spend the resources necessary to make these new technologies available to everyone who may benefit from them. However, many of the new drugs, medical devices, equipment and procedures are very expensive such that, in order to control aggregate costs, choices must be made. With constantly advancing and expensive technology, sometimes with marginal benefits only for a few, a strategy of paying for everything that may be medically beneficial will not be possible, forcing us to make difficult decisions indeed both at the individual and societal level.

1.3
Decentralization

The developments in the health care sector have made it difficult for central decision-makers (such as the provincial Ministries of Health in Canada, the NHS in the UK, etc.) to formulate and enforce rules that are restrictive enough to control costs, but not so restrictive as to be perceived as inflexible and callous by hospital managers, doctors, and patients. In many other countries, the response to this dilemma has, to a significant extent, involved an increased decentralization of funding and decision-making, either along geographic lines (as in Sweden, or in the UK during the 1990s), or to competing provider groups among which consumers are allowed to choose (the Managed Care Option in the US Medicare plan, the competing sickness funds and private insurers in the Dutch system, or the GP practices that are being given an increasingly important role in the UK during the Labor government's new NHS reforms). There has also been a revival of interest in high-deductible plans under which consumers who so desire can choose plans in which they pay a lower premium but are responsible for paying for the cost of their own care up to the deductible (so-called Consumer-Directed Health Care Plans).

Compared to other countries, Canada has been slow in adopting the approaches that have been part of this "second wave" of health system reform. Although some steps have been taken towards decentralization in most provinces, they have so far only been along geographic lines, and only with respect to the funding of hospital services. There has also been some discussion about paying for specific health services through publicly funded Medical Savings Accounts (this topic is discussed in Chapter 6). In other countries, however, there has been experimentation with a broader range of decentralized funding arrangements, including those under which consumers have a choice among competing provider groups or insurance plans, public or private (as in the UK or in the Netherlands); these are also considered in some chapters in this book.

There are a number of potential reasons why Canada has been reluctant to experiment with innovations in the funding of health care. One explanation may be its system of divided federal and provincial jurisdiction over health care. As the Dutch experience illustrates, major changes to the health care system tend to be resisted by various types of vested interest – something which can come close to bringing the reform process to a halt unless it is firmly supported by the political decision-makers. In a longer perspective, factors such as advancing medical technology and an aging population may nevertheless lead to consideration of a health system reform. The broad range of issues discussed in the chapters of this volume may be useful in moving the debate forward.

1.4
The Content of this Book

The chapters in the present volume have been written in part to contribute to the debate on health care reform in Canada, drawing on the experiences of different options of healthcare financing in other countries. While some of the chapters contain technical material, each one emphasizes a few conceptual themes that are potentially of relevance to health policy in Canada and elsewhere.

1.4.1
Private and Public Funding of Health Services

- Chapter 2: Social Health Insurance: Government Funding of Health Care

In order to consider ways in which reform could be used to improve the functioning of the health care system, one needs to understand the reasons why government, in all industrialized countries, is so heavily involved in the funding of health care, either by paying for it directly or by regulating the system through which it is paid. To economists, the question why this is so is of great interest, because so much of their work focuses on the advantages of relying on private firms in competitive markets to efficiently produce goods and services that individuals value and are willing to pay for. Health services clearly fall into this category. Why, then, do societies not simply allow their production to be governed by supply and demand in the marketplace? In Chapter 2, the answers that health economists have given to this question are reviewed, and how one can interpret the very different forms that government intervention has taken in different countries, as alternative responses to the special characteristics of health care.

Part of the reason for government intervention is due to the fact that diagnosing and treatment for many diseases would be too expensive for the overwhelming majority of the population. Therefore, there is a need for some mechanism that provides a sharing of the financial burden (risk pooling) for expensive health care – that is, some form of insurance.

The fact that there is a demand for some form of risk-pooling does not, in principle, imply that government must become involved in the funding of health care, as risk-pooling can also be provided through private markets (i.e., through private insurance plans). However, there are many reasons why private insurance is unlikely to be an effective risk-pooling mechanism in the context of health care, unless it is heavily regulated. Thus, the only real alternatives for an effective system of risk-pooling are government funding through some form of social insurance, heavily regulated private insurance, or some combination of the two.

In addition to the need for some form of risk-pooling mechanism, there is a second fundamental characteristic of health care that diminishes the potential effectiveness of a system of private competitive markets as an instrument for governing the production and supply of health services: the complexity of disease and health problems, and of the medical, surgical, and pharmaceutical technology that can be used in diagnosing and treatment. Because of this, patients typically do no have very good information about what they are buying when they seek care. The providers – on the other hand – do, and consequently, there is a problem of "asymmetric information" in this market. To decide what to "purchase", buyers must rely largely on information provided by the sellers. In this situation, they may end up making decisions that they would not have made had they been better informed. As a result, the principle that a transaction between a willing buyer and a willing seller will benefit both parties, may no longer apply. However, as this principle is the main basis for the belief in economic theory that it is efficient to allow an economy's resources be allocated in private markets through the interaction of buyers and sellers, the conclusion that it may not apply to health care suggests that a system of private markets will not work well in that sector.

Thus, a well-functioning health care system requires arrangements for effective risk pooling, and for overcoming the problem of asymmetric information in health services markets. Different countries have used very different models in designing a system that attempts to do this. In Canada, risk pooling for hospital and physician services is provided indirectly, by having provincial governments pay for them. The information asymmetry issue is addressed, at least partially, by the government paying for physician services and by funding hospitals in a way that does not give them a financial incentive to produce an overly large volume of services. Other countries have used models that are quite different (see Chapter 2).

- Chapter 3: Private Financing Outside the Publicly Funded System

To some extent, every country has a system of mixed public–private financing of health expenditures. In an implicit acknowledgement of the likely shortcomings of a risk-pooling system based purely on private insurance, most industrialized countries by now have publicly funded or publicly organized insurance plans that are available either to the entire population, or (as in the US case) to certain population groups. But private funding continues to play at least *some* role in every country. Even for those that are classified as having "single-payer" systems (such as Canada or the UK), the private share of funding ranges from 10 to 30% of the total.

As Mark Stabile discusses in Chapter 3, the way in which private and public funding of health care interact varies greatly from country to country. In some cases, the main component of private expenditure for health care is patient out-of-pocket payments of user fees charged under the public plan. In others, a significant portion of health care spending is through private insurance plans that coexist with the public plan. Mixed systems of public and private insurance, in turn, can also function in very different ways. In some countries, one important role of private insurance is to cover certain categories of health care spending (for example, pharmaceuticals and dental care) that are not covered by the public plan (Canada is an important case, as was the American Medicare plan, until recently). In others, private insurance that covers the user fees that are imposed by the public plan is allowed (for example the "Medigap" plans, marketed to beneficiaries of American Medicare; France is another example).

In a few countries, the role of private insurance is strengthened by provisions under which individuals are allowed to *opt out* of coverage under the public plan. That is, they can elect to forego public plan coverage, in return for at least some financial compensation in the form of reduced payroll taxes, premiums, or social insurance contributions. In at least two cases of this kind (Holland, US Medicare), opting out of the public plan is only allowed if the person enrolls in an approved private plan instead (being without health insurance is not allowed). Finally, there are some countries (in particular, the UK) in which some citizens have "duplicate" coverage, under which they continue to be covered by the same public plan as everyone else but are also enrolled in private insurance plans that include coverage for some of the same services that the public plan provides. An important difference here is that private plans will cover treatment in private clinics or hospitals, while the public plan only covers treatment in public facilities [3].

While the discussion of these matters in Chapter 2 considers the opting-out issue, Mark Stabile focuses on other aspects of mixed public–private funding. His chapter contains a regression exercise in which he studies the quantitative trade-off between the two sources of funding in different institutional environments, and also reviews empirical work dealing with the question what happens when the scope of public-sector coverage is restricted – that is, when certain services are "de-listed" (excluded from coverage), as has happened in some Canadian provinces in the past.

One section in Chapter 3 deals with certain issues that have become particularly controversial in places where the demand for duplicate coverage has been driven in part by long waiting lists for particular types of treatment under the public plan. When waiting lists exist in the public system, it will inevitably be the case that well-to-do individuals will try to bypass them by seeking care from private providers. What rules should apply when this happens, is something that has been heatedly debated in many countries (for example in the UK, Canada, and Australia).

One question is whether specialist doctors who are employed to provide these services in the public system should also be allowed to treat patients privately (on a part-time basis). In the UK, where this practice is allowed, studies have suggested that limits on the amount of time that salaried specialists may spend treating private patients are effective only if there is close monitoring of how the doctors spend their time. As Stabile observes, a study in Manitoba did not show this pattern; perhaps the fact that Canadian doctors are paid on the basis of fee for service in the public system is part of the reason for this.

Another issue is whether the system should allow the marketing of insurance plans that cover the cost of privately produced services that are also available through the public plan. This has been a very hotly debated question in Canada, where legislation in most provinces effectively rules out such plans [4]. As Stabile notes, the arguments against allowing those who so desire to buy services outside of the public system (and insurance that covers such services) are based either on a belief that allowing parallel private care is detrimental to the quantity and quality of care offered in the public system, or on an egalitarian belief that everyone should receive the same care when they are ill, regardless of their financial status.

- Chapter 4: Prescription Drug Financing

Steve Morgan's essay on prescription drug financing deals with a component of health care expenditures that is particularly important in a Canadian context. As he notes, the government plans that pay for general health services in most European countries (or indeed in most advanced countries outside of North America) also pay most of the cost of prescription drugs. However, Canadian provincial insurance plans (as well as, until recently, the US Medicare plan) have not included universal coverage against the cost of drugs used in an outpatient setting. Following the recommendation of the National Forum on Health some 10 years ago, however, there has been some discussion in Canada about a federal initiative to introduce some form of Pharmacare system; in the meantime, the provincial governments have gradually strengthened their own programs [5].

As Morgan discusses, demands by outpatients for pharmaceuticals have some of the same characteristics as all patients' demands for health services generally. In a given year, most people spend only a fairly limited amount of money (or none at all) on prescription drugs, though for some diseases the cost may be very large. As for the cost of health services in general, therefore, risk pooling and third-party payment of pharmaceutical costs is, potentially, both efficient and equitable. The statistics that Morgan quotes show how rapidly the significance of this issue has been growing, both as a result of the development of new and very expensive drugs, and the growing incidence of certain types of chronic condition (AIDS, diabetes, hypertension) that are treated through long-term drug therapy.

The fact that the universal provincial Medicare plans do not cover drugs does not mean that all drug costs are paid by patients out of pocket. In particular, all provinces in Canada have at least some type of coverage for specific populations (the elderly, those with low income), and many Canadians of working age have employment-related private insurance. However, as Morgan persuasively argues, there are a number of disadvantages with a system in which everyone is covered for hospital and physician services through one plan, but in which coverage for the cost of pharmaceuticals is through many different plans, and some people have no coverage at all. Such a system is likely to be complicated – and hence expensive – to administer, and is unlikely to produce a pattern of care that is efficient in the sense of minimizing the total cost of care. Moreover, incorporating pharmaceutical coverage in the provincial Medicare plans would put governments into a stronger position to influence the choice of prescriptions and to negotiate better terms for purchasing drugs from the pharmaceutical companies. The time has come, in Morgan's view, to heed the proposals to extend provincial health insurance to encompass outpatient drug coverage.

Morgan also discusses the fact that the information asymmetry between users and providers that exists for health services in general also is relevant in the case of drugs. The average consumer obviously does not have the knowledge and expertise necessary to make an informed choice of drugs, but must rely on the advice of their doctors. While doctors in Canada and the US do not have a direct financial incentive to prescribe expensive drugs (as do physicians in some other countries), they also do not have any personal incentive to take the cost of the drug into account when they prescribe, especially if the consumer is insured. In some countries, the system of paying physicians may include such an incentive. For example, in the UK some family doctors are subject to a "drug budget" for the patients on their roster, with a financial incentive to prescribe in such a way that their actual drug costs come in "under budget". Implementing such a system is easier if primary-care doctors are paid through a system that includes a capitation element, something which is not common in Canada today.

- Chapters 5 and 6: The Economics of Consumer-Directed Health Care *and* Medical Savings Accounts: Promises and Pitfalls

Although Chapters 5 and 6, by Albert Ma and by Jerry Hurley and Emmanuel Guindon respectively, are quite different in style, they implicitly relate to the same substantive question: To what extent patient cost sharing in health care promotes efficiency by giving consumers an incentive to reduce the probability that they will require health care, or to limit their utilization of health services when they are ill?

In Chapter 5, Ma discusses Consumer-Directed Health Care (CDHC) plans, most of which are variants of an old idea – that a reasonably efficient form of health insurance may be a plan under which consumers pay 100% of the cost of the health care they use, up to a fixed annual amount (the deductible), with the plan paying for all or most of any costs beyond that amount. What is new about the CDHC plans that have become increasingly common in the US in recent years is that the insurance coverage beyond the deductible is through some form of managed-care plan that restricts the consumer's choice of provider and other aspects of the care process, rather than through conventional passive coverage of the cost incurred for services supplied by any licensed provider. Thus, they represent combinations of traditional, high-deductible plans on the one hand, and managed care plans on the other hand. An additional twist in many CDHC plans is that they try to assist clients in making more cost-effective decisions about their care by acting as a source of reliable medical information.

Ma analyzes the properties of insurance plans with high deductibles with the help of some theoretical models. Consistent with published studies in the field, he shows that consumers in high-deductible plans are likely to devote more effort to illness prevention than those with conventional insurance (though this result depends on assumptions about the consumer's degree of risk aversion); that "adverse selection" may lead those with lower probability of illness to choose high-deductible plans, leading to higher premiums for those at high risk who choose more comprehensive plans; and that consumers who decide how much to spend on medical care if they fall ill early in the year should take into account the fact that higher spending will reduce their expected out-of-pocket payments in any subsequent disease episode. These results are established in elegant and easy-to-understand stylized models.

Hurley and Guindon's chapter begins with a succinct but comprehensive review of theory and evidence regarding the role of Medical Savings Accounts (MSAs) in health care financing. While the institutional arrangements that people have in mind when they discuss MSAs can vary a great deal from country to country, the common feature in all such schemes is insurance through a high-deductible plan combined with an "individual (or household)-specific account whose balances ... are normally earmarked for health care expenses". As Hurley and Guindon explain, MSAs were initially introduced in the US in response to the fact that employers' contributions to employees' health insurance premiums are treated as a non-taxable benefit – something that indirectly discriminated against high-deductible plans with low premiums. However, by allowing employers' contributions to employees' MSAs to be treated as a non-taxable benefit as well, the bias against choosing a high-deductible plan was eliminated. In Singapore and China, MSAs were introduced for different reasons: In Singapore, as a substitute for an earlier system of UK-style government funding of health care, and in China as a partial substitute for an earlier system under which most urban residents (workers and their dependents) received health care at low user fees through their employers (who before 1980 typically were either the government or a state-owned firm).

The version of MSAs that has received most attention in the Canadian health policy debate in recent years is one in which individuals' MSAs would receive regular contributions from the government. Hurley and Guindon report on an interesting set of simulation experiments to estimate the impact that such a scheme would have on aggregate health expenditure, and on the public sector's cost of health care, in Ontario. By and large, their conclusion is that MSAs are unlikely to generate significant savings in terms of public spending (partly, it appears, because the scheme they assume is one under which certain expenditure categories that currently are not publicly funded, including a large share of the cost of outpatient drugs and dental care, would be allowed). Moreover, to the extent that the high deductibles would generate savings, they would do so in a way that would expose individuals to greater financial risk and shift a share of the spending burden from those at low risk of illness to those at high risk. As the authors also stress, imposing a high deductible is an example of trying to control health care costs through *demand-side incentives* (that is, incentives on patients). In this sense, it is an approach that goes contrary to what appears to be an emerging consensus among health economists, namely that approaches that try to achieve cost control through *supply-side incentives* (that is, incentives on providers) are more likely to be effective.

However, as Ma notes in Chapter 5, high-deductible plans in the CDHC category often involve arrangements under which consumers are covered by managed-care plans (not conventional cost reimbursement plan) once they have exhausted their deductibles. Because managed-care plans typically control costs through supply-side incentives, CHDC plans thus work through a combination of demand and supply-side incentives: demand-side incentives for those whose expenditures remain below the deductible (that is, those who do not need treatment for major illness), supply-side incentives for potentially large expenditures. Such a combination may be more attractive than either plan in isolation. Moreover, it is possible to imagine flexible MSA schemes under which the government contributions to individual MSAs would be used either to pay for expenditures below a high deductible (in conjunction with a low-premium plan for high cost "catastrophic" illness), or (at the consumer's option) be immediately passed on to an insurer as a premium for a low-deductible managed care plan. In this form, the government MSA contribution would be akin to a voucher of the form envisaged under the Clinton plan for universal health coverage in the US advanced during the early 1990s, or the Dekker–Simmons plan currently being implemented in the Netherlands [6].

1.4.2
Paying Health Services Providers and Health Plans

In the later chapters the focus shifts from the mix of private and public funding of health services, to another critical issue in health system organization: What methods and principles are used in paying individual health care providers and provider groups (health plans) for the services they supply?

- Chapter 7: Physician Payment Mechanisms

The distinction between demand-side and supply-side incentives referred to above is the central theme in Pierre Léger's chapter on physician payment mechanisms. In recent years, this is an area of health policy that has received a fair amount of attention in Canada. In particular, the question whether there are better methods than "fee for service" as the way to pay physicians, particularly in primary care, has been frequently debated among policy makers, and in some provinces small-scale pilot projects have been undertaken with different payment schemes, sometimes with federal government support.

Much of the early literature in health economics was based on models in which it was assumed that health services utilization was decided on by well-informed consumers who chose what amounts to "purchase" by considering the out-of-pocket charges they faced for each unit of health services. In such models, the key question is what degree of consumer cost-sharing (that is, demand-side incentives) should be used to strike an appropriate balance between the benefits of more complete insurance (that is, lower cost-sharing), and the tendency toward inefficient over-utilization of health services that results when part of the cost is paid by a third-party insurer. Léger begins his chapter with a very clear exposition of this trade-off, and then goes on to discuss the even more difficult problems caused by the fact that, in reality, patients are not well enough informed to make health care utilization decisions on their own but must rely heavily on the advice of their doctors.

From the viewpoint of conventional economics analysis, a market in which purchase decisions are made to a large extent on the basis of advice from the seller is somewhat of an anomaly, as Evans stressed in his pioneering analysis of Supplier-Induced Demand in health care [7]. Although the seriousness of the problem of "information asymmetry" between buyers and sellers in this market can be reduced to some degree by factors such as altruism or professional ethics, those responsible for health policy in most countries where doctors are paid on the basis of fee for service (including Canada and Japan) have typically intervened to regulate the prices of physician services in order to control costs. Price controls, however, may also cause problems, and another response to the information asymmetry problem has been to pay physicians through some method that reduces or eliminates their incentive to supply and charge for a large volume of services for each patient. One such method is payment through a straight salary – that is, a system in which doctors' incomes do not depend either on the volume of services they provide, or on the number of patients they care for. Another is capitation – a method under which the doctor receives a fixed payment in advance for each patient registered on his or her list, regardless of whether or not any services are provided to the patient. Although capitation does not reward doctors for producing a large volume of services, it does give them an incentive to attract and retain a large number of patients to their practices, and it is a method that is often used by private insurers when they try to organize cost-effective networks of providers. Capitation, of course, is the principal example of an approach to cost control that emphasizes supply-side incentives.

Léger also touches on another issue that, in practice, may be very important for cost control, namely the incentives that affect the utilization of other inputs than physician services in the process of providing health care to a given population: hospital services and pharmaceuticals. As for physician services, the decisions that determine the use of hospital facilities and prescription drugs in the context of a given illness episode are typically made on the advice of a doctor. The consequences of the information asymmetry between patients and their doctors can obviously be very different with respect to the cost of these inputs than they are for physician services. Whilst doctors paid on the basis of fee for service earn a higher income the larger the volume of their own services their patients use, this is typically not true with respect to the quantity of hospital services, nor with respect to the amount of money their patients (or their patients' insurers) spend on prescription drugs. Nevertheless, doctors (particularly doctors in primary care) obviously have a major role in influencing the decisions for these inputs as well, and many provider networks in the US have contracts under which primary-care providers receive bonuses that depend on the cost of hospital services and drugs used by their patients; a similar system – referred to as "fundholding" – was used as an incentive mechanism for the capitated General Practitioners (GPs) that provided primary care to NHS patients in the UK during the 1990s.

Thus, payment methods with supply-side incentives, such as capitation and fund holding, have become more prominent in several countries over time; in the UK, their role will be even stronger in the system of so-called Practice-based Commissioning that is the centerpiece of the "new NHS" being constructed by the Labor government.

- Chapters 8 and 9: Risk Adjustment in Health Care Markets: Concepts and Applications *and* Inducing Quality from Health Care Providers in the Presence of Adverse Selection

Although the titles of the chapters by Ellis and by Glazer and McGuire are quite different, the contents are related in the sense that both deal with a similar set of problems: Those that arise when one tries to organize a system of health care financing in a population where individuals are heterogeneous in the sense of having different expected (average) health expenditures over a period of time. When these differences result from factors that either are observable to others, or are known only to the individuals themselves, then several types of problem may arise, depending on the way that the funding system is organized.

The problems that arise from differences in individual risk of illness are especially likely to be severe in a system where individuals (or families) are allowed to choose among competing health plans. Under the current Canadian system, there is no such choice. As Ellis points out, however, heterogeneity can also cause problems in a system where everybody is covered by the same government plan, but in which funding is geographically decentralized, and in which patients can choose from which provider to seek treatment. Both of these features are present in several Canadian provinces, including Alberta and Saskatchewan.

Specifically, if all or part of the cost of the population's health care is funded by provincial governments through grants to Regional Health Authorities (RHAs), two important issues arise. First, how should these grants depend on the characteristics of the population for which each RHA is responsible? Second, what arrangements should be made to cover cases where patients belonging to one RHA receive treatment in a facility located in another? The literature on risk adjustment that Ellis surveys is potentially related to the first of these issues, at least when data are available on the health care costs incurred in the treatment of given individuals over a period of time. Statistical studies of past spending can then be used to allocate provincial health care funds across RHAs in a way that "creates a level playing field" – that is, which reflects the expected health care costs (needs) of each RHA's population. For example, the allocation pattern can be designed to take account of differences in expected spending on the old versus the young, native Canadians versus non-native ones, and other factors.

Related – but slightly different – types of adjustment may be made when individuals cross RHA boundaries for certain types of care. All things being equal, total health care spending within the boundaries of large cities will obviously be higher than in rural RHAs when people living in the countryside receive treatment for serious illness in big-city hospitals. In the UK, where decentralized funding along these lines was practiced for some time during the 1990s, the approach was to make each RHA responsible for all health care costs of its population, but allowing each one to pay for specialized care provided in out-of-district facilities from the budget they had initially been allocated, according to terms negotiated in advance. (The system under which RHAs negotiated with providers regarding payment for care produced for the regional populations was sometimes referred to as the "purchaser-provider split".)

Both Ellis and Glazer and McGuire also devote attention to the difficult and more complicated problems that are likely to arise when consumers are allowed to choose among a number of competing (public or private) health plans. In particular, of course, allowing such a choice introduces the possibility of "adverse selection"; this term is used to describe the tendency for individuals with different risks of illness (different expected health care costs) to gravitate toward different types of plans. The consequences of selection in this sense are especially likely to be severe when insurers cannot tell who is at high risk, or are prevented from charging higher premiums to the high risks by regulation or for some other reason. As has been extensively discussed in the literature, adverse selection is likely to yield outcomes that not only are inequitable (in the sense that those at high risk will be paying high premiums), but also inefficient (in the sense that those who are not at high risk will be less well covered than would be desirable, or in the sense that plans that provide high-level coverage will be so expensive that no one will buy them).

Chapter 9, by Glazer and McGuire, is largely theoretical and summarizes and reviews a number of technical papers that discuss methods to overcome a particular type of adverse selection problem. Specifically, they focus on two models in which plans must offer two types of service ("acute care" and "chronic care"), and in which the "bad risks" (those whose expected health care costs are high) are particularly likely to need a large amount of one of these types of care (chronic care, in Glazer and McGuire's model). In this case, private insurance plans may try to raise their profits by providing a low standard of chronic care, so as to make themselves less attractive to the bad risks. This strategy may fail if those who are bad risks are not informed in advance of the quality of care of the two types of service that each plan offers so that, paradoxically, it may then be a good policy to withhold this information from consumers! Glazer and McGuire also consider settings in which the insurer and the "regulator" (the agency that is trying to ensure that both good and bad risks have access to the appropriate level of service) are able to observe some characteristic that enable them to estimate the probability that an individual is a bad risk. In such settings, they find that what they term "conventional risk adjustment" is not sufficient to make all plans offer the appropriate amounts of the two types of service to all clients; some plans will still try to become more attractive to good risks by offering a high standard of acute care, in the hope that the bad risks who need a large amount of chronic care will choose another insurer. An interesting insight from this type of work is that to some extent, the adverse selection problem may be overcome by "overcompensating" for patient characteristics that are known to be correlated with the risk of illness.

1.4.3
Equity Issues in the Health Care System

- Chapter 10: Equity of Health and Health Care in Canada in International Perspective

The final chapter of the book discusses a range of issues and data that are central to the health policy debate in every country: Whether the system of funding of health services contributes to reducing the degree of economic inequality. In this chapter, Eddie Van Doorslaer provides evidence on the extent to which the existing Canadian health care system has accomplished its oft-stated objective of ensuring that all Canadians, regardless of ability to pay, receive the same standard of health care when they are ill.

Demonstrating the degree to which this objective has been met is not as easy as might first be thought, even though a large amount of data on health status and health services utilization by income class is available from statistical surveys. As Van Doorslaer explains, if one simply looks at measures of utilization (probability of visiting a doctor in a year, average number of visits per year, days spent in hospital, etc.) by income class, one finds no discrimination against the poor. Indeed, data of this kind show that, on average, poor people typically use *more* health services than those with higher income. However, this pattern can largely be explained by the greater average need for health services among the poor. If one uses individuals' self-rated health (information regarding this was collected in the major survey that forms the basis for the analysis) as a proxy measure for "need", and computes standardized utilization rates that correct for need in this sense, the "pro-poor" bias largely disappears for most utilization measures. However, the corrected data do not show any significant systematic bias *against* the poor either, except for a relatively minor "pro-rich" bias for the probability of visiting a specialist. In international perspective (comparing Canada with a sample of 21 OECD countries), Van Doorslaer concludes that ". . . on the whole, Canada's performance in terms of achieving equal treatment for equal need, irrespective of income, is at least as good as that of most other countries in the study".

While this is reassuring, the conclusion that Canada's health care system has essentially eliminated any tendency for those with high income to obtain better health care refers principally to those services (of physicians, and hospital care) that are universally covered under the provincial Medicare plans under the Canada Health Act. For services that are not covered – particularly dental services – there is a strong correlation between service use and income. Data for outpatient pharmaceuticals expenditures are not as readily available, but studies conducted on more limited samples of individuals also are consistent with the pattern of higher use among those with high income. While this pattern obviously may be a cause for concern, it is not unique to Canada: Not only the US, but also many European countries have shown similar profiles.

Van Doorslaer's chapter also examines the correlation between individual health status and income or socioeconomic status. While health services appear to be allocated in a way that does not discriminate against the poor, the same cannot be said for health status: The data show a strong tendency for those with lower income to be in worse health on average than those in high-income brackets. Again, however, this is not unique to Canada, as a similar pattern typically is found not only in the US but also in most European countries.

References

1 Blomqvist, Å. (1995), Reforming Health Care: Canada and the Second Wave, pp. 165–191 in Jérôme-Forget, M., White, J., Wiener, J.M. (Eds.), *Health care reform through internal markets: Experience and proposals.* Montreal: The Brookings Institution and the Institute for Research on Public Policy.

2 Cutler, D.M. (2002), Equality, efficiency, and market fundamentals: The dynamics of international medical-care reform, *Journal of Economic Literature* **40**, 881–906.

3 Australia is an interesting case in that private insurance there only is allowed for hospital care, not outpatient care, and because, while private insurance is subsidized, those with private insurance have not technically "opted out" of public coverage. See Colombo, F. and Tapay, N. (2003), Private health insurance in Australia: A case study, OECD Health Working Papers, No. 8. Paris: OECD.

4 In a recent Supreme Court of Canada decision (*Chaoulli and Zeliotis v. A.G. Québec et al.*), the ban on private insurance was found unconstitutional when wait times are excessive. It remains to be seen whether this ruling will lead to changes in the role of private insurance. For a discussion, see Canadian Medical Association (2006), "It's about access! Informing the debate on public and private health care". CMA Task Force on the Public-Private Interface.

5 National Forum on Health (1997), Directions for Pharmaceutical Policy in Canada, in: *Canada Health Action: Building on the Legacy - Volume II - Synthesis Reports and Issues Papers.*

6 One of the most systematic and readable descriptions of the U.S. and Dutch reform models is in Flood, C.M. (2000), *International Health Care Reform: A legal, economic and political analysis.* London: Routledge, especially Ch. 3, pp. 41–126.

7 Evans, R.G. (1974), Supplier-induced demand, in: Perlman, M. (Ed.), *The economics of health and medical care,* London: MacMillan, pp. 162–173; Evans, R.G. (1984), *Strained Mercy: The Economics of Canadian Health Care.* Toronto: Butterworths, 1984.

2
Social Health Insurance: Government Funding of Health Care
Åke Blomqvist

2.1
Introduction

The question that is addressed in this survey chapter is: How, and to what extent, should the government take responsibility for funding health services in an advanced economy? In attempting an answer, it is important first to emphasize one aspect of this question that is not controversial – namely the government's role with respect to health services that have significant external effects (that is, spillover benefits to individuals other than those who receive them directly). Generally, services of this type will tend to be underproduced in an otherwise well-functioning economy based on competitive markets, unless the government takes responsibility for subsidizing them, or producing them itself. Thus, the idea that the government has a major role in the financing and production of those health services that have significant spillover effects, is beyond dispute.

What *is* controversial, however, is the government's role with respect to other types of health services. Because serious illness strikes at random, an individual's need (demand) for all such services (including those that are "private goods" with no significant external effects) is highly variable and unpredictable. For this reason, a well-functioning health care system must contain not only an efficient set of firms (hospitals, clinics, doctors' offices) for the provision of health services, but also institutional arrangements for the provision of health *insurance*. These arrangements may take the form of government funding (as payment for health services out of public funds implies that risks are pooled across all taxpayers, which is equivalent to a form of insurance). Alternatively, they may take the form of a system of risk-pooling based on private production and insurance.

The focus in this chapter is on the government's role with respect to health services that are private goods. After a brief discussion of health services with external effects, the first half of the chapter reviews the principal reasons why an unregulated system of health services funding based largely on private insurance will not function well, even when most health services are private goods. This is due to certain characteristics, both of the market for health services (information asymmetry among patients, providers, and insurers with respect to the technical

Financing Health Care: New Ideas for a Changing Society. Edited by Mingshan Lu and Egon Jonsson
Copyright © 2008 WILEY-VCH Verlag GmbH & Co. KGaA, Weinheim
ISBN: 978-3-527-32027-1

aspects of diagnosis and treatment), and of the market for health insurance (imperfect and asymmetric information regarding risks of illness), as the two are inextricably linked in determining the way in which the health care system works. One set of problems arises because patient–provider information asymmetry reduces the effectiveness of provider competition for patients as a device for controlling costs and inducing a cost-effective pattern of care. Another is due to items such as moral hazard associated with insurance and heterogeneity among patients that may cause behaviors such as excessive service utilization by patients, "cream-skimming" by insurers, and adverse selection in the consumers' choice of insurance plans.

In the second part of the chapter, alternative approaches to government participation in health care funding are discussed. One approach is for the government to pay for health services through a universal plan to which everyone is forced to belong (and which is paid for through a combination of general taxation and compulsory levies), with no – or a very limited – role for private insurance. (Examples of advanced countries that may be classified as following this model are Canada and Japan.) Another approach is one in which the funding system involves reliance both on government and on private insurance, with the latter serving either as a supplement to the government plan (the case of France), or at least partially as a substitute for it (Germany and Holland are examples of this type). Attention is also paid to the particular type of mixed approach that was envisaged in the reform proposals advanced in the United States by the Clinton administration during the early 1990s, and in Holland by the Dekker and Simmons committees, even though neither plan has been implemented in its original form. The chapter concludes with a brief summary in which comments are made on possible directions that a reform of the Canadian system of social health insurance may take in the future.

2.2
Health Services, Health Insurance, and Market Failure

2.2.1
Most Health Services are Private Goods

For many types of goods and services, government funding is justified by the fact that they are, at least to some extent, public goods. By definition, public goods have the characteristic that their production benefits not just a single individual or family, but yields benefits that are broadly shared by the society or community at large. Unless government pays for the production of such goods and services, too few of them will be produced, as individuals will tend to discount the benefits that accrue to others (the external benefits) when deciding how much to spend on them out of their own resources. Relying on government rather than on private markets for funding health care is sometimes justified by the claim that health services should be considered as being public goods.

Some health services do, indeed, have significant external benefits and therefore can be at least partly characterized as public goods. Specifically, the prevention and treatment of contagious disease do have this characteristic, to the extent that they reduce the risk that the beneficiaries will pass illness on to other people; so do screening programs to identify carriers of some diseases. In addition, certain activities that are undertaken by public health departments (which may or may not be classified as "health services") are public goods that have health benefits: examples are the enforcement of cleanliness standards in restaurants and the food industry, and the monitoring of drinking water supplies and bacteria counts in places where people swim. For all these types of service, there clearly is a case for government provision, or at least a government subsidy [1].

However, most of the health services produced in advanced countries today do not have major external benefits in this sense. The prevention and treatment of cardiovascular disease or cancer, for example, have large benefits to the patients and their families, but do not directly benefit strangers. The same is true about most interventions that deal with chronic problems (for example, joint replacements, cataract surgery, control of diabetes), including the long-term care of elderly people with disabilities. Because they do not have significant external effects in the traditional sense, the presumption in microeconomic theory would be that, other things being equal, they would be produced on an efficient scale if society simply allowed private agents to supply whatever quantities private buyers were willing to pay for.

But – as noted at the outset – even though most health services are private goods, there is another set of reasons why this standard conclusion is misleading in the case of health services. These have to do with the fact that various types of major illness occur at random, so that a well-functioning health care system must include institutional arrangements that, either explicitly or implicitly, provide people with some degree of insurance protection against the financial consequences of such illness [2].

2.2.2
The Efficiency of Risk Pooling and the Demand for Health Insurance

In standard microeconomic analysis of consumer demand, one typically studies a consumer who has a fixed budget (for example, monthly income) to allocate among different goods and services. The fixed budget, together with the prices per unit of the different commodities, can be used to define the set of all feasible combinations of quantities (units per month) that the consumer can afford. One then assumes that the consumers have given tastes (preferences) that enable them to rank all these combinations, and that their equilibrium choice is that combination of quantities that they prefer to all others that are possible, given their budget. Since it is mostly assumed that the consumers' preferences remain stable, one expects them to choose the same quantities period after a period as long as their income and the commodity prices stay the same; however, changes in income and prices will generally cause them to change the quantities purchased.

When one studies the demand for health care services, the emphasis is somewhat different. At the individual level, one does not generally expect the consumers' demand for health services to stay the same over time, even if their budget and the prices of health services stay the same. The reason, of course, is that the quantities of health services that consumers require depend primarily on whether or not they are sick. Most individuals are well most of the time, and do not use large amounts of health services even when their prices are low. However, from time to time, people fall ill. Most of the time, their problems will be minor, but on occasion a major illness will strike some. If everyone had to pay the full cost of all types of health care services out of their own pockets, the consequences of serious illness could obviously be very severe. In cases where effective treatment is very costly, many patients would be faced with the choice between either spending everything they had on health services, with little or nothing to spend on other things, or foregoing needed care, perhaps accepting pain and disability, and an increased risk of dying. For many types of disease, the cost of effective treatment if often so high that it would far exceed the resources that an average person has available, and even what they are able to borrow, so foregoing care would then be the only choice.

Even though the high cost of health care at the aggregate level is regarded as an important problem in many countries, it is still much more tractable at the aggregate (rather than the individual) level as the number of people with serious illness in any given year remains a small minority. When spread over the entire population, therefore, the resources that are needed to enable those with serious illness to be adequately treated will not constitute an intolerably large burden. This, in essence, is the reason why every modern society has some kind of mechanism of risk-pooling to share the cost of serious illness.

In tax-financed systems where all or most of these services are paid for out of general government revenue, the risk-pooling is implicit, as the burden is shifted from those who need them to the taxpayers at large [3]. However, risk-pooling can also occur through private insurance. In that case, all or most of the burden is shifted from those who are ill to those who are not but still pay the premiums out of which the insurance plans pay for the services used. The premiums, therefore, can be thought of as a type of tax that individuals pay voluntarily (as they can cancel the plan and stop paying the premium at any time). They can also be thought of as a membership fee in an ad hoc "community" which has undertaken to pay for its members' health care costs, on terms specified in the agreement written down in the insurance plan document. Individuals who believe that they are at risk for contracting serious illness are willing to pay this membership fee even when they are well, as prior membership is a condition for being covered if illness strikes.

Intuitively, most people will think of risk-pooling to pay for health services as something desirable because it is equitable: It implies a transfer from people who are lucky (who don't get sick) to those who are unlucky (who do get sick and suffer financially because they may not be able to work and, without insurance, would have to pay for the health care they need). From the viewpoint of economic theory, risk-pooling can also be efficient. In a population of risk-averse consumers with similar tastes and preferences, those who fall ill will have a more urgent need for money than those who are well. Since insurance payments effectively transfer funds from those who are well to those who are ill, the well-being of the population as a whole is therefore likely to be increased. If insurance is actuarially fair, meaning that all the money collected as premiums is transferred to those who are ill, this will happen for sure: The gains in welfare for those who receive the funds are larger than the losses in welfare corresponding to the premium payments.

A formal model that shows how the gains from insurance can be quantified is presented in Appendix 2.1.

2.2.3
The Gains from Health Insurance in Reality: Administrative Costs and Moral Hazard

In practice, the economic gains from insurance are not as large as the model in Appendix 2.1 suggests. For one thing, part of the gains will be offset by the costs of administering the insurance plans, whether private or public. Studies from the United States suggest that the administrative costs are particularly high in private plans, in part because of the money spent on marketing them. Although administrative costs are also considerable in public plans, the evidence suggests that they are much lower than in a system of competing private plans, something which constitutes an argument in favor of publicly provided insurance [5–7].

Another effect that reduces the gains from insurance is that associated with *moral hazard*, the term used to describe the tendency for the average cost of health care in an insured population to be higher than what it would be if the population was not insured. There are two types of moral hazard:

- Individuals who are insured have less of an incentive than uninsured ones to engage in behavior that is beneficial to their health and reduces the risk that they will become seriously ill. To the extent that this effect raises the risks of contracting various forms of illness, it will raise the average cost of health care in an insured population [8]. Note that, implicitly, this problem can be interpreted as resulting from imperfect information and incomplete contracts: If the insurer could costlessly observe and monitor the behavior of insured persons, then insurance contracts could be written so as to specify that they would only be valid if the insured engaged in behavior that reduced the risk of future illness. In reality, of course, many types of behavior cannot be effectively monitored, so it is not possible to enforce such contracts.
- The second type of moral hazard arises because conventional health insurance contracts take the form of an undertaking by the insurer to pay all or part of the cost of the health services incurred by the insured person. As has been extensively discussed in the literature, the fact that insurance takes this form will lead to some loss of economic efficiency, as the fact that patients do not pay the full cost of the health services they use implies an incentive to overuse them. This effect is completely analogous to the efficiency loss that arises when government subsidizes the consumption of any commodity in a perfectly competitive market in which there are no external effects.

From a theoretical perspective, a potentially more efficient form of insurance would be through a plan under which the consumer would simply receive a certain sum of money when a particular illness condition had been established, and then would be free to use the money either to pay for health services, or for any other purpose. (This is the case discussed in the formal analysis in Appendix 2.1.) The reason why such plans are not common is that illness conditions can vary so much, so that it is difficult or impossible to write enforceable insurance contracts that specify the amounts that would be payable under all types of different conditions [9]. Moreover, the information that would have to be used to determine a patient's illness condition would be in the form of a diagnosis made by a doctor based in part on the patient's description of symptoms. If the amounts paid out were to depend on the seriousness of the patients' conditions, it would be in the patients' interest to exaggerate the severity of their symptoms. Furthermore, if doctors are paid on the basis of fee for service, they also have an incentive to describe the patients' condition as serious, as this would give the patients more money out of which to pay the doctors' bills. For all of these reasons it is much simpler to design insurance plans in the conventional way, as undertakings to pay all or part of the actual cost of eligible services.

Because of the moral hazard problem, private insurance plans typically do not pay 100% of the costs incurred by the insured, but require some degree of patient cost sharing, in the form of deductibles and/or a fixed co-insurance percentage. However, patient cost-sharing of course implies a reduction in the degree of protection against the financial consequences of serious illness, so that even an optimally designed insurance plan of this kind represents a compromise: It accepts less-complete insurance in return for a more efficient pattern of health services utilization. For this reason, it is less efficient than a hypothetical (but unenforceable) optimal plan that simply pays the patient a fixed sum of money when they were ill [10–12].

Appendix 2.2 provides a formal model of the trade-off that is involved in designing a plan of this kind.

2.2.4
Information Asymmetry between Patients and Providers

In addition to the information asymmetry that exists between insurers on the one hand, and patients and their doctors on the other hand, the health care sector also is affected in a major way by the information asymmetry between patients and providers (doctors). As has been extensively discussed in the literature, patients typically do not have the specialized knowledge required to determine what the nature of their health problems are, nor what the likely outcome of different kinds of health care interventions will be. Because of the inherent uncertainty in treating illness, patients cannot tell for sure whether they were appropriately treated even after the outcome is known. Moreover, because the provision of health services often involves a very personal transaction between doctors and patients, the latter typically find it awkward to question or negotiate about both the treatment recommendations and the charges that the doctor proposes, or to look for better terms from another provider. As a result, competition among doctors for the provision of services to individual patients is not likely to be a very effective force in restraining the pricing of medical services, or in bringing about cost-effective patterns of care [13, 14]. In many countries, the tendency for price competition to be ineffective in the market for health care services is reinforced by professional associations of health care providers who discourage their members from advertising the fees they charge [15].

In a system of conventional health insurance, the information asymmetry between patients and providers may exacerbate the tendency toward an over-utilization of health services that results from the moral hazard effect. Since insured patients have less of an incentive than uninsured ones to be conservative in their use of health services, or to search for a provider that offers a lower price, doctors who have an incentive to increase the volume of services they provide, and to charge a high price for their services, will find it relatively easy to do so. The lack of effective competition as a result of the information asymmetry, and of the providers' ability to exploit their information advantage to induce patients to use more health services than they would if they had better information, is often described by saying that the market for health services gives rise to the possibility of *supplier-induced demand* (that is, unlike sellers in other markets, sellers of health services are in a position where they effective can control the demand for their own services). The potential for supplier-induced demand can be seen as another source of market failure in the health care sector, justifying a recommendation for some form of government intervention [16].

2.2.5
Managed Care as a Partial Response to Moral Hazard and Supplier-Induced Demand

Although moral hazard and providers' exploitation of their information advantage are often cited as sources of market failure, it should also be recognized that there are countries in which private markets have given rise to institutional arrangements designed to counteract the effects of these factors. In particular, some aspects of the managed-care plans that have become increasingly important in the market for private health insurance in the US can be interpreted as responses to these problems.

Managed-care plans can take many forms [17], but all of them have two features in common. First, they are based on closer contractual relationships between providers and insurers than in conventional plans. Under conventional plans of the type that were the most common form of insurance some years ago, insurers generally pay the plan's share of the cost of any services that have been provided by, or on the recommendation of, a properly licensed doctor. Although the plans might have specific limits on the amounts they would pay out to patients per unit of particular services, they typically did not prevent providers from charging higher amounts (although, of course, the patient then had to pay the difference out of pocket).

Under managed-care plans, the situation is different. For example, the contracts between the plan and the provider often specify the maximum rate that providers can charge patients for specific services, in cases where the provider is paid on the basis of fee for service. In other plans, the provider–insurer contracts specify other methods of paying for the providers' services, such as capitation (this is further discussed below), and may also contain provisions for bonuses that depend on the *ex post* cost of patient care. Through these means, the plans either place limits on the extent to which the providers can exploit their information advantage to charge high prices for their services, or reduce the incentives on them to produce high volumes of services for each patient. In addition, they often use administrative methods (such as "utilization reviews") to reduce the frequency with which certain services are used.

The second feature that characterizes all managed plans is related to the first – the plans place limits on the patients' right to choose their service provider. That is, all managed care plans either give patients no choice of provider (for example, in some Health Maintenance Organizations, patients are treated by whichever doctor is on duty when they arrive), or restrict them to seeking care from providers who appear on a list that the insurers maintain. (In some "hybrid" plans, the insurer will allow patients to seek care from providers that are not on the list, but when they do, they have to pay higher out-of-pocket charges than if they use the "preferred providers" on the plan's list.) The reason for these features, of course, is that unless they exist, providers will have no incentive to enter into the contracts that the plans use in their efforts to attain lower fees and more cost-effective patterns of care.

Some observers argue that the introduction of managed-care plans has reduced the significance of the market failures that are associated with moral hazard and patient–provider information asymmetry, and therefore have reduced the need for government intervention in the health services and insurance markets. When managed-care plans compete in the marketplace for the business of individuals, or of employers who are arranging group insurance coverage for their employees, they do so by trying to put together the most attractive combinations of insurance premiums (cost) and quality of care that they can design. While information asymmetry is still present (between providers and patients, and between insurers and individual buyers of health insurance), its significance has been reduced by the fact that negotiations regarding prices and patterns of care in a system of managed care are conducted principally between the providers and the insurance plans, not between providers and patients. Similarly, the marketing of health insurance plans in private markets more often involves employers (who can employ or consult knowledgeable experts), not individuals, on the buying side. For this reason, there are some who believe that a market-based system in which managed-care plans compete with each other in this way, is at least as likely to produce a pattern of cost-effective utilization of health care resources as a system in which the government directly provides insurance and/or health services.

2.2.6
Health Insurance and Individual Heterogeneity: Equity and Efficiency

The problems of moral hazard and information asymmetry would cause some degree of market failure in private insurance, even in a society where all individuals were similar in the sense of having the same risk of contracting different kinds of illness. However, differences in risk of illness, and imperfect information about such differences, are additional factors that may cause market failure in this sector.

Some differences in illness risk are associated with easily observable factors (age, gender, place of residence). Others can be established with reasonable reliability, though at some cost (previous history of serious illness, family illness history), while others – particularly those involving personal habits such as smoking, drinking, and exercise – will be known to the individuals themselves but are difficult for anyone else to ascertain with reliability [18, 19].

For private insurers, risk differences across individuals can matter a great deal, as the expected amount that will be paid out under a given insurance contract is proportional to the insured person's risk. For a given insurance premium, therefore, enrolling a person who is at low risk of illness will yield a higher expected profit for the insurer than enrolling a person with high risk. For this reason, private insurance plans typically do not permit "open enrollment" (that is, they will not automatically accept everyone's application to enter the plan), but instead will only allow enrollment for people who meet certain criteria related to the likelihood that they will file a claim. For individuals who are classified as being at high risk, the result is either that certain plans are not available to them, or that they have to pay above-average premiums for given plans.

An equilibrium in which different individuals pay different premiums for given insurance plans is not, in itself, inconsistent with economic efficiency as conventionally defined. It may, however, be inconsistent with many people's idea of equity, especially when the risk differences to which the premium differentials correspond are due to factors over which the individual has no control [20]. The terms that are used to describe the way that insurers try to enroll individuals at low risk ("cream-skimming"), and to discourage continued enrollment of individuals who have become classified as being at high risk ("dumping") have a negative connotation, reflecting this. In practice, however, risk differences have also given rise to severe efficiency problems in private insurance markets. Again, a major reason for this is the fact that information regarding many of the factors that give rise to risk differences is imperfect and asymmetrically distributed between the individuals who want to buy insurance and the insurers who sell it.

2.2.7
The Adverse Selection Problem

It has already been noted that administrative costs tend to be high in systems with multiple private insurance plans. These costs (which are incurred not only by the insurers but also by prospective clients) are partly attributable to what is called "underwriting" (the procedures that insurers use to try to differentiate among individuals with respect to their risk of illness). They also include payments to the actuaries who are responsible for establishing premium levels for different categories of individuals and plans. From a societal point of view, the resources used for these activities are largely wasted, as their main effect is simply to redistribute the burden of paying for health care services, with little or no effect on the total cost of care [21]. In a single-payer system where everyone automatically is covered by a monopoly government plan, these costs do not exist.

The type of market failure that has been most intensively discussed in the literature, however, arises as a consequence of residual information asymmetry that exists because individuals themselves have better information about some factors that affect their risk of illness than insurers do, in spite of the techniques that insurers use to obtain such information. In part, this information asymmetry of course exists because individuals have an incentive to not be truthful about factors that raise their risk, as a higher risk rating is likely to result in a higher premium level at best, or a denial of coverage at worst. This residual asymmetry gives rise to the problem of *adverse selection*, one that has been a prominent part of the literature on health insurance markets since the 1970s [4, 18].

Adverse selection in insurance markets results because, for a plan with a given benefit package and a given premium, those who know themselves to be at high risk will find the plan more attractive than those who know that they are at relatively low risk. (Loosely speaking, the expected benefit of belonging to the plan is higher for those at high risk because they are more likely to file claims for benefits, but individuals at high risk pay the same premium as those at low risk since, by assumption, the insurer does not have the information to tell who is in which risk category.) But suppose now that there is a choice among several alternative plans, with some having more generous benefit packages but higher premiums, while others have less generous benefit packages and lower premiums. If the premiums are at a level which would make the plans actuarially fair [22] for a person with an average risk, then those at high risk would tend to opt for the more generous (but more expensive) plans, while those at low risk would opt for the less generous, cheaper, ones (or perhaps forgo insurance altogether). This is what is referred to as "selection".

However, the systematic tendency for those at higher risk to choose the more generous plans means that, from the insurers' point of view, these plans will become unprofitable. As a result, their premiums will tend to rise, making them less attractive. Conversely, the selection effect will make the less-generous plans more attractive since those enrolled in them have lower-than-average risk. This will tend to reduce their premiums which, in turn, will further change the relative attractiveness of the plans, leading to further changes in enrollment patterns, and so on.

A general analysis of the adverse selection problem is difficult, both because insurance markets can be very complex when there are many different kinds of plans, and because it is difficult to measure the degree of information asymmetry between individuals and insurers with respect to differences in illness risk [23]. However, the general pattern that emerges from discussions of simplified models is that the equilibria that exist tend to be characterized by patterns where generous insurance plans are driven out of the market, or purchased by a very small minority of people, since adverse selection makes them very expensive. (The situation where adverse selection is severe enough to make the generous plans so expensive that nobody wants them and they disappear, is sometimes referred to as a "death spiral".) At the same time, people at low risk tend to choose plans that offer relatively incomplete insurance (for example, by requiring patients to pay a relatively large share of the costs of their care, or by stipulating that care can only be given by physicians in managed care plans who follow restrictive rules regarding patient care).

The problem with adverse selection is further analyzed in a formal model in Appendix 2.3.

2.2.8
Group Insurance as a Partial Response

In the discussion of insurance market failure due to moral hazard and patient–provider information asymmetry, it was noted that innovations in private insurance (principally in the form of managed care) had evolved to partially counteract these problems, even in cases where government had not intervened to deal with them. With respect to adverse selection, private markets have also developed a partial countervailing mechanism, namely group insurance.

The logic here is that if a common plan is offered to all members of some collective that has been formed according to some exogenous characteristic (such as all employees of a large firm, or all members of an industry-wide labor union), the adverse selection problem will largely be eliminated as long as the choice of belonging to the group is not significantly affected by the risk of illness. In the case of employment-related group insurance, the plan can include family members as well as the workers themselves, for similar reasons [25].

Although the development of group insurance can go a long way towards reducing the consequences of adverse selection, it is obviously not a perfect remedy. For one thing, many individuals (the self-employed, the unemployed, those employed in small firms) do not belong to any collective that offers group insurance. Second, as has been extensively discussed in the US literature, group insurance may reduce mobility in the labor market. The reason is that employers' group insurance plans usually do not allow automatic enrollment of new employees. Consequently, individuals who belong to a group plan that their current employer offers, and who have experienced major illness episodes, will be reluctant to leave their current job even if a better one is available, as they cannot be assured of coverage through a prospective new employer's plan. (This problem is sometimes referred to as "job lock".) [26]

A particular group for which the problem of adverse selection (as well as those of "cream-skimming" and "dumping") are likely to be especially difficult in a system that relies on private insurance, is the elderly. Because older people typically use larger amounts of health services than others, the premiums they would have to pay in a privately funded system would be quite high on average. Moreover, by the time that individuals have become old, it is relatively easy to single out those who are at high risk of illness, by looking at their past medical history. For retired people who have had significant medical problems in the past, private insurance would become either very difficult to find, or very expensive. Thus, the problems of both inequity and inefficiency of a system of health care funding through private insurance would be particularly severe for this population group. It is no accident, therefore, that even in the US, which relies more on funding of health care through private insurance than any other advanced country, there is a government-funded plan that covers everyone over age 65 years.

2.3
Different Models for Government Funding of Health Care

In the remainder of this chapter it will be assumed that, in response to the types of market failure in private insurance discussed above, the government offers citizens access to insurance through some type of publicly funded or government-organized plan. The discussion focuses on different models that have been used in designing plans that resolve or minimize the consequences of these market failures.

2.3.1
What Constitutes an Effective Funding System?

A well-functioning public plan must fulfill certain obvious criteria. First, it must be able to control the aggregate cost of health care more effectively than conventional private insurance, which means that it must have measures to counteract the cost-increasing tendencies due to moral hazard and supplier-induced demand, as well as to ensure that administrative costs, broadly defined, are kept low. Second, it must be designed so as to encourage the efficient use of resources in the health care system as a whole. In a system of private insurance, this goal may not be met very effectively if moral hazard and distorted provider incentives on the supply side are significant problems, but competition among different types of private plans can imply at least some tendency to encourage efficient resource use. If government intervention takes the form of requiring everyone to belong to the same universal plan, this effect is absent and efficient resource use must be promoted by other means.

Another criterion for a well-designed publicly organized system is that it should effectively address the equity and efficiency problems associated with differences in the risk of illness, including cream-skimming, dumping, and adverse selection. One way of accomplishing this, of course, is to force everybody to belong to the same tax-financed plan. However, it is also desirable that the system should leave room for some consumer and patient choice. For example, some individuals are less risk-averse than others; other things equal, allowing them to carry larger amounts of financial risk is efficient. Similarly, some people place a high value on being able to choose the doctor and hospital where they are treated, while others are happy to be treated by providers to whom they have been assigned. Again, it is efficient to allow the former to enroll in a plan in which they can choose their provider if they are willing to pay the extra cost of being in such a plan. Or again, some people may prefer to be treated by a doctor who does not have a financial incentive to recommend conservative patterns of treatment in order to save cost. Once more, it is efficient to allow them to choose a plan in which doctors do not have such an incentive, if they are willing to pay the extra cost.

In spite of the potential advantages of allowing some degree of consumer choice among competing insurance plans, a number of countries have organized their systems so that insurance is through a single government-funded plan that automatically covers every citizen; this is often referred to as the "single-payer" model of health funding. Three countries that fit this description reasonably well are Canada, Japan, and the United Kingdom. In other countries, however, the funding system is mixed in the sense that, although there is one or more public plans that cover some parts of the population, not everyone has to belong to these plans, and many of those not covered by the public plans have private insurance instead. Countries in this category include the US and Holland, as well as others. In the following sections, the basic features of the health care systems in the single-payer countries just mentioned are summarized, and some advantages and disadvantages of each are discussed. Consideration is then given to the models in the countries classified as mixed systems; in the cases of the US and Holland, a brief summary is provided both of the way in which their mixed systems have functioned in the past, and certain proposals for reform based on enhancement of competition among insurance plans that have figured prominently in these countries at various times.

2.3.2
Single-Payer Plans and Equity

Perhaps the most important advantage of a single universal government plan is that, by definition, it eliminates problems of cream-skimming, dumping, and adverse selection. For this reason, and also because it makes the cost of health insurance independent of illness risk, most people rate such a system highly in terms of equity, especially when, as in the cases of Canada and the United Kingdom (UK), the plans do not impose significant user fees. However, the system accomplishes this by virtue of the fact that it is a monopoly plan. With a universal government plan, private insurers are not able to compete by offering alternative plans, even when they think there would be a market for them, and individuals are not allowed the opportunity to try alternative forms of insurance that they might prefer [27]. Moreover, the equity advantage of a universal tax-financed system may be reduced to some extent if substantial excess demand develops for some services, and better-off individuals are able to turn to alternative private care (as in the UK, and to some extent also in Canada when patients receive private treatment in the US), or draw on personal contacts to "jump the queue". However, the principle of everyone having the same access to care is nevertheless highly valued by many [28].

Another dimension of equity in the health economics literature refers to the incidence of the revenue collection process associated with financing the government plan. For example, even though Japan has been classified here as a single-payer system, health funding is actually through compulsory levies payable to many different sickness funds to which individuals belong by virtue of factors such as occupation, age and residence, and so on. One of the criticisms of the Japanese system is that, even though everyone is entitled to the same package of benefits, no matter which sickness fund they belong to, people in otherwise similar circumstances may have to pay different contribution rates depending on where they live (if they are retired), or what profession they belong to. This pattern indeed seems like a violation of the principle of "horizontal equity", and exists principally for historical reasons [29].

In systems such as those of Canada and the U.K., where the government plan is financed out of general tax revenue, it is not possible to distinguish the equity concept associated with funding health care from the general question of incidence of the tax system as a whole. Indeed, even in systems where government insurance is funded, at least in part, through some form of compulsory contribution (such as a payroll tax), care is needed before one can meaningfully interpret the incidence of this contribution as a component of the equity measure for the health care system [30]. Nevertheless, it is clear that a tax-financed system of government health insurance does constitute a tool that can contribute significantly to equity: It eliminates at least a major part of the inequality in real income that would exist as a consequence of differences in the risk of illness if individuals had to rely entirely on private insurance instead.

2.3.3
Cost Control and Efficient Resource Use in the Single-Payer Case

As discussed above, in a system of health care funding through private insurance, moral hazard and supplier-induced demand are likely to produce an inefficient and costly pattern of care, especially if insurance is of the conventional type (when the insurer passively pays its share of actual health care costs) and providers are paid through fee for service (so that they have an incentive to supply a large volume of services). Insurance through a universal public system does not automatically resolve this problem, as moral hazard and supplier-induced demand may also be present in a publicly funded system. However, when all or most health care funding comes from a single public plan to which every citizen belongs, it is easier to implement measures that contain costs and promote efficiency than it is in a system of multiple private insurers.

As previously noted, one reason for this is that administrative costs tend to be lower with a single-payer plan. In addition, a monopoly public plan has more market power when negotiating over payment rates with service providers and pharmaceutical companies, and so can more easily control fees and keep aggregate costs down even when reimbursement is through fee for service.

A good example of this model is Japan, where both physician and hospital care are paid for through fee for service, but the fees are tightly regulated. To judge by aggregate statistics, this system appears to work well: Japanese health care costs as a percentage of GDP are low by international standards, and life expectancy and infant mortality rates – the most often-cited indicators of population health status – place Japan at the top in international rankings [31].

One explanation for Japan's relative success in keeping total costs down is that the fee schedule has favored outpatient care relative to hospitalization, and has provided independent family doctors with an incentive to try to keep patients out of hospital. However, critics of the Japanese system also point to other consequences of the way the fee schedule has been designed, including a pattern under which family doctors see a very large number of patients each day, but each visit is very short, and an incentive structure that results in per capita expenditure on pharmaceuticals among the highest in the world [32]. Moreover, patients in Japan have to pay relatively substantial user fees under the public plan. While user fees obviously can help to control aggregate health care costs by reducing the extent of moral hazard, they also imply a reduction in the degree of insurance protection under the plan, as discussed earlier, so that setting them at too high a level will be inefficient, and cost control through user fees is of course also considered by many to be inequitable (since the poor can be expected to reduce their service utilization more than the rich in response to given fees).

Administered or unilaterally imposed fees for health services, such as in Canada and Japan, constitute a form of price control and, according to standard microeconomic theory, price controls are likely to result in excess demand if the controlled prices are set below equilibrium levels. The literature on the Japanese system does not give the impression that this has been a major problem there, suggesting that the provider fees and user fees imposed on patients have been high enough to avoid disequilibrium. In Canada, in contrast, the price and budget controls that have been used to control aggregate costs have given rise to increasing excess demand, resulting in waiting lists for many types of hospital and specialist services. They have also led to an increasing use of emergency rooms (with long waiting times for service in many cases) for primary care, as the supply of family doctors' services has fallen behind the demand, a form of inefficiency that has been the cause of increasing dissatisfaction in recent years [33].

In the UK model of a single-payer system, the National Health Service (NHS), there are almost no user fees (as in Canada). Nevertheless, the UK also stands out as a country where the aggregate costs of health care (whether in absolute terms or relative to GDP) are comparatively low. Part of the explanation for this may be that the NHS has been using methods to pay providers that do not imply an incentive to produce high volumes of services. In particular, at the core of the NHS is a network of primary care providers (known as General Practitioners, or GPs) who are paid through a mixed system that is based predominantly on salary and *capitation*, rather than on fee for service. Under a capitation system, patients can only obtain access to primary care by signing up with a single GP for a fixed period of time. Each GP, in turn, has a contract under which the NHS will pay them a fixed capitation payment per month for each patient on their roster; in return, the GP is responsible for giving patients medical care as needed, at no additional charge. British GPs also have a "gate-keeping" role, in the sense that patients can only be given pharmaceuticals, or be treated in hospital, on the GP's recommendation.

During the 1990s, the gate-keeping role was strengthened by giving many GPs an additional budget out of which they were responsible for paying a part of their patients' drug costs and costs for certain types of hospital services [34]. Thus, under a capitation system the GPs' incentive is not to produce a large volume of services, but instead to take responsibility for the care of many patients. Similarly, the methods used by the NHS to pay for hospital services typically have not been such as to give the hospitals (and the doctors working in them) an incentive to produce large volumes of services: Many hospitals were funded through an annual budget, and hospital-based physicians were paid a fixed salary.

While the UK system has relatively low cost by international standards, its health status indicators are not quite as favorable as Japan's. Moreover, waiting lists and some degree of access problems have long been a feature of the UK National Health Service. Unlike Canada, the UK does, however, have a fairly large number of doctors who practice both in the government plans and privately, and while everyone is covered by the government plan, private insurers are allowed to offer plans that cover the same services as those offered by the NHS. Private practice and private insurance may to some extent have served as a safety valve that has relieved some of the pressure that otherwise would have been generated as a result of waiting times and access problems in the UK government plan.

Although Japan and the UK provide examples of single-payer models that have been able to effectively control total health care costs, there is much less agreement on the question which of the two is best able to ensure that health service resources are used efficiently. A definitive answer to this question may not be possible, partly because both systems are constantly evolving and being improved. Some of those who think some version of the UK system holds more promise, however, raise an interesting question. They note that one may interpret the Japanese system as one that is administered more like a conventional insurance plan (under which insured persons have free choice of provider, and providers are paid on the basis of fee for service), and the UK system as more like a managed-care plan (where insured persons face restrictions on which providers they may use, and providers are paid on the basis of methods such as capitation for primary care doctors, and annual global budgets for hospitals). However, the outcome of the competitive process among private insurance plans in the US seems clearly to favor plans of the managed-care type. Should one interpret this as a suggestion that, in the long run, some version of the UK system is more likely to show us a successful model than the Japanese approach which is based on a tightly controlled system of fee for service?

2.3.4
Cost Control and Resource Utilization in Systems of Mixed Public–Private Insurance

While there are a few countries in which government funding and regulation have rendered the role of private health insurance negligible (Japan, Italy), private insurance accounts for a non-trivial portion of what is conventionally defined as health care spending in most countries, including several of those that are often classified as single-payer systems (Canada and the UK among them). However, private insurance plays very different roles in different systems [35]. In some countries (such as Canada), most private plans act as a *supplement* to the government plan in that they provide coverage against costs that are not covered in the main government plan (such as pharmaceuticals and dental care). In others, private plans are *complementary* to the public plan in the sense that they reimburse patients for user fees that are imposed in the public plan (France is the most often-cited case in this category). In the UK, some private health plans provide *duplicate* insurance in the sense that they cover the same services that the public plan does, but in private facilities. A system in which this is allowed is regarded by many as inequitable, in that privately funded care will be used by those with private insurance in order to get treatment more quickly when there are waiting lists for publicly funded care (those with private coverage can "jump the queue"); this is likely to be the principal reason why plans that provide duplicate insurance remain illegal in most Canadian provinces. Others, however, look at private duplicate insurance as beneficial in the sense that it may reduce the demand for, and cost of, publicly funded care – an argument that is sometimes applied to the Australian case where many individuals have private hospital insurance [36].

Systems in which private insurance is used to supplement or complement the public plan or to provide duplicate coverage, are essentially variations on the single-payer principle (or, more accurately, on the model with universal compulsory public insurance). Another form of mixed system is when there is a public plan to which all citizens belong by default, but membership in the public plan is not compulsory: Anyone is permitted to *opt out* of the public plan and choose coverage through a private insurance plan instead. An essential feature of a true opting-out system is that those who opt out should be financially compensated, at least to some extent, for doing so; if they are not, then membership in the public plan is effectively compulsory (as in the UK).

As noted earlier, one argument in favor of a mixed system of this type in which individuals can substitute a private plan for the public one, is that when individuals have different tastes and preferences, it is economically efficient to offer them the opportunity to choose among many plans so that they can pick the one that best corresponds to their preferences. However, a mixed system of this kind may be advantageous even when individuals have similar preferences. The main argument that is stressed by many who favor a mixed system is that it implies competition for the government plan: The ability of private insurance plans to survive depends on whether or not they can offer more attractive combinations of premium costs and standards of care than the government plan. If they can, it is economically efficient for them to do so; if they cannot, then no harm has been done. Because of the effects of competition, a system which allows opting out may be regarded as successful even if, in the end, only a small minority of the population choose to enroll in a private plan. The reason is that, in the presence of competition from private plans, politicians and managers of the public plan have a strong incentive to operate more efficiently and reduce costs, since otherwise they will lose market share. The end result may be continued dominance by the public plan, but by a public plan that is more efficient and less costly than it would have been without the threat of competition.

At present, government plans which allow opting out in this sense exist in only a few countries, and the possibility to opt out may be limited to certain population groups only. In Germany and (until recently) in Holland, where insurance through the regular public plan requires an income-related contribution to a sickness fund, only individuals with an annual income above a certain threshold were allowed to opt out and enroll in an approved private plan instead. When they did, they no longer had to contribute to the sickness funds [37].

In the US, there is of course no universal public plan for the population as a whole. However, everyone over the age of 65 years (and individuals with certain types of disability) are covered by the federal Medicare plan, which is essentially funded out of general federal revenue plus a fixed premium payable by the consumer [38]. Since the 1970s, a limited form of opting out has existed in the Medicare plan, in the sense that individuals in the plan had the right to enroll in an approved private Health Maintenance Organization (HMO) instead; when they did, the Medicare plan transferred an annual amount to the HMO that roughly corresponded to the expected cost of the health care that the individual would have been eligible for if he or she had remained in the regular plan. Since 1997, beneficiaries have been given a wider choice of approved private plans they can opt for (the Medicare plan was at that time given a new name, "Medicare+Choice"; following additional changes it was again renamed, to "Medicare Advantage", in 2003).

Interestingly, a system of opting out also forms the basic framework for two of the most dramatic attempts at health care reform that the world has seen in the past few decades, namely the Clinton plan introduced in the US in 1992, and the Dekker–Simmons plan for reforming the Dutch health care system that was originally introduced in Holland during the late 1980s [39]. Under both the Clinton plan and the Dekker–Simmons plan, the concept of "opting out" would disappear, in the sense that all approved insurance plans (whether organized by the public or private sectors) would be treated symmetrically. However, the principle of universality would continue to apply, in the sense that everyone would be required to belong to *some* approved insurance plan, and most – but not all – of the premium cost would be paid out of government funds. Since insurance through managed care has generally been shown to be more attractive to most people than conventional coverage when the two forms have been allowed to compete (in the US system), most scenarios for how the US and Dutch systems would evolve under these reforms were based on the expectation that most people would be covered by managed-care plans. (However, under the Clinton plan, the intention was that the option of signing up for a conventional plan, with no restrictions on the choice of provider, would also have been available to every citizen.)

In the US, the Clinton plan is generally regarded as a failure, as it did not pass through Congress and the US still remains one of the few advanced countries that does not have universal health coverage. However, many of the principles on which the plan was based are the same as those that now characterize the Medicare Advantage plan for people aged over 65 years and the disabled. In Holland, the process of health care reform has been so slow that, at times, it appeared to have stalled completely. However, as of 2006 – some 20 years after the publication of the original Dekker report – the principle that sickness funds are to be organized as a system of competing managed-care plans, and that an individual can choose enrollment in any of the funds offering coverage where he or she lives, was finally implemented. For those who believe that the Clinton and Dekker–Simmons plans constituted well-designed blueprints for a system that combines the equity advantage of universal compulsory health insurance with the potential efficiency advantages of competition among multiple insurance plans, it will be very interesting to follow the performance of the reformed Dutch health care system in the future.

2.3.5
Opting Out: Cream-Skimming and Adverse Selection

Although a system that rests on individual choice among competing insurance plans may appear attractive, it will have to deal with the fact that individuals differ in terms of risk of illness, so that the incentives for cream-skimming and dumping will be present, and the adverse selection problem will continue to exist. Both, the Clinton plan and the Dekker–Simmons plan devoted considerable attention to methods that could be used to overcome these problems, at least partially [40].

Essentially, the methods they proposed consisted of devising formulae through which an individual person's expected annual cost of health care could be predicted, based not only on observable characteristics such as age and gender, but also on other factors such as aspects of the person's illness history. These estimates would then have become the basis for the contribution that the government would make to the private or public insurance plan with which people would sign up. The government contribution was intended to cover only some 80% of the cost of an average plan, and insurers would, in addition, be allowed to charge a premium directly to the insured person. Under the regulations that were proposed, this premium had to be the same for every person in the plan. That is, the insurer's revenue from insuring a given individual would consist, first, of a fixed premium that would be the same for every individual, and second, a government contribution that would differ from person to person, in a way intended the reflect differences in each person's annual health care costs. The intention of this method was to equalize, as far as possible, the profitability of insuring any given person, by means of having the government make a bigger contribution for persons at high risk, and vice versa.

If a system of this type were to work well, it would be able largely to overcome the problems of cream-skimming and dumping (as it would substantially eliminate the difference in the profitability of insuring individuals with differences in expected health care costs that depend on observable characteristics). However, since the problem of adverse selection depends on differences in expected health care costs of which individuals themselves are aware, but which cannot be observed by the insurers, differentiated premium contributions would not be a wholly effective remedy against adverse selection. Nevertheless, the selection problem would likely be less severe under this type of system than it would be if insurers were constrained to charge a total premium that was the same for everyone, as regulations in some countries require.

A system that allows individuals to choose among different insurance plans would lead different people to choose plans that would differ in various ways with respect to the degree of protection and standards of care they offered. It would, therefore, most likely result in some diversity with respect to how individuals were treated when they were sick, with the possibility that those with a lower income would opt for less-expensive plans and a lower standard of care in some dimensions than those with a higher income. Nevertheless, a system of differentiated government premium contributions at least promotes equity in the sense that it provides more support to those at high risk of illness, and by ensuring that everyone, regardless of income or employment status, at least has access to good care under some approved public plan on the same terms as everyone else.

2.4
Conclusion: The Future of Social Health Insurance in Canada

In historical perspective, Canada's health care system has performed very well compared to that of the US since the reforms that introduced the basic Canadian Medicare system were completed during the early 1970s. It has been much less costly, and has been considered by almost everyone as much more equitable than the US version because it provides every citizen with access to the same level of health care, regardless of an ability to pay.

However, in comparison with the health care systems in several European countries and Japan, the performance of the Canadian system has not stood out as exceptional. During recent years, both the UK and Japan have devoted a considerably smaller portion of their GDPs to health care than has Canada, with little or no evidence that the health status of their populations has been inferior to that of Canada. Although countries such as France, the Netherlands, and Germany devote a roughly similar proportion of GDP to healthcare as Canada, they do so even though they have a much larger proportion of elderly people than Canada, so that one would have expected their health care systems to be more expensive.

Moreover, questions are increasingly being asked about the efficiency with which health care resources are being used in Canada, as waiting lists for many types of treatment have become lengthy, and more people are finding it difficult to obtain access to primary care from a regular family doctor. The recent "Chaoulli decision" that ultimately may clear the way for an increasing role for "duplicate" private insurance can be taken as another sign that these quality issues are being taken more seriously than in the past [41]. The pressure to revamp the system so that it addresses these types of problem is only likely to become stronger over time, as new medical technologies and drugs come on stream. Many of these will be expensive, and consequently an increasing number of decisions will have to be made with regards to who will be treated, with which type of drug or technology, and how the aggregate costs will be controlled.

As is clear from the previous discussion, international approaches to designing forms of government intervention that effectively counter the market failures inherent in a purely private system have differed a great deal from country to country. In some countries (notably Japan), the system that has evolved is based on a high degree of detailed central planning and control of health service prices and the funding system. However, in many others a trend has emerged toward decentralization and variety in the funding and contracting for health services, with elements of managed care as part of the system. This certainly has been true in the US Medicare plan for the retired and disabled, as well as in the state Medicaid plans that provide access to health care for those with a low income. It has also been true in Holland. Even in single-payer systems (such as the UK and Sweden), decentralization has been strengthened and, as the UK experience shows, some of the incentive features of private managed-care plans can be mimicked in the context of a single-payer monopoly plan, by introducing capitation and gatekeeping features in primary care [42]. Pilot projects involving capitation as a method of paying for primary care have already been undertaken in some Canadian provinces. To move further in this direction may require experimentation with patient rostering (that is, restricting patients to seeking care from a single designated primary-care provider during a specific period of time). The regionalization of hospital management that is underway in almost all Canadian provinces may indirectly strengthen the trend toward use of managed-care principles, especially if organization and funding of primary care is also delegated to the regional managers.

Reform that would create the opportunity to opt out of the public plan, along the lines of what is happening in the Netherlands, or that was envisaged under the Clinton plan, is probably not going to be seriously contemplated in Canada in the medium-term future. However, the pressure in favor of allowing some variety in insurance coverage may gradually become stronger, in part because of advancing medical technology. As the range of possible treatment options grows, it will become increasingly difficult to resolve questions with respect to who is going to be entitled to what treatment in the political arena, within the framework of a single monopoly plan. The design of a model that will allow people more freedom to choose from a range of treatment philosophies will ultimately become a task that cannot be avoided, and a broad-ranging debate about how this can be accomplished without sacrificing the fundamental values underlying Canada's Medicare system could be both interesting and useful.

References

1 Hurley, J. (2000), An overview of the normative economics of the health sector, Chapter 2 in Culyer, A. J., Newhouse, J. P. (Eds.), *Handbook of Health Economics*, Amsterdam: North-Holland, Volume **1A**, pp. 55–118, contains a useful discussion of health services with public-goods characteristics. In his chapter, Hurley also summarizes the views of writers who favor somewhat broader concepts of external effects of health services utilization, some of which are based on the existence of broadly based altruistic concerns for the health of other people. These concepts are closely related to concerns

regarding the equity of the health care system.

2 In his classic 1963 article, Kenneth Arrow stressed this characteristic of the demand for health services, which he referred to as "uncertainty of demand". For a discussion, see again Hurley (2000), *op. cit.*, pp. 79–82

3 Gerdtham, U.G., Jönsson, B. (2000), International comparisons of health expenditure. Chapter 1 in Culyer, A.J., Newhouse, J.P. (Eds.), *Handbook of Health Economics*, Amsterdam: North-Holland, Volume **1A**, pp. 11–54, uses the terminology "publicly integrated systems" for the case when health services are funded by government and most services are directly produced in hospitals and other facilities that are owned by the government. Such systems are more commonly referred to as the "national health service model". The most well-known example is the UK; Gerdtham and Jönsson cite the Nordic countries and Italy as other examples.

4 Cutler, D.M., Zeckhauser, R.J. (2000), The anatomy of health insurance. Chapter 11 in Culyer, A.J., Newhouse, J.P. (Eds.), *Handbook of Health Economics*, Amsterdam: North-Holland, Volume **1A**, pp. 563–644, gives a similar example (see especially pp. 573–575). See also Hurley (2000), *op. cit.*, pp. 80–81.

5 Woolhandler, S., Himmelstein, D.U. (1991), The deteriorating efficiency of the US health care system. *New England Journal of Medicine*, **324**, 1253–1258. In this paper the systems in Canada and the US are compared in this respect; it is an often-cited study that starkly illustrates this difference. (An updated version is available in Ref. [6]). Patrician Danzon (see Ref. [7]) has argued that not all of the administrative cost in the US represents waste, however, as part of it is attributable to activities that increase consumer choice among insurance plans and make the US system more efficient in some dimensions.

6 Woolhandler, S., Campbell, T., Himmelstein, D.U. (2003), Costs of health care in the United States and Canada.

New England Journal of Medicine, **349**, 768–775.

7 Danzon, P. (1992), Hidden overhead costs: Is Canada's system really less expensive? *Health Affairs*, **11**, 21–43.

8 Zweifel, P., Manning, W.G. (2000), Moral hazard and consumer incentives in health care. Chapter 8 in Culyer, A.J., Newhouse, J.P. (Eds.), *Handbook of Health Economics*, Amsterdam: North-Holland, Volume **1A**, pp. 409–460, contains a discussion of the consequences of both this type of "ex ante" moral hazard and the second "ex post" type (see below).

9 In recent years, plans that specify large cash payouts if the holder is diagnosed with one of a specified set of "dread diseases" (such as cancer) have appeared in the market. They are, in fact, examples of this more efficient type of insurance, but their range is inherently limited to only the types of disease for which an unambiguous diagnosis can be made.

10 Zeckhauser, R. (1970), Medical insurance: a case study of the trade-off between risk spreading and appropriate incentives. *Journal of Economic Theory*, **2**, 10–26. This is the classic paper on this trade-off. Blomqvist [11] considers the generalization to non-linear insurance. Newhouse and colleagues [12] also include a discussion of a limited form of second-best optimal non-linear insurance.

11 Blomqvist, Å.G. (1997), Optimal non-linear health insurance. *Journal of Health Economics*, **16**, 313–321.

12 Newhouse, J.P. and the Insurance Experiment Group (1993), *Free For All? Lessons from the Rand Health Insurance Experiment*. Cambridge, Mass.: Harvard University Press.

13 Dranove, D., Satterthwaite, M. (2000), The industrial organization of health care markets. Chapter 20 in Culyer, A.J., Newhouse, J.P. (Eds.), *Handbook of Health Economics*, Amsterdam: North-Holland, Volume **1B**, pp. 1093–1140.

14 McGuire, T.G., Physician agency. Chapter 9 in Culyer, A.J., Newhouse, J.P.

(Eds.), *Handbook of Health Economics*, Amsterdam: North-Holland, Volume **1A**, pp. 461–536.

15 Kwoka, J.E. (1984), Advertising and the price and quality of optometric services. *American Economics Review*, **74**, 211–216. The author conducted a case study of how the intensity of competition in the market for optometric services increased (with lower prices as a result) when the right of individual physicians to advertise their services and rates was strengthened through a federal court decision in the US in 1980.

16 McGuire, T.G. (2000), Physician agency. Chapter 9 in Culyer, A.J., Newhouse, J.P. (Eds.), *Handbook of Health Economics*, Amsterdam: North-Holland, Volume **1A**, pp. 461–536, contains a detailed discussion. Supplier-induced demand is often referred to in the literature by the acronym SID, though McGuire uses PID (provider-induced demand).

17 Glied, S. (2000), Managed care. Chapter 13 in Culyer, A.J., Newhouse, J.P. (Eds.), *Handbook of Health Economics*, Amsterdam: North-Holland, Volume **1A**, pp. 707–754.

18 Van de Ven, W., Ellis, R.P. (2000), Risk adjustment in competitive health plan markets. Chapter 14 in Culyer, A.J., Newhouse, J.P. (Eds.), *Handbook of Health Economics*, Amsterdam: North-Holland, Volume **1A**, pp. 755–846, contains a detailed review of the literature on how well individual risk of illness can be estimated.

19 Ellis, R.P. (2007), see Chapter 6, this volume.

20 Blomqvist, Å.G., Horn, H. (1984), Public Health Insurance and Optimal Income Taxation. *Journal of Public Economics*, **24**, 353–373. This contains an analysis of a model in which public funding of health insurance supplements progressive income taxation as part of a policy to create a more equitable distribution of real income.

21 To the extent that predicted differences in illness risk and premium discrimination depend on life-style factors that individuals can modify (such as smoking, alcohol consumption, and perhaps some measures of physical fitness), there may be some desirable incentive effects from risk discrimination. However, in reality most factors that are used in predicting risk (such as family illness history) will be those over which individuals have no control.

22 An actuarially fair plan was defined earlier as one in which all premium revenue was paid out to plan members for covered expenses. Alternatively, it can be defined as a plan where the premium is equal to the expected value of these costs.

23 Rothschild, M., Stiglitz, J. (1976), Equilibrium in competitive insurance markets: An essay on the economics of imperfect information. *Quarterly Journal of Economics*, **90**, 281–305. This classic paper analyzes the case with only two risk classes but continuously variable degrees of coverage. In the paper by Cutler, D.M., Reber, S.J. (1998), "Paying for health insurance: the tradeoff between competition and adverse selection" (*Quarterly Journal of Economics*, **113**, 433–466), the analysis focuses on a model with only two insurance plans but a continuum of risk classes. One of the most illuminating papers on the subject is Marquis, M.S. (1992), " Adverse selection with a multiple choice among health insurance plans: A simulation analysis", *Journal of Health Economics*, **11**, 125–153, in which the author simulates equilibrium degrees of adverse selection in models where the degree of information asymmetry has been calibrated on the basis of data generated as part of the Rand Health Insurance experiment.

24 Rothschild, M., Stiglitz, J. (1976), *op. cit.*

25 Gruber, J. (2000), Health insurance and the labor market. Chapter 12 in Culyer, A.J., Newhouse, J.P. (Eds.), *Handbook of Health Economics*, Amsterdam: North-Holland, Volume **1A**, pp. 645–706. This discusses the reasons for, and the consequences of, the fact that most group health insurance in the US is employment-related.

26 Group insurance also is an imperfect remedy against adverse selection in the sense that it makes it difficult to accommodate differences in group members' preferences among different types of plans. Some choice may be possible, but if there is too much, then adverse selection will again become a problem.

27 In places where alternative private plans are illegal (as in many Canadian provinces), this is true by definition. In other places, alternative private plans are not illegal, but they cannot compete effectively with the universal government plan as the latter is offered for free to all taxpayers, while the former must charge a high enough premium to cover their cost. Thus, individuals who have private insurance plans in such countries are effectively "paying twice" for health insurance – once through the tax system, and once through premiums.

28 Although I have classified both Canada and the UK as single-payer systems with a monopoly government plan, certain types of private insurance do exist in both these countries, of course. In Canada, many people have private plans that cover items such as the cost of pharmaceuticals and dental care, neither of which are part of the provincial government plans. In the UK, many individuals also have private plans that cover items not covered in the government plan, but that may also cover private provision of the same services as those that are available free of charge from the NHS.

29 Wagstaff, A., van Doorslaer, E. (2000), Equity in health care finance and delivery. Chapter 34 in Culyer, A.J., Newhouse, J.P. (Eds.), *Handbook of Health Economics*, Amsterdam: North-Holland, Volume **1B**, pp. 1803–1862, contains a comprehensive discussion of attempts to measure health system equity, including efforts to account for the equity of government financing methods. Imai, Y., (2002), *Health care reform in Japan*, Economics Department Working Paper 321, Paris: OECD stresses

the issue of horizontal inequity in the Japanese case.

30 To construct a measure of the distributional impact of the health care system that accounts for the revenue side as well as the expenditure side, one must decide which particular sources of government revenue are used for the financing of health care (as distinct from other government spending). It is clear that, except in special cases where earmarked taxes to pay for health care exists, an answer to this question is necessarily speculative, if not conceptually ambiguous.

31 Campbell, J.C., Ikegami, N. (1998), *The art of balance in health policy: Maintaining Japan's low-cost egalitarian system*, Cambridge, UK: Cambridge University Press, and the collection of essays in Ikegami, N., Campbell, J.C., (Eds.) (1999), *Containing health care costs in Japan*, Ann Arbor: The University of Michigan Press, together provide a comprehensive discussion of the Japanese health care system in the late 1990s. A more recent brief discussion is Imai, Y., (2002), *op. cit.*

32 Part of the reason for this pattern is likely to be that in Japan, primary-care doctors both prescribe and supply pharmaceuticals to their patients, so that their income in part depends on the quantities and prices of the drugs they prescribe and supply.

33 Marchildon, G.P. (2005), *Health Systems in Transition: Canada*, Copenhagen: WHO, on behalf of the European Observatory on Health Systems and Policies, is a detailed discussion of recent trends in the Canadian system. The problems of waiting lists and lack of access to family doctors are vividly described in *Canadian Medical Association* (2006), "It's about access! Informing the debate on public and private health care", CMA Task Force on the Public-Private Interface.

34 This was the so-called "fundholding" system, which subsequently has been abolished. However, in the NHS reforms currently being implemented, groups of GPs working together in

Primary Care Trusts will have responsibilities similar to those of fundholding GPs in the 1990s. For further discussion of these payment systems and the NHS reforms since the early 1990s, see Blomqvist, Å.G. (2002), *Canadian Health Care in a Global Context*, Toronto: C.D. Howe Institute (available for downloading at www.cdhowe.org).

35 Organisation for Economic Co-operation and Development (OECD): The OECD Health Project, (2004), *Private Health Insurance in OECD Countries*, Paris: OECD.

36 Colombo, F., Tapay, N. (2003), Private health insurance in Australia: A case study. OECD Health Working Papers, No. 8. Paris: OECD.

37 One issue in this context is whether persons should be allowed to opt out of the government plan without enrolling in a private plan. Since seriously ill people are not likely to be denied care even if they are not insured, a case can be made for not allowing people to do so (in order to make sure that providers are paid in such cases). The principle that is applied in Germany and the Netherlands, namely that of only allowing persons to opt out if their annual income exceeds a given limit, is consistent with this idea.

38 Technically, Medicare is paid for out of a fund to which working Americans contribute through payroll deductions before retirement. The Medicare plan has two parts: Part A, which covers hospitalization and which does not require a premium; and Part B, which covers outpatient care, but only for those who have paid a premium. However, the premium is heavily subsidized and almost all eligible individuals choose to enroll in part B and pay the premium (which simply amounts to a deduction from the monthly Social Security check for which all Americans aged over 65 are eligible).

39 The Clinton plan and the Dekker–Simmons plan are briefly summarized in Blomqvist (2002), *op. cit.* For a more detailed and very well written exposition, see Flood, C., (2000), *International Health Care Reform: A legal, economic and political analysis*, London: Routledge. A balanced (and more recent) view of the slow progress with implementing the Dekker–Simmons plan in the Netherlands is contained in den Exter, A., Hermans, H., Dosljak, M., Busse, R. (2004), *Health care systems in transition: Netherlands*, Copenhagen: WHO Regional Office for Europe on behalf of European Observatory on Health Systems and Policies.

40 A comprehensive treatment of the techniques involved is in van de Ven and Ellis (2000), *op. cit.* In a footnote (p. 762), these authors list about a dozen countries where the question of risk adjustment for a mixed public–private system has been relevant. They also note that risk adjustment has been relevant in the context of the UK system of paying primary-care providers on a capitation basis.

41 See *Canadian Medical Association* (2006), *op. cit.* for further discussion. This decision found that provincial law in Quebec which prohibited individuals from acquiring duplicate private health insurance, was unconstitutional.

42 Proposals for health system reform in Canada based on these methods are discussed in some detail in Blomqvist (2002), *op. cit.*

Appendix 2.1
The Gains from Insurance in a Formal Model [4]

To illustrate the efficiency gains from insurance, one can consider the expected utility of a consumer who is subject to the risk of different degrees of illness. The consumer's utility is given by $u(c_i, m_i - \theta_i)$ where $i = 1, \ldots, n$ indexes different illness states, c_i is their consumption of commodities other than medical services when state i occurs, m_i is the number of units of medical services they utilize in state i, and θ_i is a parameter that represents the severity of the illness in state i (units of consumption and medical services are chosen so that each has a cost of one). We assume that

$$\frac{\partial u}{\partial c_i} \equiv u_i^c(c_i, m_i - \theta_i) > 0, \; \frac{\partial u}{\partial m_i}$$

$$\equiv u_i^m(c_i, m_i - \theta_i) > 0, \; \frac{\partial u^2}{\partial c_i^2} < 0, \; \frac{\partial u^2}{\partial m_i^2} < 0, \; \frac{\partial u^2}{\partial c_i \partial m_i} > 0.$$

State i occurs with probability p_i, so the consumer's expected utility can be written as

$$E = \sum_{i=1}^{n} p_i u(c_i, m_i - \theta_i)$$

We further assume that $\theta_{i+1} > \theta_i > \theta_1 = 0$, $i = 2, \ldots, n - 1$.

Suppose now that there is a large population of individuals with this utility function and subject to the same probabilities of illness of different severities and, for simplicity, that each has the same exogenous level of income y in each state. The opportunity then exists for risk-pooling through insurance. Specifically, we assume that insurance firms can offer contracts that either provide for a vector $z = \{z_1, \ldots, z_n\}$ of specific amounts of money, and/or payment of a share $1 - \sigma$ of the consumer's medical purchases m_i, in each state. The premium of the insurance policy is denoted by π, payable in each state. Given this, we can write $c_i = y - \pi + z_i - \sigma m_i$ for an insured consumer. Given the insurance contract, the consumer chooses m_i so as to maximize their state-specific utility, implying

$$-\sigma u_i^c(.) + u_i^m(.) = 0$$

In private insurance markets, insurers will charge premiums that are at least high enough to cover the benefits they expect to pay out to their clients, as well as the administrative costs they incur in managing the plans. That is, for any insurance contract $\{\pi, z, \sigma\}$, we will have

$$\pi \geq (1 + t) \sum_{1}^{n} p_i(z_i + (1 - \sigma)m_i)$$

where $t > 0$ represents administrative costs as a percentage of the expected payout under the plan. If the insurance market is competitive so that insurers earn zero excess profits, this condition will hold with equality. When $t = 0$ and $\pi = \sum_{1}^{n} p_i(z_i + (1 - \sigma)m_i)$, the insurance plan is said to be *actuarially fair*.

To illustrate the gains from insurance, suppose first that $\sigma = 1$ (that is, the consumer pays the full cost of their health services out of pocket), but that a competitive insurance market exists in which insurers compete by offering different vectors $z \geq 0$. Since consumers will prefer the plan that represents what they consider the best combination of state-contingent payouts and premium, the equilibrium will be one where each consumer holds that zero-profit plan which maximizes their expected utility. To find the conditions that will hold in this equilibrium, one can form the Lagrangean

$$\Psi = \left(\sum_{i=1}^{n} p_i u(c_i, m_i - \theta_i)\right) + \lambda \left(\pi - (1+t)\sum_{1}^{n} p_i z_i\right)$$

where λ is the Lagrange multiplier and we have used the assumption that $\sigma = 1$, and take its derivatives with respect to π, λ and the elements of z. Using the definitions of c_i this can be shown to imply

$$\frac{\partial \Psi}{\partial z_i} = u_i^c(.) - \lambda(1+t) \leq 0, \quad \frac{\partial \Psi}{\partial z_i} \cdot z_i = 0, \; i = 1, \dots, n$$

$$\frac{\partial \Psi}{\partial \pi} = -\left(\sum_{i=1}^{n} p_i u_i^c(.)\right) + \lambda = 0$$

as well as the non-negativity constraints $z_i \geq 0$ and the zero-profit constraint. (Terms involving the effects of changes in m_i on expected utility do not appear in these conditions because of the envelope theorem.) The two sets of n conditions in the first line together imply that, for all $z_i > 0$, the first condition holds with equality; for all terms when it does, the marginal utility of consumption $u_i^c(.)$ has the same constant value of $\lambda(1+t)$. However, when $t > 0$, it can be shown that for some of the low values of θ_i, z_i will be zero and the first condition will hold with inequality for those values of i. That is, there must then be some $u_i^c(.)$ that are smaller than this constant value. (To see this, multiply each of the first set of conditions in the first line by p_i and add them together; comparing the result with the condition in the second line when $t > 0$ implies that some of inequalities must be strict.) This implies that for $t > 0$, it is optimal for the consumer to be less than fully insured, in the sense that their marginal utility of consumption is lower in some favorable states than in others. When $t = 0$ (that is, when insurance is actuarially fair), the $n + 1$ conditions together can be shown to imply that $u_i^c(.)$ is constant for all i which in turn implies that $z_i = \theta_i$, $\forall i$. This is the case of full insurance. In the case when both goods are normal, full insurance also implies that c_i, $m_i - \theta_i$ both are constant for all i. The gains from insurance in this framework occurs because it raises average utility in the insured population (that is, it raises the expected utility of a representative individual) by transferring resources from those who are not seriously ill and otherwise would have high consumption and a low marginal utility of consumption, to those who are seriously ill and without insurance would have a low level of consumption and a high marginal utility of consumption.

Appendix 2.2
Efficient Insurance when there is Moral Hazard: A Formal Treatment

Using the same notation as before, we write the consumer's expected utility as

$$E = \sum_{i=1}^{n} p_i u(c_i, m_i - \theta_i)$$

However, because the state variables θ_i now are assumed not to be observable to insurers, insurance contracts now cannot be written in terms of unconditional state-specific payments z_i.

As noted above, one response to this restriction is for insurers to instead offer contracts that simply specify that the plan will pay a fixed share $1 - \sigma$ of the consumer's health care costs. In this case, an insurance plan consists of the two-element vector $\{\pi, \sigma\}$ specifying the premium payable, and the parameter representing the consumer's out-of-pocket share of health care costs. Consumption in state i now is $c_i = y - \pi - \sigma m_i$. For a given insurance contract, the consumer chooses medical care so as to maximize utility, implying $\sigma u_i^c(.) = u_i^m(.)$, using the same notation for partial derivatives as in Appendix 2.1. From this one can solve for $m_i = m_i(\pi, \sigma)$, for all i. It is easy to show that at the optimum with $\sigma > 0$, one will have $m_{i+1} > m_i$, $c_{i+1} < c_i$, $i = 1, \ldots, n - 1$.

Continuing to assume a competitive insurance market so that the insurers' profits are zero, we have

$$\pi = (1 + t)(1 - \sigma) \sum_1^n p_i m_i$$

Substituting $m_i = m_i(\pi, \sigma)$ into this condition, one can solve for $\pi = \pi(\sigma)$, and then, in turn, also solve for $E = E(\sigma)$. Again, assuming that the insurance markets are competitive, various combinations $\{\pi, \sigma\}$ will be offered in the market until, in equilibrium, consumers are covered by the zero-profit plan which maximizes E. That is, it will solve

$$\frac{\partial E}{\partial \sigma} = -\left(\sum_1^n p_i u_i^c(.) \cdot m_i \right) - \left(\sum_0^n p_i u_i^c(.) \cdot \frac{\partial \pi}{\partial \sigma} \right) = 0$$

(where we have once again used the envelope condition). From the zero-profit condition one obtains

$$\frac{\partial \pi}{\partial \sigma} = -(1 + t)\overline{m} + (1 + t)(1 - \sigma)\frac{d\overline{m}}{d\sigma}$$

where $\overline{m} = \sum_1^n p_i m_i$, $\frac{d\overline{m}}{d\sigma} = \sum_1^n p_i \frac{dm_i}{d\sigma}$. Substituting into the first-order condition and simplifying produces (after multiplying through by -1):

$$\left(\sum_1^n p_i u_i^c(.) \cdot (m_i - \overline{m}) \right) - t\overline{u}^c \overline{m} + (1 + t)(1 - \sigma)\overline{u}^c \frac{d\overline{m}}{d\sigma} = 0$$

where $\overline{u}^c \equiv \sum_1^n p_i \cdot u_i^c(.)$. The last two terms in this condition are negative (accounting for signs), so the equation implies that the first term, which is the co-variance between medical services utilization and the marginal utility of consumption, must be positive. That is, the consumer is less than fully insured in the sense that the marginal utility of consumption is higher when medical services consumption is high. This tendency is larger the larger in absolute value are the last two terms, the magnitudes of which depend on the extent of administration costs (t) and on the welfare loss associated with the implicit subsidy to health services utilization when the consumer is insured.

While an insurance contract that pays a fixed share of the consumer's health care costs obviously is better than no insurance, a more effective form of insurance might be a contract under which the degree of cost sharing σ varied with the amount of health care costs. One way to represent such a non-linear contract is to specify a sequence of state-specific payments z_i, but to make the payments conditional on the amounts m_i of health care spending (which *can* be observed), not on the value of the illness severity parameters θ_i (which, by assumption, cannot). However, for this to work, the sequence of payments must be structured in such a way that, when illness state i has occurred, it must be optimal for the patient to choose to spend m_i and collect z_i, rather than to spend the larger amount m_{i+1} and collect z_{i+1}. (In game theory terminology, such restrictions are known as *individual rationality constraints*). Thus, the insurance contract, as in the earlier section, would consist of a premium π and a vector z, with zero-profit condition $\pi = (1 + t) \sum_1^n p_i z_i$. With $\sigma = 1$, the consumer would choose m_i optimally, implying $u_i^c(.) = u_i^m(.)$, from which one could derive $m_i = m_i(\pi, z_i)$. The equilibrium contract would be that vector z which maximized the consumers' expected utility E subject to the zero-profit condition, and subject also to individual rationality constraints of the form

$$u(y - \pi + z_i - m_i, m_i - \theta_i) \geq u(y - \pi + z_{i+1} - m_{i+1}, m_{i+1} - \theta_i), \; i = 1, \ldots, n - 1.$$

[Although characterizing the solution (and solving a numerical version) is easier when the z_i are treated as control variables, the problem can also be expressed by allowing for policies with different state-specific cost-sharing parameters σ_i, conditional on the amount of medical care spending. The two formulations are mathematically equivalent, but the latter may be more intuitive as it looks more like conventional health insurance plans with deductibles and cost-sharing parameters that are specific to intervals of medical care spending].

The Lagrangean corresponding to this problem is:

$$\Psi = \left(\sum_1^n p_i u(y - \pi + z_i - m_i, m_i - \theta_i) \right) + \lambda \left(\pi - (1 + t) \sum_1^n p_i z_i \right)$$
$$+ \sum_1^{n-1} \gamma_i R_i \leq 0$$

where $R_i = u(y - \pi + z_i - m_i, m_i - \theta_i) - u(y - \pi + z_{i+1} - m_{i+1}, m_{i+1} - \theta_i) \geq 0$.

Taking the derivatives with respect to z_i and π produces the following first-order conditions:

$$\frac{\partial \Psi}{\partial z_i} = p_i u_i^c(.) - p_i \lambda (1 + t) + \gamma_i u_i^c(.) - \gamma_{i-1} u^c(c_i, m_i - \theta_{i-1}) \tag{A1}$$
$$\leq 0, \; i = 1, \ldots, n$$

$$\frac{\partial \Psi}{\partial z_i} \cdot z_i = 0, \; i = 1, \ldots, n, \; \gamma_i \cdot R_i = 0, \; i = 1, \ldots n - 1 \tag{A2}$$

$$\left(\sum_1^n p_i u_i^c(.) \right) + \lambda + \sum_1^{n-1} \gamma_i \frac{\partial R_i}{\partial \pi} = 0 \tag{A3}$$

where $\frac{\partial R_i}{\partial \pi} = u_i^c(.) - u^c(c_{i+1}, m_{i+1} - \theta_i)$ with $u_i^c(.) \equiv u^c(c_i, m_i - \theta_i)$, $c_i = y - \pi + z_i - m_i$, as before, and where it is understood that $y_{-1} = 0$ by definition (since θ_{-1} is not defined).

As before, the first-order conditions (A1) are stated as inequalities, since some early z_i may be zero (note the complementary slackness conditions in (A2)). The individual rationality constraints R_i also may or may not be binding; when they are not, the corresponding multiplier γ_i will be zero. Numerical solution of a model of this kind involves algorithms that must check, for each i, whether or not the individual rationality constraints are binding.

Although the conditions that characterize the equilibrium are conceptually straightforward, they are somewhat tedious; see Appendix 2.1.

Appendix 2.3
Adverse Selection: A Formal Example

To illustrate the problem of adverse selection, we consider a simplified version of the model discussed in Appendices 2.1 and 2.2. Specifically, suppose there are only two states of the world with illness severity parameters $\theta_1 = 0$, $\theta_2 > 0$. Suppose, however, that there are two populations with different probabilities that state 2 (the "ill" state) will occur, p^H (the high-risk population) and $p^L < p^H$ (the low-risk one). For simplicity, we assume that insurers can observe θ, so insurance can be in the form of a state-specific payment z_2 if the consumer is ill. However, we also assume that the insurer cannot tell in advance whether a given individual is in the high-risk or low-risk category, consistent with the assumption in the adverse selection literature.

To illustrate the adverse selection problem, consider first what an optimal insurance plan would be for the high-risk population alone. For a given insurance plan $\{\pi^H, z_2^H\}$ for this population, the expected utility of a plan member would be

$$E^H = (1 - p^H)u(y - p^H z_2^H - m_1, m_1)$$

$$+ p^H u(y - p^H z_2^H + z_2^H - m_2, m_2 - \theta_2)$$

where we have substituted $\pi^H = p^H z_2^H$, on the assumption of actuarial fairness and no transaction costs $(t = 0)$. For $i = 1, 2$ the consumer chooses m_1, m_2 to maximize state-specific utility, implying $u_i^c(.) = u_i^m(.)$, $i = 1, 2$. Again, using the principle that in a competitive insurance market the equilibrium plan in a given population will be the one that maximizes the representative consumer's expected utility, we also have

$$\frac{\partial E^H}{\partial z_2^H} = -(1 - p^H)p^H u_1^c(.) + p^H(1 - p^H)u_2^c(.) = 0$$

for the high-risk population. This equation implies $u_1^c(.) = u_2^c(.)$; together with the conditions for the consumer's optimal choice of m_i, $i = 1, 2$, this also implies $u_1^m(.) = u_2^m(.)$, which further implies $m_1 = m_2 - \theta_2$, $c_1 = c_2$, and $z_2^H = \theta_2$.

Now consider an individual with a low risk of illness p^L. For such an individual, an insurance plan $\{\pi^H, z_2^H\}$ will not seem attractive, since it has premium $\pi^H = p^H z_2^H$ while for this population an actuarially fair premium with a benefit $z_2^H = \theta_2$ would be $p^L \theta_2 < \pi^H$. However, a plan with this benefit and an actuarially fair premium for the low-risk group would not be sustainable, since the high-risk group would also want it, rather than its own plan, and the insurer does not know who is in the high-risk group. Thus, the low-risk group might prefer a plan with a lower coverage, say z_2^L, especially if it could be offered at a premium $\pi^L = p^L z_2^L$ that were actuarially fair for those in this risk class. But for such a policy to be sustainable, it must *not* be preferred by the high-risk group. The conclusion is that if there exists a *separating equilibrium* in which each risk class holds "its own" policy, then it must be the case that the policy $\{\pi^L, z_2^L\}$ bought by the low-risk population, with $\pi^L = p^L z_2^L$, would have to be such that the expected utility of a high-risk individual who held this policy must be no higher than if she held the policy designed for the high-risk group:

$$E^H(\pi^H, z_2^H) \geq (1 - p^H)u(y - p^L z_2^L - m_1, m_1) + p^H u(y - p^L z_2^L$$
$$+ z_2^L - m_2 - \theta_2)$$

where m_1, m_2 on the right-hand side have been optimally chosen, as before, according to $u_i^c(.) = u_i^m(.)$, $i = 1, 2$ with $\pi = \pi^L$, $z_2 = z_2^L$.

Although these equations may have a solution, the corresponding values may still not be a sustainable competitive equilibrium: Individuals in the low-risk category may have a lower expected utility with the policy $\{\pi^L, z_2^L\}$ than with the policy $\{\pi^H, z_2^H\}$. In that case, the conclusion in the original analysis of this type of model was that no equilibrium would exist in a competitive insurance market in this environment [24].

3
Private Financing Outside the Publicly Funded System
Mark Stabile

3.1
Introduction and the Evolution of Private Financing in Canada

Every country in the Organisation for Economic Co-operation and Development (OECD) is dealing with a health care system that is growing at a rate faster than normal economic growth. For example, Kotlikoff and Hagist note that between 1970 and 2002 health care expenditures grew 2.3 times faster than GDP in the United States, and 2 times as fast in Germany [1]. New technologies, increased demand, and increased incomes have all contributed to wealthy societies that demand more from their health care systems. These factors – together defined as growth in the health care benefit (as distinct from growth due to population changes) – account for four-fifths of total spending growth on average across the OECD [1]. Canada is no exception to this, with health care spending having increased as a share of GDP from 7% in 1975 to 10.4% in 2005 [2]. Although today we can provide treatments that were unimaginable 30 years ago, these treatments have come at a cost. Such costs have born partially by the Canadian taxpayer in the form of larger public budgets for health care, and in part by the Canadian health care consumer in the form of private payments, either through insurance companies or out-of-pocket.

As treatments continue to develop, costs continue to increase, and people expect faster and better care, Canadians and their governments have examined alternatives to the single-payer, tax-financed Medicare system that has been in place since the 1960s. The alternatives considered generally include an increased role for the private sector in the Canadian system in both the financing and delivery of care. Private delivery can be financed either privately or publicly, and should not be confused with the financing of care. The Canadian Medicare system, like many publicly financed health care systems, contains elements of both public and private delivery.

Private financing can also be both within or outside a public health care system. It can take many forms, including private financing for services that are also publicly funded (sometimes referred to as two-tier financing in Canada), paying for services not included in the publicly funded basket, user charges, medical savings

Financing Health Care: New Ideas for a Changing Society. Edited by Mingshan Lu and Egon Jonsson
Copyright © 2008 WILEY-VCH Verlag GmbH & Co. KGaA, Weinheim
ISBN: 978-3-527-32027-1

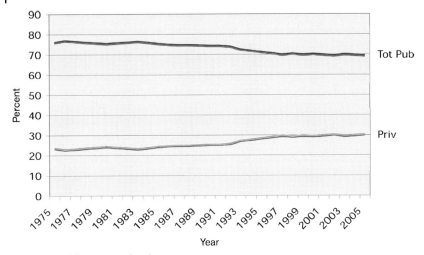

Fig. 3.1 Health care spending by source.
(Source: Canadian Institutes for Health Information: www.cihi.ca).

accounts, as well as other financing models and mechanisms. The focus of this chapter is on private financing *outside* the publicly financed health care system: private financing for services that are also publicly funded, and private financing for services not included in the publicly funded basket. The debate surrounding private financing inside of a publicly funded health care system, such as with med- ical savings accounts (MSAs) or user-fees, is the subject of other chapters in this volume. Private health care financing in Canada has grown steadily as a share of total health care spending, from approximate 24% in 1975 to 30% in 2005 (see Fig. 3.1). This figure includes all private spending, whether out-of-pocket or through a private insurance company, and includes both funding outside the public health care system and inside the system. However, as shown in Fig. 3.2, the areas of health care spending with the highest private share are drugs and other health care professionals (excluding physicians). The majority of these costs are outside the publicly funded system.

This chapter will explore the economic theory and evidence regarding supple- mental external private financing (as defined above) for health care services in Canada and elsewhere. Initially, the economic literature on supplementary private financing for health care will be reviewed, after which the debate around private financing within Canada from an economic perspective will be explored, highlight- ing trends in the de-listing of publicly funded services over the past 15 years. Next, the arguments put forth in major reviews of the Canadian health care system will briefly be reviewed, and the reasoning for the recommendations reached will be explored. Some empirical evidence using data from across the OECD will then be presented, and finally a few concluding remarks about the private financing and the Canadian health care system will be offered.

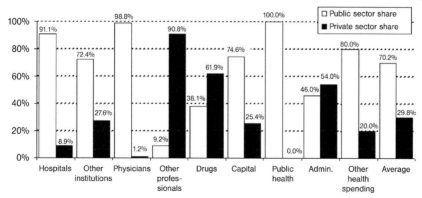

Fig. 3.2 Public and private shares of total health expenditure, by use of funds, Canada, 2003.
(Source: Canadian Institute for Health Information).

3.2
Reviewing Economic Theory and Evidence on Parallel Public and Private Financing Structures

In this section the theory and evidence on the effects of a parallel, privately financed system on the performance of the publicly financed system are reviewed. The focus here is on exploring whether the existing research supports the notion that supplemental private financing for services that are also fully insured publicly can operate without negatively affecting the publicly financed sector. No attempt will be made to evaluate the *overall* welfare effects of allowing a privately financed system. It is reasonable to assume that a privately financed system improves the welfare of those who use it. It is therefore possible that, even if the effects on the public system are negative, the overall welfare effects could be positive. However, as this is not a pareto-improvement, and empirical evidence on the take-up of privately financed care (for a review, see below) suggests that take-up is generally small and concentrated among higher-income individuals, the focus here will be on whether supplemental, privately financed services can exist without harming the public system.

Economic theory regarding the effect of introducing a private alternative for publicly financed services is ambiguous. Depending on assumptions regarding the supply of physicians, demand for services, and the magnitude of the effects of conflicting incentives on providers, the theoretical effects of private insurance suggest several possibilities. It is possible that allowing patients to seek health care outside of the public system would free-up public resources, and lead to shorter waiting times for users of both the public and private sectors. Further, it is possible that a parallel private system could serve as a benchmark against which the public system could be compared, allowing health care administrators and political leaders meaningfully to evaluate the efficiency of the public system. On the other hand, under certain assumptions, a parallel private health care system may adversely affect the public system, resulting in, at best, no decline in public waiting lists and, at worst, substantial increases. Under certain assumptions, allowing private health care would induce a shift in health care resources from the public to the private sectors. In theory, physicians may have an incentive to increase waiting lists within the public system in order to encourage patients to switch to the private system, where they can bill more than in the public sector. The existence of a private system with deregulated prices can also reduce the monopsony power enjoyed by the public system, and result in upward pressure on prices in the public system. The cream-skimming of risks by the private system can result in an increase in the per-patient cost of the cases remaining in the public system.

Finally, under certain assumptions, an increase in supply afforded by a supplemental, private system could be equally offset by an increase in demand for publicly funded health care, so that waiting lists could be unchanged. This is more likely to occur if there are complementarities in the use of private care and the use of public care. In addition, the political economy literature suggests that introducing private health care may reduce political support for the public health care system by reducing the size of the coalition that uses the public system.

To evaluate, empirically, the effects of a supplemental, privately financed system is very difficult due to a lack of counterfactuals and the multitude of differences in the interaction between publicly and privately financed systems across jurisdictions. What evidence there is however, suggests that a parallel private system does induce physicians to shift from providing services in the public to the private sector. In the United Kingdom (UK), specialists who are employed full time in the private sector may only dedicate at most 10% of their time to private surgeries. However, as Donald Light points out, this figure is almost never monitored, and there is evidence from the audit commission in the UK that public surgeons there only work 3 to 6 hours a week in the operating theater, as opposed to nearly 20 hours for general surgeons in the United States (US) [3]. Light also observes that not only are waiting lists the longest in those regions with most private providers, but they are also longest in those specialties with the most private providers [3].

Caroline Richmond observes that while almost 95% of all consultants' time is contracted to the National Health Service (NHS), 12.5% of all their surgeries are performed in the private sector [4], which suggests that the consultants perform proportionally more surgeries per paid hour in the private sector. Furthermore, the NHS allows specialists who give up one-eleventh of their salary in the public system to perform as many private surgeries as they wish, under a so-called "maximum part-time" contract, in exchange for a "full-time effort" of 35 hours' worth of work in the public system. However, because of inadequate monitoring in the public system, no one checks whether or not this requirement is fulfilled [3]. In addition, as the average NHS surgeon works 52 hours each week, those surgeons who adopt the "maximum part-time" contract devote almost one-third of their working week to private patients [3]. Even the 35 hours in the "maximum part-time" contract, may not be guaranteed, as an unspecified amount of private work may be done during NHS hours [4].

In Canada, the Manitoba Center for Health Policy and Evaluation examined the impact of a parallel private sector on cataract surgery in Manitoba during the mid-1990s. Among the results, it was found that the public waiting times for surgeons who operated in both the public and private sectors were substantially longer than for those surgeons who operated only in the public system. The authors concluded that this result "... demonstrates what can happen when surgeons have two options ... public patients waited two to three months longer than did patients whose physicians operated only in the public system" [5].

On the other hand, the evidence from Manitoba does not seem to support the claim that a private sector causes a shift in human resource from the public to the private sector.[1] The authors pointed out that, whatever the cause of the increased waiting times for surgeons who operated in both the private and public sectors, it was not caused by physicians performing fewer surgeries in the public sector. Indeed, the authors observed that physicians who operated in both sectors "... performed a higher volume of public-sector surgery than did the surgeons who operated in the public sector only" [5]. Thus, with regards to cataract surgery in Manitoba at least, the existence of a private sector does not seem to result in any decline in the supply of physician services in the public sector, though it is not at all obvious that this result is generalizable. In this case, the increased waiting times for those surgeons who operated in both sectors may be the result of increased demand for their services versus those of the public only surgeons [5], although in the absence of any data on the characteristics of these physicians it is impossible to determine if this accounts for the increased waiting times.

Besley, Hall and Preston, examined the impact of private insurance on waiting lists and concluded that: "... regions in which many are privately insured appear to put fewer resources into keeping waiting lists short." [6]. This would seem to correspond with the phenomenon observed in both the UK and New Zealand, where waiting lists were positively correlated with the level of private sector activity [7]. It should be noted, however, that this does not necessarily imply that private health care leads to a reduction in public support for public health care. Rather, it may lead to lobbying to divert resources away from areas with long waiting lists toward other areas within the public system. Thus, we would observe a correlation between waiting lists and private health care, even if we did not observe any correlation between private health care and overall spending.

Francis and Frost examined the relationship between the number of hospital beds and the magnitude of waiting lists in the Trent RHA in the UK. These authors concluded that the elasticity of the number of people on the waiting list (that is, the

---

1) Note that the existence of such a shift is likely to depend on more than just the existence of a private sector including the legislative environment, dual-practice limitations, etc.

demand for health care) was unitary with respect to the number of hospital beds [8]. Thus, as long as the number of hospital beds in the public system remains constant, the waiting lists will not decline, regardless of the private sector. Thus, introducing a private sector will only reduce waiting lists if public sector were to reduce its capacity, but at best this would have an effect on waiting times, and at worst it might increase them.

On the other hand, McAvinchey and Yannopoulos [9], found that the long-run elasticity of demand for NHS acute care with respect to the cost of waiting (a function both of time, and foregone income) were quite large. Their results suggested that a 1% decline in waiting times would lead to a 4.79% increase in the demand for NHS acute care [9]. This evidence suggest that introducing a private system which reduces waiting times in the public sector may result in an increase in demand for care in the public sector, resulting in both higher costs and longer waiting lists.

McAvinchey and Yannopoulos also examined technological change in both the public and private sectors. Using a time trend as a proxy for technological change, these authors found that costs rose twice as fast in the private health care sector as in the public sector. They concluded that "... this implies a proportionally greater expenditure on new technology in the private sector than in the NHS at least as far as acute care is concerned." [9]. This result suggests that the private sector will be able to provide more technologically intensive – that is, higher quality (in theory at least) – treatment than the public sector, and therefore may encourage more innovation.

Other evidence on how different financing systems affect the rate of technological innovation and change can be found in the literature comparing managed-care to other forms of health care financing in the United States. Cutler et al. (1998) examined rates of technological adoption for elderly patients covered by US Medicare. Their evidence suggested that managed care lowers the adoption rates of newer technologies into the health care sector [10]. Combined with lower utilization rates, this has resulted in a slower diffusion of technology. An important note here is that the comparison is not public versus private financing, but rather managed-care versus traditional fee-for-service insurance. Both, the managed-care and the traditional insurance are financed publicly in this case.

Considerable evidence suggests that private and public providers differ not only in the type of services they provide, but also in the types of patient treated. Martin and Smith [11] examined the determinants in length of stay in the NHS in Britain, and found that those patients in the NHS who had more access to NHS hospitals were likely to experience shorter lengths of stay, on average. They also found that the level of private health care facilities in the area has a positive impact on local NHS costs, suggesting that private health care tends to take the less-severe cases, and that that those who remain (in the NHS) tend to have higher average costs. This result is significant because it suggests not only that the private sector would not serve as an effective benchmark for the public sector, but also that, with the introduction of private health care, costs in the public sector would rise.

Hurley et al. [12] examined the efforts to promote private health insurance through tax subsidies in Australia, and developed lessons for Canada based on the evidence in Australia and around the world. Some of these lessons are summarized as follows:

- The potential for public cost savings through private insurance is limited. The combination of tax subsidies (currently allowed for supplemental private insurance in the most of the Canadian market), and the effects of private systems on the health care input costs (both in the short and long term) limit the potential cost savings for the public sector.
- Parallel private insurance systems are unlikely to reduce waiting times in the public sector. The authors noted that there is no conclusive evidence from Australia, or elsewhere that shows a decline in public waiting times following the introduction of a parallel private system.
- There is no straightforward way to regulate private insurers to meet public objectives. The strategic responses by insurers in Australia to regulatory efforts have hampered these efforts.
- Interactions between the public and private systems are complex and unavoidable. Through patient movement, price effects, and explicit or implicit subsidies, there will be numerous interactions between any private and public insurance systems.
- Quality plays a key role in the dynamic between public and private insurance systems. Voluntary parallel private insurance systems require there to be actual or perceived quality differences between the public sector and the private offering. Otherwise, rational consumers would prefer the paid for public offering.

Lu and Savage [13] examined the effects of the Australian reforms regarding private insurance on the public system by explicitly modeling the probability of hospital admission and length of stay for both public and private patients. The decision to take up private insurance is not random, and the authors used propensity score matching models to compare those with insurance to those without insurance (for details, see Ref. [13]). Their results indicated that, while the reforms increased the proportion of the population with private coverage substantially, the change in the use of publicly funded services was limited, with varying effects depending on the length of time that individuals held private insurance. They found robust evidence that among those with private hospital insurance, those who were privately insured for less than 2 years had public hospital utilization rates that resembled the publicly insured patients. Lu and Savage concluded that the incentives were an expensive way to reduce pressure on the public system.

Overall, the Australian experience, coupled with evidence from around the world, suggests little ability for parallel private systems to reduce public costs and public sector waiting times, and in those cases where there are reductions in public costs, these reductions come at a high price.

The distribution of insurance by payer also differs considerably by income. Flood et al. [14] noted that in Australia, prior to 1998, only 20% of people with an annual income of less than $20 000 had private coverage compared to 76% of those with an annual income of $100 000, or more. In New Zealand, approximately

37% of the total population has private coverage; among this group, about 60% are of above-average income, and 24% below-average income. Finally, in the UK, where privately insured health care exists as a parallel alternative to the publicly funded system, about 12% of the population have private insurance, with such coverage being strongly related to income. Flood et al. [14] also cited a UK study conducted in 2001 which found 40% of those in the wealthiest 10% the population to be privately insured, whereas only 5% of those in the bottom 40% had private insurance.

In summary, the literature on the impact of a supplemental, privately financed alternative for services that are also insured publicly is ambiguous, both theoretically and empirically. That said, the weight of the limited evidence available suggests that the introduction of a private system may result in a decline in the supply of medical services in the public system, resulting in longer waiting lists for public patients. On the other hand, the experience of cataract surgeons in Manitoba does not suggest that a private sector induces a decline in supply in the public sector. There also appears to be a fair degree of uncertainty surrounding the impact of waiting times on the total demand for health care, and hence private insurance. This is in part a result of the difficulty of modeling both the demand and the supply side responses to changes in waiting times.

There is some evidence that introducing or expanding private health care may induce physicians to shift services from the public to the private sector, although this evidence is by no means unambiguous. Furthermore, in such a mixed public/private system, there would exist an incentive for physicians to increase waiting lists, or at least the perceptions of waiting lists, to induce patients to shift from the public to the private sector. However, while this incentive may exist, the available evidence does not indicate that it significantly affects patient behavior. Moreover, evidence on the demand for health care suggests that the introduction of private health care would not substantially reduce waiting lists in the public system, quite apart from any effects it may have on the supply side. Finally, there is some evidence that the introduction of a private health care system may result in a more complex case-mix in the public sector, resulting in either higher public costs, or longer public waiting lists.

The weight of the evidence suggests that parallel private systems will compete for low-risk, high-profit margin patients. Problems of adverse selection, as evidenced by Cutler and Reber [15], bedevil markets where there is choice based on the comprehensiveness of the plan. More comprehensive plans (generally public plans) attract bad risks and therefore end up costing far more than benefit differences would predict. With this information as a background, the chapter now explores the nature of the private financing debate in Canada.

3.2.1
The Private Financing Debate in Canada

Why would Canada consider expanding the role for private financing in the health care sector? One could reasonably argue that a policy objective of the public health care system is to ensure that a basket of medically necessary health care services is universally provided in a timely fashion. Of course, defining "medically necessary", and "in a timely fashion" is not straightforward, and is the ongoing task of many health policy and medical experts. However, if the publicly funded health care system were able to meet this objective by the standards of the majority of Canadians, would there then be a demand for further private financing for these same services? Conversely, if the public objective is being met, is there a need to be concerned about private financing in the health care market? Of course, proponents of increased private financing for services that are also publicly financed may argue that it is because the public system is not meeting the objective of reasonable access to services that the need for increased private financing exists.

Over the past few years, the federal and provincial governments have expanded public funding in order to improve quality, accessibility and waiting times in the public system (the 2002 and 2004 health accords are examples of such agreements). Quebec has even gone further to propose guaranteed waiting times in the public system for both non-elective and elective procedures [16]. In this context of expanding resources to improve the public system, and even providing service guarantees, what is the remaining role for private financing outside the public system? Arguably, there are at least two roles. First, it will never be possible for a public system with a limited budget to provide for all services that have a positive medical benefit. Some services will not meet reasonable cost–benefit criteria for public funding, and trade-offs will always have to made by governments as to what is included in the public benefit, and what is not. For services that are not included in the public benefit, but for which there is private demand, it is reasonable to consider a role for private financing. The section on de-listing public funded services below explores this further. Second, even in the context of reasonable and universal access to public services with guaranteed waiting times, there may still be demand for faster and more extensive health care services. Indeed, Glied [17] argues that a well-functioning public system that matches the preferences of the median or mean voter will necessarily leave some people wanting more services than are provided in the public system. Is it then reasonable to allow private financing for this increased level of service?

Flood et al. [18] note that objectors to private financing for services that are also publicly funded can be categorized into two groups: communitarians, and egalitarians. Of course many participants in health policy debates may not fall into one or other of these categories, or they may fall into both, but this simple dichotomization is useful in helping to parse the arguments that follow. Communitarians are concerned primarily with ensuring the viability, quality, sustainability, and accessibility of the public system. That is, opposition to private financing for services that are also publicly funded is based on theory and evidence which suggests that allowing for private financing for services that are also publicly funded creates a negative externality on the public health care system. Elements of private financing impede the ability of the public system to meet its objectives. In economic terms, it is not possible to achieve a pareto-improvement through allowing private financing for care that is also publicly financed.

Egalitarians, on the other hand, believe that it goes against the values of the Canadian system for someone to have more or faster access to services than others based on something other than medical need (usually financial resources). Egalitarians are also concerned with ensuring a viable, high-quality, sustainable and accessible public system, but would also argue that even if the public system achieves all these goals for all who choose to use it, it is not appropriate for others to be able to buy better or faster care.

A review of the language and recommendations found in some of the commissions tasked with exploring reforms for Canada's health care system helps highlight these differences.

It its multi-volume review of the Canadian health care system, the Senate of Canada's Commission (hereafter referred to as the Kirby Commission) outlined options to be considered for financing reform prior to reaching its conclusions. In Volume 4 of the report, the Kirby Commission suggested that a number of benefits could be generated by allowing private insurance for services that are also publicly financed, including enhanced patient choice, increased competition, and improved efficiencies in the public sector. It suggested that safeguards could be put in place to ensure that:

- private insurance was administered on a non-exclusionary basis;
- no queue-jumping occurred; and
- that there was no cream-skimming of less-complicated and more profitable care by the privately financed sector [19].

The Commission presented suggestions to circumvent the potential negative aspects of supplemental private financing for medically necessary services health while maintaining the quality of publicly funded sector including:

- All doctors would be required to work a certain number of hours in the publicly funded system.
- The publicly funded system would provide a guarantee that waiting times would not exceed a certain level; otherwise, the government would be obliged to pay for treatment in the private sector.
- An independent body would be mandated to ensure that health care technology in the public sector is as good as in the private sector.

In Volume 5 of their report, following consultation and review of the possible directions for reform, the Kirby Commission reported that Canada should continue to have a single funder. It noted that having a single funder would lead to more efficient administration of health care insurance, and it would avoid adverse selection problems. It noted that very few Canadians could afford not to be covered by the public sector. It also noted that having a single funder avoids competition for doctor resources. It also recommended that provinces maintain restrictions that prevent doctors from operating in both parallel public and private systems.

One might read the evolution of the Kirby Commission's thinking on private financing to fall into the communitarian camp. The Commission presented an option of private financing for services that are publicly funded claiming, essentially, that pareto-improvements might be possible. Following further review and consultation, the Committee recommended against allowing supplemental private financing for medically necessary services, presumably because it was convinced that this would not, in fact, be the case. To be fair to the Committee, elements of the final recommendations do also speak to equality. In Volume 6, the committee notes that "... countries in which parallel private systems compete with publicly funded systems exhibit a number of problems including risk selection, cream skimming, no reduction in waiting lists in the public sector, queue jumping, and preferential treatment." [19].

The Commission on the Future of Health Care in Canada, "Building on Values," (hereafter known as the Romanow Commission [20]) also deals with the issue of private financing and delivery. Although the Commission focused more on the role for the private sector in delivery rather than financing, it does note early on in the report that, based on the evidence both in Canada and internationally, it believes progressive taxation continues to be the most effective way to fund health care in Canada. It notes that a large majority do not want to see any change in single-payer systems and that Canadians believe that ability to pay should not be the predominant factor in receiving care. To quote the commission:

> "This may be because our tax-funded universal health care system provides a kind of 'double solidarity'. It provides equity of funding between the haves and the have nots in our society and it also provides equity between the healthy and the sick." (p. 31 in Ref. [20]).

Indeed, the Commission's first recommendation on establishing a Canadian health covenant focuses on universality, equity, and solidarity (p. 48). While the Commission notes its review of the evidence on the possibility for achieving pareto-improvements through changes in financing and its conclusion that this is not the case, its primary argument for the solely publicly financed system appears to be an egalitarian one.

While there is scope for both the communitarian and egalitarian arguments in any discussion of the role of private financing for publicly funded services, the focus of this work will be on the communitarian argument and what the economic evidence can contribute to it.

3.2.2
De-Listing Publicly Funded Services in Canada

An important source of private financing for health care in Canada is for services that are not universally covered by the publicly funded system. These services, which are deemed not medically necessary, constitute most of the private spending in Canada today [21]. It is unlikely that any publicly funded health care system can afford to provide coverage for all services with a positive medical benefit. Even public systems with soft budget constraints must recognize that public programs cannot fund all health care services indefinitely. Therefore, insurers are faced with a trade-off: Do they fund as many services as possible, and ration the availability of those services so that they are difficult to access? Or, do they fund a core basket of services which are fully funded at levels which, by established clinical standards, are acceptable, and then allow other services to be partially or even fully funded by other means?

If insurance providers are to consider de-listing services, it is important to know if and how de-listing – or indeed not listing – a service will alter the demand for that service. Understanding the elasticity of demand for differing services is an important aspect of the policy-making process. If a service is particularly inelastic, then de-listing it will not affect the use of the service, but will transfer the cost of providing that service from the insurance pool (the taxpayer in a public system) to the user. In some instances, this may be desirable, but in others not. In part, this will depend on the equity consequences of the demand response. Evidence on differential responses by identifiable groups (identified by age, or income, for example) will help determine the desirability of the demand response from an equity perspective.

Publicly funded health care systems within Canada provide an opportunity to examine these demand responses. Partial or full de-listing of health care services has occurred regularly across Canadian provinces over the past 15 years. Many provinces either partially de-listed services (for example, in 1998 Ontario reduced coverage for routine eye examinations from one every year to one every other year), fully de-listed services (Alberta de-listed speech therapy for the general population in 1995), or de-listed services for some people and not others. The de-listings across provinces over time are summarized in Table ??.

In previous research with Courtney Ward, the present author exploited this variation in de-listings across provincial health care plans to provide empirical evidence on the behavioral response to provincial de-listings of health care services between 1994 and 2001 [22]. The effects of de-listing various health care services were examined across provinces and over time. The identification comes from changes within provinces over time, separate from any time trend or province specific differences in the use of health care services.

Potential changes in provincial insurance coverage (which are referred to as de-listings if the change was towards less coverage) were examined for the use of four types of health professional: physiotherapists; speech therapists; optometrists; and chiropractors. Any decrease in insurance coverage for these services was characterized as a de-listing. That is, if a province lowered the reimbursement level for the services, resulting in an out-of-pocket price increase for consumers, but still partially funded a service, this was considered a de-listing. If a province reduced the frequency with which it reimbursed a service, thereby resulting in an out-of-pocket price increase, on average, then this was considered a de-listing. If a province completely removed a service from its insurance program, it was considered a de-listing. This de-listing measure, therefore, effectively captures any increase in out-of-pocket costs for the use of these health services to individuals. Ideally, it would be possible to measure the exact price for the service faced by the individual; the de-listings could then be treated as exogenous changes in the measured price of the service. As prices for these goods in each time/province cell could not be measure, it was necessary to use the dichotomous measure of de-listing, as described here. The measure still captures an exogenous change in the price of the service, but does not allow the actual price of the service offered to be observed. One clear limitation of this analysis was that a distinction could not be made between different-sized price changes. Instead, the system measured an average effect across all de-listings, both partial and full. Findings from the RAND study suggested that the largest demand response to changes in the price of care comes from moving from zero out-of-pocket costs to a positive out-of-pocket cost [23]. Viewed in this context, the estimates of average effect may be useful in understanding how individuals respond when services go from fully covered to not fully covered.

The effects were also examined of de-listing various health care services across provinces and over time, using the 1994–1998 National Population Health Survey and the 2000/01 Canadian Community Health Survey. Each of these surveys contains detailed demographic information as well as information on the use of the four services examined. The legislative changes outlined in Table ?? were matched with the province and year information for each individual in the surveys. A multivariate framework was then used to examine the causal effects of the de-listing, separate from any time trend or province specific differences in the use of health care services.

The resulting models were variants of the following:

$$util_{itp} = \alpha + \beta delist_{ip} + \delta X_{itp} + \tau_t + p_p + \varepsilon_{itp} \tag{3.1}$$

where *util* refers to the utilization of each of the categories of services examined: optometrist, chiropractor, physiotherapist, and speech therapist. X is a vector of observable characteristics about the individual, τ is a fixed year effect to capture any differences over time in the use of these services that are common across Canada, and p is a fixed provincial effect which captures any fixed differences in the utilization of various services across provinces. Both the extensive utilization margin and the intensive margin were examined.

The results suggest that while the de-listing of services did affect utilization, the effects were not uniform across services, nor across populations. For example, while the utilization of physiotherapy and eye examinations decreased after being de-listed, the demand for speech therapy services increased. While the number of people using any physiotherapy services decreased, the number of visits among those who did use such services increased. The results are reproduced and summarized in Table 3.2.[2] The observed differences in across services have two

---

[2] For a complete description of the results, see Ref. [22].

Table 3.1 Delistings by province over time

	Physiotherapy		Optometry	
	Coverage in 1994	Changes to coverage	Coverage in 1994	Changes to coverage
British Columbia	Limit of 12 visits per year for those < 65 and 15 for those 65+	No change	Limit of 1 visit every 24 months for those 16–64 and no limit for those <16 and 64+	No change[*]
Alberta	Limit of $250 in each year	1995: not covered (only for those evaluated as high need based on a standardized assessment form)	Limit of 1 full oculo-visual exam, 1 partial vision exam and 1 single diagnostic procedure every 2 years for those >18 and < 65 and every year for those <19 and 65+	1995: No coverage for those >18 and <65 and same coverage for <19 and 65+
Saskatchewan	Not covered in private practice	No change	Not covered except for those <18 limited to one visit per year	No change
Manitoba	Not covered in private practice	No change	Limit of 1 visit every 2 years	1996: No coverage for those >18 and <65 and same coverage for <19 and 65+
Ontario	Covered in private practice	1998: Limit of 20 visits per year	An oculo-visual assessment is covered in private practice	1998: Limit of 1oculo-visual assessment and 1 follow up oculo-visual minor assessment every 2 years for those >19 and <65 and every year for those <20 and 65+
Quebec	Not covered in private practice	No change	Not covered except for those <18 and 65+ limited to one visit per year	1996: coverage changes for those <18 and 65+, who are now limited to one visit every 2 years
New Brunswick	Not covered in private practice	No change	Not covered in private practice	No change
Nova Scotia	Not covered in private practice	No change	Coverage in private practice	1997: No coverage for those >18 and <65 and same coverage for <19 and 65+
Prince Edward Island	Not covered in private practice	No change	Not covered in private practice	No change
Newfoundland	Not covered in private practice	No change	Not covered in private practice	No change

[*] In 2001, British Columbia limited patients to a combined total of 10 visits per year for chiropractic, massage, naturopathic, physical therapy or non-surgical podiatric visits.

[**] In 2001, routine optometry visits every 2 years were eliminated for everyone 16–64 years of age.

De-listing information is gathered from the legislative records for each province.

Dental		Speech Therapy		Chiropractic care	
Coverage in 1994	**Changes to coverage**	**Coverage in 1994**	**Changes to coverage**	**Coverage in 1994**	**Changes to coverage**
Not covered in private practice	No change	Not covered in private practice	No change	Limit of 12 visits per year for those < 65 and 15 for those 65+	No change[*]
Not covered in private practice	No change	Covered	1995: not covered	Limit of $300 in each year	1995: Limit changes to $200
Not covered in private practice	No change	Not covered in private practice	No change	Covered in private practice	No change
Not covered in private practice	No change	Not covered in private practice	No change	Limit of 15 visits per year based on the per visit cost of $11.56 ($12.72 in northern Man)	1996: Limit changes to 12 visits per year with a provincial spending cap on total use
Not covered in private practice	No change	Covered in private practice	No change	Limit of $220 in each year	1999: Limit changes to $150
Not covered in private practice except for those less than 10	No change	Not covered in private practice	No change	Not covered in private practice	No change
Not covered in private practice	No change	Not covered in private practice	No change	Not covered in private practice	No change
Not covered in private practice	No change	Not covered in private practice	No change	Not covered in private practice	No change
Not covered in private practice	No change	Not covered in private practice	No change	Not covered in private practice	No change
Not covered in private practice (with some coverage for those under 12)	No change	Not covered in private practice	No change	Not covered in private practice	No change

Table 3.2 The effects of de-listings on utilization

	Visited physiotherapist	Visited optometrist	Visited speech therapist	Visited chiropractor
Panel A – Use or not				
De-list	−0.005	−0.034	0.003	0.002
	[0.002]*	[0.008]***	[0.002]**	[0.004]
Observations	201541	201452	201582	201521
R-squared	0.02	0.05	0.01	0.03
Panel B – Use conditional on positive use				
De-list	0.659	0.011	0.536	−0.252
	[0.180]***	[0.014]	[0.245]**	[0.120]**
Observations	15696	76751	3205	24544
R-squared	0.06	0.02	0.07	0.07
Panel C – Use or not with income interactions				
De-list	−0.009	−0.029	0.003	−0.002
	[0.005]*	[0.010]***	[0.002]	[0.004]
De-list * Income >30K	0.007	−0.007	0.001	0.006
	[0.006]	[0.007]	[0.002]	[0.005]
Observations	201541	201452	201582	201521
R-squared	0.02	0.05	0.01	0.03
Panel D – Use conditonal on positive use with income interactions				
De-list	1.128	−0.019	0.169	−0.386
	[0.222]***	[0.017]	[0.444]	[0.242]
De-list * Income >30K	−0.701	0.046	0.645	0.186
	[0.355]*	[0.017]**	[0.635]	[0.256]
Observations	15696	76751	3205	24544
R-squared	0.06	0.02	0.07	0.07
Panel E – Use or not with age interactions				
De-list	−0.003	−0.037	0.004	0.003
	[0.002]	[0.009]***	[0.002]**	[0.004]
De-list * Age >65 years	−0.011	0.012	−0.004	−0.003
	[0.004]***	[0.027]	[0.005]	[0.006]
Observations	201541	201452	201582	201521
R-squared	0.02	0.05	0.01	0.03
Panel F – Use conditional on positive use with age interactions				
De-list	0.718	0.021	0.568	−0.210
	[0.223]***	[0.015]	[0.253]**	[0.107]*
De-list * Age >65 years	−0.339	−0.039	−0.108	−0.304
	[0.452]	[0.032]	[0.266]	[0.316]
Observations	15696	76751	3205	24544
R-squared	0.06	0.02	0.07	0.07

Notes: Robust standard errors are shown in parentheses. Other variables included in the regressions are: dummies for income, self-assessed health, age, gender, marital status and education, provincial and year dummy variables, and a constant term.
*, Denotes the coefficient is significant at the 10% level; **, denotes the coefficient is significant at the 5% level; ***, denotes the coefficient is significant at the 1% level.
Source: Ref. [22].

interesting implications when considering the role for private financing in a predominantly publicly financed model:

1. Evidence from the de-listed services examined suggests varied effects on accessibility. The absence of a demand response in some cases, even among low-income households, suggests that there was limited change in the ability to access the service following de-listing, despite a move from public to private financing for the services. In other cases, the observed decline in use suggests that concerns over accessibility are warranted.
2. In some cases, de-listing resulted in price deregulation, potentially aggravating the accessibility problems described above. As a more rigorous approach to the definition of the central core of medically necessary services evolves, more services will necessarily be de-listed. In these cases it worth considering regulation for services that have been de-listed to mitigate accessibility problems.

3.3
OECD Evidence on Private Financing

3.3.1
Introduction

The subject now turns from Canada to countries across the OECD over time, in order to better understand the potential long-term effects of private financing on public health care spending. This section of the chapter updates and extends the findings of Tuohy et al. [7], who examined the relationship between changes in private financing and changes in public spending within countries, over time. One of their major methodological findings was that it is insufficient to draw comparisons of private health care spending across nations at any given point in time. Rather, it is important to examine the dynamic effects of changes over time in private spending and public spending on health *within* given systems. These investigations builds on this methodological finding to estimate dynamics models of the relationship between private financing for health care and public financing for health care within countries over time.

Four models are used to categorize the structure of this relationship:

1. Duplicate or Parallel public and private systems: For a given range of services, a separate privately financed system exists as an alternative to the public sector.
2. Supplementary or Co-payment: Across a broad range of services, financing is partially subsidized through public payment, with the remainder financed through out-of-pocket payments and/or private insurance. The degree of Co-payment may be scaled according to the income of the patient.
3. Group-based or Primary: Certain population groups are eligible for public coverage; others rely on private insurance.
4. Sectoral or Complementary: Certain health care sectors are entirely publicly financed; others rely much more heavily upon private finance.

Table 3.3 Four categories of public-private finance

Category (OECD category mapping)[1]	Definition	Example jurisdictions[2]
Parallel public and private system (duplicate)	For a given range of services, a separate, privately financed system exists	UK, Australia
Copayment (supplementary)	Across a broad range of services, financing is partially public and partially private	Sweden, Japan
Group-based (primary)	Certain groups are eligible for public coverage, others require private purchase	Germany, US
Sectoral (complementary)	Certain sectors are primarily publicly financed, others primarily privately financed	Canada, Denmark

1) Note that OECD categories do not map is not 1-1 with the categories used in this analysis. See Footnote 4 in the text for details.
2) Note that categories are not exclusive and example jurisdictions may be placed in more than one category.

These four models have been used to structure the relationship between public and private finance to classify the countries in the OECD data base and then explicitly to test whether the relationship between private and public financing for health care differs depending on the predominant model(s) in that country. The models, definitions, and example jurisdictions are listed in Table 3.3.

The findings suggest that there is a strong relationship between increases in private financings for health care and decreases in public financing for health care. This relationship is robust to using longer lags for changes in private financing within countries over time, as well as to controlling for differing shares of in-patient funding (predominately public) across countries. Moreover, the relationship between private and public financing differs significantly depending on the structure of the public–private relationship within countries. For countries with duplicate parallel public and private systems (our reference group), the negative relationship described above holds. However, this relationship is even more negative in countries that exhibit complementary/sectoral categorization of public and private financing or primary/group-based categorization of public and private financing.

The following sections: (i) outline the empirical methodology used, (ii) describe the data; (iii) present both the updated results and the extension described briefly above; and (iv) offer some discussion based on the results, as well as some conclusions.

3.3.2
Empirical Methodology

Do public and private finance represent independent sources of funding for health care, or do they tend to substitute, or crowd each other out? There is a considerable economic literature examining the crowding-out of private funding by public programs, focusing primarily on the US [24]. Researchers have found that, in the case of the US Medicaid programs, private financing is often partially crowded out by increases in government financing. However, the opposite may also be true: that is, increases in private expenditures may lead to a decrease in public expenditure. Without resolving the issues of causality implied by the concept of "crowding out," it is possible to seek associations between changes in the public and private shares of health care expenditure over time.

These investigations build on the methodology used by Tuohy, Flood and Stabile [7], which examines the relationship between changes in private spending on health care within a country over time on changes in public spending. The estimating equation used can be represented as:

$$
\begin{aligned}
\ln(pubhs)_{it} = \alpha &+ \beta \ \ln(privh)_{it-j} + \theta \ \ln(pubsp - pubhs)_{it} \\
&+ \pi \ \ln(toths)_{it-j} + \tau \ \ln(GDP)_{it} + \delta_t + \gamma_i + \varepsilon_{it}
\end{aligned}
\tag{3.2}
$$

where i indexes an OECD country and t indexes time, $pubhs$ is the amount of public spending on health care (all dollar amounts are per capita in purchasing power parity dollars), and $privh$ is the amount of private spending on health care. Private spending is lagged (using 1-, 2- and 3-year lags) to try and account for the fact that the purpose here is to better understand the effect of private spending on public spending, and not vice versa. Whilst the use of lags does not ensure that the causal effect of private spending on public spending is being picked up, it does introduce a plausible response time between changes in private spending and changes in public spending. For example, $pubhs$ is total public spending on all goods, $toths$ is total health care spending (which is once again lagged), and GDP is the per capita GDP in each country. Each of these measures is in logs.[3] In addition, δ_t are the time dummy variables and γ_i the country dummy variables; these variables control for any changes that occurred over time that were common across all countries, and also any differences between countries that remain constant over time. For example, if all countries increased public health care spending over the 1990s, this would be picked up in the time dummies. If the UK consistently spent more publicly than other countries, this would be picked up through the country dummies. The remaining variation in spending is, therefore, within countries over time – precisely the variation required to understand the changing dynamics, or "crowd-out" within each country.

---

3) Logs were used for a number of reasons, including facilitating interpretation of the regression coefficients, and because this equation is derived from a "shares" equation (for further details on moving from the shares equation to the log-linear equation, see Ref. [7]).

Each country in the OECD database is categorized into one of the four classifications described above: parallel public and private; co-payment; group-based; and sectoral. Details of how countries are classified and why these classifications were chosen are described in an online appendix.[4] An interaction is then included between each classification and the log of lagged private spending on health care in the regression equation. In specifications that do not include country fixed effects, a fixed effect for each classification system is also included. As the classification systems and the country fixed effects are collinear, the classifications are not included when country fixed effects are included in the regression models. The resulting estimating equation is:

$$\ln(pubsh)_{it} = \alpha + \beta_1 \ln(privh)_{it-j} + \beta_2 \ln(privh)_{it-j} * \sec toral$$
$$+ \beta_3 \ln(privh)_{it-j} * co - pay + \beta_4 \ln(privh)_{it-j}$$
$$* group + \theta \ln(pubsp - pubsh)_{it} + \pi \ln(toths)_{it-j} \quad (3.3)$$
$$+ \tau \ln(GDP)_{it} + \delta_t + \gamma_i + \varepsilon_{it}$$

The coefficients β_2 through β_4 tell us whether the extent of crowding out of public health care spending by private health care spending differs by health care system classification. The coefficients are to be interpreted as relative to an omitted category, which in this case is a parallel public–private system. For example, a negative value of β_2 would mean that any crowd-out of public spending by private spending is larger in a sectoral based system than in a parallel public–private-based system.

3.3.3
Data

The analysis uses data from the OECD health database for the years 1980 through 2004. The OECD data contain information on 24 countries; Luxembourg and Iceland were excluded from the estimates, leaving a sample of 22 countries over 25 years. The data contain information on health care spending in each country that can be broken down into the public component, the private component, spending on in-patient care, out-patient care, and pharmaceuticals. As a measure of the total capacity of each country the data also include measures of GDP per capita in each year. Means and standard deviations of each of the OECD variables used in the analysis, computed over the entire sample, are presented in Table 3.4. Each of the countries in the data set is classified into one or more of the four categories used

---

4) Available at: www.chass.utoronto.ca/~mstabile/ oecd/oecddataapp.pdf. The OECD classifies private insurance as supplementary, complementary, duplicate or primary [26]). For consistency, these definitions have been mapped onto the four classifications used in this chapter as described in the Appendix. However, it is important to note that private financing, as discussed here, is broader than private insurance, and that in some cases the classifications will not overlap completely. For example, the OECD classifies Canada as "supplemental", which does not capture the fact that supplemental coverage in Canada is only available for sectors outside the legislated medically necessary sectors.

Table 3.4 Summary statistics for OECD analysis.
(Source: OECD database)

Variable	N	Mean (standard deviation)
Public expenditure on health care per capita	465	1080.559 (535.996)
Private expenditure on health care per capita	465	442.452 (422.679)
Total expenditure on health care per capita	497	1512.32 (823.816)
Public expenditure on in-patient care per capita	395	547.808 (267.753)
Public expenditure on out-patient care per capita	372	272.301 (170.046)
Public expenditure on pharmaceuticals	418	114.842 (73.301)
Total expenditure on in-patient care per capita	364	673.157 (337.390)
Total expenditure on out-patient care per capita	327	496.869 (331.948)
Total expenditure on pharmaceuticals per capita	439	201.611 (119.972)
GDP per capita	528	17888.39 (7174.145)
Government expenditure on health as a share of GDP	496	7.895 (1.754)

Sample is for OECD countries between 1980 and 2004, excluding Luxembourg and Iceland.
All dollar amounts are in purchasing power parity (PPP) dollars.

to describe the relationship between private and public financing described above. Each country can fall into more than a single category. For example, if a country has a private, parallel system available and uses co-payments in the public tier, it would fall into both the parallel and co-payment categories. Changes to the classification may result in changes in the estimation results in Eq. (3.3). One caveat to the results presented below, therefore, is that they are subject to the classifications used in this analysis and may be sensitive to changes in these classifications. Some sensitivity checks are described in the results section below.

3.3.4
The Relationship Between Private and Public Financing

The first set of models estimates the relationship between private financing for health care and public financing for health care, both at a point in time and within countries over time. As noted above, the relationship between the change in private financing and the change in public financing is, in the author's opinion, a more appropriate test of crowd-out, although the single year estimates are presented for completeness. These basic results are presented in Table 3.5, where Column 1 shows results for the single year 2002, the latest year for which relatively complete data are available. A strong negative relationship was found between the level of private financing in a country and the level of public financing, controlling for the level of public expenditure, total health expenditure, and GDP. Columns 2 through 9 present the preferred results, controlling for fixed differences between countries, and for changes in health spending over time across all countries. The models use 1-, 2-, and 3-year lags in private spending, and estimate the relationship between changes in private spending and changes in public spending within countries over

Table 3.5 Effects of private health financing on public health spending. (Source: OECD Health Database)

Dependent variable	log per capita public expenditure on health PPP								
log lagged private health care spending	-0.399	-0.292	-0.259	-0.386	-0.241	-0.157	-0.369	-0.203	-0.143
	(0.038)***	(0.019)***	(0.021)***	(0.042)***	(0.025)***	(0.026)***	(0.049)***	(0.029)***	(0.029)***
log lagged total health care spending	1.155	1.286	1.161	1.049	1.111	0.823	0.979	0.914	0.491
	(0.093)***	(0.033)***	(0.040)***	(0.098)***	(0.044)***	(0.053)***	(0.111)***	(0.052)***	(0.063)***
log public helath expenditure excluding health	-0.021	0.011	0.040	-0.024	0.058	0.139	-0.034	0.110	0.218
	(0.041)	(0.030)	(0.036)	(0.047)	(0.039)	(0.049)***	(0.057)	(0.047)**	(0.058)***
Per capita GDP	0.303	0.124	0.173	0.454	0.297	0.347	0.491	0.426	0.396
	(0.108)**	(0.048)***	(0.058)***	(0.114)***	(0.063)***	(0.079)***	(0.134)***	(0.073)***	(0.092)***
Year	2002	All	All	2002	All	All	2002	All	All
Country fixed efects	No	Yes	Yes	No	Yes	Yes	No	Yes	Yes
Regression type	OLS	OLS	GLS	OLS	OLS	GLS	OLS	OLS	GLS
Lags of private and total health spending	1 year	1 year	1 year	2 years	2 years	2 years	3 years	3 years	3 years

***indicates significance at 1%, **at 5%, and *at 10%.
Standard errors in parentheses.

time using both ordinary least squares regressions (OLS) and generalized least squares (GLS) regressions. These allow for a slightly less stringent set of assumptions about how countries differ in terms of their unobservable characteristics over time. The equation is specified in logs, so that the resulting estimates can be directly interpreted as elasticities. The estimates suggest that a 10% increase in private financing for health care in the previous year is associated with a 3% decline in public financing. The OLS and GLS estimates are quite similar. On moving to using private spending 2 and 3 years prior, there continues to be a negative and significant relationship between changes in private spending and changes in public spending on health care, with a 10% increase in private spending associated with a 1.5–2.5% decline in public spending. Again, these estimates control for differences between countries, changes in total public spending over time, differences in GDP, and general time trends that affect all countries.

3.3.5
Does the Relationship Between Public and Private Finance Differ by System Type?

The evidence above indicates a strong relationship between increases in private financing and declines in public financing for health care within countries over time. While the evidence is not strictly causal, the fact that there is a strong relationship between lagged changes in private financing and public financing suggests that public funding levels may indeed respond directly to these changes in private financing. One of the difficulties with cross-country comparisons, however, is that each country's health care financing system may operate differently. These differences may then result in differences in how countries respond to changes in private financing.

In order to assess whether different structuring of the private–public financing relationship lead to different dynamics, the countries in the OECD data were categorized into four groups, as noted above. An estimate was then made of the relationship between private and public financing, including an interaction between each of the categories for public–private financing and the log of lagged private financing, as shown in Eq. (3.3) above. The interaction between parallel systems and private financing was omitted; hence, these estimates should be interpreted as the effect of each type of system categorization relative to the omitted category of parallel public and private systems. For example, a negative coefficient on the interaction between group-based systems and private financing would indicate that the effect of private financing on public financing is stronger in countries with a group-based system than in those with a parallel public and private systems.

The main results for this section are presented in Table 3.6. There continued to be a negative and significant relationship between lagged private spending and public spending. The coefficient on lagged private spending was quite similar in magnitude to the previous estimates, which suggested that a 10% increase in lagged private financing is associated with a 3% decline in public financing (see Column 1). However, the interaction terms are revealing here. In countries with a sectoral

Table 3.6 Effects of private health care financing on public health care spending by Pub/Priv Mix. (Source: OECD Health Database)

Dependent variable	log per capita public expenditure on health PPP								
log lagged private health care spending	-0.377 (0.066)***	-0.282 (0.021)***	-0.254 (0.024)***	-0.410 (0.082)***	-0.222 (0.028)***	-0.139 (0.032)***	-0.369 (0.108)***	-0.178 (0.033)***	-0.107 (0.038)***
log lagged total health care spending	1.186 (0.112)***	1.289 (0.033)***	1.196 (0.037)***	1.142 (0.131)***	1.123 (0.043)***	0.860 (0.052)***	1.054 (0.165)***	0.930 (0.052)***	0.526 (0.063)***
log public health expenditure excluding health	-0.011 (0.050)	-0.028 (0.033)	0.005 (0.037)	-0.009 (0.060)	0.018 (0.044)	0.124 (0.051)**	-0.013 (0.079)	0.078 (0.053)	0.228 (0.062)***
Per capita GDP	0.249 (0.123)*	0.240 (0.053)***	0.256 (0.061)***	0.371 (0.138)**	0.428 (0.070)***	0.414 (0.084)***	0.422 (0.176)**	0.542 (0.083)***	0.418 (0.099)***
sectoral * log lagged private spending	0.068 (0.109)	-0.060 (0.014)***	-0.063 (0.016)***	0.060 (0.130)	-0.092 (0.019)***	-0.100 (0.025)***	-0.005 (0.160)	-0.110 (0.023)***	-0.108 (0.033)***
group * log lagged private spending	-0.075 (0.061)	-0.064 (0.016)***	-0.064 (0.019)***	-0.058 (0.073)	-0.074 (0.022)***	-0.064 (0.029)**	-0.073 (0.094)	-0.075 (0.027)***	-0.047 (0.037)
co-payment * log lagged private spending	0.022 (0.081)	0.017 (0.013)	0.007 (0.015)	0.023 (0.098)	0.021 (0.017)	-0.003 (0.023)	0.004 (0.126)	0.014 (0.021)	-0.029 (0.030)
sectoral-based [1]	-0.420 (0.683)			-0.387 (0.816)			0.011 (0.978)		
group-based	0.514 (0.399)			0.387 (0.477)			0.473 (0.608)		
copayment-based	-0.127 (0.517)			-0.180 (0.626)			-0.049 (0.791)		
Year	2002	All	All	2002	All	All	2002	All	All
Country Fixed Effects	No	Yes	Yes	No	Yes	Yes	No	Yes	Yes
Regression Type	OLS	OLS	GLS	OLS	OLS	GLS	OLS	OLS	GLS
Lags of private and total health spending	1 year	1 year	1 year	2 years	2 years	2 years	3 years	3 years	3 years

***indicates significance at 1%, **at 5%, and *at 10% standard errors in parentheses.

[1] Omitted category is parallel public-private based system.

relationship between private and public financing, there is a stronger negative relationship between private and public financing than in countries where there is a parallel-tier relationship. The sectoral countries include Canada, Denmark, Norway, and Spain. The same is true of countries with a group-based system (included are Austria, France, Germany, Ireland, the Netherlands, and the US). In countries with a co-payment structure, on the other hand, the relationship between private and public financings is not significantly different from that of a parallel private system. Using longer lags for private spending of 2 and 3 years, the coefficient on the interaction term between private spending and a sectoral system was found to be even larger (adding close to 10 percentage points to the coefficient estimate). The GLS estimates were also remarkably similar. The interaction terms clearly indicated that while systems with a parallel private structure do exhibit a negative relationship between changes in private financing and changes in public financings, this relationship was approximately 33% larger in countries with sectoral distinctions between public and private financing (and approximately 25% larger for group-based countries).

Grouping the health financing structure of each of the OECD countries is, by necessity, somewhat subjective. Many countries have some elements of many of the four categories. Attempts were made to group countries according to the predominant types of financing, conscious of the fact that changes in the grouping could potentially result in changes in the sign or significance of the interaction terms. In order to gauge whether the grouping was driving these results, some sensitivity tests were performed, focusing on the sectoral and group-based categories because of difficulties in categorizing these two groups. Each of the other countries listed in these groupings was removed one by one from the sample, before the models were re-estimated. The countries were then removed in all the potential pair combinations, and the models were again re-estimated. The purpose here was to ascertain whether the results were driven by one country, or by a group of countries that were identified as sectoral or group-based. In every case, the estimated coefficient on the interaction terms remained negative and significant, without any qualitative change in magnitude. Finally, a model was estimated where the only interaction was between Canada and lagged private financing. The coefficient estimate in this model was practically identical in magnitude and significance to the coefficient on the sectoral-based interaction with private spending (coefficient estimate of -0.07, standard error of 0.02). Thus, it can be stated with confidence that it is not a classification error that is driving the interesting result found for sectoral and group-based countries.

3.3.6
Discussion

Untangling the complex relationship between private financing for health care and public funding is a difficult, but important, task. Understanding whether private dollars add to the total pool of health care resources, or instead crowd-out public money is one key element in understanding the long-term implications of changing the private–public mix of financing. In the sections above the OECD data have been used to provide evidence on the relationship between changes in private financing over time and changes in public funding over time. A cross-country panel data set was used which allowed the control of fixed differences across countries, and global changes in health care financing. Whilst it is believed that this is the correct way to specify a "crowd-out" equation, it is important to note that it cannot be stated definitely that the relationship is the causal one, as there may be other factors that determine both private spending and public spending. Alternatively, despite using lags in private spending of up to 3 years, it may still be the case that changes in public spending cause changes in private spending. That said, robust estimates were provided of this relationship, and a strong association found between previous increases in private spending and decreases in public spending. In other words, the evidence is consistent with the hypothesis that private money partially crowds-out public dollars. While this crowd-out is not dollar-for-dollar, it is significant; estimates suggest that a 10% increase in public funding results in, on average, a 3% decrease in public funding, and this result holds across a variety of specifications.

Cross-country comparisons are often complicated by the fact that a set of national level statistics is observed, and from these statistics attempts are made to understand differences between countries. Underlying these statistics are complex funding designs, and dynamic health care systems. Whilst it can never be hoped empirically to compare health care systems across jurisdictions and to account for every detail underlying each system, the systems are classified into four broad categories in an attempt to better understand whether different types of system respond differently to changes in private financing. For this, the classification outlined by Tuohy, Flood, and Stabile [7] was used, which defined parallel private and public systems, sectoral-based private and public systems, group-based private and public systems, and co-payment systems. This classification is in keeping with the OECD classification of insurance as supplementary, complementary, duplicate or primary, as noted above. Supplemental private, as discussed above, is broader than private insurance and requires a somewhat broader classification. After categorizing each country, models were estimated to explore whether the dynamics between private and public financing differed depending on the underlying system. The findings suggested that parallel private and public systems experience the negative relationship between private and public financing described above. Interestingly, however, sectoral-based – and to some extent group-based systems – have an even stronger relationship between increases in private financing and decreases in public funding than do parallel private systems. That is, there is greater potential for crowd-out in sectoral systems such as Canada's than there is in other types of system.

These findings have important implications for Canada as the provinces begin to explore alternative financing mechanisms. First, in a system with parallel public and private tiers it does not appear to be the case that private money will be all new money entering the system. Increases in private spending are associated on average with decreases in public spending at a rate of about 30 cents on the dollar.

Although this still means that more money will be entering the system, there do appear to be declines in funding for the publicly financed health care programs. Second, sectoral systems such as Canada's appear to be harder hit. The estimates cannot tell us why this is the case, but in part it may reflect changes in the nature of health care delivery – many new treatments are being provided outside the traditional hospital and physician settings. These types of treatment will increase costs in traditionally (in Canada at any rate) less publicly insured areas such as drug programs, and may provide some relief to hospital budgets. If this is indeed the case, it would be important for future research to examine the distributional consequences of such a shift, given that patients are fully insured for care in the hospital sector, and less insured for care outside of it. Of course, there may be other explanations for the stronger findings in sectoral-based settings, and uncovering these potential mechanisms is an important area for continued research.

3.4
Overall Conclusions and Directions for Further Study

What can be concluded about the role of private financing in helping to achieve the policy goals of the Canadian health care system? In particular, does private financing offer an opportunity to enhance the goals of the public system, or to help deal with cost growth in the health care sector which has outpaced, and will likely continue to outpace, the rate of economic growth? Here, the following broad conclusions from the material presented are offered, together with some directions for further studies.

There is an important distinction to be made between private financing outside of the publicly funded health care system and private financing within the system. Financing within the public system, in forms such as user fees, tax payments, or MSAs, is beyond the scope of this chapter. The evidence presented here speaks to financing outside the public system, either for substitute care, or for services no longer covered by the public system.

The chapter reviews the evidence regarding changes in the demand for health care services in those cases where governments decide that items can no longer be funded within the public basket of services, either because they are not as cost-effective as alternative forms of care or because they are no longer deemed medically necessary. The findings suggest that the demand response to the de-listing of different types of services is not uniform. In some cases the use of services was unaffected, suggesting that accessibility was not necessarily reduced.[5] In other cases, declines in utilization are observed as a result of public de-listing, particularly among some disadvantaged populations. A blanket policy for considering the relationship between de-listing and the accessibility goals of the public system is

---

5) It is important to note that observing no overall change in utilization can mask changes across different parts of the distribution. Examining interactions between income and utilization is one test of such changes.

therefore not appropriate, and deeper consideration of the demand responses by service type is warranted.

Evidence was also presented on the relationship between increases in private financing for care and public health care financing. The evidence presented suggests that increases in private financing are correlated with decreases in public financing, although not dollar for dollar. Further, these changes differ in magnitude depending on the relationship between public and private financing within a particular health care system. The strongest relationship between increases in private spending and decreases in public spending is to be found in those systems with a predominantly sectoral distinction between public and private spending.

Likewise, the evidence was reviewed on the existence of fiscal externalities from financing private care that substitutes for care in the public system. There is an extensive, although not conclusive, literature examining many of the potential channels for a privately financed system to affect the public system. On balance, the evidence suggests that privately funded substitute care will compete for high-profit, low-risk patients, that there will be some supply shifts leading to increased cost in the public sector, and that there may be some shifting of patients across sectors by physicians. Further, there is no evidence supporting the notion that increases in private financing reduce waiting times in the public system. Presumably, there are significant benefits for those patients who choose to receive care privately, though these benefits may not necessarily be reflected in better health outcomes, but rather in greater satisfaction. The available evidence on the distribution of such benefits suggests that wealthier individuals will be the predominant beneficiaries. Moreover, the evidence presented on the relationship between increases in private funding through this mechanism and existing public funding suggests that increases in private funding are correlated with crowding-out of public funding in the order of 20%.

If, then, the existence of a privately financed alternative imposes some negative externalities on the public system, what should policy makers do? The Canadian response thus far, while varied from province to province, has been effectively to ban private financing for publicly funded care through regulations that severely limit the market for private care (see Ref. [25] for a review of the legislation in each province). Although this method removes any externality, it may be more severe than is required to maintain the integrity of the public system. As Glied [17] points out, this is effectively a tax on private health care of infinity, and while the evidence suggests that private financing imposes an externality on the public system, it is unlikely that an effective tax rate of infinity matches the harm.

Glied goes on to propose a solution that would effectively tax privately financed care at a rate that left the public system no worse off as a method of allowing possible pareto improvements in health care through the use of private financing. This solution has some attractive properties, although there would be difficult implementation issues. In particular, many health care episodes are not easily defined, and it is not clear where public care ends and private care begins and, perhaps more importantly, vice versa. Further, allowing a large-scale private alternative may reduce support for a broad-based public system. The level at which support for the public system begins to disintegrate is an open question for future research.

Flood, Stabile, and Tuohy [18] have suggested a model of concentric circles to circumscribe a role for private financing in conjunction with the public system. This model envisions various financing circles, from a core that is solely publicly funded, through mixed public and private financing, and onto fully private financing. The core of the model includes a set of services that are fully and exclusively publicly funded, and includes most complex health care episodes. However, the model also allows for the possibility of a concentric circle of publicly funded care with the option to purchase substitute care privately for a set of limited, well-defined health care episodes, where the public system is able to ensure timely and quality universal access through regulation and/or tax measures. A functioning wait-time guarantee where all citizens can acquire a specified treatment publicly at a given quality and within a set time frame would be an example of the public system ensuring timely and quality access. The recent Quebec proposal for wait times guarantees for elective surgery, coupled with a relaxation of the ban on private insurance for only these few procedures, is a *possible* working example of such a model [16] although further study is required to fully understand whether the objectives of the public system will be preserved. The model also includes a circle of mixed private and public financing where public financing covers some individuals in some circumstances, and allows for services to be privately financed for other individuals, thereby achieving full accessibility through a combination of public and private financing (the Quebec drug financing model is one example (although not a flawless one) of using mixed financing to achieve universal access).

Finally, the model includes a financing circle where care is privately financed for those services that are deemed not (or no longer) cost-effective and therefore not "medically necessary" (and perhaps de-listed) by the public system.

The Canadian health care system has been financed through a combination of public and private sources since Medicare began almost a half-century ago. The goal of the public system is to provide essential health care services in a timely fashion to all Canadians. The basket of health care services has never included all health care services of any medical value. There will always be limits to the public offering and outside these limits there is an appropriate role for private finance. Within the limits of the public offering, even a well-functioning public system will likely fall short of some patients' expectations for timeliness or intensity of service, as it balances the allocation of fixed resources across many needs. The expansion of private financing of care within this context may allow some individuals to fulfill these expectations, but at the expense of the quality and cost of care in the public sector – costs not borne by the receiver of private care through the price alone. Any role for private financing in this context must be managed in such a way as to prevent these negative externalities, and in many cases this may mean effectively banning private care. In other cases, standard mechanisms for dealing with externalities, combined with caution and careful study, may allow for some private financing without hindering the ability of the public system to achieve its goals. Well-defined public goals, such as those being developed in Quebec in response to the 2005 Chaoulli decision, combined with a fulsome program of research, will help to shape and define these boundaries.

References

1 Kotlikoff, L., Hagist, C. (2005). *Who's going broke? Comparing healthcare costs in ten OECD countries*. National Bureau of Economic Research, Working Paper #11833.

2 Canadian Institute for Health Information (2006). Quick Stats at http://www.cihi.ca.

3 Light, D.W. (1996). Betrayal by the surgeons. *Lancet*, **347**, 812–813.

4 Richmond, C. (1996). NHS waiting lists have been a boon for private medicine in the UK. *Canadian Medical Association Journal*, **154** (3), 378–381.

5 DeCoster, C., Carrière, K.C., Peterson, S., Walld, R., MacWilliam, L. (1998). Waiting times for surgery in Manitoba Winnipeg: Manitoba Centre for Health Policy and Evaluation. Accessible at: http://www.cc.umanitoba.ca/centres/mchpe/wait.htm

6 Besley, T., Hall J., Preston I. (1998). Private and public health insurance in the UK. *European Economic Review*, **42**(3–5), 491–497.

7 Tuohy, C.H., Flood, C.M., Stabile, M. (2004). How does private finance affect public health care systems? Marshalling the evidence from OECD nations. *Journal of Health Politics, Policy, and Law*, **29** (3), 359–396.

8 Francis, B.J., Frost, C. (1979). Clinical decision-making: a study of. general surgery within Trent RHA. *Social Science and Medicine*, **13**, 193–198.

9 McAvinchey, I., Yannopoulos, A. (1993). Elasticity estimates from a dynamic model of interrelated demands for private and public health care. *Journal of Health Economics*, **12**, 171–186.

10 Cutler, D.M., McClellan, M.B., Newhouse, J.P. (1998). *The costs and benefits of intensive treatment for cardiovascular disease*. National Bureau of Economic Research, Working Paper No. 6514, Cambridge, Mass.

11 Martin, S. and Smith, P. (1996). Explaining variations in inpatient length of stay in the National Health Service. *Journal of Health Economics*, **15**, 279–304.

12 Hurley J., Vaithianathan, R., Crossley, T., Cobb-Clark, D. (2002). *Parallel Private Health Insurance in Australia: A Cautionary Tale and Lessons for Canada*. Institute for the Study of Labor Research Paper, Series # 515.

13 Lu, M., Savage, E. (2006). Do financial incentives for supplementary private health insurance reduce pressure on the public system? Evidence from Australia (manuscript in preparation).

14 Flood, C.M., Stabile, M., Kontic, S. (2005). Finding health policy 'arbitrary': the evidence on waiting, dying, and two-tier systems. In: *Access to Care, Access to Justice: The Legal Debate over Private Health Insurance in Canada*, Flood, C., Roach, K., Sossin, L. (Eds.), University of Toronto Press, Toronto.

15 Cutler, D.M., Reber, S. (1998). Paying for health insurance: the tradeoff between competition and adverse selection. *Quarterly Journal of Economics*, **113** (2), 433–466.

16 Government of Quebec (2006). *Guaranteeing Access: Meeting the Challenges of Equity, Efficiency and Quality*. Ministry of Health, Quebec.

17 Glied, S. (2006). Inequalities and Externalities in Health Care Consumption. Columbia University (manuscript in preparation).

18 Flood, C.M., Stabile, M., Tuohy, C.H. (2006). Seeking the Grail: Financing for quality, accessibility and sustainability in the health care system. University of Toronto (manuscript in preparation).

19 Kirby, M.J.L. (2002). *The health of Canadian Medicare – the federal role*. Final Report to the Standing Senate Committee on Social Affairs. Science and Technology 6, Recommendations for Reform, Part II, IV and V, Ottawa.

20 Romanow, R. (2002). *Building on Values: The Future of Health Care in Canada*. Report of the Commission on the Future of Health Care in Canada.

21 Canadian Institute for Health Information (2005). *Exploring the 70/30 Split: How Canada's Health Care System is*

Financed. Canadian Institute for Health Information, Ottawa, ON.

22 Stabile, M., Ward, C. (2006). The Effects of De-listing Publicly Funded Health Care Services. In: *Health Services Restructuring in Canada: New Evidence and New Directions*, Beach, C., Chaykowski, R., Shortt, S., St. Hilaire, F., Sweetman, A. (Eds.), John Deutsch Institute for the Study of Economic Policy, McGill/Queen's University Press, Kingston.

23 Newhouse, J. (1993). *Free For All?* Harvard University Press, Cambridge.

24 Cutler, D.M., Gruber, J. (1996). Does public insurance crowd out private insurance? *Quarterly Journal of Economics*, **111** (2), 391–430.

25 Flood, C.M., Archibald, T. (2001). The illegality of private health care in Canada. *Canadian Medical Association Journal*, **164**, 825–830.

26 Colombo, F., Tapay, N. (2004). *Private Health Insurance in OECD Countries: The Benefits and Costs for Individual Health Systems*. OECD Health Working Papers, #15.

4
Prescription Drug Financing
Steve Morgan

4.1
Introduction

Drug financing policy poses many economic challenges. Not the least are the tasks of finding the resources needed to cover one of the largest expenditure components of health care, and the tools required to manage that expenditure wisely. On average, Canadians spent approximately $840 per capita on pharmaceuticals in 2006, for a total of $27 billion [1, 2]. This represents over half of what was spent on hospitals ($45 billion), and 50% more than what was spent on physicians ($19 billion) in the same year. Moreover, 2006 drug spending was nearly three times what was spent on drugs in 1996 ($10 billion). Such expenditure levels and trends reflect the rising prominence of pharmaceuticals within modern health systems and, as a result, within health care policy and health economics.

A majority of drug expenditure is spent on treatments for relatively common conditions such as high cholesterol, hypertension, heartburn, and depression [3–5]. With expenditure on such categories of medicine doubling roughly every 6 years, there is increasing interest in determining the value for money achieved from such spending [6–8]. Owing to the various imperfections on the demand and supply side of the pharmaceutical market, it is possible that agents (patients and/or their prescribing physicians) may select drug treatment options that are more costly than would be selected in a more conventional marketplace. Financing policy may contribute to or help to ameliorate such potential inefficiencies or "moral hazard" problems in the pharmaceutical sector.

Along with the rise in expenditure on common treatments, there has simultaneously been an increase in the availability and cost of drugs to treat rare, but serious, conditions. While these treatments are offered for only very small populations, they are increasingly priced not in hundreds of dollars but rather in hundreds of thousands of dollars, and thereby pose many economic and ethical dilemmas [9–11]. The costs are certainly beyond the financial reach of most individuals, and may test the limits of a society's willingness to pay for health care. Drug financing policy will therefore require mechanisms for determining what drugs should be publicly covered (or collectively, in the case of private insurance), for whom, and

Financing Health Care: New Ideas for a Changing Society. Edited by Mingshan Lu and Egon Jonsson
Copyright © 2008 WILEY-VCH Verlag GmbH & Co. KGaA, Weinheim
ISBN: 978-3-527-32027-1

under what circumstances. Whether the treatments are for common or rare conditions, setting such limits in an efficient and fair manner poses significant policy challenges [12–14].

There is an additional challenge to drug financing policy in North America because, historically, it has been distinguished from the financing of hospital and medical care. Drugs consumed within hospitals are universally publicly insured in Canada, and covered for the elderly and indigent beneficiaries of the respective public Medicare and Medicaid programs in the United States (US). Drugs purchased in the community system reside outside the Canadian "Medicare" system, and have only recently been incorporated into the US Medicare system for elderly patients [15]. The lack of universal coverage for pharmaceutical costs in Canada has caused even high-profile government inquiries to question why such a "medically necessary" form of health care would be publicly insured when in hospital, but not otherwise [16–18].

The means by which we finance pharmaceutical expenditure will have a significant impact on health care policy, equity, and sustainability over the coming years. A number of economic theories regarding the financing and reimbursement of pharmaceuticals have recently been reviewed elsewhere [13]. In this chapter, some of the basic characteristics of the pharmaceutical sector that make it distinct from other sectors of the economy – and even distinct from other components of health care – are reviewed. Various market imperfections on the demand side of the pharmaceutical sector in particular have potentially important implications for financing policy. This chapter begins with a description of drug expenditures and financing in Canada and abroad. This is followed by a review of various unique characteristics of pharmaceuticals and a discussion of the many goals that might be pursued through drug financing. The chapter concludes with a brief discussion about where Canadian pharmacare reform appears to be heading, and the major challenges that will need to be addressed on course.

4.2
Drug Expenditures and Financing in Canada and Abroad

Owing to the scale and growth rates for related expenditures, pharmaceuticals are a major challenge in health care financing. Figure 4.1 shows, graphically, the Organisation for Economic Co-operation and Development (OECD) data on pharmaceutical expenditure per capita from 1977 to 2004. The figure illustrates the average expenditure per capita for reporting OECD countries, along with the values for Canada and the US. Values are expressed in terms of year-2004 Canadian dollars per capita, and include both prescription drug expenditure and over-the-counter drug expenditure (few countries report prescription drug expenditure alone dating back further than 1990).

Averaged across OECD countries, growth in real (inflation-adjusted) expenditure per capita on pharmaceuticals has been steady over the past 30 years. In 1977, the OECD average per-capita expenditure on pharmaceuticals was $172 (measured in

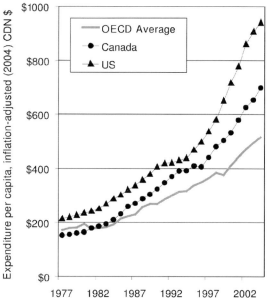

Fig. 4.1 Real (inflation-adjusted) pharmaceutical expenditure per capita, OECD countries, 1977 to 2004. Sources: Data extracted from OECD Health Data 2006: Statistics and indicators for 30 countries. OECD average based on countries reporting data in given year. Countries reporting in all 28 years: Canada, Finland, Greece, Iceland, Ireland, Norway, Sweden, and United States.

Other countries (years reporting): Portugal (27), Australia (26), Germany (26), Luxembourg (26), Netherlands (26), Denmark (25), Belgium (22), Korea (22), Japan (21), Spain (21), United Kingdom (21), Switzerland (20), New Zealand (18), France (17), Italy (17), Czech Republic (13), Turkey (11), Austria (10), Hungary (9), Mexico (6), Slovak Republic (5), and Poland (3).

year-2004 Canadian dollars). This grew at an average annual growth rate of 4.15% from 1977 to 2004, ending at $515 averaged across reporting OECD countries. Over the full period of 1977 to 2004, expenditure in Canada and the US grew more rapidly than the OECD average. Canada spent $152 per capita in 1977, while the US spent $214 per capita. By 2004, expenditures per capita were $699 and $940 in Canada and the US, respectively.

Steady and relatively rapid real growth in per-capita expenditure on pharmaceuticals among OECD countries is reflected in the gradual rise of pharmaceuticals as a share of total health care spending, as illustrated in Fig. 4.2. The average share of health spending allocated to pharmaceuticals among reporting OECD countries rose from 11.9% in 1997 to 16.7% in 2004. Growth in the share of health expenditure going to pharmaceuticals in Canada is most impressive: rising from 8.6% in 1997 (well below the OECD average) to 17.7% in 2004 (just above average). There was almost no growth in the share of US health expenditure going to pharmaceutical financing between 1977 and 1995: fluctuating between 8.5 and 9.1% over this period. Then, from 1996 to 2004, the share of US health expenditure going toward pharmaceuticals rose from 9.3% to 12.3%, moving the US much closer to

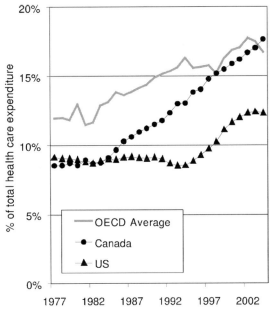

Fig. 4.2 Pharmaceuticals as a share of total health expenditure, OECD countries, 1977 to 2004. Sources: Data extracted from OECD Health Data 2006: Statistics and indicators for 30 countries. OECD average based on countries reporting data in given year. Countries reporting in all 28 years: Canada, Finland, Greece, Iceland, Ireland, Norway, Sweden, and United States. Other countries (years reporting): Portugal (27), Australia (26), Germany (26), Luxembourg (26), Netherlands (26), Denmark (25), Belgium (22), Korea (22), Japan (21), Spain (21), United Kingdom (21), Switzerland (20), New Zealand (18), France (17), Italy (17), Czech Republic (13), Turkey (11), Austria (10), Hungary (9), Mexico (6), Slovak Republic (5), and Poland (3).

the OECD average. The relatively modest share of US health expenditures allocated to pharmaceuticals has been described as the "importance of being unimportant" (until recently, that is) because these expenditures were "under the radar" of major US cost-cutting initiatives [19].

This "importance of being unimportant" can explain a number of aspects of health and pharmaceutical financing in the US and Canada. However, in view of the per-capita expenditure levels, one would be remiss to ignore the fact that the long-term stability of pharmaceuticals as a share of US health care expenditure had more to do with the fact that health care financing in the US has allowed for unusually high growth in other major components of US health expenditure (medical and hospital services) than control over pharmaceutical spending. In contrast, Canada's financing of medical and hospital services is said to have enabled government to control the growth of these components of health care [20], while the Canadian system of pharmaceutical financing has allowed for relatively rapid drug cost escalation [21].

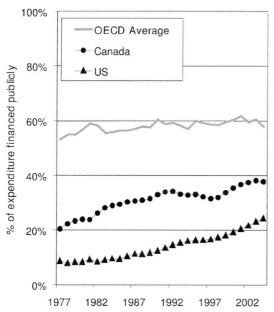

Fig. 4.3 Share of pharmaceutical expenditure financed through public sources, OECD countries, 1977 to 2004. Sources: Data extracted from OECD Health Data 2006: Statistics and indicators for 30 countries. OECD average based on countries reporting data in given year. Countries reporting in all 28 years: Canada, Finland, Greece, Iceland, Ireland, Norway, Sweden, and United States. Other countries (years reporting): Portugal (27), Australia (26), Germany (26), Luxembourg (26), Netherlands (26), Denmark (25), Belgium (22), Korea (22), Japan (21), Spain (21), United Kingdom (21), Switzerland (20), New Zealand (18), France (17), Italy (17), Czech Republic (13), Turkey (11), Austria (10), Hungary (9), Mexico (6), Slovak Republic (5), and Poland (3).

One of the major differences between American and Canadian pharmaceutical financing and pharmaceutical financing in the rest of the OECD is the level of public coverage. While direct charges by way of copayments or other forms of cost-sharing are common in virtually all OECD countries, so too is a substantial role for public drug benefit programs (or public "insurance" for pharmaceuticals). This is true in all regions except North America. For a variety of historical reasons, public drug plans pay for less than half of pharmaceutical expenditure in Canada and in the US. This is illustrated in Fig. 4.3, which depicts the average share of total pharmaceutical expenditure financed publicly among reporting OECD countries along with the public shares for Canada and the US.

4.2.1
Drug Coverage in Canada

At the core of the Canadian health care system is universal public health insurance run by the ten provinces and three territories. National standards of access to necessary medical and hospital care – without, for example, impediments such as user-charges – is guaranteed under federal–provincial cost-sharing arrangements established by the Canada Health Act [22]. Prescription drugs consumed outside hospitals are not covered by the Canada Health Act, or by any other national legislation that would ensure standards for universal accessibility. Each province or territory has therefore evolved its own public program for the coverage of prescription drugs [23, 24]. The resulting pharmacare "system" is more like a "patchwork" of private and public drug benefit programs that vary considerably across and within regions.

The largest public drug programs in Canada evolved out of provincial efforts to ensure access to necessary medicines for society's most vulnerable members – the indigent, the elderly, and the seriously ill [25]. Most provinces offer coverage for these groups with relatively modest copayments or deductibles. However, some provinces – namely British Columbia, Manitoba, and Saskatchewan – have targeted their public drug subsidies primarily toward individuals (regardless of age) who have drug costs exceeding income-based deductibles. Provincial drug programs cover from approximately 28 to 43% of prescription drug expenditure across provinces (Table 4.1). The federal government also runs specific drug benefit programs for groups such as the military, veterans, and registered aboriginal people. Because aboriginal populations in particular vary by region, the federal share of drug financing varies across provinces – from 1% in Quebec to 12% in Saskatchewan. Nationally, just under half of the population is covered by public drug plans, placing Canada (along with the US) well below the standard of near-universal public drug coverage among G8 countries [26].

Some coverage for pharmaceutical costs is offered through private insurance markets, which serve employment-related groups almost exclusively. It is estimated that approximately half of the working-age population have voluntary private drug coverage as part of employment-related benefits packages [27]. These private drug plans cover an estimated 34% of total drug expenditure in Canada. Approximately 10–20% of the population has no drug coverage of any form, and a further 10–20% have incomplete coverage, particularly for exceptionally high drug costs [27, 28]. The shares of the provincial populations that are either uninsured or underinsured for pharmaceutical costs vary by region, and are highest in Atlantic Canada (Nova Scotia, New Brunswick, Newfoundland and Labrador, and Prince Edward Island) [27, 29]. These "gaps" in Atlantic Canada's public drug coverage are partly reflected in the high shares of private drug costs for individuals residing in these provinces.

There are several potential sources of variation as to who is covered across the Canadian provinces, the primary source being provincial governments' economic ability to finance drug expenditures. For example, GDP per capita in the province of Alberta is nearly double the GDP per capita in the provinces of Atlantic Canada. Provinces therefore have significantly different levels of resources (tax bases) available for public drug benefit programs. Those provinces with greater income per capita tend to cover more people than those with lower per-capita incomes (e.g., provinces in Atlantic Canada). It has been suggested that the federal government

Table 4.1 Prescription drug expenditures and coverage by province

	2005 Population size ('000s)	2004 GDP per capita/$	2005 Rx Expenditure per capita/$	Provincial government share/%	Federal government share/%	Social insurance share/%	Private payment share/%
Alberta	3257	54 075	490	42.0	4.3	0.6	53.1
Ontario	12 541	40 346	599	43.3	1.3	0.7	54.7
Saskatchewan	994	36 749	501	38.3	12.0	0.4	49.3
Newfoundland and Labrador[a]	516	35 243	573	35.3	2.8	1.7	60.2
British Columbia	4255	35 041	421	43.9	4.6	0.4	51.2
Quebec	7598	33 856	626	37.4	1.0	13.4	48.2
Manitoba	1178	32 708	508	42.9	9.3	0.3	47.5
Nova Scotia[a]	938	30 883	576	31.5	5.2	0.5	62.9
New Brunswick[a]	752	29 900	592	29.1	4.8	0.6	65.5
Prince Edward Island[a]	138	28 106	477	28.7	4.5	1.1	65.7

a) Province in Atlantic Canada.

Data sources: Drug expenditure data from CIHI (2004) "Drug Expenditures in Canada"; population data from Statistics Canada, CANSIM, table 051-0001; income data from John R. Baldwin, Mark Brown, Jean-Pierre Maynard, and Danielle Zietsma (2004) "Catching Up and Falling Behind: The Performance of Provincial GDP per Capita from 1990 to 2003." Statistics Canada, Economic Analysis (EA) Research Paper Series: Ottawa.

could play a role in reducing this coverage variation by setting national standards for who would be covered and to what extent, and that these standards could be enforced through a cost-sharing agreement, much like the current cost-sharing agreement for hospital and medical services outlined in the Canada Health Act [17, 30]. Until such harmonization of basic entitlement to "pharmacare" occurs, provincial drug programs will continue to operate significantly different pharmacare programs that cover different components of their populations. As a result, many segments of the population will continue to be without public or private drug coverage, and access to medicines will continue to vary based on Canadians' province of residence.

4.3
Unique Aspects of Pharmaceuticals and the Pharmaceutical Sector

Understanding the motivations for, and the strengths and limitations of, different options for the financing of pharmaceuticals requires an understanding of the distinct nature of pharmaceuticals and the pharmaceutical sector. Like other aspects of health care, the demand for and use of prescription drugs differs from ordinary economic commodities in many ways. Important distinctions include the facts that the demand for pharmaceuticals is a "derived demand", an agency relationship is legally mandated on the demand-side of the prescription drug market, various types of need for pharmaceuticals imply different financial "risks", and pharmaceuticals are a component of a larger health care system and have several technical and non-technical externalities of consumption. Each of these characteristics of the sector influences drug financing policy.

4.3.1
Derived Demand

The demand for pharmaceuticals is a "derived demand" by way of the actual demand for health. That is, as with health care more generally, pharmaceuticals are not consumption goods in the classic sense. Drugs are inputs into the delivery of care aimed at restoring or maintaining health. As such, we often refer to the consumers of drugs as patients: persons receiving medicines or medical treatment to address a health problem. While consumer/patient preferences over the possible effects of pharmaceuticals are important considerations, the actual drug products themselves – tablets, liquids, injections, aerosols, creams, etc. – are of no intrinsic value. A patient derives benefit from the consumption of a drug only to the extent that the drug has the capacity to facilitate a valued secondary objective: addressing a specific health problem or risk and thereby improving or maintaining health.

That the demand for pharmaceuticals is a derived demand for health means that it is reasonable to refer to "medical necessity" when speaking about the demand for drugs. Medical necessity is a "need" defined relative to the objective of obtaining or maintaining an acceptable health status. Two dimensions of medical necessity relate to the derived demand for pharmaceuticals:

- A state of health that is currently below, or at reasonable risk of falling below, a level that could be socially validated as being acceptable health status.
- A treatment that is effective at improving or maintaining health status among those with an identified need. A drug would be a "medical necessity" (and therefore of social value) only to the extent that the treated patient suffers from the condition that the drug is indicated for, and only insofar as the drug effectively treats the given medical condition.

Consider the requirement of *need*. Because the use of medicines involves costs, inconvenience, and risk of adverse events, healthy individuals would not generally choose to consume prescription drugs. Those who would knowingly purchase medicines in the absence of medical need are likely to be suffering from one of several disorders including, for example, Munchausen's syndrome (a disorder wherein patients pretend to have illnesses in order to obtain medical care), hypochondria (a disorder wherein patients believe that they have symptoms of serious disorders despite medical reassurance and evidence to the contrary), or addiction (a disorder wherein patients have become psychologically or physically dependent on the medicine). As Robert Evans puts it, "...those who would purchase health care when they are not sick, are sick". [31].

Identifying the need for treatment with pharmaceuticals, as with other health care interventions, requires specialized knowledge and expertise. A patient may have any of a myriad signs and symptoms, often including subclinical indications of disease (e.g., those that might be determined through diagnostic tests and imaging but not otherwise felt or observable by a patient or others). Many presentations of signs and symptoms will indicate specific health problems and risks; many others will reflect experiences within the range of normal experience or of self-limiting conditions. Pharmaceuticals, for the most part, address health conditions (or health needs) that are specific. And prescription-only drugs (which account for roughly 80% of the pharmaceutical marketplace) are indicated for specific health conditions that require specialized skill in diagnosis, treatment and/or monitoring.

Being designated as a "prescription-only" drug implies that the product cannot legally be sold to a patient without the intervention of a physician. Physicians act as patients' professional agents in diagnosing conditions, determining the need for treatment, and selecting from alternative treatment options. This agency role is one of the legally mandated market imperfections in the pharmaceutical sector (albeit one that might improve market outcomes) that stems from the nature of demand for pharmaceuticals as a derived demand for health.

Derived demand and medical necessity has another implication that is increasingly being discussed in the context of pharmaceutical policy, financing, and regulation. As mentioned above, those for whom drugs might be deemed a medical necessity are in a position where their health status is below reasonably acceptable levels or at a reasonable risk of falling below an acceptable health status. The health state or health risk experienced by those in need may put them in a position of being relatively "vulnerable" in comparison to consumers of more standard goods such as automobiles, entertainment, or breakfast cereals. In the case of demand for drugs, it will often be true that the ill cannot delay consumption of treatment. Significant medical needs, in particular, tend to be urgent and pressing in the sense that any delay can be costly, potentially irreversibly so. When faced with few treatment options, seriously ill patients may face a "your money or your life" choice. This gives rise to highly inelastic demand for essential medicines, and provokes special concerns about "excessive prices" in health care markets and, in particular, the pharmaceutical sector.

It is the money or life trade-off that quite likely makes it possible for the manufacturers of new drug treatments for very serious conditions to charge vast amounts for their products. In an increasing number of cases, the cost of new drug treatments is equal to ten or more times the average annual income in even well-developed countries such as Canada [9–11]. Policy responses to this may simultaneously be to place regulatory controls on drug prices such that they cannot be deemed "excessive", while providing drug coverage and financing mechanisms that ensure patients have access to truly effective treatment options even if they are extraordinarily costly.

The second component of pharmaceuticals' derive demand and medical necessity – that a drug should effectively improve or maintain a patient's health – also has significant implications for both demand and supply. Establishing the health impact of treatment is critically important because there are certain, sometimes significant, risks associated with the consumption of pharmaceutical products. "More" is not necessarily "better" in pharmaceutical care; and, owing to this, it is generally not advisable for patients to try a variety of drug treatment options in the hope that one will cure what ails them. Given the population exposure to medicines, this cannot be ignored. Roughly two out of three Canadians will fill at least one prescription this year. Many will live longer and/or better as a result. However, no drug is perfectly safe or of value under all circumstances. Even with perfect quality control in production, adverse drug reactions occur. Indeed, adverse reactions have been estimated to be between the fourth or sixth leading cause of death in the US [32, 33]. As such, unlike the financial- and perhaps utility-loss that might be associated with random failure of a more conventional consumer product, damages done from adverse reactions from pharmaceuticals are personal, non-tradable, and sometimes severe. Various forms of regulatory intervention have been implemented to assist with the evaluation and detection of drug-related risks, including the mandated agency role of prescribing physicians [34].

Even with pre-market safety regulation and evaluation, some risks associated with drugs are, by necessity, considered acceptable. For, if the risk is of small magnitude, probability or both, it may be deemed an acceptable non-pecuniary "cost" of treatment – one borne in the hope that the expected benefits of the treatment will be larger. Some of these risks – called "side effects" – come with such frequency that they may be considered a certainty and just part of the standard impact of the medicine. Again, therapeutic choices are (ideally) to be based on determining whether the net impact of the medicine is expected to be positive.

As with the potentially negative impacts of a drug on patient health, the desired outcomes must also be measured and evaluated carefully. This is more challenging than it might appear at first glance. Any course of treatment involves an element of uncertainty – very few, if any, drugs produce desired results for 100% of the time. Moreover, a person who feels better or worse after drug consumption cannot know with certainty whether nature, placebo or the drug itself was responsible for their change in health status. This characteristic of pharmaceuticals makes them "credence goods" in economic terms – those for which the value to the consumer is difficult or impossible for the consumer to ascertain.

Patients may be able to infer whether a drug to treat a felt symptom of a condition is remedied. A patient could, for example, know that their headache went away following the use of a pain-relief medicine. Yet, even in such cases, an individual patient may not be able to determine with reasonable accuracy the comparative efficacy of treatment options because patients cannot simultaneously treat their condition with multiple options and determine from that experience which was effective – the result of such an "experiment" might indeed be worse than no treatment at all. For the majority of conditions for which pharmaceutical products are indicated, patient-evaluation will result in relatively limited information about treatment effects, particularly comparative effects.

The challenge of extracting information about drug performance is perhaps greatest for patients taking a drug product on a continuous basis to address subclinical risk factors associated with *potential* illness. In the case of preventative, long-term therapies, years may pass before the desired outcomes (lack of heart attack or stroke, for example) are realized. The task of evaluating treatment effect is near-impossible for an individual patient. For example, a drug to prevent heart attacks might lead to five in 100 people experiencing a heart attack over a 5-year period rather than seven in 100 without drug treatment. This drug may be wondrously effective by current clinical standards, but how many of 100 potential patients could verify that the product prevented *their* heart attack? Individual trial and error of such a credence good can result in false understanding of treatment effects. To know, with reasonable scientific certainty, whether a drug is comparatively safe and effective requires that thousands of patients be randomly assigned to receive various treatments, typically under circumstances where both patients and providers are unaware of which treatment is being administered to which patient.

Moreover, even if the results of scientific trials are available to consumers, understanding and keeping abreast of scientific literature requires considerable knowledge and dedication. The associated information costs are significant and growing every year. There are thousands of pharmaceutical products licensed for sale in various formulations, strengths, and brands (including "no-name" generic brands). Staying on top of the scientific literature related to medicines so that one can truly know which will be best for a given patient is, as one can imagine, near-impossible for a single person. This would certainly be so for an individual, non-expert patient.

Again, regulatory policy requires that a patient involve a prescribing physician as their agent when selecting among various treatment options.

4.3.2
Doctors as Prescribing Agent

Agency roles may not always be perfect, in this market or any other. Indeed, there are a number of common problems that exist in the agency relationship between prescribers and patients. One of the primary problems in the agency relationship is related to the time constraints and the mechanisms by which physicians are remunerated for prescribing services. While physicians surely wish to do the best they possibly can for their patients, the extent to which they actually do so is constrained in part by the financial incentives set up by remuneration policy. Doctors are not paid to study and keep abreast of the literature concerning best practices in prescribing. They are similarly not generally rewarded for taking time in the prescribing process to consult with a patient and other health professionals – most notably pharmacists and pharmacologists.

Rather perversely, in fact, the act of prescribing has become a mechanism that helps physicians to keep visits with patients short in duration. Since the 1950s, it has been acknowledged by researchers, health policy experts and medical witnesses at government investigations, that the writing of a prescription serves to "punctuate" a visit [23, 35, 36]. It marks the end of the consultation and is a symbolic aide that demarks the "act" (notably one that is ongoing between visits) of the doctor's "caring" for the patient [34]. Moreover, this is an act that the physician does not pay for. Either the patient or a third-party payer will pick up the expense of any prescribed (and dispensed) drug. Particularly when doctors are remunerated on fee-for-service (or any other mechanism that encourages practitioners to see as many patients as possible), physicians have an incentive to engage in the convenient and costless act of prescribing a drug. Thus, the allocative efficiency of pharmaceuticals prescribed will be influenced in part by physician remuneration, as well as by the methods by which pharmaceuticals are financed.

4.3.3
Types of Financial Risk

It was mentioned above that the utility or value of a drug is related to the patient's need for treatment: that is, by the patients' health status. In standard insurance market models (models of a market for instruments to reduce financial uncertainty), the consumer does not know in advance whether financial loss will occur. This is often true in health care. Before "people" become "patients" they do not typically know whether they will become sick, or with what illnesses. While such uncertainty about potential illnesses reinforces the logic of having prescribing agents in health care – concentrating information costs among prescribing agents (or independent agencies) who serve many patients (or many prescribers) reduces redundancy – it has other implications that are of more direct relevance to financing. As in other markets characterized by uncertainty, the risk of potential illness can give rise to demand for insurance to cover the financial cost associated with the need for medicines. The financial risk associated with drug treatments depends on three components: (i) the conditions for which drug treatments exist; (ii) the risk that one will have such conditions; and (iii) the cost of drugs to treat those conditions.

Historically (prior to the 1950s), most treatable illnesses were common and minor. Moreover, the treatments available at the time came at a relatively modest cost that was affordable to virtually all but those with the lowest incomes [34]. Consequently, there was little demand for pharmaceutical insurance *per se*. Pharmaceutical coverage was more of a device for subsidizing drug costs for those with the fewest means to pay and those for which the health-impact of not accessing drug treatment might be highest, namely the poor and the elderly [36, 37]. Today, there may be an increase in certain forms of "risk" associated with drug needs. One perceived reason for this is because of the rising cost of drug treatments. To understand financial risk associated with the need for pharmaceutical treatment, it is helpful to consider three types of "need" for drug treatment: (i) drugs to treat time-limited, acute conditions; (ii) drugs to treat rare disorders and diseases; and (iii) drugs to treat relatively common chronic conditions. There are other categories of treatment, such as drugs to treat lifestyle and cosmetic conditions. However, those treatment types are among the few drug categories for which there is great debate about their "medical necessity", and therefore debate about how they should fit into drug insurance programs (one should not, however, conclude that all systems avoid coverage for "lifestyle" conditions [38, 39]).

Among drugs to treat acute illnesses are some relatively high-cost treatments, such as specific types of antibiotic. Needs for these drugs are relatively uncommon and largely (though not exclusively) unpredictable. This category of medicine would constitute a classic financial "risk" *per se*. First, as was the case decades ago, most drugs used to treat occasional acute illnesses in the community setting are relatively affordable and predictable in terms of need. In comparison to the high cost of medical and hospital treatment for acute health needs (e.g., surgical treatments following an automobile accident), the cost of most drugs used in time-limited episodes is generally relatively modest. Insurance to cover drugs for such conditions is likely motivated by factors other than the classic economic value of risk-reduction in and of itself. (Such other factors might include social, health and health system related issues that will be returned to below.)

Most of the extraordinarily high cost drugs used to treat acute health needs are in fact administered within hospitals. This would include high-cost treatments for stroke, systemic infections, cancer, and many other diseases, all of which are generally administered within hospitals, and some of which are administered during the course of emergency treatment. The cost of such hospital-administered drug treatments are often viewed (and therefore and covered) as part of the hospital-based medical care that patients receive. This is certainly the case in Canada and the US, where drugs received in hospitals are covered under public or private coverage for hospital and medical services.

Yet, an increasing number of drugs to treat conditions that affect very small numbers of patients are now coming to market for use in community (or out-patient) settings at a cost of hundreds of thousands of dollars per year [9–11]. These drug treatments pose considerable financial risk, and may in and of themselves justify insurance programs. However, the nature of the "risk" of needing many of these conditions is one determined not by fate throughout the life course, but by fate at the moment of birth: most of the expensive drugs for rare diseases are for rare *genetic* conditions. Thus, most – if not all – of the actuarial "risk" that a patient will face is only faced prior to birth. At birth, one either does or does not have the condition(s) for which many of the new high-cost drug treatments are offered. Thus, the "insurance" solution for these types of risk is more of a social insurance to protect against the risk of being born with predictably high needs rather than market insurance to protect against unpredictable needs over time. Actuarially fair market insurance for many of these new high-cost drug treatments would be as costly as the treatments themselves for those born with the indicated conditions. Social insurance would transfer income from those without the indicated conditions to those with the indicated conditions *ex ante* and *ex post*. (The health and social motivates for which will be returned to below.)

Finally, a financing system may need to account for the forms of financial risk associated with drugs to treat relatively common, chronic conditions. Products for use not in singular episodes but rather over prolonged periods of time (often years), dominate the pharmaceutical market in expenditure terms. For example, drugs to treat high blood pressure, high cholesterol, heartburn, depression, diabetes, and asthma account for nearly three-fourths of total expenditure on prescription drugs in Canada [5]. All of these types of drug are often (if not exclusively) indicated for prolonged use. The predictability and persistence of the need for treatment of chronic diseases and risk factors means that the costs associated with this type of pharmaceutical care are not significant "risks" that would motivate insurance as a risk-reduction mechanism *per se*. Once diagnosed with the chronic disease, drug treatments become a predictable and common "need" that will be experienced for many years.

This is not to say that the costs of chronic disease treatments are not sometimes significant – and growing. The average costs per patient treated for many common chronic diseases and chronic risk factors have approximately doubled over the past decade [3–5]. If one happens to have multiples of these chronic needs – such as the increasingly common combination of diabetes, hypertension, high cholesterol, arthritis, ulcers, and depression – the annual costs of treatment can be measured in thousands of dollars. For, given the trends towards more expensive (and potentially more effective) treatment options over the past decade, a relatively average patient can easily incur $500 or more in drug costs for each of these common chronic conditions and risk factors [3–5]. A mechanism for financing pharmaceuticals will therefore have significant implications for the accessibility of drugs to manage common chronic conditions and the equity in how they are paid for.

4.3.4
Pharmaceuticals in the Health and Social Context

The final aspects that render the pharmaceutical sector distinct from markets for standard consumer goods concern the place of pharmaceuticals within a health care and social context. These characteristics can be considered within the economic framework of externalities in consumption. Externalities in the pharmaceutical sector exist at both the technical level and at the altruistic level.

Externalities at a technical level are those that have an impact on the well-being of others that comes by way of factors that have a direct impact on their utility, irrespective of the utility of the person consuming the product. There are various forms of pharmaceutical consumption that can affect a direct, technical impact on the welfare of others. The consumption of a medicine can have direct positive spill-over effects on the health of others or their risk of illness. An example of such positive externalities would include the fact that when a patient receives a vaccination against disease (such as a flu vaccination), this tends to reduce others' risk of infection because those vaccinated are less likely to transmit the illness. An example of negative spill-over effects would include the effects that an overuse of antibiotics can have on others: the more antibiotics are used by others in a population, the greater the chance that the bacteria will develop resistance to those antibiotics, and therefore the less protection antibiotics will offer.

Another technical eternality that is to be considered is the effect of pharmaceutical consumption, or lack thereof, on the efficiency of the health care system which is often publicly financed. The public financing of health care is motivated by various goals, including social altruistic ones that may also motivate the public financing of pharmaceuticals. But, even if one were to assume that there are no social altruistic goals motivating public coverage for pharmaceuticals *per se*, pharmaceutical use can have technical effects on the efficiency with which a population might achieve the outcomes sought through publicly financed medical and hospital care. Indeed, many forms of drug therapy do not have any direct benefit to the patient during the course of pharmaceutical treatment; instead, they have a benefit in terms of the potential to avoid future illness. While the patient would obviously benefit from a reduced future burden of illness, the economic value of medicines consumed for the purpose of prevention is typically found by way of reduced future costs of hospitalization and medical treatment associated with the downstream illness. Thus, when a drug is appropriate for reducing the risk of future illness, a patient's consumption of that drug will have a positive, technical impact on the future financial burdens of those who finance the broader health care system. Put another way, a patient's failure to take effective and appropriate drug treatment imposes a cost on that health care system by way of increasing the probability of drawing on that system.

The final forms of externalities in consumption that may occur in the pharmaceutical sector are those occurring at an altruistic level. Many of these are similar to the various forms of social altruism that motivate public cover for hospital and medical care. Altruism can take various forms in the pharmaceutical sector. There are the forms of paternalistic altruism – belief that consumers may not always know and therefore do what is best for them – that motivate regulation and the creation of various levels of agency relationships in health care. There are also good-specific forms of altruism. In the health sector, these stem from the fact that members of a society may care about those who are suffering from illness and may wish to ensure that these individuals have access to the care that might help to alleviate suffering. Finally, there are general forms of altruism that motivate considerations regarding health and financial equity. Societies may wish to achieve reasonable equity in health status and income. They may therefore wish to design financing systems that provide access to necessary health care (including pharmaceuticals) through mechanisms that do not exacerbate prevailing levels of income inequality. The fact that the consumption of effective and appropriate pharmaceuticals can affect the well-being of others, and the fact that inequality in *ex ante* risk of needing pharmaceuticals may generate significant financial hardships, may therefore affect choices concerning the systems for financing pharmaceuticals.

4.4
Considerations for Pharmaceutical Financing Reform

Under unprecedented financial pressures, there appears to be little doubt that the mechanisms by which pharmaceuticals are financed will evolve in the coming years. This is particularly true in Canada, where there have been repeated, high-profile calls for a national strategy on pharmaceutical coverage, if not a national pharmacare program [16, 28, 40–42]. As discussed above, there are many ways in which pharmaceuticals are unique products, offered in a unique marketplace. Pharmacare reforms therefore need to be designed with consideration to the distinguishing characteristics of drugs and the various goals that might be sought through a drug financing system. Hurley and colleagues recently searched literature, policy documents, and documents from agencies and stakeholder groups to identify objectives that could reasonably be considered "goals" of health care financing systems [43]. In addition to various forms of financial risk-reduction (as discussed above), many other key objectives of health care financing policy also apply to pharmaceuticals: access to care and population health, equity of finance, expenditure control, and efficiency. Because of the characteristics of pharmaceuticals and the pharmaceutical market, some financing mechanisms will serve these objectives better than others.

4.4.1
Access to Care and Population Health

While health is not determined primarily by financing, changes in financing levels and mechanisms can affect other policy goals (e.g., access to care, quality/efficiency, and income inequality) that in turn have an effect on health status. Moreover, health is such a pervasive goal in policy and even scholarly discourse that it must be included as a key objective of a health care financing system. The current Canadian (and American) "patchwork" of private and public coverage for pharmaceuticals leaves many residents without access to any coverage at all. The lack of cover for pharmaceutical costs is associated with barriers to accessing medicines and the likelihood of cost-related non-compliance [44, 45]. Moreover, the extent to which pharmaceuticals are financed through out-of-pocket charges – and the way in which those charges are determined – can have a significant impact on health outcomes and, in a related manner, the use of other health care services. For example, charges that apply to both essential and non-essential medicines are likely to reduce the use of both types of drug, and reductions in the use of essential medicines have been shown to increase the use of other healthcare services, such as emergency departments [46].

The underlying theory behind cost-sharing policies such as deductibles (either income-based or fixed) assumes that, when faced with the cost of medicines, individuals will weigh the benefits and costs of their medicines use and will rationally choose to forego their unessential medicines. However, this theory fails to account for the fact that most patients lack the full information necessary to make such crucial and potentially dangerous decisions. As a result, there have been numerous studies of patient cost-sharing policies which have demonstrated that financial disincentives, such as drug plan deductibles, cause a reduction in both essential and non-essential drug use, particularly among those with low incomes [44, 47, 48]. Reductions in essential medicine use are likely due to: (i) the sometimes-significant budgetary constraints of patients; and (ii) differences between the way in which patients and policymakers discriminate between what are "essential" and "discretionary" medicines. The manner in which patients respond to out-of-pocket charges for pharmaceuticals can lead to predictable adverse health consequences and increased total health care costs [46, 48]. Therefore, a financing mechanism that pays for essential medicines through pooled resources, thus preventing the patient from being required to make such decisions about their medication use, may be preferable.

4.4.2
Equity of Finance

Financing mechanisms have a direct effect on the distribution of health care payments (both direct and indirect) across the income distribution. Although equity is among the most commonly stated goals for health financing, the definition of equity is normative and therefore somewhat subjective. However, among policy makers and health care financing researchers the most commonly used equity principle is that payment for health care should be based on ability-to-pay rather than ability-to-benefit. Prior research on health care financing suggests that when most or all individuals, regardless of income, are covered by private insurance, it becomes a highly regressive source of financing [49]. This is because private insurance premiums (even if community rated) generally represent a larger share of income for those at the lower end of the income distribution than for those with high incomes. Public financing options, especially systems financed primarily by direct taxation such as personal income tax or social insurance, directly link ability-to-pay and total contribution to the system. In fact, many of these financing sources are designed with progressivity (individuals with higher incomes paying larger shares of their incomes than those with lower incomes) in mind. As a result, systems that rely heavily on these publicly raised sources of financing generally do well when they are evaluated according to the ability-to-pay financial equity principle [49]. Finally, deductibles under any deductible-based program will likely reduce financial equity, as payments made out-of-pocket are the most regressive form of financing. However, income-based deductibles are by their nature designed to ensure that the deductible portion of drug payments is roughly proportional to income. If these programs are well designed they may, when private and public payments are combined, be progressive: payments may be in increasing proportion to income as incomes increase.

4.4.3
Expenditure Control

Instruments of health care financing are a primary determinant of expenditure control. Different mechanisms of financing will have different implications for both the ability to limit expenditures and to increase them as needed. The data presented above, which showed growth in drug expenditure in the US, Canada, and OECD countries, illustrates one of the widely held beliefs about financing mechanisms: a single-payer system generates greater incentive and ability to control costs. This has certainly been argued as a key to the success that some countries, such as Australia and New Zealand, have had with cost control in the pharmaceutical sector [50–52].

Drug purchasers who pay all or a portion of every prescription purchased by covered populations become a form of monopsony buyer. They have influence over both manufacturers of medicines (who are anxious to have their products reimbursed) and over the therapeutic choices that patients and providers will make (who are interested in paying as little as possible for their medicines). They can then use this market "power" as the primary payer to manage costs through price negotiations [53], generic substitution programs [54], therapeutic reference pricing [55–58], and other policy tools. In using these instruments of expenditure control, the drug-purchasing agency becomes a third-party agent that intervenes in market transactions and the existing agency relationships (e.g., doctor–patient pairs) to manage expenditure. In doing so, the degree of "perfection" in this agency role might itself be evaluative. In pursuit of expenditure management, it might be argued that the agent should also achieve the various other goals of pharmacare policy: access to medicine and population health, financial equity, efficiency, etc.

In terms of the ability to control expenditures in the first instance, the power of third-party payers is significantly muted when a drug plan has jurisdiction over only a fraction of purchases made by any population group. For example, in drug plans with large deductibles (where 100% public coverage does not begin until a significant amount of money has already been spent on medicines), post-deductible incentives can influence only the minority of consumers that will reach their deductible. For many blockbuster drugs that are used at moderate cost by millions of Canadians (e.g., anti-cholesterol drugs), most consumption will fall below these large deductibles. In such circumstances, the pharmacare program will find it difficult (even likely impossible) to ensure that eligible patients receive a particular brand (or generic) under a "preferred provider" arrangement. By being unable to steer utilization toward certain products, the pharmacare program also loses its ability to negotiate lower drug prices in exchange for such "preferred provider" arrangements with pharmaceutical manufacturers. Ensuring that all patients receive cost-effective therapy, beginning with first-line treatments, requires some level of financial engagement with patients in every transaction, beginning with the first prescription.

4.4.4
Efficiency

The final goal that is an important consideration for pharmaceutical financing is overall health system efficiency. In addition to (or ultimately *because of*) the fact that some forms of user charges are associated with reduced use of both essential and non-essential medicines, the extent to which the financing of pharmaceuticals is separated from the financing of other health care services may create "silo" budgeting problems. These problems occur when cost-cutting measures in drug coverage end up producing adverse health outcomes and thereby increasing demands on other components of the health care system. Integration of the sources of funds that pay for pharmaceuticals and other health care services may produce the greatest incentive for payers to consider the total health effects of drug coverage policies. Integration of financing at the most local level has been shown to produce some desirable, and some less desirable, outcomes [59]. For example, the integration of health care delivery, including pharmaceuticals, has been one of the keys to New Zealand's success in controlling pharmaceutical expenditures during the past decade. In New Zealand, 21 District Health Boards are responsible for funding healthcare services, including pharmaceuticals, for residents in their catchment areas. Exceeding the predetermined pharmaceutical budget targets simply means there are fewer resources available to finance other health services. The result is a health care structure that provides incentive to carefully consider all the system-wide effects (both positive and negative) of any and all pharmaceutical policies [50].

4.5
Conclusion

Owing to the unique nature of pharmaceuticals and the market place in which they are bought and sold, there are potentially important roles for third-party payers that extend well beyond risk pooling or income distribution. A third-party payer can assist in the management of pharmaceutical expenditures and in the efficiency of the health care system by setting the terms of drug coverage policy. Specifically, by determining which drugs are covered, for whom, and to what extent, a drug plan can have a direct impact on the cost of pharmaceuticals, access to medicines, and the need for other health services. It may therefore play be prudent for a pharmacare system to evolve in a manner that is reasonably integrated with health care financing.

In cases where the financing of medically necessary pharmaceuticals is integrated with the financing of medical and hospital care, savings (or cost overruns) from the drug program are connected to the finances available for other components of health care. This can help to align incentives for the prudent management of total spending and for ensuring that resources available to the social insurance fund for pharmaceuticals are spent on goods that are of benefit to the population – or, at the very least, that the population is not denied cost-effective drug treatments. Given the magnitude of expenditure trends in pharmaceuticals, consideration of these trade-offs will be important to the sustainability not only of any pharmacare option to be adopted in the coming years, but also of other health care components so closely related to the use of (and related benefits from) pharmaceuticals.

References

1 CIHI (2005) *National Health Expenditure Trends, 1975–2005*, Canadian Institute for Health Information, Ottawa.

2 CIHI (2006) Canadian Institute for Health Information, Ottawa.

3 Morgan, S.G. (2005) Booming prescription drug expenditure: a population-based analysis of age dynamics. *Medical Care*, **43**, 996–1008.

4 Morgan, S. (2005) Drug expenditure trends in the Canadian Provinces: Magnitude and causes from 1998 to 2004. *Healthcare Policy*, **1**, 85–99.

5 Morgan, S., McMahon, M., Lam, J., Mooney, D., Raymond, C. (2005) Centre for Health Services and Policy Research, Vancouver, pp. 77.

6 Miller, G.E., Moeller, J.F., Stafford, R.S. (2005) New cardiovascular drugs: Patterns of use and association with non-drug health expenditures. *Inquiry – The Journal of Health Care Organization Provision and Financing*, **42**, 397.

7 Mintzes, B., Lexchin, J. (2005) Do higher drug costs lead to better health? *Canadian Journal of Clinical Pharmacology*, **12**, e22–e27.

8 Morgan, S.G., Bassett, K.L., Wright, J.M., Evans, R.G., Barer, M.L., Caetano, P.A., Black, C.D. (2005) 'Breakthrough' drugs and growth in expenditure on prescription drugs in Canada. *British Medical Journal*, **331**, 815–816.

9 Hollis, A. (2005) Drugs for rare diseases: Paying for innovation. In: Beach, C., Chaykowski, R., Shortt, S., St-Hilaire, F., Sweetman, A. (Eds.), *Health Services Restructuring in Canada: New Evidence and New Directions*. McGill-Queens University Press, Kingston.

10 Maynard, A., Cookson, R. (2001) Money or your life? The health-wealth trade-off in pharmaceutical regulation. *Journal of Health Services Research and Policy*, **6**, 186–189.

11 Berenson, A. (2006) Hope, at $4,200 a Dose. *New York Times*, October 1, 2006.

12 Syrett, K. (2003) A technocratic fix to the 'legitimacy problem'? The Blair government and health care rationing in the United Kingdom. *Journal of Health Politics, Policy and Law*, **28**, 715–746.

13 Grootendorst, P. (2006) Prescription drug insurance and reimbursement. In: Jones, A.M. (Ed.), *Elgar Companion To Health Economics*. Edward Elgar Publishing Limited, pp. 114–125.

14 Mitton, C.R., McMahon, M., Morgan, S., Gibson, J. (2006) Centralized drug review processes: Are they fair? *Social Science and Medicine*, **63** (1), 200–211.

15 USA. (2003) In: *One Hundred Eighth Congress of the United States of America*.

16 Canada. (2002) In: Commission on the Future of Health Care in Canada, Ottawa, pp. 15.

17 Canada. (2002) In: Commission on the Future of Health Care in Canada, Saskatoon, pp. 356.

18 Canada. (1997) *Canada health action: building on the legacy*. National Forum on Health, Ottawa.

19 Berndt, E.R. (2001) The US pharmaceutical industry: Why major growth in times of cost containment? *Health Affairs*, **20**, 100–114.

20 Barer, M.L., Evans, R.G., Labelle, R.J. (1988) Fee controls as cost control: tales from the frozen North. *Milbunk Quarterly*, **66**, 1–64.

21 Barer, M.L., Morgan, S.G., Evans, R.G. (2003) Strangulation or rationalization? Costs and access in Canadian hospitals. *Hospital Quarterly*, **4** (1), 10–19.

22 Canada. (2002) Health Canada, Health Policy and Communications, Canada Health Act Division, Ottawa, pp. 347.

23 Canada. (1985) *Report of the Commission of Inquiry on the Pharmaceutical Industry*, Supply and Services Canada, Ottawa.

24 Morgan, S.G., Barer, M.L., Agnew, J.D. (2003) Whither seniors' pharmacare: Lessons from (and for) Canada. *Health Affairs (Millwood)*, **22**, 49–59.

25 Grootendorst, P. (2002) Beneficiary cost sharing under Canadian provincial prescription drug benefit programs: history and assessment. *Canadian Journal of Clinical Pharmacology*, **9**, 79–99.

26 OECD (2006) OECD Health Data 2006. CD-ROM.

27 Applied Management, Fraser Group, and Tristat Resources. (2000) Health Canada, Health Transition Fund, Ottawa.

28 Canada. (1998) Directions for a Pharmaceutical Policy in Canada. In: *Canada Health Action: Building on the Legacy, Synthesis Reports and Issues Papers Volume II*. National Forum on Health, Ottawa.

29 Coombes, M., Morgan, S., Barer, M. L., and Pagliccia, N. (2004) Who's the fairest of them all? Which provincial pharmacare model would best protect Canadians against catastrophic drug costs? *Longwoods Review*, **2**, 13–26.

30 Canada. (2002) Standing Senate Committee on Social Affairs, Science and Technology, Ottawa, pp. 392.

31 Evans, R.G. (1984) *Strained Mercy: The Economics of Canadian Health Care*. Butterworths, Toronto.

32 Lazarou, J., Pomeranz, B.H., Corey, P.N. (1998) Incidence of adverse drug reactions in hospitalized patients: a meta-analysis of prospective studies. *Journal of the American Medical Association*, **279**, 1200–1205.

33 Tam, V.C., Knowles, S.R., Cornish, P.L., Fine, N., Marchesano, R., Etchells, E.E. (2005) Frequency, type and clinical importance of medication history errors at admission to hospital: a systematic review. *Canadian Medical Association Journal*, **173**, 510–515.

34 Temin, P. (1980) *Taking your Medicine: Drug Regulation in the United States*. Harvard University Press, Cambridge, Mass.

35 Canada. (1963) *Report concerning the manufacture, distribution and sale of drugs*. Department of Justice, Ottawa.

36 Canada. (1965) *Provision, distribution and cost of drugs in Canada: Royal Commission on Health Services*. Queen's Printer, Ottawa.

37 Evans, R.G., Williamson, M.F. (1978) *Extending Canadian health insurance: options for pharmacare and denticare*. Published for the Ontario Economic Council by University of Toronto Press, Toronto.

38 Daniels, N., Teagarden, J.R., Sabin, J.E. (2003) An ethical template for pharmacy

benefits. *Health Affairs (Millwood)*, **22**, 125–137.

39 Klein, R., Sturm, H. (2002) Viagra: a success story for rationing? *Health Affairs*, **21**, 177–187.

40 Canada. (2002) Prescription drugs. In: *Building on Values: The Future of Health Care in Canada – Final Report*, Chapter 9. Commission on the Future of Health Care in Canada, Saskatoon.

41 Canada. (2002) Expanding coverage to include protection against catastrophic prescription drug costs. In: *The Health of Canadians – The Federal Role: Volume 6, Recommendations for Reform*, Chapter 7. Standing Senate Committee on Social Affairs, Science and Technology, Ottawa.

42 Health Canada, Ottawa. (2005) National Pharmaceuticals Strategy (NPS). Available from: http:www.hc-sc.gc.ca/hcs-sss/pharma/nps-snpp/index_e.html.

43 Hurley, J., Abelson, J., Butler, J., Cobb-Clark, D., Contoyannis, P., Crossley, T., Giacomini, M., Grootendorst, P.L., Miller, F.A., Morgan, S., Stoddart, G., Tamblyn, R., Vaithianathan, R. (2003) In: *Report prepared for Health Canada (Project 6606-06-2000/2590194)*. Centre for Health Economics and Policy Analysis, Hamilton.

44 Adams, A.S., Soumerai, S.B., Ross-Degnan, D. (2001) The case for a Medicare drug coverage benefit: a critical review of the empirical evidence. *Annual Review of Public Health*, **22**, 49–61.

45 Kennedy, J., Morgan, S. (2006) A cross-national study of prescription nonadherence due to cost: Data from the joint Canada–United States survey of health. *Clinical Therapeutics*, **28**, 1217.

46 Tamblyn, R., Laprise, R., Hanley, J.A., Abrahamowicz, M., Scott, S., Mayo, N., Hurley, J., Grad, R., Latimer, E., Perreault, R., McLeod, P., Huang, A., Larochelle, P., Mallet, L. (2001) Adverse events associated with prescription drug cost-sharing among poor and elderly persons. *Journal of the American Medical Association*, **285**, 421–429.

47 Tamblyn, R. (2001) The impact of pharmacotherapy policy: a case study. *Cana-dian Journal of Clinical Pharmacology*, **8** (Suppl. A), 39A–44A.

48 Soumerai, S.B., Ross-Degnan, D., Fortess, E.E., Abelson, J. (1993) A critical analysis of studies of state drug reimbursement policies: research in need of discipline. *Millbank Quarterly*, **71**, 217–252.

49 Wagstaff, A., van Doorslaer, E., Van der Burg, H., Calonge, S., Christiansen, T., Citoni, G., Gerdtham, U.G., Gerfin, M., Gross, L., Hakinnen, U., Johnson, P., John, J., Klavus, J., Lachaud, C., Lauritsen, J., Leu, R., Nolan, B., Peran, E., Pereira, J., Propper, C., Puffer, F., Rochaix, L., Rodriguez, M., Schellhorn, M., Winkelhake, O., et al. (1999) Equity in the finance of health care: some further international comparisons. *Journal of Health Economics*, **18**, 263–290.

50 Braae, R., McNee, W., Moore, D. (1999) Managing pharmaceutical expenditure while increasing access. The pharmaceutical management agency (PHARMAC) experience. *PharmacoEconomics*, **16**, 649–660.

51 Brougham, M., Metcalfe, S., McNee, W. (2002) Our advice? Get a budget! *Healthcare Papers*, **3**, 83–85; discussion 87–94.

52 Birkett, D.J., Mitchell, A.S., McManus, P. (2001) A cost-effectiveness approach to drug subsidy and pricing in Australia. *Health Affairs (Millwood)*, **20**, 104–114.

53 Willison, D., Wiktorowicz, M., Grootendorst, P., O'Brien, B., Levine, M., Deber, R., Hurley, J. (2001) International experience with pharmaceutical policy: common challenges and lessons for Canada. CHEPA working paper series. Hamilton, Ontario: Centre for Health Economics and Policy Analysis, 2001. Report No. 01-08.

54 Grootendorst, P.V., Dolovich, L.R., O'Brien, B.J., Holbrook, A.M., Levy, A.R. (2001) Impact of reference-based pricing of nitrates on the use and costs of anti-anginal drugs. *Canadian Medical Association Journal*, **165**, 1011–1019.

55 Hazlet, T.K., Blough, D.K. (2002) Health services utilization with reference drug pricing of histamine(2) receptor antagonists in British Columbia elderly. *Medical Care,* **40,** 640–649.

56 Ioannides-Demos, L.L., Ibrahim, J.E., McNeil, J.J. (2002) Reference-based pricing schemes: effect on pharmaceutical expenditure, resource utilisation and health outcomes. *PharmacoEconomics,* **20,** 577–591.

57 Schneeweiss, S., Soumerai, S.B., Glynn, R.J., Maclure, M., Dormuth, C., Walker, A.M. (2002) Impact of reference-based pricing for angiotensin-converting enzyme inhibitors on drug utilization. *Canadian Medical Association Journal,* **166,** 737–745.

58 Schneeweiss, S., Walker, A.M., Glynn, R.J., Maclure, M., Dormuth, C., Soumerai, S.B. (2002) Outcomes of reference pricing for angiotensin-converting-enzyme inhibitors. *New England Journal of Medicine,* **346,** 822–829.

59 Mays, N., Mulligan, J.A., Goodwin, N. (2000) The British quasi-market in health care: a balance sheet of the evidence. *Journal of Health Services Research and Policy,* **5,** 49–58.

5

The Economics of Consumer-Directed Health Care

Ching-To Albert Ma

Abstract

This chapter presents a model of consumer-directed health care, high-deductible insurance plans. Insurance companies in a competitive market offer such plans; higher deductibles result in lower premiums. Such changes affect consumers' decisions on preventive care. It is shown that preventive care may or may not increase when consumers face more risk and lower premium. Furthermore, attention is focused on selection and cross subsidization when insurance firms offer both conventional, low-deductible and high-deductible plans. The extent of cross-subsidization may be reduced. The moral hazard effect of higher-deductible plans is also examined. Consuming more health care early within a fiscal year carries an option value. Once the deductible is reached, consumers' out-of-pocket prices are significantly lowered. Consumers have an incentive to consume more because of the option value of reduced prices later within a fiscal year. The chapter also includes a survey of recent empirical findings on consumer-directed health care.

5.1
Introduction

Consumer-directed health care is one of the latest innovations in the health market. Apparently, this innovation is a consumer revolt against managed care plans, which impose restrictions on both physician and hospital choices. Although the goal of restriction is of course cost containment and better incentives for provider qualities, consumers have begun to dislike managed-care practices, and seem to value flexibility and choice more than lower premiums.

The reaction against managed care has prompted the market to offer a family of high-deductible, insurance-managed-care plans. The typical consumer-directed health care plan has a deductible in the order of $1000 to $5000; an enrollee is responsible for the first, say, $3000 of health care expenses in a calendar year. After the deductible threshold has been reached, health care expenses will be covered for a

Financing Health Care: New Ideas for a Changing Society. Edited by Mingshan Lu and Egon Jonsson
Copyright © 2008 WILEY-VCH Verlag GmbH & Co. KGaA, Weinheim
ISBN: 978-3-527-32027-1

large percentage (say, 80%), or the enrollee's health care use may be subject to usual managed care restrictions such as use of providers within networks, authorizations, and utilization reviews. The premium of the typical consumer-directed health care plan is likely to be lower than a conventional insurance plan with a lower co-insurance rate or co-payment.

The basic idea is that a consumer enrolled in a consumer-directed health plan is responsible for the threshold amount of health care expenses. This gives complete flexibility to the consumer for which type of care is provided and from whom care is to be obtained. The consumer will be exposed to more financial risks; presumably the premium will adjust downward to account for the lower expected costs paid by the insurer. What are the other effects under consumer-directed health care? And can these be understood in terms of the common incentives in the health market such as moral hazard and adverse selection?

First, preventive care decisions – *ex ante* moral hazard – may be affected by the higher financial responsibility. One may expect that the consumer has an incentive to reduce the likelihood of falling ill. However, the consequence of high-deductible insurance plans cannot be understood entirely in terms of avoiding the loss. The risk attitude of the consumer is also relevant. In Section 5.2, a formal model to evaluate the consequence of consumer-directed health care plans on prevention is presented. It is shown that, in a competitive insurance market, a high deductible may reduce the premium in such a way that incentive to prevent illness may not increase. The outcome is analogous to a neoclassical market analysis where shifts in both supply and demand functions result in ambiguous changes in the equilibrium price and quantity.

Second, there is a worry that consumer-directed health care plans will lead to adverse selection, attracting either those who are very healthy, or those who are very sick. It is attractive to those who are very healthy because of the lower premium. It may also be attractive to the very sick because these consumers expect their health care expenses to reach the deductible level. In Section 5.3, a simple model is used to study the selection problem. The issue of cross-subsidization has been largely ignored in popular discussions. Risk sharing must involve some cross-subsidization as consumers' risks of incurring health costs are heterogeneous. In Section 5.3 it is also shown that consumer-directed health plans may lead to risk fragmentation, reducing subsidization across different risk classes.

Third, consumer-directed health care may potentially lead to a new form of moral hazard or overconsumption of health care. The deductible threshold and the subsequent low co-payment implies a set of non-linear prices for consumers. By incurring sufficient expenses to reach the threshold (say, $3000), a consumer faces a lower price of health care thereafter. There is, therefore, some option value in health care use. Early in a calendar year, a consumer may find it attractive to spend enough to reach the deductible threshold in order to enjoy the lower co-insurance rate later. Such an option value is derived formally in Section 5.4.

Section 5.5 is devoted to a survey of the existing empirical findings concerning consumer-directed health care plans. The available empirical literature is small, and studies are often limited to surveys on consumers, employers, or insurance companies. Furthermore, formal statistical studies often use data from a single employer. Nevertheless, the available evidence does reflect the theoretical findings. Broadly speaking, the effects of consumer-directed health plans on moral hazard and adverse selection are ambiguous, and selection and utilization tend to be different across plans. The evidence available now indicates that the impact of consumer-directed health plans may not exhibit clear patterns. In this chapter, attention is focused on incentive and related effects, while in Chapter 6 by Hurley and Guindon consider financing issues.

5.2
Consumer-Preventive Care Decisions

In this section, a model is presented of consumer preventive care decision under consumer-directed health care (CDHC) plans. Compared to conventional insurance or managed care, CDHC imposes more risk to consumers by letting them bear all the financial risks up to a threshold. It seems quite natural to expect that a higher financial risk will translate into a stronger incentive for consumers to prevent illness. This is the same as the basic principle that when the price of a good (likelihood of falling ill) increases, consumers tend to buy less of it (by investing more in preventive care to lower that likelihood). Nevertheless, it is known from basic economic theory that a change in the price of a good brings along an income effect, which may act against the price effect. In fact, in this section it will be shown that there is such an analogy in preventive care decisions under CDHC. While it is income effect that may counteract against the price effect in the standard demand theory, here it is the premium effect. While CDHC raises the consumer co-payment (to the full cost up to a threshold), it lowers the premium. The reduction of premium in turn affects the amount of risk that a consumer bears, and this may alter the incentives to invest in preventive care.

Here, a model is set up to illustrate these ideas, starting with a conventional insurance plan. In this plan, the consumer is charged a premium π, and in return, she bears only 20% of the health care expenditures. At this point, any moral hazard issues will be ignored, and it will be assumed that the consumer's health care expenditure is randomly distributed according to a uniform distribution on [0, 5000] if she becomes sick. Preventive care is captured by the assumption that the consumer can affect the probability of staying healthy; she has a zero medical expenditure in that state. Let p denote this probability, which is affected by the consumer's decision. If the consumer's probability of staying healthy is p, she incurs a disutility of $G(p)$ for that effort. The disutility function G is strictly increasing, strictly convex, and twice differentiable. Enough convexity is assumed in G so that the consumer's probability of staying healthy is always strictly between 0 and 1.

The consumer has wealth W. She is risk averse, and her utility function is U, which is strictly increasing, strictly concave, and twice differentiable. The consumer pays the premium up-front, and is responsible for 20% of medical expenses. If she becomes ill, and if her medical cost turns out to be c, her utility is $U(W - \pi - 0.2c)$. If she chooses an effort that leads to a probability of staying healthy p, her expected utility is

$$pU(W - \pi) + (1 - \pi) \int_0^{5000} \frac{U(W - \pi - 0.2c)}{5000} \, dc - G(p) \tag{5.1}$$

In this expression, the first term is the utility of staying healthy multiplied by that probability; the consumer simply has paid the premium π. The second term is the probability of falling ill multiplied by that expected utility, which is the average of the utility $U(W - \pi - 0.2c)$ over the range of the cost from $c = 0$ to $c = 5000$ with the density of the uniform distribution being $1/5000$.

The incentive to invest in preventive care is characterized as follows. The marginal disutility of raising the probability of staying healthy is $G'(p)$, while the marginal benefit is the difference between the expected utilities in the healthy and sick states:

$$U(W - \pi) - \int_0^{5000} \frac{U(W - \pi - 0.2c)}{5000} \, dc \tag{5.2}$$

An optimal choice of p balances the marginal benefit and the marginal disutility. For a given premium and the co-insurance rate, the consumer's optimal preventive care, in terms of the probability of staying healthy, is given by the solution p of the following equation

$$U(W - \pi) - \int_0^{5000} \frac{U(W - \pi - 0.2c)}{5000} \, dc = G'(p) \tag{5.3}$$

Given that consumers' co-payment is 20%, the premium may be determined endogenously. If the insurance market is allowed to be perfectly competitive, then the insurance companies compete by setting premiums. Each insurer therefore reduces the premium until it makes a zero profit. So, the equilibrium premium is the actuarially fair value:

$$\pi = (1 - p) \int_0^{5000} \frac{0.8c}{5000} \, dc \quad \text{which simplifies to} \quad p = 1 - \frac{\pi}{2000} \tag{5.4}$$

For a given co-insurance rate (here 20%) the premium π and preventive care p form an equilibrium if the premium lets an insurer break even given the preventive care p, and if the preventive care p is optimal given the premium. Formally, (π, p) is an equilibrium if it is the solution to simultaneous equations (5.3) and (5.4).

Equation (5.3) establishes a positive relationship between π and p; this is derived in the Appendix. Clearly, Eq. (5.4) shows a negative relationship between π and

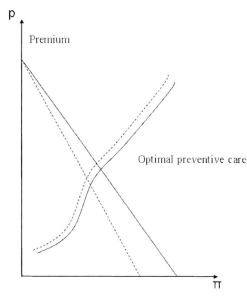

Fig. 5.1 Equilibrium premium and preventive care.

p, and therefore the equilibrium must be unique. If these relationships are represented in a plane with π on the horizontal axis, and p on the vertical axis (as in Fig. 5.1), the upward-sloping solid line is Eq. (5.3), while the downward-sloping solid line is Eq. (5.4). There is a unique intersection point, which is the equilibrium.

Next, the equilibrium in the CDHC regime is considered. Consider a typical contract: a deductible of $1000, a co-insurance rate of 20% thereafter, and all assumptions regarding health care expenditures and preferences are maintained. Under this scheme, the consumer's expected utility becomes

$$
\begin{aligned}
& p U(W - \pi) + (1 - p) \left[\int_0^{1000} \frac{U(W - \pi - c)}{5000} \, dc \right. \\
& \left. + \int_{1000}^{5000} \frac{U(W - \pi - 0.2c)}{5000} \, dc \right] - G(p)
\end{aligned}
\tag{5.5}
$$

The difference from Eq. (5.1) is that here the consumer's utility is $U(W - \pi - c)$ when health expenditure c is below $1000, and the incentive to incur preventive care becomes stronger. The marginal benefit from preventive care for a given premium is

$$
U(W - \pi) - \left[\int_0^{1000} \frac{U(W - \pi - c)}{5000} \, dc + \int_{1000}^{5000} \frac{U(W - \pi - 0.2c)}{5000} \, dc \right]
$$

The consumer's optimal choice of preventive care is given by the first-order condition:

$$U(W - \pi) - \left[\int_0^{1000} \frac{U(W - \pi - c)}{5000} \, dc \right.$$

$$\left. + \int_{1000}^{5000} \frac{U(W - \pi - 0.2c)}{5000} \, dc \right] = G'(p) \tag{5.6}$$

For the same premium, the consumer's incentive to invest in preventive care is stronger: the left-hand side of Eq. (5.6) is larger than that of Eq. (5.3). As the consumer must bear more financial risks, she has a stronger incentive to reduce the probability of falling ill.

An insurer is responsible for 80% of the consumer's health care cost when it exceeds $1000. The determination of the premium in the competitive market is again given by the zero-profit condition:

$$p = (1 - \pi) \int_{1000}^{5000} \frac{0.8c}{5000} \, dc \quad \text{which simplifies to} \quad p = 1 - \frac{\pi}{1920} \tag{5.7}$$

An equilibrium in the CDHC regime is a premium and a level of preventive care that satisfy both Eqs. (5.6) and (5.7). Again, a graphical approach can be used, and the optimal preventive care Eq. (5.6) sets up a positive relationship between p and π, while the premium determination Eq. (5.7) establishes a negative relationship. As in conventional insurance, the intersection of the positively-sloped, optimal preventive care dashed line and the negatively sloped, premium dashed line yields the equilibrium.

How is the equilibrium under CDHC different from conventional insurance? This can be studied in terms of how Eq. (5.6) is related to Eq. (5.3). The optimal preventive-care line in the CDHC regime is an upward shift from the conventional insurance line; the upward-sloping dashed line is above the solid line. For a given value of the premium, because the left-hand side of Eq. (5.6) is larger than in Eq. (5.3), the value of p that satisfies Eq. (5.6) must be larger than the one that satisfies Eq. (5.3). Hence, the entire locus that describes the consumer's optimal preventive care as a function of the premium must shift up when conventional insurance is changed to CDHC. (Note that typically the shift is not parallel.)

It is easy to compare the premium equation under CDHC [Eq. (5.7)] with that under conventional insurance [Eq. (5.4)]. The two lines have the same vertical intercept in the π-p space, but the premium line under CDHC is less steep.

A shift from conventional insurance to CDHC must reduce the equilibrium premium. Nevertheless, the effect on preventive care is less clear. In Fig. 5.1, in a CDHC equilibrium preventive care has decreased from that under conventional insurance. The determination of equilibrium preventive care depends on the consumer's attitude towards risk. Furthermore, because CDHC involves a discrete change from conventional insurance, the usual local measures of risk aversion are insufficient for characterizing the change in optimal preventive care. However, by lowering the premium, the reference point of the consumer's wealth has increased, and the consumer may actually become less risk averse. When the consumer is willing to bear more risk, she may choose to reduce preventive care effort. For a modest change in premium, perhaps due to cross-subsidization across heterogeneous groups in a large organization, consumers will likely increase preventive effort.

5.3
Selection and Cross-Subsidization

In this section, selection in CDHC plans compared to conventional insurance plans will be discussed. If the probability of staying healthy is allowed to be heterogeneous, then there are two types of consumers: (i) more healthy consumers who have a probability of staying healthy p_H; and (ii) less-healthy consumers who have a corresponding probability p_L, with $0 < p_L < p_H < 1$. These probabilities cannot be altered by the consumer. There are equal proportions of more and less healthy consumers in the population.

An insurance company cannot observe the consumers' type. If the insurance market is continued to be assumed competitive, then the premium will be set at the actuarially fair level. As in Section 5.2, the conventional insurance coverage will again be used as a benchmark; the consumer will be covered for 80% of the health care cost when she becomes sick. For CDHC, the consumer is allowed to bear the full cost when the medical expense is below $1000, and 20% thereafter.

Consider now a conventional insurance policy that covers all consumers. Because the premium cannot be based on the consumer's type, it must cover the expected expense of the average consumer. When the consumer is sick, the expected expense is $2500, but the policy only covers for 80%. So, the expected payment by the insurance company is $2000 conditional on the consumer falling ill. Now, the probability of staying healthy is either p_H or p_L. When there are equal proportions of healthy and less healthy consumers, the population average probability of staying healthy, is $(p_H + p_L)/2$. The fair premium of a 20% co-payment insurance contract to cover the entire population is

$$\pi_{\text{ins}} = \left[1 - \frac{p_H + p_L}{2}\right] 2000 \tag{5.8}$$

The consumer's expected utility from such a contract is

$$p_t U(W - \pi_{\text{ins}}) + (1 - p_t) \int_0^{5000} \frac{U(W - \pi - 0.2c)}{5000} \, dc \tag{5.9}$$

where t denotes the type and is either L or H, and the value of the premium π is in Eq. (5.8). The equilibrium premium is higher than the actuarially fair level for the health type, which is $(1 - p_H)2000$. Because of asymmetric information, the healthy consumers are subsidizing the less healthy ones.

Now, consider the typical CDHC contract. Here, the 20% co-payment takes effect after the first $1000 of medical expenditure. Conditional on a consumer falling ill, the expected payment is

$$\int_{1000}^{5000} \frac{0.8c}{5000} \, dc = 1920 \tag{5.10}$$

If both types of consumers are enrolled in a CDHC plan, the premium that breaks even is

$$\pi_{\text{cdhc}} = \left[1 - \frac{p_H + p_L}{2}\right] 1920 \tag{5.11}$$

The consumer's expected utility from such a contract is

$$p_t U(W - \pi_{\text{cdhc}}) + (1 - p_t) \left[\int_0^{1000} \frac{U(W - \pi - c)}{5000} \, dc \right.$$

$$\left. + \int_{1000}^{5000} \frac{U(W - \pi - 0.2c)}{5000} \, dc\right] \tag{5.12}$$

where $t = L, H$.

The CDHC plan has a lower premium, and imposes more financial risks on consumers. However, the extent of cross-subsidization is less, as the premium is lower. When the CDHC plan is offered, it may well be that both types of consumer prefer it to the conventional plan. That is, for $t = L, H$, the expression in Eq. (5.12) may be higher than in Eq. (5.9). This is referred to as a *CDHC pooling equilibrium*.

The CDHC plan is more attractive to the more healthy consumers. In fact, if the CDHC was preferred by the less healthy type L consumers, it would also be preferred by type H. The converse is not true, and when the expression in Eq. (5.12) is higher than in Eq. (5.9) for a type H, the reverse may hold for a type L. Then, the pooling – both types of consumers joining the CDHC plan – fails to be an equilibrium. That is, at the pooling premium level under CDHC, the less healthy type L does not find it optimal to switch. The premium level calculated in Eq. (5.11) will not be an equilibrium.

A CDHC plan may only attract the more healthy consumers, while the less healthy consumers stay with the conventional insurance plan. This is referred to as a *separating equilibrium*, where each type of insurance plan attracts one type of consumer. The equilibrium premium level in the conventional plan is

$$\pi_{\text{ins}}^s = [1 - p_L]2000 \tag{5.13}$$

as only the less healthy consumers are enrolled. On the other hand, the CDHC equilibrium premium is

$$\pi_{cdhc}^{s} = [1 - p_H]1920 \tag{5.14}$$

In a separating equilibrium, the type L consumer will prefer the conventional plan to the CDHC plan:

$$p_L U\left(W - \pi_{ins}^{s}\right) + (1 - p_L) \int_0^{5000} \frac{U(W - \pi - 0.2c)}{5000} dc$$

$$\geq p_L U\left(W - \pi_{cdhc}^{s}\right) + (1 - p_L) \left[\int_0^{1000} \frac{U(W - \pi - c)}{5000} dc \right. \tag{5.15}$$

$$+ \left. \int_{1000}^{5000} \frac{U(W - \pi - 0.2c)}{5000} dc \right]$$

The type H consumer will prefer the CDHC plan to the conventional plan:

$$p_H U\left(W - \pi_{cdhc}^{s}\right) + (1 - p_H) \left[\int_0^{1000} \frac{U(W - \pi - c)}{5000} dc \right.$$

$$+ \left. \int_{1000}^{5000} \frac{U(W - \pi - 0.2c)}{5000} dc \right] \tag{5.16}$$

$$\geq p_H U\left(W - \pi_{ins}^{s}\right) + (1 - p_H) \int_0^{5000} \frac{U(W - \pi - 0.2c)}{5000} dc$$

The pair of inequalities in Eqs. (5.15) and (5.16) are *incentive constraints*. A separating equilibrium, in which the more healthy type picks the CDHC plan while the less healthy type picks the conventional plan, must satisfy these constraints, together with the premiums determined in Eqs. (5.13) and (5.14).

Given that $p_H > p_L$, and that $\pi_{ins}^{s} = [1 - p_L]2000 > \pi_{cdhc}^{s} = [1 - p_H]1920$, it is indeed possible to find preferences such that the two incentive constraints are satisfied. The more risky, lower premium plan is selected by the more healthy consumers, while the less risky, higher premium plan is selected by the less healthy.

In a separating equilibrium, each insurance plan just breaks even, and cross-subsidization does not occur. Compared to the conventional insurance benchmark, the departure of the more healthy consumers for the CDHC plan raises the premium for the less healthy consumers who remain with the conventional plan. The less healthy consumers must become worse off when the CDHC plan implements a separating equilibrium.[1]

---

[1] There should be no concern with the existence of competitive equilibria here. Rothschild and Stiglitz [10] is the classic reference on this issue.

5.4
Health Care Demand and Non-Linear Prices

In this section, the consumers' demand for health care is studied when they are enrolled in high-deductible CDHC plans. This begins with a standard, static model of consumer usage of health care when the price depends on the amount of usage, and is then extended to a dynamic version, exploring consumers' intertemporal decisions.

5.4.1
A Static Model of Demand

Let q denote the medical care that a consumer purchases. If the price of medical care is normalized to 1, then a typical CDHC scheme is defined as follows. A consumer is responsible for all medical expenditures under $1000; thereafter, she pays at a co-insurance rate of 20%. Let $\theta V(q)$ represent a consumer's benefit when she purchases q units of health care, where the parameter θ measures the intensity of demand, and $V(q)$ is an increasing and concave function.

Under the CDHC scheme, when $q < 1000$, the consumer is responsible for the full cost of treatment. So, when the consumer purchases q units of treatment, her utility is given by $\theta V(q) - q$, for $q \leq 1000$. If she purchases more than 1000 units of health care, her utility is $\theta V(q) - 1000 - 0.2(q - 1000)$, since she is responsible for 20% of the cost above 1000 units.

How does the consumer decide on the optimal health care in the standard model? The marginal benefit of health care is always $\theta V'(q)$. For later use, it should be noted that the marginal benefit schedule is increasing in θ. Although a higher value of θ indicates a stronger demand for care, the marginal cost depends on the level of purchase. If $q \leq 1000$, this is 1, the normalized price of health care; if $q > 1000$, it is 0.2, as the consumer only pays at the 20% co-insurance rate. In each case, the consumer's optimal choice of quantity equates the marginal benefit and marginal cost.

Due to the non-linear price of medical care, however, the consumer's optimal decision may become discontinuous. For any value of θ, the consumer must consider whether it is worthwhile to consume the full $q = 1000$ units; doing so will result in the price reduction (health care at 20%) for units thereafter. This is illustrated in Fig. 5.2, where the downward-sloping line is the marginal benefit schedule $\theta V'(q)$, and a higher value of θ corresponds to an upward shift of the entire marginal benefit schedule. On the vertical axis, two points have been labelled, at prices equal to 1 and 0.20. If the price of medical care was always 1, the consumer would purchase 800 units because $\theta V'(800) = 1$. Similarly, if the price of medical care was always 0.20, the consumer would purchase 1250 units because $\theta V'(1250) = 1$. Nevertheless, to obtain the price reduction, the consumer must purchase at least 1000 units. How should the consumer decide whether it is worthwhile to go beyond the first 800 units of health care?

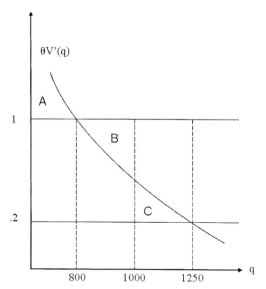

Fig. 5.2 Optimal quantity decisions under CDHC.

The total benefit from a purchase of q units is the area under the marginal benefit schedule.[2] The net benefit of purchasing 800 units at the full price of 1 is the area labeled A in Fig. 5.2; this is the total benefit substracting the total cost. Now, for the next 200 units above $q = 800$, the marginal benefit is actually below the full price of 1; the consumer experiences a reduction in her total net benefit when she purchases the next 200 units. This is a deadweight loss, and is the area labelled B in Fig. 5.2. After she has purchased 1000 units, the price for the consumer drops to 0.2, when the optimal quantity is given by $q = 1250$. The net benefit for those 250 is the area labelled C in Fig. 5.2.

There are two possible choices for the consumer. Either she can purchase 800 units at the price of 1, or she can keep on purchasing until the price falls to 0.20, for a total of 1250. Which is more attractive depends on the total (utility) cost that the consumer must incur to obtain the final total (utility) benefit due to the lower price. The net (utility) benefit of purchasing above 800 units is the difference between areas C and B. Again, area B is the net loss due to the high price for those 200 units beyond $q = 800$; area C is the net benefit for going beyond $q = 1000$. So, if area C is greater than area B, the consumer will purchase 1250 units, paying $1000 for the first 1000 units and $50 (=250 \times 0.20$) for the next 250 units. On the other hand, if area C is less than area B, the consumer only purchases 800 units, and the total expenditure is $800.

The marginal benefit schedule in Fig. 5.2 is the most interesting case. Depending on the sizes of B and C, the consumer may decide to stay with a quantity below

---

2) The total benefit is $\theta V(q) = \int_0^q \theta V(x)\, dx$, which is the area under the $\theta V(q)$ schedule.

1000, or go beyond it. There are two other, more extreme possibilities. First, the demand for health care may be so strong that the marginal benefit schedule is very high. For a sufficiently high value of θ, the consumer may decide to purchase more than 1000 units even when the price is 1. Here, of course, the actual demand will definitely be larger than 1000. Graphically, this corresponds to a case where area B vanishes. Second, the demand for health care may be so little that the consumer purchases less than 1000 units even when the price is 0.20. This corresponds to the case where area C does not exist.

There is a unique threshold value of the demand intensity parameter θ at which the consumer is just indifferent between consuming 850 units of health care and 1250 units. At this threshold level, the areas of B and C are exactly the same. If the actual value of θ is below the threshold, the optimal choice is 850 units; otherwise, it is 1250.

Generically, the consumer never finds it optimal to consume at exactly 1000 units. Because of the discrete reduction in the price of health care from 1 to 0.20 when q reaches 1000, the consumer either buys a quantity strictly less than 1000, or a quantity strictly larger than 1000. This is a strong prediction of the property of CDHC. Under a non-linear price schedule in a CDHC plan, consumers never purchase an amount of health care to reach exactly the point when the price begins to drop.

5.4.2
A Dynamic Model of Demand

Now consider the consumer's dynamic decisions. It can be demonstrated that, under CDHC, a consumer has an incentive to increase consumption in an early period for the option of consuming more health care at a lower price in the future. Here, a two-period model is used where, in each period the consumer chooses the health care quantity; these are q_1 in period 1 and q_2 in period 2. The total benefit is $\theta_1 V(q_1) + \theta_2 V(q_2)$, where θ_1 is the demand intensity in period 1, and θ_2 the demand intensity in period 2. First, θ_1 is fixed, after which, θ_2 is allowed to follow a distribution on an interval, $[\underline{\theta}, \overline{\theta}]$ with density $f(\theta)$. It is assumed that in period 1, the consumer does not know the value of θ_2. However, at the beginning of period 2, the consumer is able to observe θ_2 before she makes the decision on health care consumption.

The CDHC policy is the same as in Section 5.4.1; that is, if the quantity of health care is below 1000, the price is 1; otherwise it is 0.2. The accounting of the quantity accumulation is over the entire two periods; the price reduction from 1 to 0.2 occurs whenever the total quantity is above 1000. This may occur in either period 1 or period 2, or not at all.

For any given consumption level q_1 in period 1, the consumer's optimal decision in period 2 is derived, after which the way that q_1 is chosen by the consumer is examined. The model in Section 5.4.1 will be adapted for the analysis.

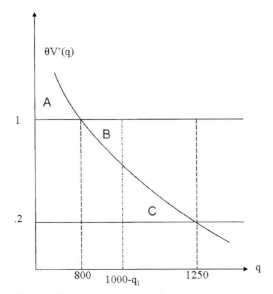

Fig. 5.3 Optimal second period decisions.

When q_1 units of health care have been chosen, the price falls to 0.2 if $q_1 >$ 1000. However, the more interesting case is when q_1 is less than 1000, where the consumer must purchase $1000 - q_1$ more units at the full price before the price falls to 0.2. In Fig. 5.3, Fig. 5.2 has been adapted to illustrate this situation. The two areas B and C are now different, as the extra quantities in period 2 to be purchased before the price reduction is only $1000 - q_1$; the corresponding vertical line has moved to the left. As a result, area B becomes smaller, while area C becomes larger.

Any given care quantity q_1 chosen by the consumer in the first period is associated to a threshold value of $\theta(q_1)$. At this demand intensity, the consumer will be indifferent to purchasing a lower quantity at full price of 1 and purchasing a high quantity at the lower price of 0.2. In other words, for a given q_1, $\theta(q_1)$ is the demand intensity at which areas B and C are identical. The threshold $\theta(q_1)$ is a decreasing function in q_1. A higher value of q_1 makes it that much easier for the consumer to reach the 1000 units level for the price reduction. As a result, for a less intense demand in the second period, the consumer may still want to go beyond the 1000 unit level. A lower threshold implies a higher level of consumer surplus due to the lower price.

A higher level of quantity in the first period brings in a higher option value. The consumer now finds it easier to choose optimally a high enough quantity to qualify for the lower price. This option value is in addition to the intrinsic benefit of health care. This is an incentive for overconsumption during the first period, despite the consumer bearing the full cost. By consuming beyond where the marginal benefit is equal to 1, the consumer incurs some deadweight loss but gains the option value in the possible consumption of medical care at the lower price of 0.2. An expression for this option value is derived in the Appendix.[3]

5.5
Empirical Studies of Consumer-Directed Health Care

In this section, the available evidence of consumer-directed health care is surveyed. Perhaps the benchmark for all studies is the RAND experiment which, to the author's knowledge, is the only randomized experiment on health insurance. Many types of insurance treatments were included in the RAND experiment. In fee-for-service plans, consumers were subject to free care, 25%, 50%, and 95% co-insurance rates with maximum annual out-of-pocket expenditures (up to $1000 in 1974); beyond the annual expenditure cap, care expenditure was fully reimbursed. Manning et al. [5] found that the group of consumers paying 95% co-insurance did have fewer office visits, lower outpatient and inpatient expenses, and a lower likelihood of incurring any medical or inpatient expenses.

The RAND experiment did demonstrate a "price" effect on the use of medical care, although it was conducted quite some time ago and current practices of managed care under CDHC plans were not part of the experiment design. There is, however, little reason to believe that the price effect would be seriously affected by managed care practices that apply beyond the deductible in current CDHC plans. Newhouse [6] advocated that high-deductible plans should be regarded as complementary to managed care, as the choice of the deductible threshold affects risk sharing. The 100% cost shares in the expenditures before the deductible provides price incentives, while managed care may be used to control those expenditures beyond the deductible.

Although current enrollment in CDHC plans is still relatively small (about half a million at the end of 2004, according to America's Health Insurance Plans), enrollment has been growing rapidly. More recent studies on CDHC plans tend to be surveys on plans and consumers, as well as on a single employer. Rosenthal and Milstein [9] conducted a national survey of three types of CDHC plans these were health reimbursement accounts, tiered-benefit, and premium-tiered models. The first type resembles the model presented above, while tiered models adjust the premium or the contribution to network restrictions. Rosenthal and Milstein [9] reported that in their survey the majority of enrollees were in the tiered models. Information support is emphasized by CDHC plans, a feature that the RAND experiment could not have considered. Access to information about typical medical procedures and service costs is provided by plans, but information from specific providers is typically unavailable. Comparative cost information would have allowed consumers to "shop" around effectively. Perhaps, due to business practice and the

---

3) Ellis [2] is a general model for coverage ceiling and deductible in health insurance.

complexity of medical services, comparative cost information would not be expected to be made publicly available.

Lo Sasso et al. [4] conducted site visits during the spring and summer of 2003 at four firms offering CDHC plans to employees. The visits yielded useful information about plan characteristics and selection problems. Two sites reported favorable selections: enrollees who chose CDHC plans over conventional Preferred Provider Organizations (PPOs) and Health Maintenance Organizations (HMOs) tended to incur much lower medical expenses (up to 50% over the average over the year prior to the introduction of CDHC plans). Basic managed care styles are still used by CDHC plans when enrollees have reached their deductible, and hence CDHC plans will not replace managed care. Nevertheless, the methodology of this survey must be interpreted with caution. The firms in the survey were not from a random sample, and voluntary participation might have biased the reported savings, with firms that had been "successful" in cutting costs being more willing to participate. Furthermore, all data were reported by firms, as primary data collection was infeasible in the study.

Another survey examined the employees' experiences with CDHC plans. Fowles et al. [3] sent a six-page questionnaire to Humana Inc. employees aged 18 years and over who were eligible for health benefits. The survey was conducted in 2001 after an open enrollment period. Information about employees such as sociodemographic characteristics (age, gender, race, education, and insurance coverage), health status, care utilization and plan preferences was collected. With a response rate of over 65%, Fowles et al. correlated the plan choices using logistic regressions.

Only 7% of respondents chose the new CDHC plans after open enrollment. These people tended to be more healthy, less likely to have a chronic condition, and less likely to have had recent medical visits. Enrollees in the new CDHC plans thought that the lower premium was a significant factor in their decision. Information support was also a critical factor for consumers; those who chose CDHC plans found the electronic enrollment process and benefit information easier to understand and use.

Two studies have examined the experiences of large employers. For example, in 2002 the University of Minnesota added a CDHC plan to the existing PPO, an HMO and a set of tiered benefit plans. Parente et al. [7] investigated the characteristics of enrollees who had chosen the CDHC plan compared to those who had not, with the data deriving from a telephone survey of about 900 employees, and about 45% of the respondents being enrolled in the CDHC plan. The survey results then were combined with payroll information for logistic estimations. In the Minnesota experience, CDHC plans were not disproportionately chosen by the young and healthy, although they were more attractive to wealthy individuals and those who valued choices and flexibility. The study did not include actual health status prior to enrollment in CDHC plans. In a follow-up study, Christiansen et al. [1] examined the experiences of University of Minnesota enrollees. Consumer experience information was obtained by a survey, whereby those consumers en-rolled in CDHC plans generally reported a satisfactory experience, although only a minority used the on-line information. The turnover rate among consumers in

CDHC plans, however, was higher, with 8% leaving CDHC plans compared to 5% among enrollees of other plans.

Parente et al. [8] used claims data to assess the effects of CDHC plans on medical expenditures and utilization at the University of Minnesota. In this common pre-post study design, the authors identified three cohorts: (1) those University of Minnesota employees enrolled in an HMO plan between 2000 and 2002; (2) those enrolled in a PPO plan from 2000 to 2002; and (3) those enrolled in either an HMO or PPO plan in 2000 and in the CDHC plan in 2001 and 2002. A difference-in-difference methodology was used to identify the effect of CDHC on medical cost and utilization relative to other plans. Total expenditures for CDHC enrollees were lower than PPO enrollees but higher than HMO enrollees, yet CDHC enrollees had higher hospital costs and admission rates than either group. So, the main conclusion was that CDHC plans seemed to be a viable alternative.

Tollen et al. [11] studied the experiences of about 10000 Humana Inc. employees and their dependents during the benefit years beginning July 2000 and July 2001. Claims and administrative data were used to assess risk fragmentation, and prior claims (care costs), and prior utilization (admissions, average length of stay, outpatient visits, and prescriptions) were combined with demographic data. The study results showed that enrollees of CDHC plans had lower prior-year usage (by 60%) and lower spending (by 50%) than those in traditional PPOs, even though the two groups had similar demographic characteristics. The study was limited to the prior experiences of enrollees; this focus did not permit an analysis of the impact of CDHC plans on utilization.

The above studies on the University of Minnesota and Humana Inc. complemented each other, as while the former focused on the impact, the latter focused on selection. Each, however, examined one large employer and consequently the relevance of these results on the general population remains an open question. The available evidence on the moral hazard and adverse selection of CDHC plans is limited. Perhaps, in a market-driven health care sector, the test for CDHC plans is their survival. Nevertheless, once public services such as Medicare and Medicaid use these plans, the policy implication of CDHC plans becomes important. At this point, it seems prudent for policy makers to adopt a "wait and see" approach. So far, the experiences of CDHC seem to suggest the lack of very strong or clear impact on either adverse selection or moral hazard.

5.6
Conclusion

The potential policy benefits of CDHC plans include their affordability, their ability to empower consumers to select providers, and the provision of coverage for catastrophic events. However, public health researchers and economists have pointed out the potential problems of CDHC. Because health care use is highly skewed, with a small number of users incurring a large proportion of expenses, CDHC may lead to risk fragmentation, attracting primarily consumers who do not expect to incur large expenses. On the other hand, CDHC is often tied to a medical savings or reimbursement account, which may be funded by an employer. Because enrollees may not pay the full cost of the premium, and because balances of a medical savings account can be rolled over or withdrawn with tax advantages, CDHC plans may also attract both healthy and less healthy enrollees.

This chapter has presented three theoretical models to evaluate the incentives of preventive care, selection and cross-subsidization, and option value under a high deductible. The empirical findings appear to be broadly consistent with the theoretical results. Upon the introduction of a high deductible, consumers experience a lower premium. This then interacts with consumers' risk attitudes. Preventive care may then either increase or decrease, and CDHC plans may not always lead to more preventive care. Selection is related to cross-subsidization across different risk classes. The impact of CDHC plans on selection may lead to reduced cross-subsidization, which then raises the premium of a high-risk class and lowers the premium of a low-risk class. Adverse selection and risk fragmentation may indeed occur. Finally, a high-deductible health insurance policy implies non-linear prices for consumers. Reaching the deductible is an option that consumers will consider, after which moral hazard takes on a new route. Excessive spending early in a fiscal year may be valuable for the option of lower prices later in the fiscal year.

It seems unlikely that CDHC plans will overtake conventional insurance or managed care plans to become the dominant form of health care coverage for Americans. Some consumers do value flexibility however, and the new information support system in CDHC plans may encourage these consumers to take charge of their health care. Consumer-directed health care plans can be expected to complement managed care.

Acknowledgments

For their comments, I thank Chris Auld, Mingshan Lu, and participants of the Banff International Health Economics Workshop, September 2006. Financial support from the Institute of Health Economics, Alberta, Canada is gratefully acknowledged. Ideas and opinions in this paper do not represent the views of the funding institute.

References

1 Christiansen, J.B., Parente, S.T., and Feldman, R. (2004). Consumer Experiences in a Consumer-Driven Health Plan, *HSR: Health Services Research*, **39**(4), Part II, 1123–1139.

2 Ellis, R.P. (1986). Rational Behavior in the Presence of Coverage Ceilings and Deductibles, *The RAND Journal of Economics*, **17**(2): 158–175.

3 Fowles, J.B., Kind, E.A., Braun, B.L., and Bertko, J. (2004). Early Experience with Employee Choice of Consumer-Directed Health Plans and Satisfaction with Enrollment, *HSR: Health Services Research*, **39**(4), Part II, 1141–1158.

4 Lo Sasso, A.T., Rice, T., Gabel, J.R., and Whitmore, H. (2004). Tales from the New Frontier: Pioneers' Experiences

with Consumer-Driven Health Care, *HSR: Health Services Research*, **39**(4), Part II, 1071–1089.

5 Manning, W.G., Newhouse, J.P., Duan, N., Keeler, E.B., and Leibowitz, A. (1987). Health Insurance and the Demand for Medical Care: Evidence from a Randomized Experiment, *The American Economic Review*, **77**(3): 251–277.

6 Newhouse, J.P. (2004) Consumer-Directed Plans & The RAND Experiment, *Health Services Research*, **23**(6), 107–113.

7 Parente, S.T., Feldman, R., and Christiansen, J.B. (2004a). Employee Choice of Consumer-Driven Health Insurance in a Multiplan, Multiproduct Setting, *HSR: Health Services Research*, **39**(4), Part II, 1091–1111.

8 Parente, S.T., Feldman, R., and Christiansen, J.B. (2004b). Evaluation of the Effect of a Consumer-Driven Health

Plan on Medical Care Expenditures and Utilization, *HSR: Health Services Research*, **39**(4), Part II, 1189–1209.

9 Rosenthal, M. and Milstein, A. (2004). Consumer-Driven Plans: What's Offered? Who Chooses? Awakening Consumer Stewardship of Health Benefits: Prevalence and Differentiation of New Health Plan Models, *HSR: Health Services Research*, **39**(4), Part II, 1055–1070.

10 Rothschild, M., and Stiglitz, J. (1976) Equilibrium in Competitive Insurance Markets: An Essay on the Economics of Imperfect Information, *Quarterly Journal of Economics*, **00**(90), 629–649.

11 Tollen, L.A., Ross, M.N., and Poor, S. (2004). Evidence about Utilization and Expenditures. Risk Segmentation Related to the Offering of a Consumer-Directed Health Plan: A case Study of Humana, Inc., *HSR: Health Services Research*, **39**(4), Part II, 1167–1187.

Appendix

Equation (5.3) yields a positive relationship between π and p. Let

$$W(p;\pi) \equiv pU(W-\pi) + (1-p)\int_0^{5000} \frac{U(W-\pi-0.2c)}{5000}\,dc - G(p)$$

Let $p(\pi) = \arg\max_p W(p;\pi)$. Then $p'(\pi) = -\frac{W_{p\pi}(p;\pi)}{W_{pp}(p;\pi)}$, where the subscripts denote the second-order partial derivatives. Since $G(p)$ is convex by assumption, W is concave in p, so that $W_{pp} < 0$.

Next, we have

$$W_{p\pi}(p;\pi) = \int_0^{5000} \frac{U'(W-\pi-0.2c)}{5000}\,dc - U'(W-\pi) > 0$$

where the inequality follows from the concavity of U. So we have $p'(\pi) > 0$. The optimal preventive care is positively related to the premium.

An expression is derived for the option value of the first-period quantity in the dynamic model of consumer demand under CDHC. For any given q_1, let the threshold be $\hat{\theta}(q_1)$: for $\theta < \hat{\theta}(q_1)$, the consumer optimally chooses q_2 with $q_1 + q_2 \le 1000$; for $\theta > \hat{\theta}(q_1)$, $q_1 + q_2 > 1000$. Let $U^L(\theta) = \max_{q_2}\theta V(q_2) - q_2$. Let $U^H(\theta;q_1) = \max_{q_2}\theta V(q_2) - (1000 - q_1) - 0.2(q_2 - 1000)$. These are the indirect utility functions given the demand parameter θ and the first-period quantity q_1. The first indirect utility function U^L is a function of θ alone, since for $\theta < \hat{\theta}(q_1)$

the optimal quantity in the second period together with q_1 do not exceed 1000. The second indirect utility function U^H does depend on q_1. The consumer needs only purchase $(1000 - q_1)$ more units to qualify for the lower price of 0.2. By the Envelope Theorem, the partial derivative of U^H with respect to q_1 is 1.

Now, consider the expected utility in the second period for a given q_1. This is

$$W(q_1) \equiv \int_{\underline{\theta}}^{\hat{\theta}(q_1)} U^L(\theta) f(\theta) \, d\theta + \int_{\hat{\theta}(q_1)}^{\bar{\theta}} U^H(\theta; q_1) f(\theta) \, d\theta$$

The derivative of W is

$$W'(q_1) = (U^L(\hat{\theta}) f(\hat{\theta}) - U^H(\hat{\theta}; q_1) f(\hat{\theta})) \hat{\theta}'(q_1) + \int_{\hat{\theta}(q_1)}^{\bar{\theta}} \frac{\partial U^H(\theta; q_1)}{\partial q_1} f(\theta) \, d\theta$$

The term inside the brackets on the right-hand side is zero: by definition, at $\hat{\theta}$, the consumer is just indifferent between consuming optimally an amount less than 1000 and more, $U^L(\hat{\theta}) = U^H(\hat{\theta}; q_1)$. The partial derivative of U^H with respect to q_1 is 1. So, the derivative of W is actually $1 - F(\hat{\theta}(q_1)) > 0$, where F is the distribution function of θ.

6
Medical Savings Accounts: Promises and Pitfalls

Jeremiah E. Hurley and G. Emmanuel Guindon

6.1
Introduction

Medical savings accounts (MSAs) are a contentious method for financing health care. Advocates of MSA-based financing argue that MSAs offer considerable benefits over traditional comprehensive insurance coverage, including increased health system efficiency, better expenditure control, more choice and increased quality, all while not unduly compromising equity. Detractors, of course, argue the opposite: that MSAs will lead to less efficiency, higher expenditures, reduced access for many, and serious inequity in the finance and use of health care. These differing judgments are rooted in a number of factors: differing ideological commitments; differing assessments of the ability of individuals to overcome sources of market failure in health care; and, importantly, a weak evidence base that yields contested conclusions. This chapter distills what is possible from existing evidence regarding the effects of MSAs, especially with regards to their use within publicly financed health care systems.

MSA schemes include two essential features: (i) an individual (or household)-specific account, the balances (which can accumulate over time) of which are normally earmarked for health care expenses; and (ii) a high-deductible, catastrophic insurance plan. An individual uses MSA funds (and personal resources if the MSA funds are not adequate) to pay for health care expenses below the deductible and, if required, cost-sharing above the deductible. The catastrophic policy covers extraordinary, high-cost care. MSAs can be integrated into virtually any system of health care finance, with myriad variations of this two-part design depending, for instance, on the source of the contributions to individual MSA accounts (taxes, employers, individuals), the source of the catastrophic insurance (public, private), the extent of cost-sharing required by the catastrophic insurance, regulations regarding how the MSA balance can be spent (health care only; health care and other goods and services), the tax treatment of MSA contributions, withdrawals and interest earned, and the range of insurance choices that individuals have alongside MSAs.

MSAs come in many varieties, and under many labels. In the United States (US), for example, such plans are now called "Health Savings Accounts" (HSAs), whilst in Canada they have been called "consumer allowances." MSAs are one type of "consumer-directed" health plan which are designed to give consumers the incentive to make "financially responsible" choices when considering alternative costly health care services [1, 2]. The financial incentive is created by including high levels of consumer cost-sharing in the financing arrangements. Increasingly, such plans also attempt to provide consumers with information regarding health care options. (See Chapter 5 for a further discussion of consumer-directed health plans.)

Historically, the origins of MSAs lie at least in part in idiosyncrasies of the United State's system of health care finance. In the US, employer contributions to health insurance benefits are not taxable income, so such benefits are effectively purchased with pre-tax income. Those purchasing insurance in the individual market and those paying out-of-pocket, however, must purchase insurance and care with after-tax dollars. MSAs financed with tax-deductible contributions were proposed as a way of eliminating the asymmetrical treatment of such purchases in the US.

Conceptually, the broader appeal of MSAs lies in their claimed ability to counter the incentive for increased health care utilization (typically interpreted as moral hazard) associated with low-cost-sharing comprehensive insurance, while mitigating some of the inequities associated with standard cost-sharing policies. MSAs do this by forcing individuals to purchase routine health care at full price, limiting the role of insurance to low-probability, high-cost events, but allowing individuals to accumulate funds in tax-preferred accounts to finance such purchases. Advocates argue that, compared to comprehensive insurance, MSAs will decrease health care costs, increase systems efficiency, increase choice, increase access to care, and lead to a better quality of care [3–6]. Detractors, of course, argue quite the opposite: that MSAs will lead to higher costs, compromise equity utilization and financing, and do little to improve quality or other aspects of system performance [7–10]. Nonetheless, the enticing promises of MSA advocates have generated international interest in MSA financing both in long-established systems of public and social insurance struggling with rising costs and ever-expanding health care interventions (for example, Germany, Netherlands, Australia) and less-developed countries that are attempting to develop systems of health care finance.

For all the debate, the actual use of MSAs remains remarkably limited. Only three countries – Singapore, China and the United States – either finance a measurable (though still small) proportion of health care using MSAs, or are strongly committed to policies to expand the use of MSAs substantially. Furthermore, rigorous empirical evidence regarding the effects of MSA financing is largely non-existent.

This chapter reviews current knowledge and evidence related to the performance of MSAs, with particular reference to the potential integration of MSAs into publicly financed health care systems. The focus on MSAs within publicly financed health care systems derives from the continuing debate in Canadian health policy regarding the potential use of publicly financed MSAs in Canada, and more generally from the fact that, if MSAs are ever to become an important source of finance in developed countries other than the United States, they will have to be integrated into systems of public finance.

6.2
MSA Financing Internationally

Despite much policy attention, as noted above, few countries finance health care using MSAs, and even in those settings MSAs account for a small minority of health care finance. Following Singapore's introduction of MSAs during the mid-1980s, it took more than a decade for other countries to embrace MSAs. During the mid-1990s, China embarked on an ambitious health insurance experiment in which health accounts played an important role, the US began pilot experiments with MSAs, and South Africa briefly expanded their use. As a prelude to reviewing the current evidence, the MSA designs in Singapore, China, the United States and South Africa are briefly described, and the qualitative and quantitative roles that MSAs play in their systems of health care financing are examined.

6.2.1
Singapore

In 1984, Singapore became the first (and, to date) only country to introduce universal and compulsory MSAs. In Singapore, MSAs form one part of a large social insurance system founded on a government-prescribed savings program administered by the Central Provident Fund (CPF). The CPF was set up during the 1950s with an initial objective to increase savings. At present, the CPF runs three accounts:

- The *Ordinary account*, for housing, investment and education purposes.
- The *Medisave account*, the MSA program covering a portion of health care expenditures.
- The *Special account* for pension payments and special circumstances.

The CPF is financed by both employers' and employees' contributions, with a designated proportion going to each fund. The mandatory contribution in 2006 for an individual under the age of 55 years, for example, was 33% of annual income (20% from employee, 13% from employer) up to a maximum of S$4 500 per month.[1] All those in the paid workforce (including the self-employed)[2] must contribute to Medisave; the unemployed do not contribute.

In addition to furthering the mandatory savings objective of all the funds in the CPF, an additional objective of Medisave was to increase the personal responsibility of health care users [11] by increasing the extent of cost-sharing for many Singaporeans who had previously been covered by a public insurance program. As

1) As of October 20th, 2006, 1 S$ = 0.71 Cdn$ = 0.64 US$.
2) Prior to 1992, contributions for the self-employed were voluntary.

such, Medisave funds can be used to pay for a limited set of health care services, and the program requires considerable cost-sharing even for many of these services. When MSAs were first introduced in 1984, Medisave funds could be used to pay only for acute in-patient hospital care in government facilities [12]. Since then, subject to some limits, Medisave eligibility has been extended to care in most hospitals, including private hospitals and in all classes of wards. Beginning in 2002, the prohibition on using Medisave funds for out-patient care was relaxed; Medisave can now be used to finance a limited set of out-patient services (e.g., hepatitis B vaccinations, maternity predelivery expenses, renal dialysis, HIV anti-retroviral drugs, chemotherapy and radiotherapy). However, primary care, accident and emergency charges, long-term hospital care and traditional Chinese medicine, remain excluded [12]. Even for eligible services, Medisave imposes coverage limits that result in significant cost-sharing. Such cost-sharing amounts to about 50 to 60% of expenditures for MSA-eligible services in private hospitals, and 20 to 30% in a non-subsidized ward of public hospitals [12]. Medisave funds can be used to cover health care expenses of all family relatives [12].

One peculiar aspect of MSAs in Singapore is a limit on the total amount (S$30 500 in 2006) that an individual can accumulate in their Medisave account.[3] Excess contributions are reallocated to an individual's ordinary account [12]. Some withdrawals for non-health care expenses are permitted beginning at the age of 55 years, provided that a minimum amount (S$27 500 in 2006) remains in the account for health care expenses (see Ref. [13] for a detailed overview of withdrawal limits). The balance remaining at the time of an account holder's death is exempt from estate taxes and is paid to the account holder's inheritors.

Since 1984, Singapore has introduced three additional funds that complement Medisave: Medishield, Medifund, and Eldershield. Medishield, introduced in 1990, is a voluntary catastrophic health insurance scheme. The plan is fairly restrictive in the sense that it imposes limits to claims per individual (per year and per lifetime), has a maximum age of entry of 75 years and coverage ends at 80. Medishield premiums, which vary by age groups, can be paid from an MSA. Medifund, introduced in 1993, is an endowment fund for the poor that provides financing to individuals unable to pay the high-out-of-pocket expenses required by Singapore's system of finance. Finally, Eldershield, introduced in June 2002, is an insurance scheme that provides financial assistance to individuals who become severely disabled (it does not cover those already disabled at the time of its introduction).

In summary, although the MSA system in Singapore is universal and compulsory, it constitutes only a small proportion of the overall system of finance. MSAs (Medisave) have never accounted for more than 10% of total health care spending, and Medishield and Medifund combined account for no more than 2% of total health spending [14]. The remainder of the health care expenditures is financed by employer benefits, government subsidies, out-of-pocket payment, and private insurance [15]. Indeed, most health care expenditures are financed by out-of-pocket

---

3) The average MSA balance in 2005 was S$10 600 [12].

spending, which represents approximately 70% of all health care spending [14]. For a more complete description of MSAs in Singapore, see Ref. [12].

6.2.2
China

MSAs were introduced in China during the mid-1990s as part of a package of reforms that addressed the breakdown of the health care financing system following economic liberalization in the 1980s. Prior to economic liberalization, almost all rural and urban individuals in China were covered by some form of health insurance. The commune-based cooperative medical scheme (CMS) provided coverage to agricultural workers; the Labor Insurance Scheme (LIS) provided coverage to employees and retirees of state-owned enterprises with more than 100 employees and to their dependents; and the Government Insurance Scheme (GIS) provided coverage to government employees, retirees, disabled veterans, and university teachers and students. The CMS was financed via a prepayment plan generally funded from three sources: premiums (0.5–2% of a peasant family's annual income); a collective welfare fund, funded by each village following State guidelines; and subsidies from higher-level government structures. During the mid-1970s, the CMS provided health insurance coverage to about 90% of rural villages [16]. The GIS and LIS each provided comprehensive benefits with minimal cost sharing. For the most part, health care services were free, with the exception of dependents of employees or retirees who were required to pay out-of-pocket for 50% of their health care expenses. The GIS was financed by general government revenues, and the LIS was financed by enterprises. Each organization under the original GIS and LIS systems was self-insured; it was responsible for the health-care payments of their employees under GIS or LIS.

The 1980s transformation of the Chinese economy placed substantial strains on the health care system, such that by the 1990s health insurance coverage in rural areas had virtually collapsed. In 1993, less than 10% of the rural population had any health insurance coverage, and health insurance coverage had also decreased in urban areas, albeit less dramatically [17].

This situation prompted the Central government to embark on an ambitious program of health insurance reforms, and in 1995 a pilot health insurance experiment was launched in the cities of Zhenjiang and Jiujiang. This experimental plan provided mandatory medical insurance coverage for all employees through a single, city-wide insurance plan. It also provided coverage to retirees, disabled veterans, and university students. The city-based experimental plans, which effectively replaced GIS and LIS into these cities, contained three key components:

- MSA: An individual MSA for each subscriber financed by employer and employee contributions.
- Deductible: When the MSA funds were exhausted, beneficiaries were required to pay up to 5% of their annual salary out-of-pocket for health care expenses.

- Catastrophic insurance: A citywide Social Risk Pooling Account (SPA), financed also by employer and employee contributions, pooled insurance funds across all subscribers for health expenses above the deductible, subject to a decreasing rate of co-insurance paid (up to 20%) by the individuals. For retired employees, the deductible was waived [18].

In addition to this MSA-based insurance scheme, the reform introduced a variety of other mechanisms to contain costs. An essential drug list was developed which consisted of about 1400 Western pharmaceutical productions and about 500 manufactured Chinese medicines. Drugs on the list could be purchased using MSA funds, but drugs not on the essential drug lists had to be paid out-of-pocket [18]. In 1997, the health care reimbursement system for in-patient care funded by the SPA changed from being essentially retrospective based on fee schedules to one based on prospective global budgets [19]. A cost-sharing of 20% was introduced on expensive technological procedures (even for those whose spending reached catastrophic levels) [18]. A more complete description of the Zhenjiang and Jiujiang experiment can be found in Refs. [18, 20, 21].

During late 1996, the State Council expanded the urban health insurance experiment, whereby 40 cities out of the 57 eligible reformed their GIS and LIS, with most introducing MSAs loosely based on the Zhenjiang and Jiujiang experiment [18].

In 1998, nationwide urban reforms began with aim of transforming the existing GIS and LIS into a new Basic Medical Insurance (BMI). This BMI retained the main features of the health insurance pilot experiments [i.e., individual MSAs and catastrophic insurance (SPA)], but cities were given considerable flexibility to adapt BMI to their local context. In fact, most cities chose not to adopt a three-tier system [MSA, deductible, catastrophic insurance (SPA)] like that of Zhenjiang and Jiujiang. Rather, most opted for a "compartmental model" based on the experience of the city of Hainan, whereby MSA and SPA are service-specific. Here, MSA funds are used to pay mostly for out-patient services and small uncovered services, while the SPA is used to pay for in-patient services and larger out-patient expenses up to some pre-defined maximum (between 30000 Chinese Yuan (CNY) and 50000 CNY, depending on the city) [19].[4] The SPA is associated with a deductible (400 CNY) and decreasing co-payments, ranging from 15%, 9%, 5%, and 0% [22].

By the end of 2003, most cities had reformed their health insurance systems, and approximately 110 million individuals were covered by these new schemes [19]. In parallel, the central government pushed supply-side reforms aimed at reducing costs in the hospital and pharmaceutical markets [22].

Despite the reform efforts of the central government, insurance coverage for urban residents continued to fall (from about 70% in 1993 to about 50% in 2003).

---

4) In October 2006, 1 CNY = 0.142 Cdn$.

For rural residents, coverage increased marginally but still stood at abysmally low levels in 2003 (about 20%) [22].[5] The combination of low coverage rates and high out-of-pocket payments (estimated at 70% of all health care financing [22]) mean that MSAs play a minor role in China's overall system of health care finance. Current estimates put the MSA share of total financing at less than 8% [26].

6.2.3
United States

Medical Savings Accounts were first introduced in the United States in 1996. Unlike Singapore, and to a lesser extent China, MSAs in the US are voluntary and operate in parallel with more traditional forms of health insurance. The growing interest in MSAs, HSAs and related consumer-directed health plans has been spurred in part by a backlash against managed care which, during the 1990s, came to dominate US health care. Currently, there are two main types of MSAs in the United States: Health Reimbursement Accounts (HRAs) and Health Savings Accounts (HSAs).

HRAs are employer-funded and -owned accounts authorized in 2002. Funds can only be used for health care expenses and year-end account balances carry over, but unused funds revert to the employer at retirement or termination. Because accumulated funds are lost on retirement, termination or job change, the incentive to reduce utilization so as to accumulate funds is substantially blunted compared to usual MSA designs. HRAs are primarily used with catastrophic, high-deductible insurance plans [1].

HSAs are owned by individuals and can be incorporated into plans obtained through both the group and individual insurance markets. Beginning in 2007, Medicare beneficiaries will also have the option to choose an HSA. HSA regulations and options have changed frequently since they were introduced. At the time of writing, in order to be HSA-eligible, a plan must: have a minimum deductible of US$ 1050 for an individual and US$ 2100 for a family (in 2006), and a maximum limit on out-of-pocket spending of US$ 5250 for single coverage and US$ 10 500 for family plans.[6] For group plans, both employees and employers can contribute funds to an individual's HSA; for plans obtained in the individual market the holder can

---

5) In October 2002, the government introduced a New Cooperative Medical System (NCMS) piloted in about 300 (out of 2000) counties with the objective of extending it to all counties by 2010. Financing is once again from three sources (household, local government and central government); enrolment is voluntary, and was approximately 70%; the designs vary across counties, but about 80% of the counties include a family savings plan. For details, see Refs. [22, 24]. Private health insurance coverage is limited, but growing. In 2003, 5.6% (urban) and 8.3% (rural) of the population had some private health insurance coverage. Private health insurance is used both as primary insurance not eligible for public insurance and as supplementary insurance for those who have public health insurance [25].

6) This includes out-of-pocket spending on eligible health services; it does not include insurance premiums.

contribute funds. Annual contributions are limited to US$ 2850 for individuals and US$ 5450 for families. Unused balances can be carried over year-to-year, invested in a variety of financial instruments, and neither the contributions themselves nor the interest earned are subject to tax. HSA funds can be used to pay for eligible health care services as well as non-health care services. Withdrawals made for non-eligible goods and services are subject to taxation and, for those aged under 65, a penalty [1, 27].

Although MSA plans have been promoted in the US for a decade, the take-up has been slow until recent reforms that created HSAs [1]. During the late 1990s, Congress sponsored a pilot project to establish tax-preferred MSAs for the self-employed and employees of small firms covered by high deductible insurance [28]. In 1997, Congress approved the further pilot project targeted at Medicare beneficiaries [29]. Despite much enthusiasm, in both pilots MSAs uptake remained well below expectations. Indeed, participation rate were so low that the US General Accounting Office (GAO) was unable to conduct planned evaluations of the pilot projects [28]. However, since the creation of HSAs in 2004 (which have fewer restrictions than the previous MSA plans), the growth has been rapid. It is estimated that the number of enrollees and dependents covered by an HSA-eligible plan rose from approximately 438 000 in September 2004 to about 3 million in early 2006 [27]. The majority of these policies were sold through the individual insurance market, but more recently group-based HSAs have outpaced individual plans. Still, HSAs are currently a tiny portion of the overall private insurance market for those under the age of 65 (approximately 210 million people).

6.2.4
South Africa

MSAs first appeared in South Africa during the mid-1990s, and South Africa's regulatory environment formally made provision for them in 1998. Although the use of MSAs initially grew rapidly in South Africa, a government review issued in 2002 severely curtailed MSA growth. The Department of Health inquiry examined South Africa's experience with MSAs and decidedly rejected their expansion [30]. The Department was concerned that substantial financial resources were being diverted away from risk-pooling schemes. The Department also found that administration companies charged unusually high administration fees for managing MSAs, and it rejected the notion that self-insurance can reduce costs. The Department inquiry issued the following recommendation:

> "Medical savings accounts are clearly problematic in a number of important areas of policy and consumer protection. *It is therefore recommended that the current policy be revisited with a view to phasing them out of medical schemes, or at the least substantially diminishing their impact on risk pools and contribution costs. The focus of health policy needs to be on risk-sharing and cost containment. None of these key health policy objectives can be achieved through medical savings accounts"*. (emphasis in original) (p. 123, Ref. [30].)

6.2.5
Summary

This short review has highlighted the limited extent to which MSA-based financing is used internationally at both the extensive and intensive margins. At the extensive margin, only four countries currently have any experience with MSA financing; at the intensive margin, MSAs play a very minor financing role (as measured by proportion of finance accounted for by MSA or proportion of people enrolled in MSA plans) in each of these settings. The designs of the MSA plans differ importantly across settings and, with the exception of the US, depart importantly from the prototypical, textbook MSA. In particular, in Singapore, which makes the most extensive use of MSAs, these funds can be used to pay for only a limited set of health care services. In China, many plans actually limit catastrophic coverage, leaving very high users of care exposed to substantial financial risk. No setting currently uses publicly financed MSAs; in all cases MSA contributions come from one or both of individuals and employers. Finally, the future role of MSAs is uncertain in some of these settings. As noted, South Africa made an explicit policy decision to restrict MSAs severely. And in China, where MSAs have been a core part of health care reform for the past decade, international agencies such as the World Health Organization are more cautious about expanding their use further as health reforms continue [31]. Gottret and Schieber [32] conclude, in an extensive review of health care financing, that the experiences thus far indicate that MSAs can function primarily as a supplementary method for increasing insurance coverage.

6.3
MSA Financing and System Performance

6.3.1
The Evidence Base

The virtual absence of high-quality evidence documenting the effects of MSA financing makes it difficult to assess the performance of MSAs. Both, the limited quantity of evidence and the generally poor quality of that evidence (as judged by the standards of program evaluation) mean that assessments of MSA performance are highly contested. Further, because MSAs are founded on a belief in the efficacy of individual-level, demand-side market competition in health care, judgments (both pro and con) are often influenced as much by preconceived ideological positions as by hard facts.

Because Singapore has the longest experience with MSA financing, its system has undergone more scrutiny than any other [8, 9, 11, 12, 33–36], but limited access to the data has made evaluation difficult. China's implementation of MSAs is now growing sufficiently mature that an increasing number of studies are available [37–39]. The MSA literature from the US consists mainly of analytic commentary and proposals [3, 40–42], reports of the experiences of private firms that have limited scientific validity and generalizability [1, 40], or predictions based on simulation models [43–50]. As noted earlier, two pilot projects (one targeted at the self-employed and one at Medicare beneficiaries) failed to generate meaningful results because of insufficient enrolment [51, 52]. Although the uptake of HSAs has been growing rapidly in the US since 2004, and HSAs are heavily promoted by current policy, at this early stage there is little evidence regarding the effects of HSA financing in the US [27]. Finally, in response to numerous calls in recent years to replace Canada's current system of comprehensive public insurance with publicly financed MSAs [4–6, 53, 54], an analogous literature consisting of analytic commentary and policy simulations has emerged in Canada regarding publicly funded MSAs [4–7, 53, 55–59].

This evidence base is weak for a number of reasons. The implementation of MSAs, even when done on a pilot basis, has not been accompanied by any systematic evaluation employing rigorous evaluation methodologies. With a few exceptions, the methods and data used in assessing MSAs largely remain descriptive with accompanying commentary, anecdote and interpretation. This is nowhere more evident than in the extended debate regarding Singapore's MSA experience [8, 9, 11, 33, 60]. The lack of good evaluation design is particularly problematic because MSAs have seldom been implemented in isolation. Rather, their implementation has been accompanied by broader system reforms, making it difficult – if not impossible – to isolate the impact of MSAs on relevant outcomes. This has been a particular problem in interpreting the experience of Singapore and China, both of which implemented important supply-side policies simultaneously with MSAs. The generalizability of each country's experience to many of the policy contexts in which MSA financing is debated can also be questioned. Important variations in design across Singapore, China and the US limit the ability to build evidence on the impact of key parameters of MSA design. Further, the "counterfactual" against which MSAs are being compared in many of the evaluations is not relevant to many new settings contemplating MSA financing, especially those with well-established system of public or social insurance. Evaluations of China's experience, for instance, compare MSA schemes against a situation in which the majority of individuals had no insurance. Drawing inferences from such a setting to systems universal coverage though public or social insurance, or even in the US with its complex insurance system, is fraught with problems. Hence, even if good evidence exists, drawing policy implications for quite distinct settings is not straightforward.

With these cautions noted, in the following sections the evidence relevant to judging MSA financing is reviewed and interpreted. The review draws on existing country experiences, simulation-based evidence, and the more general empirical and analytical literature on health care financing, health care demand and insurance. In their archetypal design, MSAs are just a high-deductible insurance policy accompanied by a tax-preferred vehicle to save for out-of-pocket expenditures. Hence, the more general literature on health care demand and insurance is relevant to an analysis of MSA financing.

The review emphasizes four key objectives, or criteria, commonly associated with systems of health care finance: (i) expenditure control; (ii) efficiency in financing and health service production and use; (iii) patient choice/access; and (iv) equity. These objectives are not universally embraced (nor are they the only relevant objectives), but they are important in most health care systems. Further, these objectives will be interpreted within the policy framework of countries such as Canada and other OECD countries with public or social insurance systems that stress universal access to needed health care services (especially physician and hospital services) without undue financial hardship to individuals.

6.3.2
MSAs and Expenditure Control

The demand-side cost-sharing integral to MSAs is intended to control health care expenditures by: (1) reducing the utilization of health care services; and (2) stimulating price competition among providers who compete for the business of cost-conscious consumers. As summarized by Folland, Goodman and Stano:

> "Advocates of MSAs argued that comprehensive, tax-subsidized insurance creates substantial moral hazard and ineffective incentives for efficient consumption of care. In contrast, the lure of potential distributions from an MSA, like spending one's own dollars, provides the individual with an incentive to become a prudent user of care. In principle, patients will be less likely to consume unnecessary or marginally beneficial care, and stronger market forces will help restrain prices (p. 425, Ref. [61].)

The evidence from settings that have implemented MSAs, and the broader experience with demand-side, competition-based approaches to health care financing suggest that MSAs will not be effective in controlling expenditures, especially compared to comprehensive public insurance.

Singapore is commonly cited to support the claim that MSA-induced competition will control health care expenditures. It is often noted, for instance, that Singapore maintains a modern health care system while spending less than 4% of its GDP on health care (e.g., Ref. [33]). The balance of evidence, however, suggests that MSAs have not been effective in controlling costs in Singapore. First, as noted, MSAs in Singapore account for 10% or less of total health care expenditure [8, 14, 15]. It is unlikely that the method of finance used for such a small segment of expenditures could exert a strong effect on trends in overall health care expenditures. Second, the existing evidence on the impact of MSAs on expenditure trends is disputed. Although Massaro and Wong [33] argued that MSAs did help to control expenditures in Singapore, others have challenged this conclusion. In fact, Hsiao [9] even argued that the rate of increase in health expenditures per capita increased following the introduction of MSAs in 1984. Barr [11] notes that, by 1993 – some 9 years after the introduction of MSAs – increasing costs arising from increased physician fees and the over-adoption of expensive new technologies as hospitals competed with each other led the government to conclude that: "Market forces alone will not suffice to hold down medical costs. . . the government has to intervene directly to structure and regulate the health system." (Singapore Ministerial Committee on

Health Policy 1993, as quoted in Ref. [11]). Barr argues that that Singapore's ability to control costs has resulted not from MSA financing, but rather from a series of supply-side regulatory initiatives that control, for instance, the introduction of technologies, physician supply, physician fees, and the number of hospital beds [11]. This is consistent with the relative success of supply-side cost-control initiatives in publicly financed systems during the 1990s and to the experience of the US in the mid-to-late 1990s when health care cost inflation fell to historically low levels as managed-care and related initiatives, which rely heavily on supply-side approaches, exerted strong influence.

While there is some evidence that expenditures decreased where the MSA insurance schemes in China were pilot tested, some analysts similarly attribute such effects to a variety of supply-side reforms intended to control costs that were contemporaneous to the introduction of MSAs [38, 62].

Although the US experience with HSAs is too young to have generated evidence of their impact on health care expenditures, a few points deserve mention. Although some private firms report cost-savings, these are not based on proper evaluations and likely represent at least in part selection effects and cost-shifting onto other payers – individual MSA account holders in particular who previously had comprehensive insurance. Some expenditure discussions also focus on health care expenditures only, and do not include the cost of the substantial public subsidy to MSA/HSA plans in the US. Gruber [48], for instance, estimates that the annual subsidy to HSA insurance premiums and to HSA contributions amounts to US$ 12 billion in tax expenditures. Finally, US-based simulation exercises generate mixed results with respect to expenditure savings, with predictions sensitive to MSA design and behavioral assumptions regarding utilization responses and selection into voluntary MSAs. Kendix and Lubitz's [47] examination of the introduction of MSAs for Medicare beneficiaries predicted modest savings at best, that strong selectivity effects and weak utilization responses severely limit expenditure savings, and there was no scenario under which Medicare saved money when MSAs were offered by private insurers. Keeler et al. [63], using the RAND Health Expenditures Simulation Model, found that if all insured non-elderly Americans switched to MSAs, then health care expenditures would decline by between 0 and 13%, but that taking into account selection patterns in a voluntary program, health spending would change by +1 to –2%. Both, Ozanne [45] and Nichols et al. [44] have predicted that introducing MSAs in the non-elderly population would reduce expenditures modestly (by 2–6%). Overall, the results are not reassuring that MSAs will be especially effective in either reducing or controlling expenditures. This is particularly true given that most MSA plans are voluntary and subject to self-selection whereby the relatively healthy adopt MSA plans. In addition to mitigating promised expenditure reductions, self-selection can affect the viability of some plans. Zabinski et al. [46], for example, found that if MSAs are offered alongside comprehensive plans, biased MSA enrollment could lead to premium spirals that would drive out comprehensive coverage. Evidence suggests that voluntary MSA enrolment is subject to self-selection, though the seriousness of this selection and its consequences are not known. Doherty and McLeod [64] found that MSAs in South Africa selectively attracted low-risk individuals, while initial evidence on HSA enrolment indicates that they attract relatively wealthy, healthy individuals [65].

6.3.2.1 Publicly Financed MSAs

Advocates of publicly financed MSAs in Canada have argued that such a plan will reduce public health care expenditures compared to the current system of publicly financed comprehensive insurance [5, 6, 66]. However, a growing body of simulation-based Canadian studies concludes that, under many plausible scenarios, publicly financed MSAs would increase public health care expenditures relative to the current system of public finance (even though health care utilization is assumed to fall). Reductions in public expenditures arise only under designs with considerable cost-sharing and under the assumption that government can capture all of the savings from reduced utilization.[7]

Deber et al. [7] simulated the introduction of publicly funded MSAs in the province of Manitoba, based on plans advocated by MSA proponents that included the following features:

- the plan included physician and hospital services,
- enrollment was mandatory,
- the deductible equaled the mean expenditure level within age–gender cells,
- the public contribution to individuals' MSAs was equal to 80% of the mean annual expenditure level in an individual's age–gender category, leaving an individual's corridor (the difference between the MSA contribution and the deductible) equal to 20% of the mean annual age–gender-adjusted expenditure,
- the government clawed back 50% of unspent MSA contributions.

Even under the extreme assumption that utilization fell to zero for all individuals whose actual spending in the current system is less than their MSA deductible, MSA financing was estimated to increase per-capita public expenditures; for example, by 12% for 25- to 35-year-old males, and by 15% for females aged 75 years or over. Total health care spending, including both public and private, rises even more since some individuals now must pay out-of-pocket for services that previously were fully publicly insured. Making the MSA plan expenditure-neutral for the public sector requires the deductible to be increased to unacceptable levels: from \$54 to \$ 1171 for 25- to 35-year-old males, and from \$ 3203 to \$ 8768 for females aged 75 years or

7) It is important to distinguish government outlays as part of its public health care insurance program (which increase), from spending on health care services itself, which is assumed to decrease by definition under MSAs in the simulations. The difference between these two amounts represents a redistribution through the tax system from the general public to those who accumulate unused funds in their MSAs. This redistribution, which is discussed in more detail below, creates equity effects but not efficiency effects. The reduction in health care consumption creates both efficiency and equity effects; these are also discussed in more detail below. Note also that all of the simulations ignore the administrative costs associated with MSA-based financing, which would be expected to increase compared to the current system.

over. Hence, individuals in each group were left with annual out-of-pocket liabilities of $ 390 and $ 4179, respectively.

Zaric and Hoch [58], also using data from Manitoba and a similar plan design, examined the impact on system costs of a number of MSA design parameters, including the MSA contribution, the deductible, and the government clawback rate. Under a range of reasonable parameter values, these authors found public-sector expenditures higher under MSA financing, unless the rate government claw back of unspent MSA contributions was greater than 50%; in some simulations the break-even claw back rate was over 80%.

To some extent, these findings are not surprising given that the plan designs examined are *ex ante* expenditure-increasing. Hurley et al. [59] used four years' of data from Ontario to examine MSA plans in which the government is assumed to capture the savings associated with reduced utilization, the government allocates its health care budget through a process that, *ex ante* is actuarially fair, MSA contributions are assumed to be age, gender and health-status adjusted, and the assumed reductions in utilization range from one-half to one times the difference in utilization observed in the RAND HIE between those with free care and those who faced 95% cost-sharing [67]. In the budget process, government first sets the deductible based on last year's utilization; it then calculates expected catastrophic payment and sets these funds aside; it then allocates to MSAs the remaining funds. At the start of the year, therefore, expected total government health care spending equals the budget. MSA plans that provide the same level of coverage as the current system of finance (i.e., no cost-sharing) increase public expenditures by 4–6%. Plans that incorporate a $500 annual deductible are predicted to reduce public expenditures by 4–8%. That is, under reasonable assumptions publicly funded MSA plans of this design can modestly reduce public expenditures, but only by introducing cost-sharing which, as discussed below, also creates efficiency and distributional effects.

6.3.3
MSAs and Efficiency

MSAs are intended to enhance efficiency through three primary channels: (i) the cost-sharing imposed by MSAs is intended to increase allocative efficiency by reducing unnecessary utilization (and the associated welfare loss); (ii) the competition among providers induced by now cost-conscious consumers is intended to increase responsiveness of providers to consumer preferences, again enhancing allocative efficiency; and (iii) MSA-induced price competition is intended to increase supply-side technical efficiency in the production of health care.

Currently, there is no explicit, direct evidence of the effect of MSAs on either allocative or technical efficiency within health care systems. Conjectures regarding the efficiency effects of MSAs are therefore based primarily on the broader literatures on the effects of cost-sharing and demand-side competition in health care. These are some of the most debated areas of health economics, with schools of thought roughly dividing between: (i) those who argue that health care markets are not that much different than markets for standard commodities, who therefore ascribe large welfare losses to insurance-induced moral hazard that is best addressed with demand-side cost sharing, and who believe in the efficacy of traditional consumer-based competition; and (ii) those who question either one or both of the magnitude of welfare losses associated with moral hazard or the effectiveness of demand-side cost-sharing to increase efficiency, and who argue that health care markets are sufficiently distinct as to render traditional consumer-based competition, on net, to be welfare decreasing. The present authors subscribe more to the second school of thought, and consequently argue below that MSAs are unlikely to achieve important efficiency gains and risk important inefficiencies.

MSAs and the associated increase in cost-sharing will decrease health care utilization. Evidence continues to document, however, that demand-side cost-sharing does not selectively reduce unnecessary or inappropriate utilization [68–71]. Rather, cost-sharing reduces utilization of both necessary and unnecessary services. This implies that the cost-sharing-induced utilization reductions under MSA financing are, on net, not efficiency enhancing. This has been the longstanding view of many health economists who have questioned the validity of traditional welfare comparisons based on the demand curve for health care [72]. In this view, although moral hazard is a source of market failure, it is best addressed with supply-side policies rather than demand-side cost-sharing. In addition, Nyman's [73] analysis of the demand for health care insurance, which accepts the normative significance of the health care demand curve, argues that the traditional analysis of moral hazard overstates the efficiency losses associated with insurance-induced increases in utilization (and hence the potential gain from reducing utilization via cost-sharing) because it ignores income effects. Furthermore, Newhouse, has recently argued that for many health services, including effective preventive services and many drugs, optimal cost sharing is considerably less than suggested by the RAND HIE, and may be zero [74]. Broad access to, and compliance with, treatment regimes for such services and health care products are, on net, both health-improving and cost-reducing. In combination, all of these considerations call into question whether the decreases in utilization under MSAs would on net be efficiency-enhancing.

Similarly it can be argued that, on balance, both consideration of the informational problems that consumers face in health care markets and the performance of health care systems over the past three to four decades seriously question the claim that patient-level, demand-side competition will enhance technical efficiency in production. Recent attempts in many systems to exploit competitive forces to improve system performance have not relied primarily on such demand-side competition. Rather, they have relied on competition among large purchasers; in the US through the growth of managed care, and in other settings through purchaser–provider contracting approaches. These reforms were motivated in part by the perceived failure of traditional demand-side competition which, in many health care markets, was associated with higher prices (for example, physician fees were frequently positively rather than negatively correlated with physician supply [72, 75]), wasteful duplication among hospitals, and questionable increases in spending on new technologies [61, 76, 77]. These findings appear to have been mirrored in Singapore's early experience with MSAs, which led the Ministry of Health to adopt a stronger regulatory approach to the supply-side [11]. Similarly, the studies conducted by Kessler and McClellan [78] found that, whilst some forms of hospital competition in the US reduced costs without reducing measured quality, demand-side competitive strategies, such as those which dominated prior to the 1990s, were associated with increased costs. Only after the early 1990s, with the spread of managed care and the development of large health plan purchasers that could extract price concessions, did cost-reducing effects of competition emerge along with important increases in measured quality. These effects were strongest in markets with the greatest penetration by HMOs, which rely on supply-side rather than demand-side regulatory approaches to control utilization and expenditures. Hence, the question is not a simple one of whether competition can be beneficial in health care. Some types of competition can be beneficial, but it depends crucially on the nature of the competition – among whom, on what dimensions of care, and so forth. In our judgment, evidence on the effects of the type of consumer-based competition at the heart of MSAs challenges the claim that MSAs will be efficiency enhancing.[8]

6.3.4
MSAs Choice and Access

Advocates of MSAs emphasize the potential for MSA funds to increase choice and access to a wide range of health-related services (for example, drugs, non-physician health professionals and, potentially, even health club memberships). In many situations, MSAs can offer individuals greater flexibility in the range of health care services that they can purchase at (public) subsidy. However, the impact on a person's choice set clearly depends critically on what is already covered under the financing approach that MSAs are replacing, and on the goods and services eligible for MSA spending. In both Singapore and China, the use of MSA funds has been restricted to only a subset of basic health care services. In the US, the services covered by HSA-eligible plans are very similar to traditional health care plans [27], and HSA funds can be used without penalty only for medical services as defined by the Internal Revenue Service. Hence, as currently designed, MSAs have not substantially expanded the set of "covered" services compared to traditional insurance. In settings such as Canada, which concentrate public coverage in physician and hospital services, public MSAs funds could be used to purchase, drugs, dental care and other services that must currently be paid for privately.

The real benefits of such an expansion in the choice set would be unevenly distributed among the population. The biggest gainers would be those who currently

8) Also, given the marginal role of MSAs in each of the systems that currently employs them, it is unlikely that MSAs could induce the types of competitive pressure necessary to materially affect overall system efficiency.

use few services insured under the comprehensive insurance (public or private) and demand high levels of uninsured health care services. MSA financing will allow these people to use MSA dollars to pay for previously uncovered services, with no reduction in previously insured services. However, those people who already use a high volume of insured services can finance this increased choice of uninsured services only by reducing their demand for insured services. Further, increased consumer cost-sharing under MSAs would reduce the ability of many individuals to finance non-insured services out-of-pocket. In other words, MSAs can shrink the feasible choice set for high users of care.

The impact of MSA financing on choice is therefore more complicated than is often portrayed in the literature, and is all the more so when interest earned on MSA balances, potential tax consequences and related matters are incorporated into the analysis.

6.3.5
MSAs and Equity

In health care finance, equity is interpreted as entailing contributions according to a person's ability to pay, while equity in health care utilization entails utilization in accordance with needs. Although, not universally held, these are the predominant equity principles that guide health care systems internationally, particularly among developed countries.

A number of features of MSA financing compromise equity in finance and the use of health care. Cost-sharing particularly has an adverse effects on the poor, both fiscally in terms of utilization and ultimately in terms of reduced health status [68, 70, 79]. The design of MSAs mitigates the effects of requiring individuals to pay the full cost of care up to the deductible, but it does not remove them.

Simulation models of the effects of introducing voluntary MSAs alongside traditional comprehensive insurance consistently predict that low-risk, high-income individuals financially benefit the most, whereas high-risk, low-income individuals suffer the most financially [44–46]. This pattern in rooted in a number of features of MSAs. Contributions to the MSA are commonly a percentage of earnings up to a maximum annual amount, so that the wealthy often contribute more. Contributions (and the associated withdrawals for health care consumption) are not taxed, which generates a greater gain at the margin for the wealthy than for those of low income. The wealthy are on average healthier, so they have less need to draw down MSA balances, and this leads to a greater accumulation of funds over time. Such an accumulation is particularly attractive if the MSA balances can be spent on non-health care consumption (as is currently the case in Singapore; in the US, those aged over 65 can do so without penalty). It is perhaps not surprising, therefore, that in some instances MSAs have been marketed to high-income individuals primarily as tax-preferred savings vehicles [80]. In Singapore, Medisave balances across income groups tend to mirror the distribution of income because mandatory contributions are based on an individual's income [12]. As a result, wealthier individuals have higher monthly contributions, which allows them to benefit more from the tax exemption and from the tax-free interest on their balances. A similar pattern of benefit is noted by Yi et al. [20] in their analysis of equity in the Chinese MSA system.[9] In the US, wealthy individuals disproportionately choose MSAs and HSAs [27, 28]. Those who enrolled in HSA-eligible plans indicated that they would recommend HSAs to healthy individuals but not to those "… on maintenance medication, with chronic conditions, with children, or who may not have the funds to meet the high-deductible". [27].

These issues play out somewhat differently under publicly financed MSAs. Contributions to finance the MSA system are based on the tax system, which is linked to income. In Canada, for instance, the incidence of financing for public health care is roughly proportional (progressive income taxes are offset by a regressive sales taxes). However, if public contributions to individual MSAs are risk-adjusted, then transfers to the MSAs of those with higher expected needs (who, on average have lower income/wealth) would be greater than those with lower needs (who, on average, have higher income/wealth); hence, this would mitigate some of the negative equity effects that arise when contributions are a positive function of income. Even so, compared to the traditional tax-financed systems, many publicly funded MSAs tend to redistribute public resources in ways that disproportionately benefit healthier, wealthier, and younger members of society.

For example, Hurley et al. [59] found that, under a publicly funded MSA plan which required no out-of-pocket costs (and which increased overall public expenditures by 5.8% compared to the current system), the average increase in public subsidy was: (i) larger for those in excellent health than for those in poor health; (ii) larger for low users than high users of care; (iii) larger for the young (aged 18–25 years) than the elderly (those aged over 65); and (iv) roughly equal for those in the highest income quintile compared to those in the lowest income quintile. A similar pattern of redistribution of public funds also held for the MSA plan with a $500 deductible; however, in addition individuals now incurred out-of-pocket costs which, in absolute dollar terms, were equal for those people in excellent and poor health and high and low income, but considerably larger for high users than low users and for elderly compared to the young. Making the deductible proportional to income (but equal to $500 on average across the whole population) ameliorates some of these effects, especially across income groups (public subsidy falls 20% for the highest income group and increases 1% for the lowest), but it is still the case that high users and elderly users both receive less public subsidy and pay more out-of-pocket than do low users or those aged under 25.

In general, publicly funded MSAs both redistribute public resources and require out-of-pocket contributions in a manner contrary to common notions of distributive equity in health care financing.

---

9) The analysis indicated that the MSA system was more equitable than the system that predated MSAs. However, the Chinese MSAs were regressive and the authors argue that the same funds could have provided better coverage if a higher proportion has been allocated to the social risk pool.

6.4
Conclusions

MSA have been – and continue to be – heavily promoted as a method of finance that can address many of the challenges facing modern health care systems. Although MSAs have been oversold, whatever their virtues it is essential to recognize what they are – a high-deductible, catastrophic insurance plan with a tax-preferred vehicle to assist saving for expenditures below the deductible. Compared to comprehensive insurance, MSAs *by design* shift financial risk onto the consumers. To pretend that MSAs can provide all the risk-sharing of comprehensive insurance, improve efficiency and reduce costs is misleading. An assessment of MSAs (as with any method of finance) must begin with the objectives of the system, and MSAs do not fare well when compared against the core objectives of most publicly financed health care systems, which stress equity in finance, allocation according to need, equitable access, risk reduction, efficiency, and health gains. Rather, MSAs are more attractive in settings that stress autonomy, market choice, and related principles. Whether MSAs are judged superior will depend on the weight given to competing objectives. In Singapore, for example, MSAs were intended as much to further national savings goals as to finance health care or pool risks.

MSAs are also premised on a highly contested view with regards to the operation of the health care insurance and health care service markets. MSAs are only compelling when accompanied by a firm belief that a key health policy problem is too much health insurance, and that health care markets can – and should – function just as markets for common consumer goods. Absent these points, and the case for MSAs falls away.

Finally, the experience with MSAs raises serious doubts as to whether they ever will – or should – play a major role in health care financing. As noted by Adam Wagstaff from the World Bank, despite much enthusiasm, thus far MSAs have played only a limited role in practice [14]. Similarly, Gottret and Schieber [32] concluded that the experience thus far suggests that MSAs can function primarily as a supplementary method of finance. In contrast to a decade ago, support is waning for further integrating MSAs into China's reforming system of health care finance [31]. In the US, the early evidence is that HSAs are attractive to that limited segment of the population which is wealthier, healthier, and low health care users) [27]. Overall, this review of current experience finds little compelling evidence to support the widespread adoption of MSA-based financing, especially within public or social systems of health care finance.

Acknowledgments

This chapter was originally prepared for the Workshop on Health Care Financing, Banff, Alberta, September 14–15, 2006. The authors thank Vicki Rynard, Albert Ma and conference participants for their helpful comments.

References

1 Buntin MB, Damberg C, Haviland A, Lurie N, Kapur K, Marquis MS. *"Consumer-Directed" Health Plans: Implications for Health Care Quality and Cost.* 2005. Santa Monica, CA, RAND Corp and California Health Care Foundation.

2 Buntin M, Damberg C, Haviland A, Kapur K, Lurie N, McDevitt R, et al. Consumer-directed health care: early evidence about effects on cost and quality. *Health Affairs* 2006; **25**: W516–W530.

3 Feldstein M. *Balancing the Goals of Health Care Provision.* 2006. National Bureau of Economic Research, NBER Working Paper 12279.

4 Gratzer D. It's time to consider Medical Savings Accounts. *Canadian Medical Association Journal* 2002; **167**(2): 151–152.

5 Ramsey C, Esmail N. *The Alberta health care advantage: an accessible, high quality, and sustainable system.* 81. 2004. Vancouver, Fraser Institute.

6 Owens D, Holle P. *Universal Medical Savings Accounts: Consumerizing Medicare to End Waiting Lists and Improve Service.* 2000. Frontier Centre for Public Policy.

7 Deber RB, Forget EL, Roos LL. Medical savings accounts in a universal system: wishful thinking meets evidence. *Health Policy* 2004; **70**(1); 49–66.

8 Hsiao WC. Behind the ideology and theory: what is the empirical evidence for medical savings accounts? *Journal of Health Politics, Policy and Law* 2001; **26**(4): 733–737.

9 Hsiao WC. Medical savings accounts: lessons from Singapore. *Health Affairs (Millwood)* 1995; **14**(2): 260–266.

10 Maynard A, Dixon A. Private health insurance and medical savings accounts: theory and experience. In: Mossialos E, Dixon A, Figueras J, Kutzin J (Eds.), *Funding Health Care: Options for Europe.* Buckingham: Open University Press, 2002.

11 Barr MD. Medical savings accounts in Singapore: a critical inquiry. *Journal of Health Politics, Policy and Law* 2001; **26**(4): 709–726.

12 Reisman D. Payment for Health in Singapore. *International Journal of Social Economics* 2006; **33**(1-2): 132–159.

13 Singapore Ministry of Health. *Medisave Withdrawal.* Singapore Ministry of Health. 2006. 5-9-2006.

14 Wagstaff A. *Health Systems in East Asia: What Can Developing Countries Learn From Japan and the Asian Tigers?* 2005. Washington, DC, The World Bank, Policy Research Paper 3790.

15 Lim MK. Shifting the burden of health care finance: a case study of public–private partnership in Singapore. *Health Policy* 2004; **69**(1): 83–92.

16 Liu Y, Mao Z, Nolan B. *China's Rural Health Insurance and Financing: A Critical Review.* 2004. Washington, DC, The World Bank.

17 The World Bank. Rural Health Insurance – Rising to the Challenge. *Rural Health in China: Briefing Notes Series,* 2005.

18 Tang S, Cheng S, Xu L. *Developing Urban Social Health Insurance in a Rapidly Changing Economy of China: Problems and Challenges.* International Conference on Social Health Insurance in Developing Countries. 2005. Berlin, Germany.

19 Liu G, Nolan B, Wen C. *Urban health insurance and financing in China.* 27-7-2004. Washington, DC, The World Bank.

20 Yi Y, Maynard A, Liu G, Xiong X, Lin F. Equity in health care financing: evaluation of the current urban employee health insurance reform in China. *Journal of the Asia Pacific Economy* 2005; **10**(4): 506–527.

21 Yip WC, Hsiao WC. Medical Savings Accounts: Lesson from China. *Health Affairs* 1997; **16**(6): 244–251.

22 The World Bank. Rural Health Insurance – Rising to the Challenge. *Rural Health in China: Briefing Notes Series,* 2005.

23 Brown PH, de Brauw A. *Implementing the New Cooperative Medical System in China.* 2005. Colby College, Department of Economics, Working Paper.

24 Zhengzhong M. *Pilot Program of NCMS in China: System design and progress.* World Bank China Rural Health Study. 2005. Washington, DC, The World Bank.

25 Hu T-W, Ying X. Private health insurance and its potential in China. In: Prekek AS, Scheffler R, Bassett M (Eds.), *Private Voluntary Health Insurance in Development: Friend or Foe?* Washington, DC, The World Bank, 2006.

26 National Health Accounts. *National Health Accounts – Preliminary estimates.* 2006.

27 Government Accountability Office. *Consumer-Directed Health Plans – Early Enrollee Experiences with Health Savings Accounts and Eligible Health Plans.* 2006. Washington, DC, United States Government Accountability Office, Report GAO-06-798.

28 Minicozzi A. Medical savings accounts: what story do the data tell? *Health Affairs (Millwood)* 2006; **25**(1): 256–267.

29 Fuchs B, James JA. *Health Savings Accounts: The Fundamentals.* 11-4-2005. Washington, DC, The George Washington University. National Health Policy Forum Background Paper.

30 Department of Health. *Inquiry into the various social security aspects of the South African health system.* 2002. Pretoria, Department of Health.

31 World Health Organization. *Implementing the New Cooperative Medical Schemes in rapidly changing China – Issues and Options.* 2004. Beijing, Office of the World Health Organization Representative in China.

32 Gottret P, Schieber G. *Health financing revisited: A practitioner's guide.* Washington, DC, The World Bank, 2006.

33 Massaro TA, Wong YN. Positive experience with medical savings accounts in Singapore. *Health Affairs (Millwood)* 1995; **14**(2): 267–272.

34 Nichols L, Hong PK, Prescott N. *Medical Savings Accounts for Developing Countries.* 1997. Washington, DC, The World Bank.

35 Schreyogg J, Lim MK. Health Care Reforms in Singapore – Twenty Years of Medical Savings Accounts. *Dice-Report-Journal for Institutional Comparisons* 2004; **2**(3): 55–60.

36 Dong W. Can health care financing policy be emulated? The Singaporean medical savings accounts model and its Shanghai replica. *Journal of Public Health (Oxford)* 2006; **28**(3): 209–214.

37 Liu Y, Hsiao WC, Eggleston K. Equity in health and health care: the Chinese experience. *Social Science and Medicine* 1999; **49**(10): 1349–1356.

38 Meng Q, Rehnberg C, Zhuang N, Bian Y, Tomson G, Tang S. The impact of urban health insurance reform on hospital charges: a case study from two cities in China. *Health Policy* 2004; **68**(2): 197–209.

39 Yu H, Gong Y. Lessons from a health insurance experiment in China. *Abstracts, Academy of Health Services Research and Health Policy Meeting,* 2001; **18**: 90. Available at: http://www.academyhealth.org/arm/ViewAbstract.cfm?uid=GWHSR0001653. Accessed March 15, 2007.

40 Physician Payment Review Commission. *Medical Savings Accounts. Annual Report to Congress.* Washington, DC, Physician Payment Review Commission, 2006: 113–133.

41 Pauly MV, Goodman JC. Tax credits for health insurance and medical savings accounts. *Health Affairs (Millwood)* 1995; **14**(1): 126–139.

42 Cogan JF, Hubbard RG, Kessler DP. Making markets work: five steps to a better health care system. *Health Affairs (Millwood)* 2005; **24**(6): 1447–1457.

43 American Academy of Actuaries. *Medical Savings Accounts: Cost Implications and Design Issues.* 1995. Washington, DC, American Academy of Actuaries.

44 Nichols L, Moon M, Wall S. *Tax-Preferred Medical Savings Accounts and Catastrophic Health Insurance Plans: A Numerical Analysis of Winners and Losers.* 1996. Washington, DC, Urban Institute, Working Paper 06571-002.

45 Ozanne L. How will medical savings accounts affect medical spending? *Inquiry* 1996; **33**(3): 225–236.

46 Zabinski D, Selden TM, Moeller JF, Banthin JS. Medical savings accounts: microsimulation results from a model with adverse selection. *Journal of Health Economics* 1999; **18**(2): 195–218.

47 Kendix M, Lubitz JD. The impact of medical savings accounts on Medicare program costs. *Inquiry* 1999; **36**(3): 280–290.

48 Gruber J. *The Cost and Coverage Impact of the President's Health Insurance Budget Proposals.* 2006. Center on Budget and Policy Priorities.

49 Parente ST, Feldman R, Christianson JB. Evaluation of the effect of a consumer-driven health plan on medical care expenditures and utilization. *Health Services Research* 2004; **39**(4 Pt 2): 1189–1210.

50 Cardon J, Showalter M. Insurance Choice and Tax-preferred Health Savings Accounts. *Journal of Health Economics*, 2006; **26**(2): 373–379.

51 Medicare Payment Advisory Commission. *Medical Savings Accounts and the Medicare Program.* 2000. Washington, DC, Medicare Payment Advisory Commission.

52 General Accounting Office. *Medical Savings Accounts: Results from Surveys of Insurers.* 1998. Washington, DC, US General Accounting Office, Report GAO/HEHS-99-34.

53 Skinner BJ. *Improving Canadian Health Care: Better Ways To Finance Medicare.* 2002. Halifax, Nova Scotia, Atlantic Institute for Market Studies, Background Paper #12.

54 Manzankowski D. *A Framework for Reform.* Edmonton: Government of Alberta, 2001.

55 Reuber GL, Poschmann F. *For the good of the patients: Financial incentives to improve stability in the Canadian health care system.* 2002. Toronto, C.D. Howe Institute.

56 Hurley J. Medical savings accounts: approach with caution. *Journal of Health Services Research Policy* 2000; **5**(3): 130–132.

57 Shortt SE. Medical Savings Accounts in publicly funded health care systems: enthusiasm versus evidence. *Canadian Medical Association Journal* 2002; **167**(2): 159–162.

58 Zaric GS, Hoch GS. Medical Savings Accounts: Opportunities for cost savings? *International Transactions in Operational Research* 2006; **13**(6): 493–513.

59 Hurley J, Guindon GE, Rynard V, Morgan SM. *Publicly Funded Medical Savings Accounts: Expenditure and Distributional Impacts.* 2007. Hamilton, ON: McMaster University Centre for Health Economics and Policy Analysis, Working Paper #07-01.

60 Pauly MV. Medical savings accounts in Singapore: what can we know? *Journal of Health Politics, Policy and Law* 2001; **26**(4): 727–731.

61 Folland S, Goodman A, Stano M. *Economics of Health and Health Care.* 5th edn. 2007.

62 Liu G, Cai R, Chao S, Xiong X, Zhao Z, Wu E. China's urban health insurance reform experiment in Zhengjiang: cost and utilization analysis. In: Hu T-W, Hsieh C (Eds.), *The Economics of Health Care in Asia-Pacific Countries.* Northampton, Mass: Edward Elgar Publishing, 2002: 143–158.

63 Keeler EB, Malkin JD, Goldman DP, Buchanan JL. Can medical savings accounts for the nonelderly reduce health care costs? *Journal of the American Medical Association* 1996; **275**(21): 1666–1671.

64 Doherty J, McLeod H. *Medical Schemes.* South African Health Review 2002. Durban: HST, 2003: 41–66.

65 Government Accountability Office. *Consumer-Directed Health Plans – Early Enrollee Experiences with Health Savings Accounts and Eligible Health Plans.* GAO Report to the Ranking Minority Member, Committee on Finance, US Senate. GAO-06-798. 2006. Washington, DC, United States Government Accountability Office.

66 Migué JL. *Funding and Production of Health Services: Outlook and Potential Solutions.* 2002. Ottawa, Ontario, Commission on the Future of Health Care in Canada, Discussion Paper No 10.

67 Newhouse JP. *Free for all? Lessons from the RAND Health Insurance Experiment.*

Cambridge, Mass.: Harvard University Press, 1993.

68 Rice T, Morrison KR. Patient cost sharing for medical services: a review of the literature and implications for health care reform. *Medical Care Reviews* 1994; **51**(3): 235–287.

69 Rice T, Matsuoka KY. The impact of cost-sharing on appropriate utilization and health status: a review of the literature on seniors. *Medical Care Research Reviews* 2004; **61**(4): 415–452.

70 Stoddart GL, Barer ML, Evans RG. *User Charges, Snares and Delusions: Another Look at the Literature.* 1994. Toronto, The Premier's Council on Health Well-being and Social Justice.

71 Lexchin J, Grootendorst P. Effects of prescription drug user fees on drug and health services use and on health status in vulnerable populations: a systematic review of the evidence. *International Journal of Health Services* 2004; **34**(1): 101–122.

72 Evans RG. *Strained Mercy: The Economics of Canadian Health Care.* Toronto: Butterworth, 1984.

73 Nyman J. *The Theory of Demand for Health Insurance.* Stanford, CA: Stanford University Press, 2003.

74 Newhouse JP. Reconsidering the moral hazard-risk avoidance tradeoff.

Journal of Health Economics 2006; **25**(5): 1005–1014.

75 Pauly MV, Satterthwaite MA. The pricing of primary care physicians' services: A test of the role of consumer information. *The Bell Journal of Economics* 1981; **12**(1): 488–506.

76 Robinson JC, Luft HS. The impact of hospital market structure on patient volume, average length of stay, and the cost of care. *Journal of Health Economics* 1985; **4**(4): 333–356.

77 Benjamini Y, Gafni A. The diffusion of medical technology: A "Prisoner's Dilemma Catch". *Socio-Economic Planning Science* 1986; **20**: 69–74.

78 Kessler DP, McClellan MB. Is hospital competition socially wasteful? *Quarterly Journal of Economics* 2000; **115**(2): 577–615.

79 Tamblyn R, Laprise R, Hanley J, Abrahamowicz M, Scott S, Mayo N, et al. Adverse events associated with prescription drug cost-sharing among poor and elderly persons. *Journal of the American Medical Association* 2001; **285**(4): 421–429.

80 Prescott N, Nichols L. International Comparisons of Medical Savings Accounts. In: Prescott N (Ed.), *Choices in Financing Health Care and Old Age Security.* Washington, DC, The World Bank, 1998: 19–32.

7
Physician Payment Mechanisms
Pierre Thomas Léger

7.1
Introduction

Health-care expenditures have grown considerably over the past few decades, and now constitute an important and rising share of GDP in many developed countries. The fact that many countries spend a considerable share of their GDP on health care is not necessarily alarming. However, if total consumption of medical services is inefficiently high, then controlling the growth of health-care expenditures is welfare increasing as such funds may be put to better use elsewhere. There are many reasons why the consumption of medical services may be inefficiently high. The most cited reason is that insured individuals do not face the true cost of medical services and thus are likely to over-consume – this is known as the ex-post moral-hazard problem. In order to reduce this over-consumption, one policy option is to increase the price paid by consumers by having them bear part of the costs, for example, through a co-payment. Co-payments, where patients pay a percentage of their medical expenditures, can be used to better align the price paid by the consumer with the true cost of the medical services. Measures, such as co-payments, which seek to control consumption (and consequently the cost) of medical services through the price paid by consumers are known as demand-side cost-sharing mechanisms [1]. Although these mechanisms may be effective in reducing total consumption, they have the disadvantage of increasing the financial risk faced by consumers. That is, individuals who suffer from severe illnesses may be faced with large medical expenditures. Consequently, demand-side cost-sharing policies may reduce over-consumption but sacrifice some of the benefits of health insurance.

Physician payment mechanisms, where the provider bears some financial risk associated with medical treatment, may serve as a more effective tool in reducing excessive consumption of care. Such supply-side cost-sharing mechanisms may have advantages over demand-side cost-sharing mechanisms for several reasons. First, physicians may in practice have more control than their patients over the type and quantity of medical services consumed, especially in an emergency setting. Second, physicians may be better at assessing the risks and advantages of different

Financing Health Care: New Ideas for a Changing Society. Edited by Mingshan Lu and Egon Jonsson
Copyright © 2008 WILEY-VCH Verlag GmbH & Co. KGaA, Weinheim
ISBN: 978-3-527-32027-1

medical procedures. Furthermore, physicians or physician groups, are seen as better able to bear financial risks than are individual patients [2]. By shifting the responsibilities/incentives to physicians, controlling costs need not necessarily imply less than full insurance for patients.

In this chapter we examine different payment systems directed at physicians, and their likely effects on physician behavior and patient well-being. Before doing so, we present a general framework and describe the efficient provision of medical services and the first-best insurance contract. The first physician payment mechanism that we present is the traditional fee-for-service (or cost-reimbursement) payment mechanism, where physicians are paid for each service they provide and bear no financial risk. We then examine pre-payment systems such as capitation and fully-prospective payments. In these settings, physicians are paid a given amount for each patient they enlist into their practice or for each patient they treat, while subsequently bearing all costs associated with treatment. Finally, we examine mixed-payment systems, where physicians receive a given amount for each patient they treat as well as a partial reimbursement of costs. For each physician payment mechanism, we examine the incentives they create, including how they are likely to affect the provision of medical services, physician referral decisions and patient selection. We also discuss how results are likely to change when considering such things as information asymmetry, provider altruism and diagnostic ability, physician monitoring and medical malpractice, and competition between providers. Although this chapter focuses on the theoretical foundations of physician payment mechanisms, we discuss related empirical findings throughout.

7.2
A Basic Model of Health-Care Provision and Consumption

In this section, we present a general framework to study medical-care provision and consumption. We then briefly present the first-best insurance contract as well as its feasibility in a real-world setting. In later sections, we adapt this general framework to different physician payment mechanisms and compare them to the first-best.

In our simple model, consumers are assumed to have preferences over health (H) and consumption (X) represented by the utility function:

$$U(H, X) \tag{7.1}$$

where $U_H > 0$, $U_{HH} < 0$, $U_X > 0$, $U_{XX} < 0$ and $U_{HX} > 0$.

The consumer's health is assumed to be a decreasing function of illness severity θ and an increasing function of medical treatment q. That is,

$$H = h(\theta, q) \tag{7.2}$$

where $\frac{\partial h}{\partial \theta} < 0$ and $\frac{\partial h}{\partial q} > 0$. A patient who does not suffer any illness is assumed to have health equal to H^0 [3]. The consumer is healthy with probability d and ill with probability $(1 - d)$. If the consumer is sick, he/she draws an illness severity θ from a known distribution $\Gamma(\theta)$. The patient with income I can purchase medical-care services at a per-unit price p (we normalize the price of the consumption good X to 1). Thus, the patient's expected utility is given by:

$$EU = dU(H^0, X) + (1 - d) \int_\theta U(h(\theta, q), X) d\Gamma(\theta)$$

where

$$X = I - pq \tag{7.3}$$

A consumer who is ill and suffers from an illness of severity θ maximizes his/her utility [Eq. (7.1)] by choosing a quantity q of medical services such that [4]:

$$\left(\frac{\partial U}{\partial h}\right)\left(\frac{\partial h}{\partial q}\right) = p\left(\frac{\partial U}{\partial X}\right) \tag{7.4}$$

or

$$\frac{\left(\frac{\partial U}{\partial h}\right)\left(\frac{\partial h}{\partial q}\right)}{\left(\frac{\partial U}{\partial X}\right)} = p \tag{7.5}$$

Equation (7.5) simply states that the individual will consume medical services up to the point where the marginal rate of substitution of medical services for consumption is equal to the price of medical services.

Given that there exists a unique utility-maximizing quantity of medical services for each illness–severity price pair, we can use Eq. (7.5) to define a demand function:

$$q = q(\theta, p) \tag{7.6}$$

We can show that the amount of medical services demanded will be decreasing in price ($\frac{\partial q}{\partial p} < 0$) and increasing in illness severity ($\frac{\partial q}{\partial \theta} > 0$). That is, the demand curve is downward-sloping in price and will shift outwards as the illness severity increases.

In Fig. 7.1, the efficient consumption level of medical services for a patient who suffers from illness severity θ is given by the intersection of the demand curve and the marginal-cost curve (mc) (which simply gives the per-unit-cost of producing medical services and is equal to the competitive price p^*) and is denoted as $q^*(\theta, p^*)$, or simply q^* [5].

Although the above solution characterizes the efficient consumption of medical services, uninsured individuals are subject to significant financial risks. That is, their consumption of medical services, as well as their consumption of non-medical goods, will depend on the illness severity that they experience. In order to increase their expected utility, risk-averse patients will wish to purchase health insurance. Health insurance allows patients to receive medical services at either reduced cost or free of charge in exchange for an up-front payment.

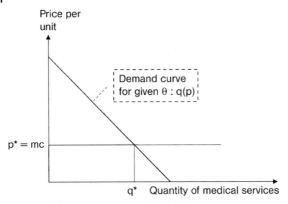

Fig. 7.1 Efficient consumption of medical services.

Suppose that individuals can purchase an actuarially fair insurance policy which covers all medical expenses. An actuarially fair insurance policy in such a case is one which charges the consumer an up-front premium α that exactly equals his/her expected medical expenses. Mathematically, α is defined by:

$$\alpha = (1 - d) \int_{\theta} p^* q(\theta, p) d\Gamma(\theta)$$

As a result, the patient's budget constraint previously given by Eq. (7.3) can now be written as:

$$I = X + \alpha$$

If illness severities were verifiable and contractible, then a patient could be forced to consume the efficient quantity of medical services according to the demand function given by Eq. (7.6) evaluated at the competitive price p^*. Consequently, the actuarially fair insurance premium would be given by:

$$\alpha^* = (1 - d) \int_{\theta} p^* q^* (\theta, p^*) d\Gamma(\theta)$$

Notice that, in the presence of insurance, the patient's consumption is constant across illness severities as medical services are now provided free of charge. Furthermore, the insured patient will now choose the quantity of medical services to satisfy the first-order condition given by Eq. (7.4), but where the price of medical services is set to zero to reflect the fact that he/she receives treatment free of charge:

$$\left(\frac{\partial U}{\partial h} \right) \left(\frac{\partial h}{\partial q} \right) = 0 \tag{7.7}$$

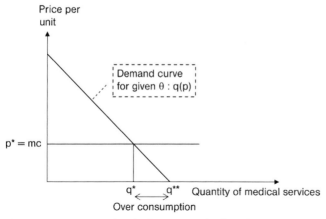

Fig. 7.2 Consumption of medical services under full information.

Equation (7.7) states that the fully-insured patient will consume medical services up to the point where the marginal benefit of health-care services is zero (which we denote as q^{**} in Fig. 7.2). Patients will wish to over-consume medical services beyond the efficient level simply because they do not face the true cost of medical services. In other words, patients will wish to consume units of care even if the cost to produce such units is greater than the value they attribute to them. As noted in the Introduction, this phenomenon is known as the ex-post moral-hazard problem.

The above analysis illustrates in a simple way that health-care insurance comes at a cost: the over-consumption of medical services. Obviously, the actuarially fair insurance premium will need to reflect this over-consumption and will be given by:

$$\alpha^{**} = (1 - d) \int_{\theta} p^* q^{**}(\theta, 0) d\Gamma(\theta)$$

That is, the actuarially fair insurance premium which takes into account the overconsumption of insured individuals will be greater than the actuarially fair insurance premium which would result if patients could somehow be forced to consume the efficient amount of medical services (α^*). It can also be shown that the consumer's expected utility would be greater under the efficient provision of care $q^*(\theta, p^*)$ and its corresponding insurance premium α^* than it would be if he/she were allowed to choose his/her own level of consumption of medical services $q^{**}(\theta)$ but faced a higher insurance premium α^{**}.

In fact, in a seminal article on health insurance, Arrow (1963) shows that an optimal insurance contract is characterized by an illness-contingent reimbursement policy [6]. More specifically, the insurance contract would specify a reimbursement schedule where a given amount of money would be transferred to the patient depending on his/her illness severity θ, i.e.,

$$reimbursement = g(\theta)$$

A patient with illness severity θ and receiving a reimbursement in the amount of $g(\theta)$, could purchase health-care services directly at market price p^*. Such a policy would maintain the benefits of full insurance (i.e., the consumer would not face any financial risk associated with illness) while maintaining the correct incentives for consumption (i.e., eliminate ex-post moral-hazard).

Although such an insurance contract is optimal from a theoretical stand-point, it is not feasible simply because it would be almost impossible – or at the very least very expensive – for an insurance provider to verify the patient's illness severity with precision prior to reimbursement.

Because illness-contingent contracts are not feasible, different policies have been put into place in an attempt to reduce the over-consumption of medical services. As mentioned in the Introduction, one of the ways to reduce ex-post moral-hazard is to introduce demand-side cost-sharing such as co-payments. By forcing patients to pay for a portion of their medical expenses, it is hoped that individuals will reduce their consumption to more efficient levels. If the patient were forced to pay for a portion γ of his/her medical consumption, the patient would consume care (under full information) such that:

$$\left(\frac{\partial U}{\partial h}\right)\left(\frac{\partial h}{\partial q}\right) = \gamma p \left(\frac{\partial U}{\partial X}\right) \tag{7.8}$$

Denote the level of consumption chosen by the patient facing a co-payment of γ to be q^{***} [7]. In Fig. 7.3, we can see that the patient would consume more than the efficient level but less than the fully insured patient.

Although demand-side cost-sharing may help to reduce the over-consumption of medical services, it nonetheless has several disadvantages. First, by increasing the co-payment rate (γ), patients face greater financial risk and thus lose some of the

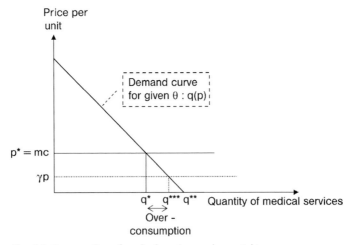

Fig. 7.3 Consumption of medical services under partial insurance.

benefits that full insurance gives them. Furthermore, patients may not necessarily dictate the quantity of medical services they consume. If patients partially or fully delegate their decision-making responsibilities to their physicians, or they lack information about their illness and/or the benefits of medical treatment, then introducing higher co-payments may not sufficiently reduce their medical-care consumption. How much patients rely on the advice or recommendations of their physicians is ultimately an empirical question – and one to which we return in detail later on.

7.3
Traditional Fee-For-Service (FFS)

Physicians in many countries have traditionally been paid on a fee-for-service (FFS) basis. Although this system is now somewhat less popular than before, it remains the predominant payment mechanism in many countries including Canada and the United States. With this type of payment mechanism, physicians are paid a fee for each service they provide, and it is thus considered a retrospective form of payment. For simplicity, one can express the physician's per-patient revenue in a FFS setting as:

$$\pi^{ffs} = Fq - cq$$
$$= (F - c)q$$

where F denotes the fee paid to the physician per service q provided and c denotes the constant marginal cost per service. In such a setting, providing more services is associated with greater income for the physician as long as $F > c$ [8, 9]. Consequently, physicians may wish to increase the number of services provided to their patients – even if such services are not justified from an efficiency standpoint (i.e., even if the services that are provided yield less benefit to the patient then they cost to provide).

In the following two subsections, we examine how physicians may be able to persuade their patients to consume excessive amounts of care in order to increase their own revenues. In the first subsection, we assume that patients can fully assess their illness severity and the quantity of services they should consume. In the second subsection, we relax these assumptions and assume that patients are less informed about their health status and/or the benefits of medical interventions than their physicians. In the final subsection, we examine a series of related issues and extensions.

7.3.1
Fee-For-Service and Perfect Information

Because of the monopolistic power they hold, physicians may be able to "force" their patients to consume more than the efficient amount of care *even if* patients are fully informed and must pay the full cost of medical services. Physicians may hold a certain amount of monopolistic power in the sense that patients may be unwilling to readily leave for an outside physician because they have developed a valued patient–physician relationship, because of search costs associated with finding a new physician, or because of the uncertainty that exists as to what type of physician they would get if they left their current physician for a new one. As a result, physicians may successfully opt for a "take-it-or-leave-it" strategy with their patients.

In order to highlight the effect of monopolistic competition on the consumption of medical services, we assume that the patient is uninsured, has suffered an illness severity θ^1, and faces a market price of p^* per unit of q [10]. The utility maximizing patient would choose $q^1(\theta^1, p^*)$ of medical services, which would provide him/her with post-treatment utility:

$$U^1 = U(h(\theta^1, q^1), I - pq^1)$$

Suppose that the patient could expect to receive post-treatment utility equal to $\overline{U}$ (where $\overline{U} < U^1$) if he/she left his current physician for another one. Consequently, the physician may "force" their patient to consume medical services up to q^2 without the risk of losing them, where:

$$\overline{U} = U(h(\theta^1, q^2), I - p^*q^2)$$

As a result, the physician can increase their income from $(F - c)q^1$ to $(F - c)q^2$ [11].

7.3.2
Fee-For-Service, Imperfect Information and Supplier-Induced Demand (SID)

Physicians often have privileged information or expertise which they may exploit to encourage an inefficiently large consumption of medical services – a phenomenon known as supplier-induced demand (SID) [12]. A physician may be able to influence the demand for medical services either by manipulating information about the patient's illness severity and/or by manipulating the expected returns associated with medical treatment. In order to highlight the effect of SID and to isolate its effect from those of insurance, we assume that the patient chooses the level of medical care to consume and must pay for all his/her medical services. Recall that under full information a patient having suffered from illness severity θ and facing market price p^* would choose the efficient quantity of medical services $q^*(\theta, p^*)$. Now suppose that the patient, having insufficient information about his/her illness severity, accepts the physician's diagnosis. A physician who reports to the patient that he/she suffers from illness severity θ^+ rather than the true illness severity θ, essentially shifts the patient's demand curve from $q(\theta, p)$ to $q(\theta^+, p)$. Consequently, the patient will choose q^+ instead of q^*, thereby increasing the physician's income from $(F - c)q^*$ to $(F - c)q^+$ (as is shown in Fig. 7.4).

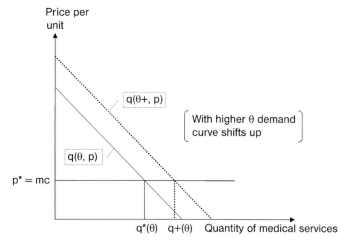

Fig. 7.4 Consumption of medical services with supplier-induced demand.

Given that the physician's income is an increasing function of the quantity of medical services that they recommend to their patient, a completely selfish physician would wish to exaggerate the patient's illness severity without limit. There are several explanations as to why the physician's desire or ability to do so is in fact limited. One possible explanation is that physicians may have some altruistic feelings towards their patients, or bear psychic costs associated with information manipulation [12]. This is especially plausible if the patient must pay a portion of his/her medical expenses and/or suffers some negative health effects from the over-consumption of medical services. An alternative explanation is simply that manipulating information requires costly physician effort [13]. If this is the case, physicians must weigh the benefits of increased revenues with the costs associated with information manipulation.

The physician's ability to induce demand may also be limited by their patient's unwillingness to accept any diagnosis or treatment recommendation. In fact, physicians who attempt to manipulate information excessively may risk losing their patients. As shown by Rochaix (1989), the threat of seeking a second opinion from another physician may serve as an implicit monitoring device and may limit the physician's ability to provide excessive treatment [14]. Because physicians face uncertainty as to the patient's likelihood of consent, Rochaix also shows that only a small number of patients need be sufficiently informed to limit excessive recommendations.

Regardless of the conclusions drawn above, one should expect that the physician's ability to manipulate information and/or the patient's willingness to acquiesce to their physician's recommendations will be greater for insured patients than uninsured. An insured patient is likely to care less about over-consumption of medical services than an uninsured patient, given that the latter must not only consider the effect of over-consumption on his/her health (or time) but must also pay for it.

7.3.2.1 Empirical Evidence of Supplier-Induced Demand

Many studies have attempted to test whether, and to what extent, physicians are able and/or willing to manipulate signals in order to increase medical-care consumption and their income. In order to do so, most have relied on either a change in physician supply or a change in the fees paid to physicians.

The examination of how physicians react to changes in the supply of physicians is often centered around the idea that physicians will increasingly wish to manipulate information (induce demand) as their income is threatened by competing physicians. If the demand for medical services is very high, or the supply of physicians is low, physicians may not need to induce demand to fill their schedule and maximize their income. However, when faced with falling demand or increased competition by other physicians, the benefits to inducing demand become greater [15]. Although evidence of SID is mixed, several studies are worth noting. Gruber and Owings (1996) used cross-state variation in birth rates to test whether obstetricians who practiced in states with greater declines in birth rates were more likely to deliver babies via a Cesarian section, which is more lucrative than a vaginal delivery [16]. The authors found that a 10% decrease in the fertility rate is associated with a 0.6% increase in the probability of a Cesarian section. Yip (1998) found that when fees to thoracic surgeries were reduced, thoracic surgeons were able to recoup 70% of their lost income through increased volume [17]. Although these studies suggested that SID does in fact exist, the estimated effects were nonetheless relatively small. As noted by Auld, Emery and Lu (1999), "The key question is whether this [is] enough to justify a radical departure from FFS payment for physician services?" [18].

7.3.3
Other Issues and Extensions

In the above analysis, several important assumptions were made to simplify the analysis. One assumption was that there is only one type of provider and that physicians have perfect diagnostic abilities. In addition, other issues such as prevention and innovation were excluded from the analysis. In this section, we briefly discuss these issues.

In the general framework discussed above, the physician's decision was limited to the quantity of medical services to be provided. However, general practitioners (GPs) also often serve as gate-keepers to specialty and inhospital care. Different physician payment mechanisms may affect not only the level of care provided by GPs but also their referral decisions. Examining the effect of different payment mechanisms on referral rates to specialists or hospital care is important because a significant proportion of all visits to primary-care physicians result in a referral [20]. Furthermore, hospitalizations account for a large portion of total health-care expenditures, even though they are a relatively rare occurrence ([1], p. 40).

In a recent study, Blomqvist and Léger (2005) presented a model with two types of provider: generalists and in-hospital specialists [19]. Although generalists may be more efficient at providing care for relatively mild illnesses, in-hospital specialists may be more cost-effective for relatively more severe illnesses. Furthermore, physicians are assumed to have more precise information about their patients' illness severities and the appropriate types of care than are patients themselves. More specifically, patients are assumed only to be able to distinguish between different classes of illnesses (or intervals of illness severities). In the traditional FFS system, GPs will have an incentive to exaggerate their patients' illness severities in order to increase their revenues. GPs are limited in their ability to induce demand because: (i) patients are assumed to be able to grossly evaluate their illness severity; and (ii) excessive exaggeration of the illness severity would lead the patient to seek in-hospital specialty care. The authors found that GPs paid by FFS would over-provide treatment yet also under-refer patients to specialty care. This general finding was consistent with several empirical studies which showed that physicians in a FFS setting were less likely to refer than those who were paid by capitation [21]. The issues of physician payment mechanisms and their effect on referral rates are discussed further in Section 7.4.3.

Allard, Jelovac and Léger (2006) provide a model where GPs differ in their diagnostic ability and their altruism, and where illness-severity is allowed to evolve over time [22]. In their model, high-ability GPs can better distinguish whether a patient should receive general care or be referred to specialty care. First, they solved for the efficient treatment and referral strategies conditioning on the GP's level of diagnostic ability. The authors then examined GP behavior under different payment mechanisms, including FFS. They found that the FFS system led relatively selfish GPs to systematically treat their patients (i.e., not refer to patients to specialty care), while leading GPs who were both relatively altruistic and had a low diagnostic ability to systematically refer their patients to specialty care. Nonetheless, relatively altruistic and able physicians followed their diagnostic findings when making treatment and referral decisions. The authors found that, for certain types of physician (i.e., for certain levels of physician altruism and diagnostic ability), the FFS system led to outcomes which coincided with the first-best. Nonetheless, other types of physicians were found to both under- and over-refer relative to the first-best.

Another issue which has been somewhat ignored in the literature is the link between the FFS system and its disincentive for physicians to undertake preventive measures. Because physicians are remunerated for each service they provide, any measure which may decrease future demand for medical services will be revenue-decreasing. Finally, FFS mechanisms often leave little incentive for physicians to delegate tasks to more efficient providers or to innovate in an effort to reduce costs [23, 24].

7.4
Capitation and Fully Prospective Payments

As discussed in detail in Section 7.3, traditional insurance and the FFS payment scheme are associated with the well-known moral-hazard problem and SID, respectively. In order to deal with both of these issues, different supply-side cost-sharing payment mechanisms have been proposed and often implemented. One of the most popular is *capitation*, where physicians are prepaid a fixed amount for each patient they enlist into their practice, and where the payment is set to reflect the patient's expected medical expenditures for a predetermined period of time [25]. In return, the physician is obliged to provide the patient with care "as needed" during the predetermined period, without any marginal reimbursement [26]. With an up-front payment, the physician is therefore responsible for all medical expenses incurred by the patient. In such a system, the physician bears the entire financial risk of treatment and consequently, will wish to control costs in order to increase their revenue [27–29].

Prospective payment systems are very similar to capitation payment systems, but are based on a single episode of care. More specifically, the physician receives a prospective payment based on the patient's expected cost for his/her condition, but in return is responsible for providing care without any further compensation. Thus, as in the capitation payment system, physicians are the residual claimants (or payers) and bear all financial risks associated with care. One important difference between the two systems is that capitation payments are paid prior to the patient's realization of illness whereas, prospective payments are paid after the realization of illness but prior to treatment and are based on the patient's illness. In the following discussion, attention is focused on the capitation payment system while returning to the prospective payment system in the subsections below.

Suppose, as before, that the patient is ill with probability $(1 - d)$, and if ill, draws an illness severity θ from a known distribution $\Gamma(\theta)$. Further suppose that illness severities are bounded by θ^L and θ^H (i.e., $\theta \in [\theta^L, \theta^H]$) and that each illness severity is associated with an appropriate (or efficient) level of care $q^E(\theta)$. In such an environment, the expected cost of treating the patient is given by:

$$E(cq) = (1 - d) \int_{\theta^L}^{\theta^H} cd^E(\theta)d\Gamma(\theta)$$

where c denotes the per-unit cost of medical services.

Under a capitation payment system, a physician who enlists a patient into their practice receives a net per-patient payment of:

$$\pi^{capitation} = R - cq \tag{7.9}$$

where R denotes the capitation payment [30]. If the capitation payment R reflects the patient's expected expenses plus some fixed margin m (i.e., $R = (1 - d) \int_{\theta^L}^{\theta^H} cq^E(\theta)d\Gamma(\theta) + m$), the physician's per-patient expected income under appropriate treatment is given by:

$$E(\pi^{capitation}) = R - E(cq)$$
$$= m$$

In such a setting, a purely selfish physician's optimal strategy is to tell their patient that they suffer from θ^L and to recommend the corresponding level of care $q^E(\theta^L)$ [31]. Consequently, the physician's per-patient net payment would be:

$$\pi^{capitation} = R - cq^E(\theta^L) > m$$

while the patient's post-treatment health would be $h(\theta, q^E(\theta^L))$ [32]. The patient's post-treatment utility would be equal to $U(h(\theta, q^E(\theta^L)), I - \alpha)$ where $\alpha = R$.

Capitation payments, as with other pre-payment schemes, have been empirically linked to reduced levels and/or quality of care. To cite but a few examples, Hillman, Paul and Kerstein (1989) found a 7% reduction in hospital days when comparing capitation with FFS in a Health Maintenance Organization (HMO) setting (HMOs are organizations that serve both as insurers and health care providers) [33]. By using data from the Rand Health Study, Manning et al. (1987) found substantially lower expenditures when patients were cared for by physicians in an HMO setting (characterized by prepayment plans) compared to those cared for by physicians paid by FFS [34]. Prepayment schemes have also been associated with lower rates of discretionary surgeries [35, 36] and less-intensive therapy in outpatient mental-health care [34]. Finally, patients assigned to HMOs rather than to FFS physicians were typically less satisfied with their care [34, 37].

7.4.1
Limits to the Under-Provision of Care

Although theoretical and empirical results suggest that physicians may wish to provide less care in a capitation system than in a FFS system, several reasons may explain why the under-provision of care may not be as drastic as first expected. For example, physicians may provide more care than predicted by the simple analysis given above because of: (i) the physician's altruistic motives or medical ethics; or (ii) medical malpractice suits and physician monitoring. We examine both of these issues in the following subsections [38].

7.4.1.1 Physician Altruism and Medical Ethics
In Eq. (7.9), we specified a selfish physician's revenue function, where physicians were assumed to ignore their patients' benefits from treatments. Many have argued that such a framework is unrealistic and that physicians are likely to value both their own welfare and their patients' health. As a consequence, we re-specify the physician's per-patient objective function in terms of utility, which is a function of both the physician's net revenue and the patient's health:

$$V(\pi, h) = \delta(R - cq) + (1 - \delta)h(\theta, q)$$

where $\delta \in [0, 1]$ denotes the relative weight that the physician puts on their revenue. A physician with $\delta = 0$ can be considered a perfect agent to his/her patient in the sense that they behave uniquely in the patient's best interests [39]. The more a physician is altruistic towards their patient, the less they will under-provide care. Similarly, one can think of medical ethics as playing an important role in limiting the under-provision of care. For example, physicians may be unwilling to provide less than a specified amount of care (which is likely to be illness-specific) [40].

7.4.1.2 Medical Malpractice Suits and Physician Monitoring

Because prepayment schemes such as capitation may encourage the under-provision of care, medical malpractice litigation and/or physician monitoring may be necessary in order to limit the under-provision of care. In fact, Ellwood and Paul (1986) note that at least one major insurance carrier believes that medical malpractice suits are more likely to be won if physicians practice under systems with cost-sharing and cost-containment [42]. In addition, Davis (1990) and the U.S. Senate have recommended that physicians who practice under supply-side cost-sharing (such as capitation) be monitored [41]. In fact, physicians who practice under cost-sharing schemes are both subject to internal monitoring by their HMOs and by Physician Payment Review Commissions (PPRC) (PPRCs are government agencies which monitor physicians who practice under certain prepayment schemes and who treat Medicare patients [42]) [43, 44].

In this section, we discuss the effect of monitoring mechanisms on physician behavior – whether they be internal mechanisms within the health-care organization, government mechanisms such as PPRCs, or private mechanisms such as medical malpractice suits [45]. Several reports have examined physician monitoring, and medical malpractice, including the seminal study by Danzon (1990) [46]. In the article by Blomqvist (1991), physicians are fined a given amount of money if their patient's post-treatment health outcome is sufficiently different from his/her expected outcome (what is known as an "outcome-oriented" criteria) [32]. The author shows that the first-best outcome can be reached if fines are paid directly to the government and the government pays a subsidy to the physician that is observable to the HMO. In Blomqvist's model, physicians may be successfully sued even if they have behaved appropriately. However, these false convictions are due to the randomness of treatment and individual's expectations about outcomes. Furthermore, each physician is subject to constant monitoring, and post-treatment health is costlessly observed.

Léger (2000) examines physician monitoring in a model where physicians are paid by capitation and where physician monitoring is endogenous and costly [47]. In the first version of the model, the monitoring of physicians is conducted by a third party. In this simple version, very large fines can lead to outcomes where all physicians behave appropriately and where no monitoring exists. In a more complex version of the model, where the monitoring is conducted internally by the HMO, very large compensations may lead these organizations to manipulate information in order to win compensation, even in the absence of negligent care. Léger shows that there may exist a fine such that the capitation payment system Pareto dominates the traditional FFS payment mechanism. At this level of fine, the patients receive the same level of treatment they would under the FFS, but at a lower cost.

7.4.2
Patient Selection and Up-Coding

The analysis above assumes implicitly that physicians are randomly assigned patients and that capitation payments (or prospective payments) reflect their patients' true expected costs of treatment. However, neither of these assumptions need necessarily hold. To allow for a more complete analysis, we modify Eq. (7.9) such that the physician's per-patient net revenue is given by:

$$\pi^{capitation} = R_i - cq_i$$

where the capitation payment R_i is patient-specific and reflects patient i's expected expenses $E(cq_i)$. Suppose further that the patient's expected expenses under appropriate treatment are a function R of two types of characteristics: (i) commonly observable characteristics X_i; and (ii) characteristics ε_i which are observable to the physician but unobservable to the insurance provider or third-party payers, where $\varepsilon \sim G(\mu_\varepsilon, \sigma_\varepsilon)$. Thus, the patient's expected expenses are given by:

$$E(cq_i) = R(X_i, \varepsilon_i)$$

However, because ε_i is unobservable to the insurer or third-party payer, a capitation payment set to reflect patient i's expected expenses can only be based on X_i and the expected value of ε_i. Therefore,

$$\begin{aligned} R_i &= R(X_i, E(\varepsilon_i)) \\ &= R(X_i, \varepsilon_\varepsilon) \end{aligned}$$

and the physician's revenue can be re-written as:

$$\pi^{capitation} = R(X_i, \mu_\varepsilon) - cq_i$$

As a result, a physician providing appropriate treatment will make positive profits if $\varepsilon_i | X_i < \mu_\varepsilon$, and negative profits if $\varepsilon_i | X_i > \mu_\varepsilon$.

In order to maximize their expected earnings, a physician would like to select patients who have low values of ε (are "unobservably" more healthy) in each class of observable characteristics (i.e., $\varepsilon_i | X_i < \mu_\varepsilon$). Although it may be illegal to do so, physicians may be able to encourage certain types of patient to join their practice, while discouraging others from not joining, through a variety of instruments including the choice of services to offer. For example, "unobservably" healthy individuals may care more about location and hours-of-operation, while "unobservably" unhealthy individuals may care more about technology. This phenomenon is known as "cream-skimming" [48].

Ellis (1998) examines issues of selection and treatment in a model where two different providers (in his case, hospitals) compete for patients under several payment schemes [49]. More specifically, he examines provider incentives on both the intensive margin (how much care the provider will give) as well as the extensive margin (who the provider will treat). If providers are paid under a fully prospective system, they will wish to "dump" high-severity patients. That is, they will turn away patients who have high expected expenses. On the other hand, they will over-provide care to low-severity patients in order to attract them (cream-skim). Furthermore, the author shows that under general conditions, physicians will wish to provide too few services (skimp) to relatively high-severity patients. Finally, the author shows that, compared to a traditional cost-based reimbursement scheme such as FFS, capitated physicians will provide fewer services to all types of patient.

Recall from the above discussion that prospective payments, unlike capitation payments, are based on the patient's diagnosis, but are determined prior to treatment. This type of payment mechanism has been in use in the United States at the hospital level, where hospitals receive a prospective payment based on the patient's diagnosis-related group (DRG) when treating a medicare patient. Even if hospitals or physicians may not be able to attract relatively low-cost patients within one of these DRGs, they may be able to exaggerate the patient's condition such that they receive a larger payment. In the hospital setting, such systematic up-coding of diagnosis group has led to what is known as the "DRG creep" [50].

7.4.3
Other Issues: Referrals and Diagnostic Ability

The models discussed above were limited to one type of provider. As discussed in Section 7.3.3, patients may seek care from different types of providers such as GPs and a variety of specialists. In the static framework discussed above, physicians paid by capitation faced incentives which led to the reduction of medical services compared to FFS physicians. As a result, capitation payment systems were viewed as a potentially important way of reducing total medical expenditures. This result may not necessarily hold when considering all types of care and providers. Capitated physicians are not generally financially responsible for specialty and hospital expenditures incurred by their patients. Thus, a capitated physician faces every incentive to refer their patients to specialty care and/or to hospital, which may in turn increase total medical expenditures.

Blomqvist and Léger (2005) also considered a case where physicians were paid by capitation and where the insurance provider (the HMO) took a more active role in managing care [20]. Physicians paid by capitation will: (i) downplay the patient's illness severity when the patient's illness is not serious enough to justify in-hospital specialty care; but (ii) exaggerate the patient's illness severity if there is ambiguity as to whether or not the patient should receive in-hospital care. This may explain why HMOs that pay their physicians by capitation also impose second-opinion requirements on their physicians in order to limit the excessive hospitalization. These findings were consistent with empirical evidence which suggested that GPs paid on the basis of FFS were less likely to refer patients to other providers than were GPs paid on the basis of capitation [51].

Allard, Jelovac and Léger (2006) also examined the treatment and referral behavior of GPs who practiced under capitation [22]. They found that capitated GPs would wish to systematically over-refer patients to specialty care. Although such behavior may be undesirable in most settings, the authors found that the GPs' strategy may coincide with the efficient treatment and referral strategy if their diagnostic ability was imprecise, the probability of a high-severity illness was high (or the probability that a mild illness will worsen over time is high), and/or the cost of specialty care was relatively low.

7.5
Mixed-Payment Systems

In the above analysis two important simplifying assumptions are made. First, the payment mechanism is either completely based on a FFS system (a form of retrospective payment system whereby the physician faces no financial risk of treatment), or a capitation or fully prospective system (a form of payment system whereby the physician faces all the financial risk associated with treatment). That is, the analysis excluded payment systems which include both retrospective and prospective forms. Second, medical care was assumed to be unidimensional and could be purchased at a given price. In this section, we relax the first assumption and show that a mixed-payment system which has both a prospective and a retrospective component may be necessary for efficiency in a setting characterized by physician altruism and/or moral-hazard. Finally, we relax the second assumption by introducing a more complete health-production function, where the patient's health depends not only on the quantity of medical services he/she receives but also on the physician's effort. We then review the literature which allows for both types of care and show that a mixed-payment system is required in order to encourage the efficient provision of both dimensions of care.

7.5.1
Physician Altruism and a Mixed-Payment System

In Section 7.4.1.1, the physician's utility function was augmented to include the patient's health. In this section, we re-examine the effect of physician altruism in a setting where physicians may be paid by FFS, capitation, or a combination of the two.

Suppose that the physician's utility function is given by:

$$V(\pi, h) = \delta(R + Fq - cq) + (1 - \delta)h(\theta, q) \tag{7.10}$$

where, as before, R represents a capitation payment, F represents a marginal reimbursement (or FFS rate) per unit of q, c represents the marginal cost of treatment, and δ represents the physician's altruism parameter [52].

For simplicity assume that the patient's utility function is separable in health and consumption:

$$U(H, X) = h(\theta, q) + X$$

and that he/she faces a budget constraint of:

$$X = I - cq$$

where the price of medical services is set equal to the marginal cost.

Note that in such a setting, a patient who consumes medical care efficiently will consume care up to the point where its marginal benefit is just equal to its marginal cost:

$$\frac{\partial h}{\partial q} = c \tag{7.11}$$

Now suppose that the physician is somewhat altruistic (i.e., $\delta \in (0, 1)$) and decides on the patient's behalf how much medical services the patient will consume and that the patient is fully insured (i.e., $X = I - \alpha$). In such a setting, the physician will choose the quantity of medical services to maximize [Eq. (7.10)] that will satisfy the following condition:

$$\delta(F - c) + (1 - \delta)\frac{\partial h}{\partial q} = 0 \tag{7.12}$$

Notice that if $F > c$, then $\frac{\partial h}{\partial q}$ must be less than 0 for Eq. (7.12) to hold. That is, the physician makes the patient consume too much care to the point where the marginal benefit of care is actually negative. If the physician is fully altruistic (i.e., $\delta = 0$), then the utility maximizing quantity is given by $\frac{\partial h}{\partial q} = 0$. Either way, the physician's utility maximizing quantity is greater than the efficient level [53].

In order for the utility maximizing quantity [Eq. (7.12)] to coincide with the efficient quantity [Eq. (7.11)], the following condition must hold:

$$\delta(F - c) + (1 - \delta)c = 0 \tag{7.13}$$

which implies that $F < c$. To induce the physician to provide the efficient level of medical services, the marginal reimbursement must be less than the marginal cost (i.e., the physician must make a loss on every unit of care he/she provides). However, given that physicians will make negative profits under such a marginal reimbursement policy, physicians will need to receive an up-front payment to ensure their participation. Thus, when $F < c$, $R > 0$. Finally, notice from Eq. (7.13), that the difference between the marginal payment and the marginal cost is increasing in the physician's altruism parameter. Thus, in order to induce the efficient provision of medical services, more altruistic physicians must face a greater loss for each unit of medical care they provide (yet, must also receive a larger up-front payment) [54].

7.5.2
Physician Effort and Mixed-Payment Systems

As mentioned previously, we assumed from the start that medical care was unidimensional, could be purchased at a market price p, and could form the basis of a contract. In reality, some types of care are difficult to observe and cannot be reimbursed on a per-unit basis. To reflect the multidimensionality of care, several recent reports have separated health care into medical services q (for example, actual treatments and procedures, diagnostic testing...) and physician non-contractible effort, e.

To reflect the multidimensionality of care, the patient's health production function is augmented from Eq. (7.2) to include both of these components and is represented by:

$$h = h(\theta, q, e)$$

Although physicians may not be remunerated directly for the amount of effort they exert, physician effort is considered a valued input by patients. In the following section we examine several models which integrate the idea of multidimensional care. Although the models presented below consider a mixed-payment system, they differ in several respects including: (i) who decides on the level of care; (ii) informational assumptions; (iii) the role of altruism and medical ethics; and (iv) the role of competition.

7.5.3
Physicians Decide on Medical Services and Effort

In McGuire (2000), the number of patients (n) that a physician attracts is directly related to the net benefit (NB) that they provide to their patients [10]. More specifically, the physician's net revenue (π^{Total}) is given by the number of patients (n) multiplied by the net per-patient revenue ($\pi^{per-patient}$):

$$\pi^{Total} = n(NB) * \pi^{per-patient} \tag{7.14}$$

The net benefit received by a representative patient is assumed to be the difference between the benefits (B) received (which are a function of the quantity of medical services q and effort e received) and the cost of treatment (which is uniquely a function of quantity q):

$$NB = B(q, e) - pq \tag{7.15}$$

where p denotes the price paid by the patient per-unit of medical care q received.

McGuire then defines a mixed-payment system which allows for both a prospective (R) and a retrospective (Fq) component. The physician's net per-patient revenue is thus:

$$\pi^{per-atient} = R + Fq - cq \qquad (7.16)$$

where c denotes the per-unit cost of medical services. In such a setting, a fully prospective payment, such as capitation, is given by $R > 0$ and $F = 0$. A fully retrospective payment system, such as FFS, is given by $R = 0$ and $F > c$. Finally, a mixed-payment system is generally defined by $R > 0$ and $F < c$.

In this model, the physician is assumed to choose both the effort and the quantity of medical services to provide, and the physician's choice of q and e are assumed to be observable to the patient prior to his/her choice of physician. As a result, q and e directly affect the number of patients that the physician will attract. Given this set-up, a revenue-maximizing physician chooses e and q to maximize Eq. (7.14) subject to the patient's net-benefit function [Eq. (7.15)] and the mixed-payment system [Eq. (7.16)].

In a fully prospective system (i.e., $R > 0$ and $F = 0$), the physician must provide enough quantity q and effort e to attract patients. Although more quantity, q, increases the number of patients they attract, they receive no marginal reimbursement for its provision. As a result, the physician will provide too much effort and too little quantity. Under a fully retrospective system (i.e., $R = 0$ and $F > c$), the opposite will hold. That is, the physician will under-provide effort and over-provide medical services. Now, consider the case of a mixed-system where $R > 0$ and where $F < c$. An increase in the prospective payment will increase the level of effort the physician will provide. Furthermore, by decreasing the level of reimbursement, the amount of q will decrease. Using these two instruments, one may be able to achieve the targeted levels of both observable and unobservable components of care.

McGuire makes the simplifying assumption that potential patients can perfectly observe each physician's choice of quantity and effort prior to selecting their provider. This assumption, however, is unlikely to hold in the reality. The author further supposes that the number of patients that a physician will attract is an increasing function of the amount of effort and quantity they provide, which implies that competing physicians are passive.

7.5.4
Physicians Make Effort Decisions Prior to Patients' Treatment Decisions

In a seminal article, Ma and McGuire (1997) build a model in which health-care providers interact with patients and insurance providers with several interesting features [55]. Like McGuire (2000), two different types of medical care are valued: (i) medical services q which can form the basis of the physician's remuneration (such as the number of visits or the number and type of procedures); and (ii) physician time and effort e which is often unobservable (or at least not verifiable) and thus cannot directly form the basis of the physician's remuneration. Unlike McGuire (2000), however, the authors assume that the patient chooses q following the physician's choice of e, and that the reported quantity of medical services q need not correspond to the true amount provided.

In the model, the physician chooses effort e to maximize his/her utility given by:

$$V = (1 - d)[R + Fq^r - cq - \Lambda(e)] \tag{7.17}$$

where $(1 - d)$ denotes the patient's probability of illness, R denotes the prospective payment, F denotes the marginal payment per unit of reported treatment q^r, q denotes the actual amount of treatment provided, c denotes the per unit cost of treatment, and $\Lambda(e)$ denotes the cost of providing e units of effort. Finally, by allowing $F = v + c$, we can interpret v to be the margin over cost which the physician receives per unit of reported treatment.

The patient chooses treatment q to maximize his/her expected utility given by:

$$EU = (1 - d)U(I - \alpha - \gamma q^r - \theta + B(q, e)) + dU(1 - \alpha) \tag{7.18}$$

where I denotes the patient's state-independent income, α denotes the insurance premium, γ denotes the co-payment rate, θ denotes the monetary equivalent of the health shock, and $B(q, e)$ denotes the benefit associated with treatment q and effort e.

In this model, the physician announces his/her level of effort, which is followed by the patient's choice of treatment. Once these choices have been made, the patient and physician must agree on the level of treatment to report to the authorities. A physician who receives a positive payment for each unit of treatment reported (i.e., $v + c \geq 0$) would like to over-report the quantity of care they actually provide (i.e., $q^r > q$). However, such a report would never be accepted by the patient, given the presence of a co-payment rate γ (in fact, the patient would wish to under-report the true level of treatment). Thus, when $v + c \geq 0$, the true level of treatment will be reported ($q^r = q$) and the physician's utility will be reduced to:

$$V = (1 - d)[R + vq - \Lambda(e)]$$

Two distinct scenarios must be examined to derive the optimal payment mechanism: (i) the case where effort and treatment are complementary; and (ii) the case where they are substitutes. First, consider the case where effort and treatment are complementary and the physician makes a positive return on each treatment quantity they provide (i.e., $v + c \geq 0$). In order to increase their patient's demand for treatment, the physician must increase the level of effort they provides. Thus, by increasing the margin, the social planner (or the insurance provider) can induce the physician to provide valued, yet not remunerated, effort. If treatment and effort are substitutes, then physicians would wish to decrease their level of effort in order to induce positive consumption of treatment. To counteract this incentive, physician cost-sharing would be necessary (i.e., $v < 0$). Obviously, the level of physician cost-sharing is limited by the truth-telling constraint (i.e., $v < 0$ but must also satisfy $v \geq -c$) [56].

7.5.5
Physicians Decide on Effort While Patients Decide on Quantity (Simultaneously) in a Model with Endogenous Competition

Allard, Léger and Rochaix (2006) examine provider and patient behavior in a dynamic setting where physicians repeatedly compete for patients in a mixed-payment system [57]. In this model, patients value both the quantity of medical services they receive and the level of effort provided to them by their physician. Unlike the studies cited above, the authors assume that physician effort is unobservable to the patient prior to the patient's quantity decision. Furthermore, patients must attempt to predict what level of effort they would receive from a new physician if they actually left their current physician for an unknown outside one [58]. Physicians are characterized by an individual-specific ethics constraint. The authors also allow for switching costs (i.e., both financial and psychic costs associated with leaving one physician for another) and uncertainty in the treatment–outcome relationship. In their model, the prospective payment compensates for the physician's effort (which is non-contractible and thus cannot be remunerated on a per-unit basis), while the retrospective payment compensates the physician for the observable quantity provided. When switching costs are small and the treatment–outcome relationship is certain, the authors show that all physicians will provide their patients with the appropriate level of care, irrespective of their ethics constraint. In the presence of switching costs, the effect of competition is dampened, leading to some heterogeneity in treatment (i.e., some patients receive more care than others). When the treatment–outcome relationship is uncertain, physicians will over-provide care in order to limit the amount of patient turnover (a form of defensive medicine) [59]. Thus, this report suggests that competition between providers may limit the physicians' ability or desire to under-provide care in a mixed-payment system. This result may help to explain why pre-payment schemes have managed to compete with more traditional, cost-based reimbursement schemes [60].

7.5.6
Empirical Evidence

Although the empirical literature that examines the effects of a mixed-payment system on physician behavior is quite sparse, a new report by Fortin, Jacquemet and Shearer (2005) provides some important insights. Here, the authors analyze the effects of the introduction of a mixed-payment system (in competition with a traditional FFS system) on specialists' behavior [62]. More specifically, the authors examine in a structural model, the effect of introducing a voluntary mixed-payment system, whereby specialists accepted a lower FFS rate in return for a per-diem payment, on the treatment behavior of specialists in Quebec. The authors estimate the effect of the introduction of the mixed-payment system on both: (i) the total hours of work and the number of clinical services provided (i.e., the extensive margin); and (ii) the time spent per service (i.e., the intensive margin). By controlling for the voluntary nature of the mixed-payment system, they find that the introduction of a mixed-payment system leads to an increase in the number of hours of work, as well as the time spent per service for surgeons who chose the mixed-payment system. However, it also led to a reduction in the total number of services provided for this group. The authors then used their results to simulate the likely effects of a mandatory mixed-payment system, and predicted both a reduction in the number of services and the time devoted to them. The preliminary results, however, only included estimates on surgeons and did not consider general equilibrium effects which may be important.

7.6
Concluding Remarks

In this chapter we have reviewed the literature on payment mechanisms and examined its likely effects on provider behavior and patient's consumption of medical services. In the first section, we introduced a basic model of health-care consumption and showed that insured individuals would wish to consume care beyond efficient levels – the well-known moral-hazard problem. Although, in theory, one could design an insurance contract to encourage the efficient provision of care, such a contract is considered unfeasible given its informational requirements. In order to maintain the benefits of insurance while reducing the excessive consumption of medical services, we examined the likely effects of three commonly studied and used types of payment mechanisms – namely FFS, capitation, and mixed-payments – on provider behavior, including the provision of care and referral rates. We also examined how predictions derived from the basic model changed when introducing such things as multiple providers, competition, altruism, and monitoring.

As discussed above, FFS payment mechanisms may actually encourage the over-consumption of care (even beyond that which results from moral-hazard). We showed that physicians may be able to encourage the over-consumption of care either by exploiting their monopolistic power or by manipulating information about the patient's illness severity and/or the efficacy of treatment (what is known as supplier-induced demand). This ability or desire to encourage excessive consumption of medical services is likely tempered by the physician's altruistic feelings for his/her patients and/or competition between providers. Fee-for-service physicians, may however be less likely to depend on referrals to specialty care (than are physicians paid under capitation or mixed-payment systems). We also showed that capitation payment mechanisms, whereby physicians are paid a given amount for each patient they enlist into their practice, but must provide care without any marginal reimbursement (for a pre-determined period of time), generate incentives which basically run in the opposite direction to those generated by FFS. In such a setting, physicians will wish to under-provide care in order to maximize their income. As in the FFS case, the ability to do so is also likely tempered by physician altruism and competition between providers. It may also be limited by physician monitoring and/or the threat of medical malpractice litigation. Finally, we examined mixed-payment systems whereby physicians are paid partly on a prospective basis and partly on a retrospective basis. By providing only a partial reimbursement of costs, we showed that mixed-payment systems can be used to encourage the efficient level of "observable" types of care (such as procedures) while also encouraging the efficient provision of unobservable (or at least non-contractible) types of care (such as physician time and effort).

Although many theoretical and empirical questions remain unanswered, the literature is quite clear that financial incentives for physicians matter. More specifically, FFS payment mechanisms appear to encourage supplier-induced demand and excessive use of care. On the other hand, capitation payment mechanisms appear to reduce the provision of care and some excessive use of specialty and in-hospital care. Finally, the use of mixed-payment systems appear to reduce the quantity of services provided while increasing the quality of care provided.

Acknowledgments

I am grateful to participants of The Banff International Workshop on Health Care, especially Mingshan Lu and my discussant Tom McGuire. I also thank Rob Clark, Marie Allard, Pierre-Yves Geoffard and Shannon Seitz for the their thoughtful suggestions. Part of this research was undertaken while I was a visiting researcher at Paris-Jourdan Sciences Économiques (PSE) and I thank them for their hospitality. Financial support from the Social Science and Humanities Research Council of Canada (SSHRC), le Fonds québecois de la recherche sur la société et la culture (FQRSC), HEC Montréal and The Institute of Health Economics is gratefully acknowledged.

References and Footnotes

1 See Part II of Newhouse, J. P. (1993) *Free For All? Lessons from the RAND Health Insurance Experiment*, Harvard University Press, Cambridge, for a thorough discussion of the effects of patient cost-sharing on the use of medical services.

2 Ellis, R.P., McGuire, T.G. (1986) Provider Behavior under Prospective Reimbursement: Cost Sharing and Supply. *Journal of Health Economics*, **5**, 128–151.

3 Note that, unlike most goods, health-care services are considered a derived good as they do not directly increase utility but rather increase health, which in turn increases utility.

4 Obviously, a patient who does not suffer an illness shock (where $d = 1$) will dedicate all of his/her income to consumption (i.e., $X = I$ and $q = 0$).

5 For simplicity, we assume that the marginal cost of medical services is constant (i.e., that the production cost of medical services is constant) and that the market for such medical services is competitive. Consequently, the competitive price for medical services will be equal to the marginal cost.

6 Arrow, K. (1963) Uncertainty and the Welfare Economics of Medical Care. *American Economic Review* **53**, 941–969.

7 The actuarially fair insurance premium associated with q^{***} is given by $\alpha^{***} = (1 - d) \int_\theta p^* q^{***}(\theta, \gamma p^*) d\Gamma(\theta)$.

8 Pauly, M. V. (1970) Efficiency, Incentives and Reimbursement for Health Care. *Inquiry*, **7**, 114–131.

9 Note that for consistency, we have taken the liberty of changing the authors' notation when reviewing the relevant literature.

10 The model presented in this section is based on Program II in McGuire, T.G. (2000) Physician Agency. In: *The Handbook of Health Economics*, Vol. 1, Culyer, A.J., Newhouse, J.P. (Eds.), Elsevier Science B.V., Amsterdam, pp. 461–538.

11 The above argument relies on the assumption that patients cannot resell physician services to other patients. Given that physician services are heterogeneous, diagnostic specific and by nature inherently non-tradeable, such an assumption is both reasonable and realistic [Gaynor, M. (1994). Issues in the industrial organization of the market for physician services. *Journal of Economics and Management Strategies*, **39**, 211–255).]

12 Evans, R.G. (1974) Supplier-induced demand: some empirical evidence and implications. In: *The Economics of Health and Medical Care*, Perlman, M. (Ed.), MacMillan, London, pp. 162–173.

13 Stano, M. (1987) A further analysis of the physician inducement controversy. *Journal of Health Economics* **6**, 229–238.

14 Rochaix, L. (1989) Information asymmetry and search in the market for physician services. *Journal of Health Economics*, **8**, 53–84.

15 Increased competition between providers will also increase the patient's threat of leaving for an outside physician, thus tempering some of the physician's ability to induce demand.

16 Gruber, J., Owings, M. (1996) Physician financial incentives and Cesarean section delivery. *Rand Journal of Economics*, **27**, 99–123.

17 Yip, W. (1998) Physician responses to medical fee reductions: changes in volume and intensity of supply of Coronary Artery Bypass Graft (CABG) surgeries in the medicare and private sector. *Journal of Health Economics*, **7**, 675–700.

18 Auld, M.C., Emery, J.C.H., Lu, M. (1999) Paying for Physician Services in Canada, University of Calgary (unpublished manuscript).

19 Frank, P., Clancy C.M. (1997) Referrals of Adult Patients from Primary Care: Demographic Disparities and their Relationship to HMO Insurance. *Journal of Family Practice*, **45**, 45–53, report that 4.5% of all visits to primary care in the US resulted in a referral to specialty or hospital care.

20 Blomqvist, Å., Léger P.T. (2005) Information Asymmetry, Insurance and the Decision to Hospitalize. *Journal of Health Economics*, **24**, 775–793.

21 Grembowski, D.E., Cook K., Patrick D.L., Roussel, A.E. (1998) Managed Care and Physician Referral. *Medical Care Research and Review*, **55**, 3–31.

22 Allard, M., Jelovac, I., Léger, P.T. (2007) Physician Payment Mechanisms: Dynamics, Diagnostic Ability and Altruism, HEC Montréal (unpublished working paper).

23 Feldstein, P.J. (2004) *Health Care Economics*, 6th edition, Thomson Delmar Learning, p. 221.

24 For a specific discussion about the link between physician payment mechanisms and technology adoption, see Selder A. (2005) Physician reimbursement and technology adoption. *Journal of Health Economics*, **24**, 907–930.

25 See Chapter on *Risk Adjustment* by Ellis (in this book) for a complete review of the theoretical and empirical literature on how fees are (should be) calculated and set in such an environment.

26 Selden, T.M. (1990) A Model of Capitation. *Journal of Health Economics*, **9**, 397–409.

27 A more comprehensive form of capitation payment system was introduced in the UK and was known as the fund-holding system. In this system, a partnership of physicians received a fund for each patient they enlisted into their practice. In return, the partners were responsible for four types of expenditure: (i) staff employed by the partnership; (ii) prescription drugs; (iii) many types of outpatient care, and (iv) inpatient care for many types of procedure [see Crump, B.J., Cubbon, J.E., Drummond, M.F., Hawkes, R.A., and Marchment, M.D. (1991) Fundholding in general practice and financial risk. *British Medical Journal*, **302**, 1582–1584, for a more comprehensive description of the fundholding system]. Croxson, B., Propper, C., and Perkins, A. (2001) Do doctors respond to financial incentives? UK family doctors and the GP fundholder scheme. *Journal of Public Economics*, **79**, 375–398, estimate the effects of the introduction of the fundholding system on physician behavior and show, controlling for the fact that participation in the fundholding system by physicians was voluntary, that fundholders responded to financial incentives (by altering their admission behavior).

28 Health Maintenance Organizations (HMO) often use group-based incentives where a group of physicians share a bonus when total expenditures fall below some predetermined level [see Gaynor, M., Rebitzer, J.B., and Taylor, L.J. (2004) Physician Incentives in Health Maintenance Organizations. *Journal of Political Economy*, **112**, 915–931 for a recent article on the topic).

29 Another payment mechanism which is not covered in this chapter, but that may also lead to the underprovision of care, is salary. Salaried physicians may face little incentives to see many patients or to schedule more visits [Hickson, G.B., Altemeier, W.A., and Perrin, J.M. (1987) Physician Reimbursement by Salary or Fee-for-Service: Effect on Physician Practice Behavior in a Randomized Prospective Study. *Pediatrics*, **80**, 344–350]. They may also have too great an incentive to refer patients to specialty care.

30 Alternatively, one could also interpret Eq. (9) as the physician's utility function, where q includes the physician's time and effort and c denotes the per-unit cost (in monetary terms) of time and effort.

31 One can think of this effect as being similar to the supplier-induced demand effect discussed above, but where the physician attempts to shift the patient's demand curve for healthcare services inwards instead of outwards.

32 In such an environment, the patient might recognize his/her physician's strategy as being (partially) invariant to his/her true illness severity. Thus, the physician's recommendation of care is likely to be suspect. Although deriving an optimal insurance policy is not the goal of this section, it would be characterized by a specific reimbursement amount (i.e., a given amount of money to be transferred from the insurance provider to the patient) that would be transferred to the patient upon illness *but* would not depend on the patient's illness severity or treatment received. [Blomqvist, Å. (1991), The doctor as double agent: Information asymmetry, health insurance, and medical care. *Journal of Health Economics*, **10**, 411–422].

33 Hillman, A.L., Pauly, M.V., Kerstein, J.J. (1989) How to financial incentives affect physicians' clinical decisions and the financial performance of health maintenance organizations? *New England Journal of Medicine*, **321**, 86–92.

34 Manning, W.G., Newhouse, J.P., Duan, N., Keeler, E.B., Leibowitz, A. (1987) Health insurance and the demand for medical care: evidence from a randomized experiment. *American Economic Review*, **77**, 251–274.

35 Luft, H. (1981) *Health Maintenance Organizations: Dimensions of Performance*, Wiley, New York.

36 Siu, A. (1988) Use of the hospital in a randomized trial of prepaid care. *Journal of the American Medical Association*, **259**, 1343–1346.

37 Several papers have examined the effect of capitation payments on treatment costs and patient outcomes for mental health patients. Although some evidence suggests that capitated patients utilized less inpatient services [Warner, J.P., King, M., Blizard, R., McClenahan, Z., and Tang, S. (2000) Patient-held shared care records for individuals with mental illness: Randomized controlled evaluation. *British Journal of Psychiatry*, **177**, 319–324]), the effect of capitation on quality of care is unclear [Chandler, D., Hu, T., Meisel, M., McGowen, M., and Madison, K. (1997) Mental health costs, other public costs, and family burden among mental health clients in capitated integrated service agencies. *Journal of Mental Health Administration*, **24**, 178–188].

38 Another important factor which may limit the underprovision of care in a supply-side cost-sharing environment setting is physician competition. This issue is discussed in greater detail in Section 7.5.

39 Blomqvist (1991) considers an alternative specification where the physician is a double agent – that is, they weigh the benefits to their patients with the revenues of their hospital/health care organization (see [32] for the complete citation).

40 Physicians may also be limited in their ability to underprovide care if manipulating information concerning the patient's illness severity is costly in terms of effort (i.e., the ability for the physician to shift the patient's demand curve inwards is costly).

41 Ellwood, P.M., Paul, B.A. (1986) Commentary: But what about quality? *Inquiry*, Spring, 135–140.

42 Davis, K., Rolland, D. (1990) *Health Care Cost Containment*, Johns Hopkins University Press, Baltimore.

43 Gold, M., Hurley, R., Lake, T., Ensor, T., Berenson, R. (1995) A national survey of the arrangements managed-care plans make with physicians. *New England Journal of Medicine*, **333**, 1678–1683.

44 Gold, M., United States Physician Payment Review Commission, Mathematica Policy Research Inc., and Medical College of Virginia (1995) *Arrangements between managed care plans and physicians: results from a 1994 survey of managed care plans*, Selected External Research Series 3, Physician Payment Review Commission, Washington D.C.

45 Under fee-for-service, physicians do not have any incentive to under-provide care. As a result, medical malpractice is associated with negligent care, not with strategic behavior.

46 Danzon, P.M. (1990) *Medical malpractice: theory, evidence and public policy*, Harvard University Press, Cambridge, MA.

47 Léger, P.T. (2000) Quality Control Mechanisms under Capitation Payment for Medical Services. *Canadian Journal of Economics*, **33**, 564–588.

48 For a more detailed discussion of patient selection, see Van de Ven, W. P. M. M., Ellis, R.P. (2000) Risk Adjustment in Competitive Health Plan Markets. In: *The Handbook of Health Economics*, 34 Vol. **1**, Culyer, A. J., Newhouse, J. P. (Eds.), Elsevier Science B.V., Amsterdam.

49 Ellis, R.P. (1998) Creaming, Skimping and Dumping: Provider Competition on the Intensive and Extensive Margins. *Journal of Health Economics*, **17**, 537–555.

50 See Dafny, L.S. (2005) How Do Hospitals Respond to Price Changes? *American Economic Review*, **95**, 1525–1547, for a recent article on the subject.

51 As noted previously, physicians in the UK fundholding received a budget for each patient they enlisted into their practice. In return, physicians were responsible for many types of medical expenditures, including specialty care and some hospital care. In a setting such as this, physicians are likely to under-refer to costly specialty or hospital care. This is consistent with empirical findings which suggest that gatekeepers who face financial-risks when they refer are less likely to do so

[Hurley, R.E., Freund, D.A., Gage, B.J. (1991) Gatekeeping Effects on Patters of Physician Use. *Journal of Family Practice*, **32**, 164–170; Gravelle, H., Dusheiko, M., Sutton, M. (2002) The demand for elective surgery in a public system: time and money prices in the UK National Health Service. *Journal of Health Economics*, **21**, 423–449].

52 A more complete form of physician altruism could include the patient's entire utility, and not just his/her health, and would be given by: $V(\pi, h)$ $\delta(R + Fq - cq) + (1 - \delta)U(X, h(\theta, q))$. If patients are fully insured, both forms are equivalent as the patient's consumption of other goods is constant and is independent of his/her medical-care consumption.

53 McGuire, T.G. (2006) *Physician Fees and Behavior: Implications for Structuring a Fee Schedule*, Department of Health Care Policy, Harvard Medical School (unpublished manuscript).

54 A similar argument can be made to limit supplier-induced demand and moral hazard (see McGuire (2006) [53] for a more complete discussion).

55 Ma, C-t. A., McGuire, T.G. (1997), Optimal Health Insurance and Provider Payment. *American Economic Review*, **87**, 685–704.

56 Ma and McGuire (1997) also examine the effect of medical ethics and competition (see [55] for the complete citation).

57 Allard, M., Léger, P.T., Rochaix, L. (2006) Provider Behaviour under Competition, HEC Montréal (unpublished manuscript).

58 Ma and McGuire (1997) (see [55] for the complete citation) also examine competition between providers in a mixed-payment system, but where physician effort is observable prior to the patient's quantity decision. Unlike Allard, Léger and Rochaix (see [57] for full citation), the patient's outside option is not endogenously determined.

59 Defensive medicine is generally used in a context where physicians over-provide care in order to protect themselves against unfair medical malpractice litigation. In this set-up, physicians over-provide care in order to protect against adverse patient health-outcomes (resulting from uncertainty in the treatment–outcome relationship) which could result in a patient seeking care elsewhere.

60 Although not covered in this chapter, mixed-payment systems may also help balance incentives for quality across different services when the desired outcomes for some tasks are more easily observed than for others [Eggleston, K. (2005) Multitasking and mixed systems for provider payment. *Journal of Health Economics*, **24**, 211–223].

62 Bernard, F., Jacquemet, N., Shearer, B. (2006) Compensation, Incentives and the Practice Patterns of Physicians: Theory and Evidence from Micro-data, Université Laval (unpublished manuscript).

8
Risk Adjustment in Health Care Markets:
Concepts and Applications
Randall P. Ellis

8.1
Overview

This chapter summarizes the recent literature on risk adjustment, synthesizing the theoretical and empirical literatures, and emphasizing areas of current research and policy interest. The chapter relates optimal risk adjustment to the previous theory and empirical work. The section describing empirical estimation covers the choice of an objective function, the different types of information that can be used, conceptual issues, estimation, and validation. The chapter concludes with a detailed discussion of risk adjustment applications in Canada, the US, Netherlands, and Germany.

8.2
Introduction

This chapter provides an overview of the theory and practice of risk-adjustment models for health care systems. After first defining risk adjustment and discussing its importance, the theory, empirical estimation, and international applications of risk adjustment are described. In the theoretical section, an attempt is made to motivate why risk adjustment is important, and to clarify the links between the theoretical and empirical risk adjustment literatures. In the empirical section, the different information sets that can be used for risk adjustment are first summarized, after which details are provided of how risk-adjustment formulas are estimated and used to predict health care spending. In the international applications section, some examples are provided of how risk-adjustment models are used worldwide in practice, and both the opportunities and limitations of risk adjustment identified.

Financing Health Care: New Ideas for a Changing Society. Edited by Mingshan Lu and Egon Jonsson
Copyright © 2008 WILEY-VCH Verlag GmbH & Co. KGaA, Weinheim
ISBN: 978-3-527-32027-1

8.2.1
What is Risk Adjustment?

Within this chapter, *risk adjustment* is broadly defined to mean "the use of patient-level information to explain variation in health care spending, resource utilization, and health outcomes over a fixed interval of time, such as a year." This definition focuses on what are often called "population-based models", which is to say the utilization of services by an individual rather than a group. Episode-based predictive models and models using grouped data are not considered here.

There is considerable diversity in the literature about what is meant by risk adjustment. In their review, van de Ven and Ellis [1] focus on using risk adjustment to pay competitive health plans, and define the term *risk adjustment* narrowly to mean "...the use of information to calculate the expected health expenditures of individual consumers over a fixed interval of time (e.g., a month, quarter, or year)." Glazer and McGuire [2, 3] define risk adjustment as paying a provider a price "...conditioned on observable characteristics of the enrollee or patient." According to the classic book on risk adjustment, written by the US physician Lisa Iezzoni, the terms "risk adjustment" and "severity adjustment" can be used interchangeably, although risk adjustment is more commonly used. In the health services research literature, the terms "case mix adjustment" is often used instead [4]. Among economists, "risk adjustment" is often – but not always – limited to uses for payment: the creation of formulas to be used for capitation payment. Risk-adjustment models used for payment purposes, have also been referred to as "health-based payment" [5, 6]. In Europe and Canada, the terminology "needs-based payment" is often used [7, 8]. Health-based payment is but one application of how explicit risk-adjustment formulas can be used. In recent years the terminology "predictive modeling" has come to be used in the US for models designed for predicting health care utilization without regard to whether the predictive model will be used for payment.

The different terminology that has been used to talk about risk adjustment, primarily from a US perspective, is organized in Fig. 8.1 The terminology "predictive modeling" is broader, and includes case identification models used to identify

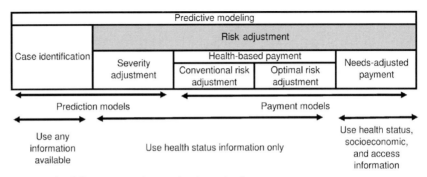

Fig. 8.1 The different terminologies related to risk adjustment.

high-cost cases without any regard to incentives. For this purpose almost any information available can be used, including other endogenous variables such as lagged spending or use of procedures information.

In the risk adjustment literature, two different questions are often asked:

1. What is the predicted resource use for individual XYZ? Having a good prediction model to answer this question can be useful for many reasons, and an abundant literature has developed classification systems and estimation methods that attempt to answer this question well.
2. What is the best payment formula to use for capitated payments for individual XYZ? Answering this question is a recent literature on optimal risk adjustment [2]; this chapter discusses models useful for answering both types of question: risk adjustment prediction models and risk adjustment payment models.

The different terminology is also related to the information used for prediction and payment. As elaborated upon by van de Ven and Ellis [1], there are many different types of information that can be used to predict health care service utilization. Variation in health care use can be decomposed both conceptually and empirically into variation due to patient characteristics, provider characteristics (e.g., specialists, general practitioners, hospitals, nurses), and the nature of the services actually provided (such as their pricing, intensity and duration). Depending on the purpose, all of this information may be useful for prediction. Patient characteristics can be further decomposed into variations due to the underlying health status of the patient, socioeconomic variables (such as income and education), enabling information (such as benefit design and geographic location that affect access and utilization), and patient tastes. The best set of information to use depends upon the intended use. Health-based payment models and severity adjustment models restrict the information set to only use health status. Needs-adjusted payment, which is widely used in Europe, broadens the information to reflect further demographic variables such as income, race, geography, and access (e.g., distance). The choice of information may also affect the desired empirical specification to be used.

8.2.2
How are Health Risk-adjustment Models Used?

Economists tend to focus on the uses of risk-adjustment models for purposes of payment, whereas the majority of use in practice is for other purposes. Risk-adjustment models are used in the US commercial sector for measuring quality, case management, disease management, high-cost case identification, underwriting, plan selection by employers, and provider profiling. The answer to the question: "How many resources is person XYZ expected to use next year?" is valuable for all of these uses. One way of documenting how risk adjustment is used in practice is to quantify its use on the web. A web search using Google on September 6th, 2006, found the 259 000 hits on "risk adjustment" + "health". Of these, the word

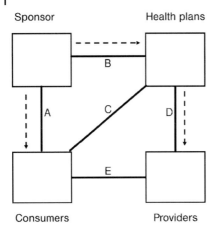

Fig. 8.2 Four agents, five primary contracting relationships (A–E), and three possible uses of risk-adjusted payments.

"payment" appeared in 45% of the web sites, while the word "quality" appeared in 73%. More than half of the health risk adjustment web sites mention "quality" without mention of the word "payment". This highlights that risk-adjustment predictive models are increasingly being used extensively for many diverse purposes. Thomas et al. [9] provides a useful review of different models.

There are many ways in which risk-adjustment models can be used for payment. In Fig. 8.2, an organizational framework from van de Ven and Ellis [1] is used to consider the relationships between the various agents in health care markets. There are four primary contracting agents in each health care system: consumers; providers; sponsors; and health plans. The solid lines in Fig. 8.2 reflect five possible contractual relationships among these agents. Consumers and providers are well-known participants in health care markets. *Consumers* receive health care services, choose providers and service quantities, and collectively contribute toward the cost of health care. Consumers generally contract with at least one sponsor, and may or may not contract directly with health plans. *Providers* provide the actual health services and accept payments from health plans. They contract with consumers and health plans.

A *sponsor* plays the critical role of accepting contributions from each consumer that may not be equal to their expected cost of health care. The sponsor makes payments to a health plan that need not be equal to the contribution by a given individual. As such, the sponsor plays the extremely important role of redistributing the burdens of premium contributions by consumers, generally subsidizing high-risk and low-income consumers by low-risk and high-income consumers.

The *health plan* also plays an important role. This is an intermediary that takes payments from the sponsor or from consumers, and pays providers. Any agent contracting with providers for services can be considered a health plan, and if the sponsor pays providers directly, then it has merged the role of sponsor and health plan. Health plans need not bear any financial risk. In the US, they may be simple financial intermediaries who transfer risk back to the sponsor.

Risk-adjustment payment models can potentially be used for each of the five contracting relationships shown in Fig. 8.1. The primary use in many countries is on payments from sponsor to health plans. This is commonly called capitation payment, as payments by the sponsor are calculated on a per capita (per person) basis. For example, in Germany, Netherlands and the US Medicare program, risk-adjustment payment models are used to calculate payments by public or quasi-public organizations to health plans. In relatively few settings in the US, a single employer makes capitated payments to multiple health plans [10, 11].

Risk adjustment can also be used for other contractual relationships. In the US, risk-adjusted payments are often made by a health plan to networks of providers, such as hospital or primary care networks. In the UK and the Netherlands, primary care doctors receive capitated payments for broad sets of out-patient services. Risk adjustment also plays a key role in most "pay for performance" programs, which are discussed briefly below in the review of US experience.

As van de Ven and Ellis [1] highlight, fees, risk-sharing and other non-capitated payments are often used in combination with risk-adjusted capitation. For example, capitation payments may be calculated for only the facility-based spending by a government, or primary care providers may share the risk that costs are higher or lower than the capitated amounts. Although such partially capitated models are discussed briefly below in the empirical section, following the literature, the theoretical discussion focuses on pure capitation models.

8.3
Theory

In recent years there has been a burgeoning of theoretical analyses of risk-adjustment payment model incentives. This section does not attempt to provide an exhaustive review of that literature, but rather provides a conceptual overview of some of the key issues that have been studied, and the insights from that work. Attention is focused here on the particular issues of perfect versus imperfect information, imperfect signals available to the regulator, the incentive problems that health based-payments are intended to correct, and the strategic responses to risk-adjusted payments.

In this section a simplified framework is employed which uses primarily a graphical approach. Focus is centered on the case where there are only two states of the world, two types of health care goods, two types of consumer, and two possible signals about consumer types. Following the recent literature, it is assumed that the only information that is *contractible* – and hence usable for paying capitated health plans – are the signals about consumer types. Realized states of the world, actual levels of spending on each type, and true patient types are not observable to the payer. Even if they are observable to all agents, including the sponsor, they may nonetheless not be contractible.

It is assumed that consumers can find themselves in one of only two possible states of the world; for concreteness, these are called "healthy" and "diabetic". Healthy consumers use only general practitioner (GP) services and cost α per year, whereas diabetic consumers use both GP and specialists services (SP), and cost $\alpha + \beta$ per year. Hence, α is the annual cost of healthy consumers under a given set of incentives, while β is the incremental cost of diabetes. Using the terminology of Glazer and McGuire [12], GPs would be the acute care service, while specialists would be the chronic care service used more intensively by high-risk types. In the terminology of Jack [13], GPs would be "regular care", while specialists would be "acute care." The key assumption is that one service (here called specialist care) is used more intensively by high-risk types than the other service (GPs).

It may also be assumed there are only two types of consumer, called "low-risk" and "high-risk". Initially, focus is centered on the simple case where low-risk types are always healthy and high-risk types are always diabetic. While it is true that there is no uncertainty (risk) in this polar case, it is still convenient to think of each type as potentially having a distribution across different states of the world. A richer model, as in Glazer and McGuire ([12], henceforth GM), has both high- and low-risk types having some non-zero probabilities of being diabetic and healthy, but the simple model developed here captures the essential features needed for talking about risk adjustment. Most of the useful insights arise due to imperfect signals about patient types rather than due to uncertainty about how consumer types are related to which state of the world consumers find themselves in. For pedantic simplicity, it is also convenient to assume that both types are equally common in the population, thereby saving another parameter.

This situation is shown in Fig. 8.3, where healthy (low-risk) consumers consume at point A using only GP services, and diabetic consumers (high-risk) consume at point B. Later, it becomes significant when the assumption is made that diabetics use more of both GP and SP, and not only SP. Note that, so far, it is only the variation in consumer health status that drives the variation in demand for different types of care. Differences in tastes and income may also affect the utility of different states of the world, and hence the use of health care services. Various reports have considered models where patients differ not only in health status but also in taste parameters [12–14].

The optimal risk-adjustment formula to use depends on the objective function of the sponsor, as well as the cost structure, competition, health plan and consumer objective functions, the information (signals) available to sponsor, consumers, and health plans, and the strategic behavior allowed by the health plans. The next section begins by considering the polar cases, where signals are either totally uninformative or perfectly informative about consumer type. Initially, health plans are assumed not to have any strategic behavior possible. Later, imperfect signals are introduced and different forms of strategic behavior allowed.

Throughout this section, an assumption is needed about the health plan's objective function. Although a more general framework might have the health plan caring about both patient benefits and profits [15], in a static model the conceptually

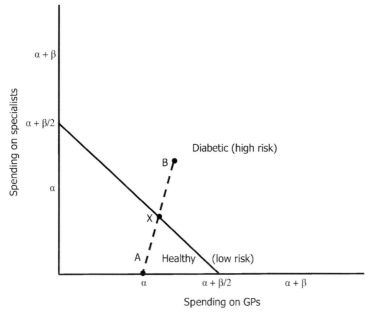

Fig. 8.3 No risk adjustment when quantities of each service supplied are exogenous. The health plan is reimbursed by the simple average cost. The average services provided at X are for the entire population.

straightforward assumption is that health plans maximize profits, or what is also known as "net revenue".

The objective function of the sponsor is initially assumed to be very simple. The sponsor wishes to simply pay each health plan the expected value of each signal for each consumer, which is what is GM have termed *conventional risk adjustment* [12]. GM and others may note that this is a naïve and inferior objective function for the sponsor, but it is nonetheless the most common one. As this objective and the implied behavior assumption about the sponsor are central to many empirical models of risk adjustment, it is also an important one to start with.

8.3.1
No Risk-Adjustment Signals

The simplest case is one in which the GP and SP services provided to each type of consumer are exogenous to (independent of) payments and information, and there are no signals about consumer type available. If quantities of care offered are unaffected by capitation payments, then it does not matter whether consumer types are observable or unobservable by the health plan or consumers at the time that plan enrollment decisions are made. Under pure capitation, health plan budgets are set prospectively and will equal the expected amount of $R = \alpha + \beta/2$ per person, where this formula reflects the equal prevalence in the population of high- and low-risk types.

This no-risk-adjustment situation is shown in Fig. 8.3, where X is the average quantity of services consumed. As long as the proportion of high-risk types enrolling in the plan is no greater than the population average, then the plan can at least break even by subsidizing the losses on high-cost types with the savings on the low-cost types. Economists would point out that X is not incentive-compatible for all possible plans: plans will not want to participate if they have a higher proportion of diabetics than the population average used for payment. Accommodating such plans creates the desire for risk adjustment by the sponsor.

Of course a profit-maximizing health plan would prefer not to have to enroll high risks. Under the stated assumptions, plans do not have any tools available for avoiding diabetics, as no information is available *ex ante*. With no risk adjustment, health plans are forced to carry out the key role of redistributing funds from low- to high-risk consumers. Shen and Ellis [16] explore how a profit-oriented health plan would prefer to exclude high-risk types based on observable signals, but they assume that plans can perfectly select which consumers to avoid or "dump." Almost all countries and markets prohibit explicit dumping of high-risk consumers. Settings where the exclusion (dumping) of high-risk types is allowed include the individual and small employer markets in the US, commercial health plans in Chile, Columbia, and India, and supplementary health insurance policies in many countries.

8.3.2
Perfect Signals

It may now be assumed that health status signals S are costlessly available to all agents (consumers, health plans and sponsors) at the beginning of each period, and that these signals are informative about each patient's risk type. In the simplest case there are only two possible signals, so that S takes on values of either 0 or 1. It is assumed initially that the signal S is perfectly informative, so that a value of 1 (0) perfectly classifies a consumer as a high- (low-) risk type. This is often called "perfect information".

With perfect information by all agents, the sponsor wishing to pay health plans the expected cost will pay a risk-adjusted payment of $R_i = \alpha + \beta S_i$ for each consumer i. Since signals are perfect, then the implied payment parameters are $R_1 = \alpha$ and $R_2 = \alpha + \beta$. This is the conventional risk-adjustment solution, calculating α and β so as to just pay the average cost of each signal. Even if health plans (or regions) vary in the proportions of high- and low-risk types, payments will equal costs. Since profits on each type of consumer are zero, a health plan should be just indifferent to enrolling consumers who have low- or high-risk signals. Conventional risk adjustment with perfect information and solves the objective of eliminating the incentive problem facing profit maximizing health plans to selectively avoid or "dump" unprofitable consumers when the signals used are the only information known to health plans, and costs of treating patients are exogenous.

The large literature on the calculation of conventional risk-adjustment formulas, including the US Medicare and the Dutch risk-adjustment payment formulas, are calculated while implicitly using assumptions similar to those used here. It is straightforward to calculate the α and β parameters empirically using a regression approach. Recent theoretical research has greatly expanded the understanding of risk-adjustment incentives and possible corrections to it. The following sections highlight various extensions involving imperfect signals, provider distortions of services available, and heterogeneous tastes.

8.3.3
Exogenous Imperfect Signals, Exogenous Service Quantities

The above model assumes that the signals are perfectly informative: once the signal is observed, then the true type of each consumer is known and perfect risk adjustment is feasible. Unfortunately, the norm is that signals are highly imperfect. Empirical studies repeatedly find that, even for serious chronic conditions such as AIDS, diabetes, multiple sclerosis and quadriplegia, less than 75% of consumers with these diagnoses coded in one year have the same information coded the following year [17, 18]. Even signals of serious illness are highly imperfect.

There are two broad possibilities for why signals are imperfect. Signals may exogenously misrepresent true patient risk types, or signals may be endogenously (intentionally) chosen by the health plan or providers so as to influence payments. GM [12] examined the concept of exogenous imperfect risk-adjustment signals. In expanding the notation of this chapter, suppose that proportion γ_i of type i consumers have a signal $S = 1$. In order for the signal to be informative, we need proportion $0 \leq \gamma_L < \gamma_H \leq 1$. The polar case $\gamma_L = 0$ and $\gamma_H = 1$ corresponds to the perfect information case just considered. Empirically, it is widely found that some low-risk types have a false positive signal $(0 < \gamma_L)$, and many high-risk types have false negative signals $(\gamma_H < 1)$. This means that those with a signal $S = 1$ will contain both H and L types, and the average cost of those with $S = 1$ will be less than $\alpha + \beta$. As shown in Fig. 8.4, starting from the point X where no information is available, improving risk-adjustment signals will better differentiate between low- and high-risk types, reducing the calculated payment for healthy signals $(S = 0)$ toward α and increasing the calculated payment for $S = 1$ toward β. Under these assumptions, the proportion of a plan with high-risk signal $S = 1$ would be $(\gamma_H + \gamma_L)/2$, the average cost of those signal $S = 1$ would be $R_1 = \alpha + \beta$ $\gamma_H/(\gamma_L + \gamma_H)$, while the average cost of signal $S = 0$ would be $R_0 = \alpha + \beta (1 - \gamma_H)/(2 - \gamma_{L-}\gamma_H)$, which yields the correct weighted average of low- and high-cost types.

Imperfect risk-adjustment signals create problems for conventional risk adjustment, and three types of problem have been emphasized in the literature. One common complaint of managed-care plans is that their decentralized information

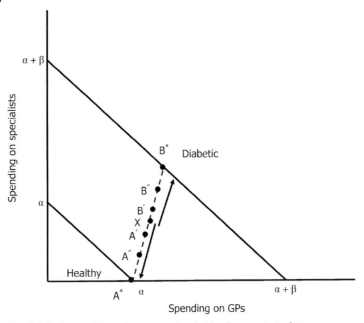

Fig. 8.4 Perfect and imperfect conventional risk adjustment. Perfect risk adjustment (A*, B*) is just the limiting case of improving information (X → A′ → A″ → A* for low-risk types and X → B′ → B″ → B*) so that payments by the sponsor for each type more closely match costs.

systems mean that they have fewer high-risk signals (i.e., more false negatives) than traditional health plans. Newhouse [15] discusses the profitability of selection by health plans when they have only a small amount of private information, and finds that profits are highly non-linear, with a small quantity of private information being very profitable [15]. Both, GM [12] and Frank, Glazer and McGuire [19] highlight how imperfect signals, in combination with strategic behavior, create significant distortions in health services; this point is highlighted after considering endogenous risk-adjustment signals.

8.3.4
Endogenous Risk-Adjustment Signals, Exogenous Service Quantities

Among actuaries and policy makers, one of the great concerns with implementing risk adjustment is over the problem of endogenous signals, which is to say that the information used to make payments is influenced by the payment formulas themselves (e.g., Ref. [20]). For example, following the introduction of diagnosis-related groups (DRGs) in the US, there is convincing evidence of a meaningful increase in the apparent coded severity of hospitalized patients due to the new incentives which raised Medicare payments by a few percentage points. Similar concerns arise with the policy implementation of risk-adjusted payments. The pattern of information used for calibrating the models may differ from the pattern that will arise after risk-adjusted payments are introduced. Concern over this endogeneity has been a major force in the US in its choice of risk adjusters for its Medicare program. (See, for example, Ref. [21], p. 56 for a discussion of Medicare's adoption of the Principal Inpatient Diagnostic Cost Group (PIPDCG) model.) This concern was a major factor in the Medicare program's choice of payment formulas that intentionally ignored diagnoses predictive of lower cost conditions.

In terms of the simplified model used here, endogenous signals would mean that health plans would wish to increase the proportion of high-risk types $\gamma'_L > \gamma_L$ and $\gamma'_H > \gamma_H$ reported beyond the levels used to calibrate the models, γ_L and γ_H. The reported proportion of high-risk enrollees has increased, and there will be an overpayment to the health plans until payments are recalibrated. Such recalibration to accommodate coding prevalence changes is what took place with DRGs during the late 1980s, and in 2006 the Medicare program expanded to use diagnoses from all encounters.

Concern about endogenous signal changes in response to the US Medicare capitation formula in 2004 was the principal reason why Medicare implemented a "fee-for-service (FFS) correction" factor in the original payment formula. This adjustment factor remained at 5% for three years, but was reduced to 2.9% for 2007, suggesting that the impact was relatively transitory and modest [22].

8.3.5
Health Plan Response to Capitation Payments: Proportional Adjustment

It is a widely held belief that the quantities and qualities of health care services will respond to payment incentives. Ellis and McGuire [23] model partially altruistic providers as responding to lump sum payment incentives by reducing the quantities of care relative to fee-based services. Newhouse [15] extended this discussion to health plan behavior in response to capitated payments. The classic supply-side response to capitation would be a reduction in spending on all types of service. This possibility is shown in Fig. 8.5, where spending on both diabetics and healthy types is reduced in response to moving from fees to capitated payments. As the quantities of services are no longer exogenous, distinction can be made between the initial fee-based quantities (A^0, B^0) from the capitation-induced quantities (A^1, B^1). Costs parameters for each type also change, from (α^0, β^0) to (α^1, β^1).

There is a significant empirical literature that has worried about estimating this plan-level change in spending in response to capitation incentives, building on the approach of Lee [24]. Recent studies by Terza [25] in this area, using non-parametric techniques, have further extended this approach. The hallmark of the method has been to model total health spending, allowing for a uniform proportional or absolute reduction in spending in response to capitation incentives. Empirical plan selection models that estimate how total health care spending differs between managed care, indemnity and other types of health plan work on the assumption of a simple proportional or additive adjustment to total costs. It is not uncommon to calculate the cost savings of health maintenance organizations (HMOs) or other

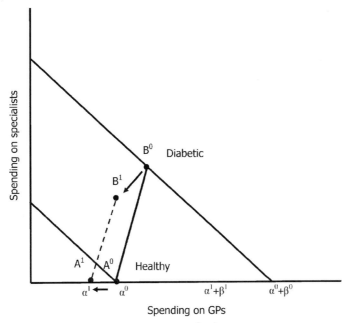

Fig. 8.5 Capitated quantities of services (A^1, B^1) will differ from quantities offered under Fee-For-Service (A^0, B^0) due to supply-side moral hazard. A simple selection model might have all spending reduced by the same percentage amount. Conventional risk adjustment will yield correct payments if capitated quantities are used.

plan types with an additive constant in either a linear or loglinear model. This corresponds to assuming that all costs are adjusted additively or proportionally for all types of consumers. (For a discussion of such results for managed care, see Ref. [26].)

If health plans respond to capitation incentives by reducing spending on all types of services uniformly, then this does not create particular problems for risk adjustment. A uniform reduction can be accommodated by reducing the payment parameters (α, β) proportionally. This type of correction is reflected in the US Medicare adjustments to the AAPCC during the 1980s and 1990, where payments were reduced by 5% to accommodate expected response by capitated health plans [22].

8.3.6
Strategic Response by Health Plans to Capitation Payments

Glazer and McGuire [12] highlight that health plans can behave strategically in how generously they provide each type of specific health care service. Regulators may be able to prohibit the dumping of unprofitable consumers, but they cannot easily prevent health plans and providers from increasing or decreasing the availabilities

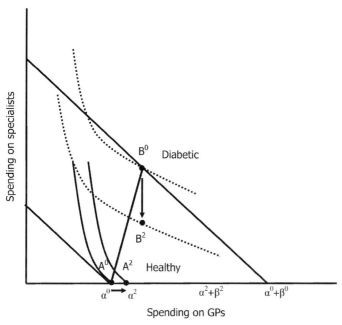

Fig. 8.6 Conventional risk adjustment with quantities of services offered strategically determined. Unless true types are observable, imperfect signals will tend to cause health plans to oversupply GP services attractive to the healthy (supplying A^2 rather than A^0), while un-
dersupplying specialist services (B^2 versus B^0) used by diabetics.

of certain specialists or types of service. If certain types of consumer are unprofitable
because risk adjustment is imperfect, then health plans have an incentive to avoid
enrolling or treating these consumers by reducing the provision of the health
care services that are most attractive to them. In the present model, rather than
reducing spending on all types of service proportionally, the health plans will have
an incentive to reduce spending on SP because it is used more heavily by high-risk
types. At the same time, plans will have an incentive to compete to attract low-
risk types, by oversupplying GP services to the healthy. This process may, or may
not, result in an increase in GP services being made available to high-risk types,
depending on whether the health plan is able to differentiate the services offered
to the two observable types. This subtle issue underlies a key difference between
the studies of GM [12] and Ma [27]. GM assume that, even though plans know the
signal of a consumer, they are not able to differentiate the quantity of services (GP
and SP) offered to a given signal type. Hence, GM assume plans cannot offer GP
services more generously to the $S = 0$ than the $S = 1$ consumers, while Ma assumes
that they can. This leads to different conclusions about plan rationing and optimal
payments.

Three new insights follow from the GM framework. The first insight is that each
consumer type can be thought of as having a set of indifference curves between

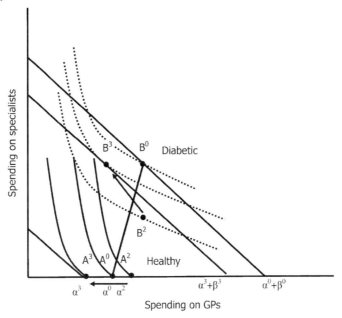

Fig. 8.7 Optimal risk adjustment with quantities of services strategically determined. By increasing the payments for diabetics to β^3, which enables B^3 rather than B^2, and reducing the payment for healthy consumers to enable only A^3, health plans can be made indifferent to enrolling healthy or diabetic consumers and induced to provide efficient services to both types.

GP and SP services. For a given level of spending, there will be some optimal combination of GP and SP services that maximizes consumer utility, and those quantities of good will differ by consumer type. It is natural to ask in this framework whether the amounts offered are the utility maximizing quantities under different payment formulas. Indifference curves are shown in Fig. 8.7, illustrating that the initial allocation at B^0 need not be welfare-maximizing for high-risk types: there is no particular force under FFS reimbursement ensuring that quantities provided are efficient. Indeed it is known that, in general, fully insured patients will tend to receive too much treatment of both services.

A second insight is that if risk adjustment is perfect, then capitated health plans will compete by offering services to each type where welfare is maximized. (This result is not shown graphically.) With complete information, health plans will wish to maximize consumer welfare for the same reasons that competitive firms do so. As long as health plans are indifferent between enrolling a given consumer, then they will try to do the best thing by them.

The third insight of GM is that if signals are imperfect, then health plans will distort quantities in an inefficient way. As shown in Fig. 8.7, the quantities of SP will be greatly reduced (to point B^2), to deter high-risk types, while quantities of GP will tend to be increased (to A^2) in an attempt to attract the low-risk types. Note the key role of consumer choice; because consumers can be attracted to a better set of services offerings, then health plans will compete in this dimension. If payment formulas are recalibrated using the new service quantities, then conventional risk-adjustment formulas will validate the results of this form of health plan competition by reducing payments for $S = 1$ signals, and increasing them for $S = 0$ signals, confirming the service intensity choices of the health plans. Alternatively, if the conventional risk-adjustment formula continues to be based on a distinct FFS sample, as is true for the US Medicare program, then the formula may misrepresent the costs of both types when they are enrolled in the capitated plans. Even though the sponsor is breaking even conditional on the signals, they are not maximizing consumer welfare.

8.3.7
Optimal Risk Adjustment

In order to solve this service distortion, GM broadens the sponsor's objective function. They introduce the concept of "optimal risk adjustment" in which the sponsor's goal is to maximize consumer welfare rather than to just break even. Instead of restricting the sponsor to consider only unbiased risk-adjustment formulas, they allow the sponsor to make payments for some signals that differ from the expected cost of each signal.

The GM optimal risk-adjustment solution to this distortion is to use the structure of demand and the exogenous signal reporting process to overpay systematically for signals $S = 1$, while underpaying for $S = 0$. For each observed signal $S = 1$ implying a high-risk type, the health plan should be compensated for more than the incremental cost of that consumer, to cover the inferred presence of other high-risk types in the same plan. This overpayment for $S = 1$ will make the health plan more willing to enroll high-risk types, and to offer more SP services that will attract them.

The GM [12] optimal risk-adjustment equilibrium for this simplified example is shown in Fig. 8.7. It is useful to contrast the conventional and optimal risk adjustment results. Continuing with the previous example with imperfect signals, consider the case where $\gamma_L = 0$ but $\gamma_H = 1/2$. This corresponds to the case where half of all diabetics have a signal reporting their type, but half do not. There are no false positives. Assume that the regulator calculates conventional risk-adjustment payments based on unbiased estimates using the imperfect signal S using FFS data. In this case, conventional risk adjustment would pay $\alpha^0 + \beta^0$, for those with $S = 1$, and pay $\alpha^0 + (1 - \gamma_H) \beta^0$ for the $S = 0$ types. If the plan simply enrolled a representative mix of high- and low-risk types, then it would break even. If instead the plan is able to discourage some of the true high risks from enrolling, then for the extra share of its enrollees with $S = 0$, it could receive $\alpha^0 + (1 - \gamma_H) \beta^0 > \alpha^0$ for the low-risk types it enrolls, making a profit. Hence, in order to achieve this, the plan would reduce SP and increase GP spending, offering a service mix such as A^2 and B^2 in Fig. 8.7.

The GM solution to this incentive is to overpay for the high-risk types, making them sufficiently attractive as to encourage plans to compete for them. If α^0 and β^0 were the optimal levels of spending to achieve, then the solution would be to pay α^0 for the $S = 0$ types, and $\alpha^0 + \beta^0/\gamma_H = \alpha^0 + 2\beta^0$ for the $S = 1$ types. Note that by overpaying twice, the expected difference in costs for the high signal, the regulator undoes the disincentive to attract high-risk types. In general, the FFS level of services would not be as desired, and an alternative level such as A^3 and B^3 in Fig. 8.7, where $\alpha^3 < \alpha^0$ and $\beta^3 < \beta^0$.

Although attractive conceptually, achieving the first best in practice may be difficult, for reasons that GM and others acknowledge. Knowing the optimal consumption points A^3 and B^3 may not be feasible, and the structure of the information set, such as the rates of true- and false-positive signals, may not be known to the sponsor. The optimal risk-adjustment payment can be very sensitive to the degree of imperfect signaling. For small γ_H, it may be necessary to greatly overpay $S = 1$. In some situations, underpayment for low risks may also be needed, which imposes non-negativity constraints on payments. Still, the GM solution points to the direction that should be considered by sponsors where health plans compete to avoid high-risk types: overpay for high-risk-type signals and underpay for low-risk-type signals relative to conventional risk adjustment, in order to encourage desirable competition to attract high-risk-type consumers. In Chapter 9, Glazer and McGuire provide an important extension to the GM framework that encompasses optimal risk adjustment when there is non-contractible service quality, and not just service non-contractible quantity.

8.3.8
Taste and Income Variation

Taste or income variation can be introduced into the problem by adding consumer heterogeneity. For example, Fig. 8.8 illustrates the case where there are two types of healthy enrollees, whose preferred bundles of services are A' and A'' and two types of diabetics, preferring B' and B''. Payments based on a binary signal cannot achieve the first best allocations of both GP and SP for all four types of consumer. If averages for each signal are paid, then health plans will have an incentive to compete to attract consumers with lower tastes for services.

8.3.9
Rationale for Focusing on High-Cost Conditions

The data in Fig. 8.8 can also be used to show the implications of adding further types. Suppose that, instead of taste variation, there are now two different types of healthy consumer (e.g., healthy and healthy with allergies), with optimal choices A' and A'', with still only one diabetic type at B'. (B'' may be ignored for this discussion.) It might very well be that signals which distinguish B' from A' and A'' are much more reliable than those distinguishing A' from A''. This could justify developing payment models that recognize distinctions of diabetics B', but ignore minor differences among the healthy. This is the approach that has been taken in the Netherlands and the US Medicare program, both of which have focused on paying more for only the highest cost conditions.

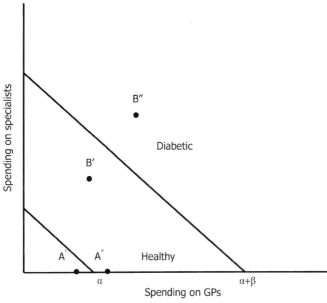

Fig. 8.8 Risk adjustment with taste or income heterogeneity. Optimal service choices for two alternative diabetic types are B′ and B″, while optimal service choices for two healthy types are A′ and A″. With only two signal values, plans cannot offer efficient quantities of services to all four types. Health plans will have an incentive to compete to be most attractive to the lower cost types, A′ and B′.

8.3.10
Optimal Risk Adjustment in Settings with Non-Competing Health Plans

Before continuing, it is useful to consider the relevance of the GM service competition from the point of view of other countries. Risk adjustment is used in Canada and Europe in settings where health plans do not choose services so as to actively compete for enrollees. In Canada and Scandinavia, budget allocations are primarily geographic, while in Netherlands and Germany – even though there are many competing health plans – selective contracting is rare, so that health plans do not have available tools that enable meaningful service distortion so as to attract profitable enrollees. Hutchison et al. [8], when discussing Canada, go so far as to assert "For health care funding allocations to geographically-defined populations, risk adjustment is irrelevant." Is this true?

There are two important ways in which risk adjustment remains important even for Germany, Canada and other regions without meaningful service level competition. One reason is that there may be historic reasons (geography or employment) why populations in some regions or health plans differ that are not captured well by simple risk-adjustment models. As documented below under the international review, even geographic areas may vary significantly in their disease patterns. and hence costs. Another reason is that consumers may temporarily or permanently migrate to use a different region or plan. It is not uncommon for consumers to use a hospital or specialist from a different region, or a different health plan, and the internal transfer payments among regions or health plans are tricky to calculate. Individuals migrating across regional borders will tend to differ from the average. For example, chronically ill patients often relocate to be close to centers of excellence that specialize in their illness. The effort that hospitals or providers work to attract consumers from neighboring regions is also a strategic decision, possibly influenced by the payment system. Recognizing this health distribution and choices being made in the risk-adjustment formula may be important.

GM [12], and especially Glazer and McGuire [2], emphasize that optimal risk adjustment is more about recognizing that unbiased payment should not be the primary objective of the sponsor, but rather a more fundamental objective of maximizing consumer welfare that should drive payment calculations. Canadians and Europeans may assign more importance to equity than efficiency goals in their objective function, but that does not reduce the desirability of acknowledging the value of a broader objective function than just minimizing individual level variance in plan profitability, or at the other extreme paying regions or health plans without regard to the healthiness of their enrollees.

8.4
Estimation Issues

This section highlights some of the results that bear on the estimation and interpretation of risk-adjustment models. Much of these data were reviewed by van de Ven and Ellis [1] until 1999 whilst, for the US, more recent reviews and comparisons of different risk-adjustment models have been provided by Cumming et al. [28], in their report to the Society of Actuaries, the studies of Thomas et al. [9, 29] on provider profiling, and the policy review of Newhouse [21]. Chapter 7 in this book, by Léger, on provider payment also has a direct bearing [30]. In addition, Rice and Smith [31] conducted a very useful overview of risk-adjustment techniques outside of the US. Other articles on other specific countries are discussed below.

Empirical models of risk adjustment must address five issues in model estimation:

- The choice of the objective function to be optimized.
- The choice of risk adjusters (signals to be used for prediction).
- The conceptual framework, including the classification system and whether to use mutually exclusive rate cells or additive prediction models.
- Econometric specification, including non-linear estimators and endogenous plan selection corrections.
- Methods of evaluation and prediction.

The following discussion centers on the coverage of these five topics.

8.4.1
Choice of the Objective Function to be Optimized

The theory section above has emphasized the choice of the objective function for the sponsor, and the consideration of the allowed risk selection problem that is being solved. Very few empirical studies have estimated "optimal risk-adjustment" models that reflect any objective function other than being budget-neutral and maximizing predictive power (e.g., the R-square). The two notable examples are: Glazer and McGuire [32], which estimates a "minimum variance optimal risk-adjustment" model using Medicaid data that seeks to maximize the R^2 while maintaining the first best incentive for service provision; and Shen and Ellis [16], which estimates a "cost-minimizing risk-adjustment model" which minimizes the financial cost to the sponsor when capitated, risk-selecting plans compete against an open enrolling FFS plan, as is true for the US Medicare program.

European countries often pursue equity objectives that are not easily summarized in a welfare function to be maximized. Many of the risk-adjustment formulas reviewed by Rice and Smith [31] reflect transfers and subsidies to increase service provisions to underserved populations (low-income households, underserved rural areas, and minority status consumers, for example.) These models are implicitly using more complex objectives than maximizing simple predictive power.

Implicit in the choice of most objective functions is the choice of the dependent variable – which variable is being predicted. In the payment literature, total annual spending – including in-patient, out-patient and pharmacy spending – is the most common dependent variable, although in some settings visits, admissions, or other measures of utilization are predicted.

8.4.2
Choice of Risk Adjusters

As better information and larger samples have become available, there has been a progression towards more elaborate information sets being used for empirical risk-adjustment models. Many researchers have suggested that diagnoses come as close as any widely available measure of consumer health status, and hence diagnoses from insurance claims are the most widely used set of information beyond demographic variables. Pharmacy information is sometimes used in place of diagnosis information, although prescription practice is perhaps more subject to variation across doctors and over time than diagnostic coding. Self-reported health status is attractive conceptually, although surveys are more expensive to collect than diagnoses and pharmacy use. Another concern is that consumers may only imperfectly differentiate among illness severities or imprecisely recall doctor's advice and diagnoses. The information sets used by 12 risk-adjustment models used primarily in the US are summarized in Table 8.1 [33–47]. Each of the widely used models tends to be given an acronym, and there are typically many variants of each modeling framework. Here, only the acronyms used, without elaborating on the details of each model.

Table 8.1 Overview of major US claims-based risk-adjustment mode s

Acronym	Key reference	Name	First referenced	Rate cell or linear regression?	Age/ gender	In-patient diagnoses	All diagnoses	Pharmacy	Proc codes
CI	33	Charleson Index	1987	Regression	X	X			
DCG	34	Diagnostic Cost Group	1989	Regression	X	X			
ACG	35	Adjusted Clinical Group	1991	Rate cell	X	X	X		
CDS	36	Chronic Disease Score	1992	Regression	X			X	
HCC	44	Hierarchical Condition Categories	1996	Regression	X	X	X		
CDPS	45	Chronic and Disability Payment System	1996	Regression	X	X	X		
GRAM	46	Global Risk Assessment Model	1996	Regression	X	X	X		
CD-RISC	47	Clinically Detailed Risk Indication System for Cost	1997	Regression	X	X	X		
CRG	39	Clinical Related Group	1999	Rate cell	X	X	X	X	X
ERG	40	Episode Risk Group	2001	Rate cell	X	X	X	X	X
RxGroups	37	RxGroups	2001	Regression	X			X	
RxRisk	38	RxRisk	2003	Regression	X			X	

The three earliest risk-adjustment models [Charleson Index (CI), Diagnostic Cost Groups (DCGs), and Adjusted Clinical Group (ACG)] emerged in the US during the 1980s and early 1990s, using diagnoses as reported on insurance claims [33–35]. Pharmacy information was first used in 1992, and has been an active direction for model estimation in recent years [36–38]. Some recent risk-adjustment models [Clinical Risk Groups (CRGs), Episode Risk Groups (ERGs)] combine different information sets, such as pharmacy plus diagnoses [39, 40]. Alternative models which use functional status and disability measures are not shown in the table (for discussion and evaluation, see Ref. [41]). Other models using self-reported health status information included the Short Form 36 (SF-36), which was developed at the New England Medical Center [42]. Within Table 8.1, predictive models that use lagged spending information are not included, although this framework is often used (such models are discussed briefly below). The predictive power of various data sets is also evaluated below when discussing evaluation tools.

8.4.3
Conceptual Framework and Classification Systems for Empirical Models

The risk-adjustment models defined in Table 8.1 differ not only in the information set used, but also in how the information is used for prediction. Two fundamental approaches are used: (i) a rate cell approach; and (ii) linear prediction formulas.

In the rate cell approach, each consumer is classified into a unique group, with groups chosen so as to most usefully distinguish patient severity or cost. Consumers are typically assigned to one rate cell based on a complex sorting algorithm in which the most complex or highest cost patients are identified first, and remaining consumers are filtered through a succession of screens until lower-cost and less-severe individuals are eventually exhaustively assigned to a rate category. The most ambition rate cell approach, the CRG framework, uses over 700 rate cells to classify individuals. A rate cell approach allows the cost of each person in a rate cell to be calculated using a simple weighted or unweighted average of the cost of all consumers in that rate cell.

The primary alternative conceptual approach for estimating risk adjustment models is to use linear or non-linear additive models, in which a long array of binary or possibly continuous signals are used in a regression framework to predict spending. Some of the additive models use over 200 risk adjusters (signals) for prediction. The predicted cost or service utilization of an individual is then the fitted value of the model for that individual.

Rate cell approaches have the advantage of simplicity to estimate, but suffer from being less predictive than additive models. Even with 700 rate cells, there are simply too many combinations of even the 20 most common conditions ($2^{20} = 1\,048\,576$) to be able easily to capture all of the diversity of consumer types. One strength of the rate cell approach can be that, under certain conditions, a single rate cell can contain a relatively homogeneous set of consumers to price and evaluate. However, a weakness is that for many conditions (e.g., asthma, diabetes, mental illness), consumers with this condition as well as other more serious ones will be spread out over multiple rate cells. Additive models can accommodate an enormous diversity of patient types, while interactions can capture possible non-linearities.

Conditional on the same set of information (diagnoses or drugs), risk-adjustment models also differ significantly in how they use this information. Most systems impose hierarchies on the information so that more-serious conditions take precedence over less-serious conditions. Much of the cleverness, clinical coherence and predictive power are related to the choice of these categories.

Once a rate cell or additive approach, and a classification system have been selected, there remain issues about over which time period the information will be used. The US Medicare program and many other risk-adjusted payment models use a prospective framework, in which information from a base period (usually one year) is used to predict spending from the subsequent period. The main alternative framework is to use concurrent (sometimes called retrospective) information for prediction, where the diagnoses or other information from a year is used to predict spending or utilization from the same year. The principal argument for prospective models is that it is easier for the sponsor, and only predetermined information can be used to influence selection choices. The argument in favor of concurrent models is that they are much more highly predictive than prospective models.

8.4.4
Econometric Specification Issues

Risk-adjustment models have been the subject of many refinements on econometric techniques, with the large number of zero values, the skewed distributions, heteroskedasticity, and sample selection issues all attracting frequent attention.

The simplest and most common approach is ordinary least squares (OLS) in which the dependent variable is untransformed spending. This approach has the major advantage of being rapid and simple to estimate, interpret, and explain to non-econometricians; indeed, it is the approach used by the US Medicare program [41]. Ash et al. [34] established the concept that in order to obtain unbiased estimates for consumers where some have partial year eligibility, then the correct approach within an OLS setting is to annualize costs by deflating by the fraction of the year eligible, and then to weight the observation by this same fraction. This weighted annualized regression can be shown to generate unbiased means in rate cells, and corresponding linear regression models.

Manning et al. [48] contains the classic discussion of why OLS can be inefficient in small samples. The two-part loglinear model proposed by Duan et al. [49] is the classic discussion of this model, and also develops the smearing correction to ensure that model predictions are not too seriously biased. Subsequent studies [50–52] have highlighted the importance of correcting the mean not only for skewness but also for heteroskedasticity. Both, Fishman et al. [53] and Basu et al. [54] are recent examples contrasting various refined econometric specifications.

Despite all of these refinements, OLS remains very popular. Why is this? One reason is that with very large sample sizes, the inefficiency of OLS and concerns about overfitting due to a few very high outliers are nullified. The large sample

Table 8.2 Predictive power of various information sets and various models. Dependent variable: 1997 annualized total covered charges

	Weighted OLS	OLS	Square-root model (hetero-skedasticity-corrected)	Two part linear model	GLM with link = log, dist = normal
Partial Year Eligibles included?	Yes	No	No	No	No
Sample mean	6886	5063	5063	5063	5063
No. of observations	1 380 863	1 273 471	1 273 471	1 273 471	1 273 471
	R^2	R^2	R^2	R^2	R^2
Age and gender only	0.011	0.010	0.009	0.010	0.010
Prior year total covered charges[1]	0.089	0.096	0.113	0.120	0.105
Diagnoses organized by DCG/HCC[1]	0.104	0.108	0.103	0.107	0.105
Covered charges by DCG/HCC[1]	0.099	0.107	0.103	0.105	0.095
Covered charges by Place of Service[1]	0.140	0.145	0.136	0.145	0.126
Covered charges by Physician Specialty[1]	0.142	0.152	0.143	0.152	0.131
Covered charges by Type of Service[1]	0.150	0.155	0.146	0.154	0.134
All of the above except diagnoses[1]	0.154	0.160	0.151	0.160	0.138
"Kitchen sink": All of the above[1]	0.169	0.171	0.161	0.169	0.147

1) All regressions included a constant and 21 age–gender dummy variables.
Source: Ref. [54] and Table 8.1.

sizes and large number of parameters also make some of the non-linear estimators difficult to estimate using conventional statistical packages. A second reason to prefer OLS is that, for large samples, the findings will be relatively robust to the econometric specification. Five econometric specifications on nine alternative sets of regressors, as developed by Ellis and McGuire [55], are contrasted in Table 8.1.

The first column in Table 8.1 uses the weighted least squares, including partial year eligibles. The second estimation approach uses simple OLS, and excludes people with fractional years of eligibility. This approach focuses on people with the most complete information, and uses a sample that is also used by the remaining three approaches. The third estimation approach is a heteroskedasticity-corrected square-root model, as described by Veazie et al. [56]. The square root of actual covered charges is regressed on the given set of independent variables, and the squared residuals from this regression are then regressed on the fitted value, called say G. Heteroskedasticity-corrected predictions of spending from this model are the squared fitted predictions, G_i^2, plus the predicted variance for each observation $s^2(G_i)$. The fourth model uses a "two part OLS with smearing" as described by Manning [57] and Buntin and Zaslovsky [58]. The first stage is a probit model of the probability of any spending, and the second stage is a linear model of spending among those with positive spending. The fifth specification uses a generalized linear model (GLM) evaluated by Buntin and Zaslovsky with the linear portion transformed using the log transformation, and additive errors assumed to be normally distributed, hence $Y = \exp(X\beta) + \epsilon$. Ellis and McGuire [55] also tried estimating two part log models and GLM models with alternative link and distribution functions, although these models either did not converge or had very poor or negative R^2 values. Similar problems with these models were found by Veazie et al. [56].

Several results are shown from Table 8.1. First, all of the various econometric specifications shown achieve a very similar R^2 for each information set. Conventional risk-adjustment models using diagnoses or lagged spending do much better than age and gender alone, but less well than using disaggregated spending information. Even if sponsors might never want to use lagged spending signals for payment purposes, health plans that have this information available can use it for the prediction and identification of profitable and unprofitable consumers given the signals used for risk adjustment. A third and final observation is that there are diminishing returns to adding more information set as explanatory variables, with the highest prospective R^2 achieved in this US Medicare sample at only about 17%.

The last econometric specification issue to be discussed is the appropriate correction for sample selection. Terza [25] has been one of many advocating that risk-adjustment models should be corrected for selection bias. Since HMOs and unmanaged FFS plans have different styles of care, they will tend to attract systematically different types of people who may differ in their tastes for those styles. Moreover, it well predicted by the above theory models that there will be behavioral responses by HMO providers to the incentives of capitation that will cause them to offer different quantities of care than will FFS providers. The existence of these selection and moral hazard differences is certain, but it is an empirical question as to whether these differences are large and seriously bias estimates, or whether they are small. The magnitude of these differences is examined below.

8.4.5
Methods of Evaluation and Prediction

A significant literature on how to compare and evaluate risk-adjustment models has developed. Cumming et al. [28], in their US study for the Society of Actuaries, include a good discussion of different metrics and illustrate their use. Ash et al. [34] used not only individual R^2 as a metric, but also defined and used grouped R^2, which is to say how well the models perform for mutually exclusive partitions of an entire sample. The mean absolute deviation (MAD), as well as the standard error of the regression, is also common [28, 34]. Finally, the literature often reports what are called "predictive ratios"; these are the ratios of predicted to actual spending or utilization [34]. An ideal model would have predictive ratios close to one for every group of possible interest.

There is a decided danger of overfitting with econometric models, given how skewed both the dependent and the independent variables are. In order to evaluate the degree of overfitting, researchers often compare the ordinary R^2, MAD and predictive ratios not only for the estimation sample, but also with a reserved split sample not used for model development or estimation. The validated R^2 and other measures of predictive power is often significantly lower, (5–50 % lower), than the development sample R^2.

The validated R^2 from three different research studies are shown in Figs. 8.9 and 8.10. The first set of bars are from Berlinguet [59], who studied three diagnosis-based risk-adjustment models (ACGs, DCGs, and CRGs) in three provinces of Canada. The second set of bars are from Wasem et al. [60], who report on their comparison of seven diagnosis- and pharmacy-based risk adjustment models in Germany. The final set of bars is from Cumming et al. [28], who evaluated seven diverse risk-adjustment models for the US Society of Actuaries. The figures reveal several points:

- There are distinct differences among the risk-adjustment models in terms of their predictive power.
- The models using combinations of information, such as the CRG the RxGroups_ IPHCC and the ERG, tend to do better than models using only one type of information.
- Concurrent models (Fig. 8.10) perform much better than prospective models.

8.4.6
An Extended Example

Every country that has implemented more elaborate risk adjustment using diagnoses or pharmacy information started out by using only demographic information such as age and gender. It is useful to see an example of how risk adjustment can

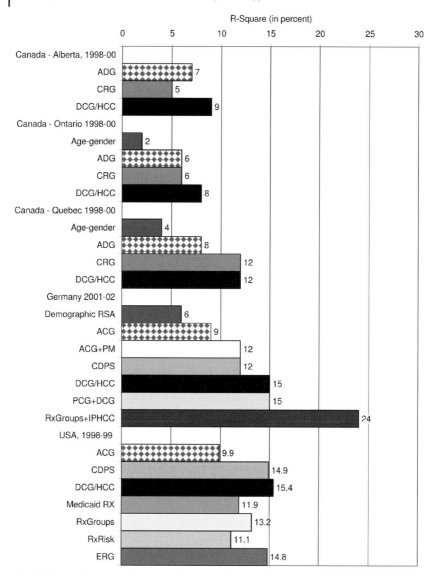

Fig. 8.9 Predictive power (R-square) of prospective risk adjustment models in three countries. For details of abbreviations, see text and Table 8.1 [28, 59, 60].

improve upon age and gender prediction. Figure 8.11 illustrates the pattern of average annual spending by one-year age groups from a sample of 14.6 million privately insured individuals in the US. This figure (which was generated at DxCG using the MEDSTAT Marketscan data from 2004) is unusual for the US in that the commercial under-age 65 years sample has been pooled with the MEDSTAT Medicare sample, which is a sample of primarily privately insured individuals aged

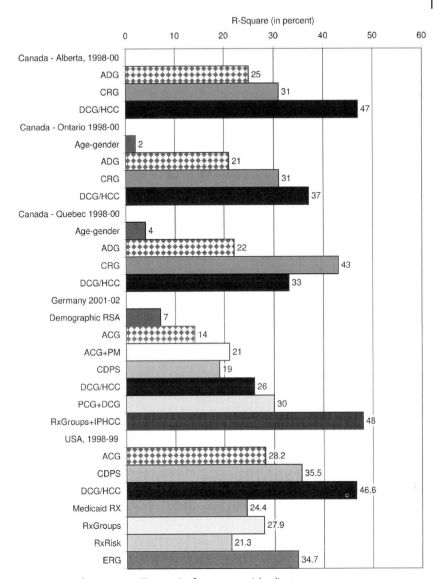

Fig. 8.10 Predictive power (R-square) of concurrent risk adjustment models in three countries. For details of abbreviations, see text and Table 8.1 [28, 59, 60].

over 65. Some subjects in this Medicare eligible sample are still working, some are retirees over age 65 and still covered by their employer, and some are in Medicare supplementary policies. Numerous patterns will strike the reader, but several deserve note. First, costs increase with age, although not monotonically, and a simple linear or quadratic age specification cannot hope to capture the complex shape. Second, women of child-bearing age are distinctly more expensive than males of

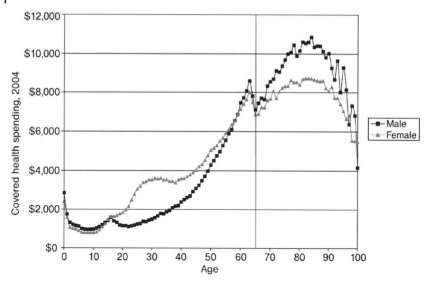

Fig. 8.11 US privately-insured health care spending, by age and by gender. 2004 MEDSTAT Marketscan data (N = 14.6 million). Notes: Plots show weighted average annu- alized health care spending by one-year age intervals, for males and females. Age is beginning-of-year age. Total health spending includes covered in-patient plus out-patient plus pharmacy covered spending. Sample is merged MEDSTAT commercially insured (under age 65) and MEDSTAT Medicare sam- ples. Discontinuity at age 65 reflects both a sample discontinuity as well as benefit and utilization changes. (Source: Author's own calculations at DxCG, Inc.).

the same age, but still relatively low cost relative to the elderly. Third, males over age 65 are more expensive than females. Finally, there appears to be a tapering off in average spending at about age 85 years.

Figure 8.12 is similar to Fig. 8.11, except that it focuses on the under-65 population and instead of showing the graph by gender, it shows the curve for five types of health plan. Each of the lines is drawn with at least 100 000 enrollees, so the patterns are highly stable across age groups. The figure suggests that enrollees in each of the five plan types are relatively similar up until age 40, at which time there is a divergence of HMO and point-of-service (POS) with capitation plans from the rest. By age 40 there is about a 20% discrepancy between the HMO and POS with capitation plan from the other three plan types. Whether this difference is due to the selection of healthier people conditional on age, to taste differences, or due to supply side moral hazard response to incentives, is unclear.

Figure 8.13 provides one answer to this question. Instead of plotting actual spending by age and plan type, the figure shows the risk-adjusted spending by age and plan type. Risk adjustment in this example was performed using the DCG/HCC concurrent risk-adjustment model. The five lines are much closer together, differing by less than 5% across plan types. There is still a difference at age 40, but it is much smaller. This modest difference, once spending is risk adjusted, suggests that most of the 20% observed difference is due to selection differences and not to taste nor

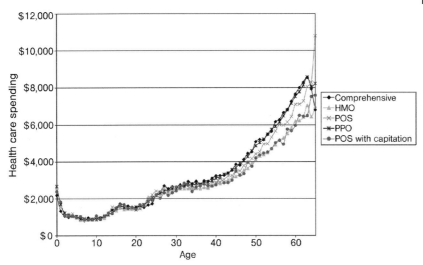

Fig. 8.12 US privately-insured health care spending by age, by health plan type. 2004 MEDSTAT Marketscan data (N = 13.0 million). Notes: Plots show weighted average annualized health care spending by one-year age intervals by five major health plan types. Age is beginning-of-year age. Exclusive provider organization (EPA) and miss-ing plan type observations omitted. Total health spending includes covered in-patient plus out-patient plus pharmacy covered spending. Sample is 2004 MEDSTAT commercially insured (under age 65) sample. (Source: Author's own calculations at DxCG, Inc.).

moral hazard. The implied cost savings from the HMO and POS with capitated from the most common plan type of preferred provider organizations (PPOs) is less than 5%, with a modest gradient upward with age.

It is commonplace for others to be critical of risk-adjustment model developers because they ignore sample selection when estimating their models. The above graphical results suggest that sample selection corrections will result in relatively modest errors in the estimated models – errors that are much smaller than differences across age, disease, or gender. Adding in a few more interaction terms to more accurately predict spending may be as valuable as incorporating selection effects into the original models.

8.5
Country Experience with Risk Adjustment

In this section, the experiences of six countries that have used risk adjustment in different ways are discussed. Some of the key features of segments in each of these countries are summarized in Table 8.3. The systems implemented are by no means uniform, and there are numerous differences in the number of agents, whether competing health plans or regional orientation is used. Discussion of the history and use of risk adjustment in each country is provided below.

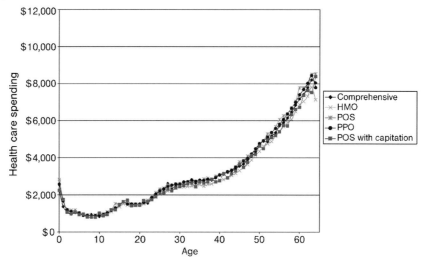

Fig. 8.13 Risk-adjusted US privately-insured health care spending, by age and by health plan type. 2004 MEDSTAT Marketscan data (N = 13.0 million). Notes: Plot shows risk-adjusted weighted average annualized health care spending by one-year age intervals by five major health plan types. Average spending at each age was deflated by the ratio of the plan-specific average age-specific relative risk score to the overall age-specific average relative risk score. Risk scores calculated using the concurrent HCC model of DxCG release 6.1 software. Age is beginning-of-year age. Exclusive provider organization (EPA) and missing plan type observations omitted. Total health spending includes covered in-patient plus out-patient plus pharmacy covered spending. Sample is 2004 MEDSTAT commercially insured (under age 65) sample. (Source: Author's own calculations at DxCG, Inc.).

8.5.1
Canada

Canada does not offer multiple competing health plans in any of its provinces, and hence one might expect the provinces to have minimal incentives for selection. Despite this, a modest selection problem still exists, arising from consumer choice of residence, and consumer choice of providers. Canada is also interesting in that its health care system is similar to that of many other countries with a social insurance program, including countries as diverse as Australia, France, Norway, and Taiwan. Health system financing, publicly funded services and delivery systems in Canada vary across the provinces. While there is some variation in financing systems across provinces, there are many similarities. Here, the focus is primarily on Alberta.

A stylized view of Alberta Canada's health care system using the previously discussed four agents in health care markets is depicted in Fig. 8.14. All residents are automatically covered by the province in which they reside, and payments are collected from all workers and employers through mandatory social insurance premiums and general income taxes. The province's ministry of health, Alberta Health and Wellness (AHW), pays for most physician- and office-based services using a fee

Table 8.3 The practice of risk adjustment in six countries

Current risk-adjusters

				Country			
	Canada (Alberta)	Germany	Netherlands	Switzerland	United Kingdom	United States (Medicare)
	Age/gender Disability Income	Age/gender Disability Aborigine	Age/gender Region Pharmacy In-patient diagnoses	Age/gender Region	Age/gender Prior utilization Local factors	Age/gender All-encounter diagnoses
Rate cell or regression model	124 rate cells	Rate cell	Regression model	Rate cell	Rate cell	Regression model
Individual or grouped data	Individual	Individual	Individual	Individual	Group	Individual
No. of health plans/funding regions	9 RHA (2006)	292 Sickness funds (2004)	25 private health insurance funds	166 sickness funds	303 Primary Care Trusts	314 (2006) Medicare Advantage plans
Open entry for new health plans? (subject to certain conditions)	No	Yes	Yes	Yes	No	Yes
Open enrollment every month/.../year	–	Year	Year	Half-year	No open enrollment guarantee	Monthly
Mandatory or voluntary membership	M	V for high income	M	M	M	V
Implementation date	1985	1994	2004	1993	1991	2004

RHA: Regional Health Authority.

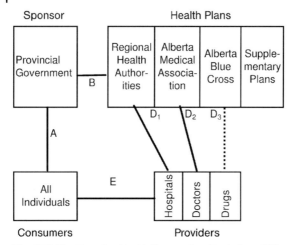

Fig. 8.14 The Canadian Health System. A stylized view of Alberta, 2006.

schedule managed by the Alberta Medical Association. In addition to using fees, the provincial government also allocates annual budgets to nine (previously 17) regional health authorities (RHAs). RHAs are responsible for spending on hospitals, continuing care facilities, home care, public health, community rehabilitation, mental health and a portion of cancer care, which together comprises 56% of the total AHW spending [61]. Prescription drugs are not included as a benefit for all residents, but are covered for those aged over 65 with a copayment through an arrangement with Alberta Blue Cross. In addition to this publicly funded system, consumers as individuals or with sponsorship from their employers, are allowed to purchase supplementary insurance that covers pharmacy costs and certain uncovered services.

Two issues create an interest in risk adjustment in Alberta: in its allocation among the RHA; and in its payments to primary care providers. The allocation of AHW funds among the RHA is complicated by the fact that residents do not choose where to live randomly, and need not necessarily seek care in the RHA in which they live. Patient choice of facility implies a need to ensure fair payments to each facility given the case mix of patients that they manage, treat or refer.

AHW has explored this geographic selection bias, and finds evidence of it [62]. In particular, they find persons with more serious chronic illnesses are more likely to live in urban areas, and that certain diseases vary significantly across RHAs. Evidence provided by comparing summary statistics across RHAs, where the highest and lowest rates observed have been chosen, is shown in Table 8.4. (Sample sizes in each RHA exceed 20 000, and hence these differences are all statistically significant at high levels of confidence.)

Geographic variation within Alberta, in terms of urban versus rural, and distances from rural areas to urban hospitals, are probably greater than in many other countries (such as the Netherlands) that are more homogeneous in their access. The Alberta experience reminds us that consumers do sort themselves geographically in meaningful ways. It should be emphasized that the Alberta regional

Table 8.4 Evidence of geographic risk selection in Alberta, Canada [61]

Risk category	RHA rate	
	Highest	Lowest
Average age (years)	36.7	25.2
Proportion over age 65 (%)	14.7	2.1
Proportion with pregnancy diagnosis (%)	3.6	1.9
Proportion of diabetics with chronic complications diagnosis (%)	13.2	8.1%

RHA: Regional Health Authority.

allocation formula *does* take into account the age distribution of the population in each RHA. The differences in age across the RHAs are taken not as a problem with unpriced risk heterogeneity by itself, but rather as a signal that consumers are sorting themselves geographically, and that this creates potential selection problems for Alberta.

8.5.1.1 Role of Risk Adjustment in Canada

Only Alberta and Saskatchewan appear to be using population-based capitation formulas in allocating funds to health authorities. RHA budgets in Alberta are currently allocated using demographic risk adjuster information. A rate cell approach is used in which the rate cells are based on age, gender, and four socioeconomic categories that reflect income and "aboriginal" (i.e., Native American) status. AHW has considered methods that more accurately measure health risk in order to improve the fairness of compensation regions and providers for seriously ill, high-expenditure patients. The Calgary Regional Health Authority in Alberta was one of the participants in the study conducted by Berlinguet et al. [59] of diagnosis-based risk-adjustment models, funded by the Canadian Health Services Research Foundation (CHSRF), as discussed above. AHM also conducted its own evaluation of risk-adjustment models from 2002 to 2004, but has not yet moved beyond using only demographic information for budget allocations to the RHA. Recent initiatives emphasizing primary care and coordination among diverse providers also highlight the role of risk adjustment.

A recent review found British Columbia to be the only province using diagnosis-based risk adjustment for paying physicians, although many alternative payment formulas are being used [63]. Risk adjustment was tested as part of a demonstration project on primary care that started in British Columbia in 1998. Reid et al. [64, 65] evaluated a diagnosis-based risk-adjustment model using the Adjusted Clinical Group (ACG) classification system on data from Manitoba and British Columbia. British Columbia uses a capitation formula: "a physician funding methodology based on the patient population served, as opposed to the number of services provided". The B.C. Ministry of Health received $9.6 million from the Federal Health Transition Fund for a primary care demonstration project to explore new and innovative approaches for paying for primary health care delivery. The formula uses the ACG case-mix system to calculate payments that are based on each consumer's age, gender, and diagnoses codes [66].

8.5.2
USA Medicare

The USA Medicare program was one of the earliest adopters of capitated payments, and provides a useful case study for other countries. This program covers almost 40 million individuals who are either aged, disabled or have end-stage renal disease (ESRD). Prior to 1985, when "at-risk" HMOs were first permitted, the traditional indemnity Medicare program resembled the Canadian system, with a government sponsor raising revenue from taxes and insurance premiums, fully insuring geographically defined insurance carriers (health plans) who were contracted to pay services mostly on a FFS basis. There was no incentive for traditional Medicare plans to control costs.

Legislative changes to Medicare were adopted in 1985 to improve cost containment by encouraging competing managed-care health plans. These reforms permitted Medicare HMOs to receive capitation funding and be "at-risk" for the cost of their enrollees. The Medicare Managed Care program, now called Medicare Advantage (MA), enrolled about 5.6 million (15%) of the Medicare population in 2002, and since then has had a relatively stable enrollment. Health plans participating in this program are closely regulated in terms of the benefits they can offer and premiums they can charge. Open enrollment is required, but MA plans are allowed to compete in many other ways. For example, health plans have the right to market directly to consumers, or to locate their offices in more or less convenient sites. MA plans are also given the right to choose counties to enter or exit from, to choose additional benefits (such as drug coverage) not offered by indemnity Medicare, to choose the enrollee premium, and to selectively contract with providers. From the start, payments to the MA plans by the government were risk adjusted to reflect the county, age, gender, disability, and institutional status of the health plan's enrollees, using a formula called the Adjusted Average Per Capita Cost (AAPCC).

8.5.2.1 Early Concerns About Biased Selection

Since its inception, policymakers have been concerned about whether risk adjustment using the AAPCC, which uses only demographic information, was sufficient to reduce selection incentives and avoid overpayment of managed-care plans. Early evidence clearly indicated that the HMOs were attracting healthier than average enrollees even within each rate cell. An important study conducted by Brown et al. [67] concluded that, rather than saving money (as intended), the Medicare managed-care program was actually costing the Medicare program 5.7% more than it would have been if Medicare offered FFS alone. The analysis by Brown et al. linked survey and claims information, and found that HMO consumers were relatively satisfied with their HMOs, there were no clear quality differences, and that HMOs successfully reduced the use of certain resources, such as in-patient days. Several further government and academic studies further documented risk-selection problems with the program.

The major concern in the US with regards to managed-care plans is that selective contracting permits plans to distort services and provider availability in ways that encourage favorable selection. This level of service distortion is the primary focus of Glazer and McGuire [11, 12], and reflects a concern expressed by Newhouse [15] and others. Empirical evidence on the nature of this selection is limited. Cao and McGuire [68] use Medicare FFS claims to detect that rates of spending on certain chronic diseases and certain services are higher in the FFS sector when a higher proportion of individuals are enrolled in HMOs, suggesting service and provider type distortions as predicted by the theory. Recent evidence of a different selection activity is provided by Dallek and Dennington [69], who find that Medicare managed-care plans had primary care physician turnover rates averaging 14%, with rates of over 20% in five states. These extremely high turnover rates on primary care physicians must disrupt the continuity of care, and also discourage continued enrollment by those who are more seriously ill.

8.5.2.2 Risk Adjustment in the US Medicare Program

The US Medicare program reacted to the evidence of biased selection in their M + C program in several ways. During the early and mid-1990s, the program funded five major studies of different risk-adjustment models, using a wide range of approaches that included in-patient diagnoses, all encounter (in-patient and out-patient) diagnoses, survey methods, risk-sharing models, and prior year spending models [70–72]. Legislated changes in 1997 mandated a transition to health status-based risk adjustment. Starting in 1998, the Medicare program slowed the rate of increase in payments, largely eliminating the perceived overpayment, and changing the mechanism for calculating each country's average payment. Medicare also began laying the foundation for implementing risk adjustment by requiring that the M + C plans provide in-patient diagnoses starting in 1998, and all encounter diagnoses in 2000 (see Chapter 3 in Ref. [70]). In January 2000, the Medicare program implemented the Principal Inpatient Diagnostic Cost Group (PIPDCG) model, and used it for payment of 10% of the total amount to MA plans. Pope et al. [41] provide a careful description of the framework and the effort that went into trying to reduce the incentives to distort treatment and diagnoses and "upcode" patient severity. Rather than jumping from a demographic to a diagnostic-based risk-adjustment formula in one year, implementation called for the gradual phasing in of the new formula over seven years. While initially only 10% of the capitated payments were based on the diagnoses, in 2007 all of the risk adjusted payment is diagnosis-based.

While initially only in-patient diagnoses were used, since 2004 the payment formula has relied on all diagnoses, and hence it is called an "all encounter model". The Medicare program decided to use a relatively simplified classification system called the CMS-HCC model, a simplified version of the Diagnostic Cost Group/ Hierarchical Condition Categories (DCG/HCC) [6, 43, 44]. Kanika Kapur, a researcher at the RAND Corporation, summed up the reasons for the choice of this model as "...CMS chose the DCG/HCC model for Medicare risk adjustment, largely on the basis of transparency, ease of modification, and good clinical coherence." [72].

The CMS-HCC model is a prospective model, so that demographics and diagnoses from a base year are used to predict payment for a given individual during the following year. Payments are calculated prospectively each January, using data from the previous calendar year. Retrospective adjustments are used to reflect late-arriving data relevant to payment. To simplify the data burden on health plans, instead of requiring that the full set of all 15 000 ICD-9-CM diagnosis codes be provided, approximately 3300 valid diagnoses are clustered into 64 disease groups (HCCs). Regressions were used to generate cost weights on each of these disease groups, together with demographic categories, selected disease interactions, and age–disease interactions. These HCC cost weights are cumulative, in that predictions are the sum of the contributions of each factor rather than cost weights on mutually exclusive categories. Five variants of the basic model are used, with separate payment weights for continuing and new Medicare enrollees, ESRD enrollees, long-term institutionalized, and participants in "specialty organizations" (which also use self-reported frailty measures).

Data from managed-care plans paid using the CMS-HCC formula have not yet been available to independent researchers for analysis, so it is early to assess the impact and success of the new risk-adjustment formula. The primary concern when it was implemented was that health plans would take advantage of the system and increase the coding intensity of enrollees. In order to offset this, Medicare reduced predicted payments by 5% for each of the first three years. For 2007, they have announced that only a 2.9% offset will be used, suggesting that the coding escalation was not as significant as originally feared. For 2007, a newly recalibrated risk-adjustment formula is also being used that updates the cost weights using more recent data.

8.5.3
USA Privately Insured

The USA privately insured population has an extremely complex set of institutions providing health care. No overview can possibly capture its full complexity, although Cutler and Zeckhauser [73] provide an excellent summary. The way in which the four classes of agent interact in this market differs from the US Medicare is illustrated in Fig. 8.15. The sponsor in almost all cases is the employer, but in some cases (e.g., New Jersey) the state sponsors individual and small firm coverage by creating a separate insurance pool to subsidize this group. Other states mandates require that all insurers offer individual or small group coverage at a community rate, either independently or as part of a larger pool. This effectively forces health plans to become sponsors for this type of consumer. More commonly, employers in the US are able to choose whether to offer insurance or not, and in only a few states is there a tax or penalty to employers who choose not to do this.

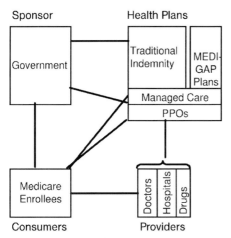

Fig. 8.15 The US Medicare system, 2006.

Employers are able to choose from a large number of competing health plans. Long ago, most consumers enrolled in indemnity plans which offered coverage for any services desired by plan enrollees, subject to deductibles and copayments. Today, most consumers are in some form of managed care, often called HMOs, in each geographic area. Numerous further refined health plan contracting forms, such as PPOs, exclusive provider organizations (EPOs) and POS health plans differ in how much choice the consumer is given, the levels and variation in demand-side cost sharing, and the tightness of the provider panel that is included. Overall, about half of all employees have a choice of health plans through their employment.

The USA differs from Canada and most European countries in that there is much less emphasis on equity goals and weaker efforts to equalize access to health care. Health care is not uniformly viewed as a merit good to which all are entitled with the same level of access. Instead, freedom of choice and honoring individual heterogeneity of tastes is revealed to be highly valued. While there is certainly a great deal of dissatisfaction with the current system and its enormous inequities in access, leaders remain reluctant to introduce major reform.

Formal risk adjustment is used very rarely by private employers [10]. Glazer and McGuire [11] highlight that employers are generally able to negotiate premiums with health plans or have experience rated premiums that implicitly risk adjusts the payments for the riskiness of the enrollees. Also, while formal risk adjustment is only rarely used for payments from employers to health plans, it is widely used for contracting between health plans and provider groups, or for calculating capitated payments to doctors, hospitals and other provider groups.

One new area in which risk adjustment is increasingly being used in commercial health plans is in the calculation of provider quality measures and "pay for performance" measures. Increasingly, providers are being offered bonuses for holding down hospitalization rates, achieving targets for vaccinations and screening, and reducing costs. Recent experience in the USA with bonus and performance–reward payment systems find mixed evidence of its effect [74]. Kapur [72] discusses the need for careful risk adjustment to avoid creating undesirable selection incentives under pay-for-performance programs.

8.5.4
The Netherlands

The Netherlands health care system has two broad systems: (i) a compulsory insurance system of "sickness funds" with careful sponsorship and regulation by the government; and (ii) a voluntary, private insurance system that is much less tightly sponsored and regulated. Eligibility for the two systems is based on income, with income thresholds varying across population subgroups (employees, self-employed, elderly). A person who is eligible for the compulsory system is not eligible for the voluntary system, and vice versa. The structure of the compulsory system is shown in Fig. 8.16. The key decision-making agents in the Dutch health care system are consumers, who enroll in health plans as individuals (plus non-employed partner and non-employed children); employers and a central insurance fund, which serve as sponsors; and 25 non-profit sickness funds (health plans).

Since the early 1990s there has been a slow movement toward managed competition in the Netherlands. The key responsibilities of paying and contracting with providers has been gradually transferred from central government to competing risk-bearing sickness funds. The bulk of the health care financing comes through payroll taxes, levied on earned income, shared between the employee and their employers. A Central Insurance Fund uses prospective formal risk adjustment to reallocate money among the funds. Although in 1992 only age and gender were used to calculate payments, there was a gradual increase in the use of other signals,

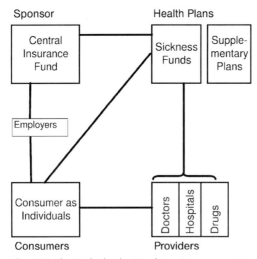

Fig. 8.16 The Netherlands, Mandatory insurance system, 2006.

as described by van de Ven et al. [75, 76]. Along with improved risk adjustment, greater risk has also been imposed on the sickness funds. Whereas originally only 3% of the risk was passed on to health plans, in 2003 the sickness funds' financial risk averaged 52%.

The Netherlands is notable for its gradual enhancements to the risk-adjustment formula used. In 1992, only age and gender were used, but the following new risk adjusters were added over time: region; being an employee (yes/no); disability (all in 1995); age/disability (in 1997); and Pharmacy-based Cost Groups (PCGs) (in 2002). In 2004, DCGs using only in-patient diagnoses were added. Both systems are relatively simple, with only 13 categories of drug and nine categories of diagnoses used. Despite this, PCGs and DCGs are used together to predict an individual's subsequent year expenses. They substantially reduce predictable profits and losses, and reduce the incentives for selection [76].

8.5.5
Germany

Germany has both a social health insurance (GKV) system that covers about 90% of the population, and a private health insurance system (PKV) that is only available to high-income consumers [77]. The structure of the social health insurance system is highlighted in Fig. 8.17; the system is funded primarily by a payroll tax that varies across health plans, called "sickness funds". Whereas prior to the health insurance reforms in 1996, employers played an important role as sponsors, since

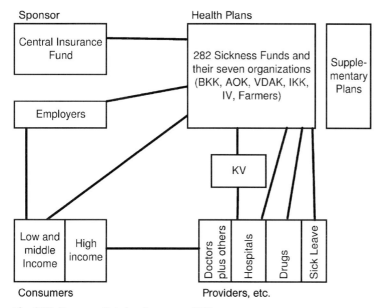

Fig. 8.17 Germany, Statutory Insurance, 2006.

then consumers have been allowed to make choices of health plan without regards to their employment. Consumers make choices as family units, not individuals. Employers contribute half of the payroll tax payments for health insurance, but are not allowed legally to restrict or influence the choices of their employees.

There are over 200 competing sickness funds (health plans), broadly organized into seven classes, each of which has its own history and association [78]. For the most part, the origins of these plans are unimportant for a high-level overview. It is significant that this different history means that each plan tends to have a systematically different group of consumers, so that risk differences across plans are large, even without intentional selection efforts. Currently, there are the first signs of a small degree of selective contracting by health plans with providers.

Risk adjustment is used in Germany at three stages. The primary use is by the sponsor (the central insurance fund), to reallocate funds among competing sickness funds. In addition, capitation payments are used for transferring money to the regional Kassenärztliche Vereinigungen (KV) associations of physicians. Capitation formulas are also currently used in calculating ceilings on total physician payments, which are often binding.

Since 1994 a central insurance fund, that is external to the rest of the financing system and hence cannot endure any deficits, has reallocated money between sickness funds. The central insurance fund acts as if it had received the income-based payments directly from all of the employees and employers, and pays all of the health plans a needs-based amount that is determined by a demographic risk adjuster. Payments for each individual are based on the average cost of the rate cell that the individual falls in; each of 670 rate cells are defined by age, gender, disability pension status, and entitlement to sickness allowances. Buchner and Wasem [79] note that the system equalizes about 92% of the income variation, and that about 70% of the redistribution is due to morbidity differences across plans.

There is relatively little evidence of selection problems in Germany, perhaps because of its structure. While there are many plans, they mostly have very similar benefits and identical provider networks. Buchner and Wasem point out that KV local sickness funds remove much of the risk from the sickness funds, and ensure uniform provider incentives [79]. The KV local sickness funds transfer financial risk back onto providers through their ex-post pricing system. There is enormous dissatisfaction with this mechanism among physicians, and so reforms to this payment approach are a priority.

One empirically validated selection problem in Germany is the difference in characteristics between those choosing private insurance and those choosing the social insurance program. Buchner and Wasem [79] note that, among high-income workers who have the choice, individuals are much more likely to choose private insurance, while families are more likely to choose social insurance. Hence, the average number of persons per contract is 1.18 in the private insurance system (which charges a fixed premium) versus 2.22 in the social insurance system (which collects the premium as a percentage of income). While segmentation of the wealthy, healthy and single contracts from the rest of the population is not a major problem for their system, it does reduce the solidarity contribution (cross-subsidy) from these low-cost individuals to the remainder of the population.

In 2002, the German government passed legislation mandating that they move to a more comprehensive risk adjustment formula in 2009, and legislation enacting this mandate was passed in early 2007. The existing payment formula between the central insurance fund sponsor and the sickness funds will be revised to use a diagnosis and pharmaceutical information, where the choice of indicators is constrained by legislation to include only those conditions costing more than 50% above the average. The reform bill also changes how payments to physicians will be made, with a reduced emphasis on local geographic organizations of physicians. Currently, these agents receive payments that are calculated using only the characteristics of employees in each region, and even basic demographic information such as the number of children, people with chronic conditions, and the unemployed are not reflected. Risk adjustment in Germany may also start to be used to calculate more refined payments to office-based physicians. As of 2006, physicians received FFS reimbursements subject to fixed caps by specialty on allowed total revenue. Under the recent reforms, payments to primary care providers will change to use a quarterly fee for each patient seen, a step towards capitated payment for office-based care, although currently this is proposed to be done without any risk adjustment. The new structure of Germany's provider payment system and health plan choice will increase the role of risk adjustment for many uses.

8.5.6
Lessons from Country Experiences

While summarizing the experience of many diverse countries is difficult, a few themes are worth highlighting. One is that countries differ dramatically in the settings and problems that they face, and also in their reasons for using risk adjustment. It is important to recognize these differences, and to adjust the objective functions for optimal risk adjustment appropriately. In order to achieve equity goals and to ensure efficient payments when the initial levels of per capita spending are inefficient, may require corrections to the formulas generated using conventional risk adjustment.

Whilst every country started out with a relatively simple risk-adjustment formula, such as that based only on age and gender, many have progressed over a period of years from a demographic-only risk adjustment to diagnosis- (US, Netherlands, Germany) or pharmacy-based groups (Netherlands). Hence, many countries are considering their next steps, and the interest and adoption of capitation-based payment seems to be accelerating in many cases.

The US Medicare program is an example of adjusting the overall level of risk-adjusted payments to avoid overpaying its capitation. Both, under demographic- and diagnosis-based groups, the predicted spending was reduced by 5% to reflect differences between the capitated and non-capitated spending levels. Although this is not the same as optimal risk adjustment, which might take into account more sophisticated coding creep and other forms of strategic behavior, it is a step in that direction, and indeed it may be all that is feasible given the limited information available to policy makers. In this respect, the research community can help by conducting further research that will provide the policy makers with more information concerning the nature of strategic behavior and the relevant parameters to the cost and provision processes.

8.6
Conclusions

Currently, the available literature on risk adjustment is diverse in nature, and rapidly growing in extent. Whilst it is impossible to summarize the extensive information provided, it may be useful to mention a few common themes and directions for future research. The major new direction for risk-adjustment payment models is to incorporate richer and more explicit objective functions than simply to maximize the predictive power. Optimal risk adjustment is an important concept – not only for theoretical research but also for policy applications of risk adjustment. The uses to which models will be put should play an important role in their design and estimation.

Today, risk-adjustment and other predictive models are increasingly used for diverse, non-payment purposes. Controlling for quality [81], detecting performance improvements [82], ranking and rating providers [83], measuring selection incentives [55, 84, 85], and identifying and managing those patients at greatest risk of health deterioration, are all important uses of the frameworks that have been used here. Although few academic studies have been conducted on either the conceptual basis or empirical development of models for these more practical uses, it will be interesting to monitor the findings of economics and health service studies over the next few years.

Acknowledgments

The ideas expressed here are the author's own and do not necessarily reflect those of Boston University, nor any other organization. The authors thanks Pierre-Thomas Léger, Thomas McGuire, Nazmi Sari, and participants at the Banff International Workshop for their useful comments on an earlier draft. Note: The author is a consultant at a company that licenses software to implement risk-adjustment models.

References

1 Van de Ven, W., Ellis, R.P. (2000) Risk adjustment in competitive health plan markets. In: Culyer, A.J., Newhouse, J.P. (Eds.), *Handbook of Health Economics*. North Holland, Amsterdam.

2 Glazer, J., McGuire, T.G. (2006) Optimal risk adjustment. In: Jones, A.M. (Ed.) *The Elgar Companion to Health Economics*. Edward Elgar Publishing Co., Gloucester, UK.

3 Glazer, J., McGuire, T.G. (2007) Chapter 9 in this book.

4 Iezzoni, L.I. (2003) *Risk adjustment for measuring health outcomes.* 5th edn. Ann Arbor, MI: Academy Health HAP.

5 Kronick, R., Dreyfus, T. (1997) *The Challenge of Risk Adjustment for People with Disabilities: Health-Based Payment for Medicaid Programs.* Princeton, N.J. Center for Health Care Strategies.

6 Ash, A.S., Ellis, R.P., Pope, G.C., Ayanian, J.Z., Bates, D.W., Burstin, H., Iezzoni L.I., McKay, E., Yu, W. (2000) Using diagnoses to describe populations and predict costs. *Health Care Fin. Rev.*, Spring **21**(3), 7–28.

7 Hurley J., Hutchison B., Giacomini M., Birch S., Dorland J., Reid R., Pizzoferrato G. (1999) *Policy Considerations in Implementing Capitation for Integrated Health Systems.* Canadian Health Services Research Foundation, June.

8 Hutchison B., Hurley J., Reid R., Dorland J., Birch S., Giacomini M., Pizzoferrato G. (1999) *Capitation Formulae for Integrated Health Systems: A Policy Synthesis.* Canadian Health Services Research Foundation, June.

9 Thomas, J.W., Grazier, K.L., Ward K. (2004) Comparing accuracy of risk-adjustment methodologies used in economic profiling of physicians. *Inquiry*, **41**, 218–231.

10 Keenan, P.S., Beewkes Buntin, M.J., McGuire, T.G., Newhouse, J.P. (2001) The prevalence of Formal Risk Adjustment. *Inquiry*, **38**, 245–259.

11 Glazer, J., McGuire, T.G. (2001) Private employers don't need formal risk adjustment. *Inquiry*, **38**, 260–269.

12 Glazer, J., McGuire, T.G. (2000) Optimal risk adjustment of health insurance premiums: an application to managed care. *Am. Econ. Rev.*, **90**(4), 1055–1071.

13 Jack, W. (2006) Optimal risk adjustment in a model with adverse selection and spatial competition. *J. Health Econ.*, **25**, 908–926.

14 Biglaiser, G., Ma, C.T.A. (2003) Price and quality competition under adverse selection: market organization and efficiency. *RAND J. Econ.*, **34**(2), 266–286.

15 Newhouse, J. (1996) Reimbursing health plans and health providers: efficiency in production versus selection. *J. Econ. Lit.*, **34**, 1236–1263.

16 Shen, Y., Ellis, R.P. (2002) Cost minimizing risk adjustment. *J. Health Econ.*, **21**, 515–530.

17 Kronick, R., Gilmer, T., Dreyfus, T., Lee, L. (2000) Improving health-based payment for Medicaid beneficiaries. *CDPS Health Care Fin. Rev.*, **21**, 29–64.

18 Ozminkowski, R.J., Smith, M.W., Coffey, R.M., Mark, T.L., Neslusan, C.A., Drabek, J. (2000) Private Payers Serving Individuals with Disabilities and Chronic Conditions. Report prepared under contract #HHS-100-95-0044 between the U.S. Department of Health and Human Services (HHS), Office of Disability, Aging and Long-Term Care Policy (DALTCP). at http://aspe.hhs.gov/daltcp/reports/privpay.htm.

19 Frank, R., Glazer, J., McGuire, T.G. (2002) Measuring adverse selection in managed health care. *J. Health Econ.*, **19**, 829–854.

20 Ingber, M. (1998) The current state of risk adjustment technology for capitation. *J. Ambul. Care Manage.*, **21**, 1–28.

21 Newhouse, J. (2002) *Pricing the Priceless: A Health Care Conundrum.* MIT Press, Cambridge MA.

22 Centers for Medicare and Medicaid Services (CMS). (2006) Announcement of Calendar Year (CY) 2007 Medicare Advantage Capitation Rates and Medicare Advantage and Part D Payment Policies, April. Downloaded on August 23, 2006. http://www.cms.hhs.gov/MedicareAdvtgSpecRateStats/Downloads/Announcement2007.pdf.

23 Ellis, R.P., McGuire, T.G. (1986) Provider behavior under prospective reimbursement: cost sharing and supply. *J. Health Econ.*, **5**, 129–152.

24 Lee, L.F. (1983) Generalized econometric models with selectivity. *Econometrica*, **51**, 507–512.

25 Terza, J.V. (2002) Alcohol abuse and employment: a second look. *J. Appl. Econometrics*, **17**, 393–404.

26 Glied, S.A. (2000) Managed Care. In: Culyer, A.J., Newhouse, J.P. (Eds.), *The Handbook of Health Economics*. North Holland, Amsterdam.

27 Ma, C.-A. (2003) Managed care and shadow price. *Health Econ. Lett.*, **7**, 17–20.

28 Cumming, R.B., Knutson, D., Cameron, B.A., Derrick, B. (2002) A comparative analysis of claims-based methods of health risk assessment for commercial populations. Research study sponsored by the US Society of Actuaries. http://www.soa.org/ccm/cms-service/ stream/asset?asset_id=9215098&g11n.

29 Thomas, J.W., Grazier, K.L., Ward K. (2004) Economic profiling of primary care physicians: consistency among risk-adjusted measures. *Health Serv. Res.*, **39**, 985–1003.

30 P.-T. Léger (2007) Chapter 7 in this book.

31 Rice, N., Smith, P. (2001), Capitation and risk adjustment in health care financing: an international progress report. *Millbank Q.*, **79**, 81–113.

32 Glazer, J., McGuire, T.G. (2002) Setting health plan premiums to ensure efficient quality in health care: minimum variance optimal risk adjustment. *J. Pub. Econ.*, **84**, 153–175.

33 Charlson, M.E., Pompei, P., Ales, K.L., MacKenzie, C.R. (1987) A new method of classifying prognostic comorbidity in longitudinal studies: development and validation. *J. Chron. Dis.*, **40**, 373–383.

34 Ash, A.S., Porell, F., Gruenberg, L., et al. (1989) Adjusting Medicare capitation payments using prior hospitalization data. *Health Care Fin. Rev.*, **10**(4), 17–29.

35 Weiner, J.P., Starfield, B.H., Steinwachs, D.M., Mumford, L.M. (1991) Development and application of a population-oriented measure of ambulatory care case mix. *Med. Care*, **29**, 453–472.

36 Von Korff, M., Wagner, E.H., Saunders, K. (1992) A chronic disease score from automated pharmacy data. *J. Clin. Epidemiol.*, **45**, 197–203.

37 Zhao, Y., Ellis, R.P., Ash, A.S., Calabrese, D., Ayanian, J.Z, Slaughter, J.P., Weyuker L., Bowen, B. (2001) Measuring population health risks using inpatient diagnoses and outpatient pharmacy data. *Health Serv. Res.*, **26**, 180–193.

38 Fishman, P.A., Goodman, M.J., Hornbrook, M.C., Meenan, R.T., Bachman, D.J., O'Keeffe-Rosetti, M.C. (2003) Risk adjustment using automated ambulatory pharmacy data: the RxRisk model. *Med. Care*, **41**, 84–99.

39 Averill, R.F., Goldfield, N.I., Eisenhandler, J., Hughes, J.S., Shafir, B.V., Gannon, D.E., et al. (1999) *Development and evaluation of clinical risk groups (CRGs)*. 3M Health Information Systems, Wallingford, CT.

40 Symmetry Health Data Systems, Inc. (2001). *Episode risk groups: ERG user's guide*. Phoenix, AZ: Symmetry Health Data Systems, Inc.

41 Pope, G.C., Ellis, R.P., Ash, A.S., Liu, C.F., Ayanian, J.Z., Bates, D.W., Burstin, H., Iezzoni, L.I., Ingber, M.J. (2000) Principal inpatient diagnostic cost group models for Medicare risk adjustment. *Health Care Fin. Rev.*, **21**, 93–118.

42 Ware, J.E., Gandek, B. (1998) Overview of the SF-36 Health Survey and the International Quality of Life Assessment (IQOLA) Project. *J. Clin. Epidemiol.*, **51**, 903–912.

43 Pope, G.C., Ellis, R.P., Ash, A.S., Ayanian, J.Z., Bates, D.W., Burstin, H., Iezzoni, L.I., Marcantonio, E., Wu, B. (2000) Diagnostic cost group hierarchical condition category models for Medicare risk adjustment. Final Report to Health Care Financing Administration, December.

44 Ellis, R.P., Pope, G.C., Iezzoni, L.I., Ayanian, J.Z., Bates, D.W., Burstin, H., Ash, A.S. (1996) Diagnosis-based risk adjustment for Medicare capitation payments. *Health Care Fin. Rev.*, **12**, 101–128.

45 Kronick, R.T., Dreyfus, T., Zhou, Z. (1996) Diagnostic risk adjustment for Medicaid: the disability payment system. *Health Care Fin. Rev.*, **17**, 7–33.

46 Hornbrook, M.C., Goodman, M.J., Fishman, P., Meenan, R., Greenlick, M.R.

(1998) Development and estimation of a global risk adjustment model. *Abstr. Book Assoc. Health Serv. Res. Meet.*, **15**, 227.

47 Carter, G.M., Bell, R.B., Dubois, R.W., et al. (1997) *A Clinically Detailed Risk Information System for Cost*. DRU-1731-1-HCFA. RAND, Santa Monica, CA.

48 Manning, W.G., Newhouse, J.P., Duan, N., Keeler, E.B., Leibowitz, A. (1987) Health insurance and the demand for medical care: evidence from a random-ized experiment. *Am. Econ. Rev.*, **77**, 251–277.

49 Duan, N., Manning, W.G., Morris, C.N., Newhouse, J.P. (1983). A comparison of alternative models for the demand for medical care. *J. Bus. Econ. Statist.*, **1**, 115–126.

50 Mullahy, J. (1998) Much ado about two: reconsidering retransformation and the two-part model in health econometrics. *J. Health Econ.*, **17**, 247–282.

51 Manning, W.G., Basu, A., Mullahy, J. (2005) Generalized modeling approaches to risk adjustment of skewed outcomes data. *J. Health Econ.*, **24**, 465–488.

52 Manning, W.G., Mullahy J. (2001) Estimating log models: To transform or not to transform? *J. Health Econ.*, **20**, 461–494.

53 Fishman, P., Sloan, K., Burgess, J., Jr., Zhou, C., Wang, L. (2006) Eval-uating alternative risk assessment models: Evidence from the US Vet-eran Population, Group Health Center for Health Studies working paper, May, 2006, available at: http://www.centerforhealthstudies.org/ctrstaff/fishman.html.

54 Basu, A., Manning, W.G., Mullahy, J. (2004) Comparing alternative mod-els: Log vs. Cox Proportional Hazard. *Health Econ.*, **13**, 749–765.

55 Ellis, R.P., McGuire, T.G. (2007) Pre-dictability and predictiveness in health care spending. *J. Health Econ.*, **26**, 25–48.

56 Veazie, P.J., Manning, W.G., Kane, R.L. (2003) Improving risk adjustment for Medicare capitated reimbursement

using nonlinear models. *Med. Care*, **41**, 741–752.

57 Manning, W.G. (1998) The logged de-pendent variable, heteroskedasticity, and the retransformation problem. *J. Health Econ.*, **17**, 283–296.

58 Buntin, M.B., Zaslovsky, A.M. (2004) Too much ado about two-part models and transformation? Comparing meth-ods of modeling Medicare expenditures. *J. Health Econ.*, **23**, 525–542.

59 Berlinguet, M., Preyra, C., Dean, S. (2005) Comparing the value of three main diagnosis based risk adjustment systems (DBRAS). Canadian Health Services Research Foundation (CHSRF) report. www.chsrf.ca/final_research/ogc/pdf/berlinguet _final.pdf.

60 Wasem, J., Lauterbach, L.M., Schrader, W.F. (2006) Klassifikationsmodelle für Versicherte im morbiditätsorientierten Risikostrukturausgleich. (Classifica-tion models for risk adjustment in the morbidity-oriented risk structure reconciliation.) Wissenschaftliches Institut der AOK (WIdO). Down-loaded on 8/17/2006 at http://wido.de/fileadmin/wido/downloads/pdf_ggw/wido_ggw_aufs1_0205.pdf.

61 Alberta Health and Wellness (2003) Health and Wellness, http://www.health.gov.ab.ca/.

62 Chowdhury, T., Fatoo, H., Friesen, D., Yang, Q., Kramer, G. (2003) *An eval-uation of risk adjustment groupers in a publicly funded health system: A case study using Alberta data, Alberta Health and Wellness*. iHEA Poster Presentation, June.

63 Canadian Institute for Health In-formation. (2005) The Status of Alternative Payment Programs for Physicians in Canada. http://dsp-psd.pwgsc.gc.ca/Collection/H115-13-2003E.pdf.

64 Reid, R.J., MacWilliam, L., Verhulst, L., Roos, N., Atkinson, N. (2001) Perfor-mance of the ACG case-mix system in two Canadian Provinces. *Med. Care*, **39**, 86–99.

65 Reid, R.J., Roos, N. P., MacWilliam, L., Frohlich, N., Black, C. (2002) Assessing population health care need

using a claims-based ACG morbidity measure: A validation analysis in the Province of Manitoba. *Health Serv. Res.*, **37**, 1345–1364.

66 Lu, M., Moores, D.G., Reid, R., Woodhead-Lyons, S.C., Zhang, J.X. (2002) A Review of Capitation in Alberta: A Report to the APP Subcommittee of Alberta Health & Wellness and the Alberta Medical Association, pp. 1–77.

67 Brown, R., Bergeron, J.W., Clement, D.G. (1993) Do health maintenance organizations work for Medicare? *Health Care Fin. Rev.*, **15**, 7–24.

68 Cao, Z., McGuire, T.G. (2002) Service-level selection by HMOs in Medicare. *J. Health Econ.*, **22**, 915–931.

69 Dallek, G., Dennington, A. (2002) Physician withdrawals: a major source of instability in the Medicare+Choice program. The Commonwealth Fund, New York.

70 Medicare Payment Commission (1998) Report to the Congress: Medicare Payment Policy.

71 Pope, G.C., Adamache, K.W., Khandker, R.K., Walsh, E.G. (1998) Evaluating alternative risk adjusters for Medicare. *Health Care Fin. Rev.*, **20**, 109–129.

72 Kapur, K. (2005) *Risk Adjustment Methods and their Relevance to Pay-or-Play Supplement E to the Report: Challenges and Alternatives for Employer Pay-or-Play Program Design: An Implementation and Alternative Scenario Analysis of California's Health Insurance Act of 2003 (SB 2).* Report written for the California Health Care Foundation and the California Managed Risk Medical Insurance Board Project Team. www.ihps.org/pubs/2005_Apr_IHPS_SB2_ESup_Risk_Adj.pdf.

73 Cutler, D., Zeckhauser, R. (2000) The anatomy of health insurance. In: *Handbook of Health Economics*, Volume **IA**, Culyer, A., Newhouse, J.P. (Eds.), Elsevier, Amsterdam, pp. 563–643.

74 Rosenthal, M.B., Frank, R.G., Li, Z., Epstein, A.M. (2005) Early evidence with pay-for-performance: From concept to practice. *JAMA*, **294**, 1788–1793.

75 Van de Ven, W.P.M.M., Beck, K., Buchner, F., et al. (2003) Risk adjustment and risk selection on the sickness fund insurance market in five European countries. *Health Policy*, **65**, 75–98.

76 Van de Ven, W.P.M.M., van Vliet, R.C.J.A., Lamers, L.M. (2004) Health-adjusted premium subsidies in the Netherlands. *Health Affairs*, **23**, 45–54.

77 Busse, R., Riesberg, A. (2004) Health care systems in transition: Germany. Copenhagen, WHO Regional Office for Europe on behalf of the European Observatory on Health Systems and Policies.

78 Fuerstenberg, T., Rochell, B., Roeder, N. (2007) Ambulatory and hospital care in the Federal Republic of Germany. *Am. Heart Hosp. J.*, **5**, 22–26.

79 Buchner, F., Wasem, J. (2003) Needs for further improvement: risk adjustment in the German health insurance system. *Health Policy*, **65**, 21–35.

80 Alberta Health and Wellness (2005) 2005–2006 Regional Health Authority Global Funding, Methodology and funding manual, April.

81 Murgolo, M. (2002) MCBS highlights: comparison of Medicare Risk HMO and FFS enrollees. *Health Care Fin. Rev.*, **24**, 177–185.

82 McKillop, I., Pink, G.H., Johnson, L.M. (2001) The financial management of acute care in Canada: A review of funding, performance monitoring and reporting practices. Ottawa, Ontario: Canadian Institute for Health Information, 2001.

83 Shwartz, M., Ash, A.S., Pekoz, E. (2006) Risk adjustment and risk-adjusted provider profiles. *Int. J. Healthcare Tech. Manage.*, **7**, 15–42.

84 Eggleston, K. (2000) Risk selection and optimal health insurance-provider payment systems. *J. Risk Insur.*, **67**, 175–198.

85 Eggleston, K., Bir, A. (2007) Measuring selection incentives in managed care: evidence from the Massachusetts State Employee Health Insurance Program. *J. Risk Insur.* (in press).

9

Inducing Quality from Health Care Providers in the Presence of Adverse Selection

Jacob Glazer, and Thomas G. McGuire

9.1
Introduction

In many countries, residents choose a health plan or sickness fund through which to receive health insurance benefits. These choices are regulated and at least partially paid for by governments and employers. Collective financing of health care redistributes the burden of cost from the sick to the healthy and from the poor to the rich, in comparison to a system with no insurance where everyone pays their own way. At the same time, societies seek the virtues of markets: choice, innovation, and cost and quality competition from their health insurance plans. Melding these desires for both a fair and controlled, and an efficient and innovative, health insurance sector is a central and common problem facing all developed nations. As Rice and Smith [1] point out, a common approach to this problem consists of national governments collecting the funds to pay for health care, but then passing responsibility for the purchasing of health care to a local organization, a private insurance plan, as in the federal Medicare program in the United States, local government in the United Kingdom, Canada and Australia, or sickness funds as in Germany, Israel, Netherlands, and Belgium. Governmental involvement intends to distribute the cost burden fairly, and competition among the decentralized participants is intended to promote efficiency.

One of the major concerns with such a policy is adverse selection [2, 3]. Generally, health plans or sickness funds may take actions to discourage or encourage potential enrollees from joining, and these actions may have efficiency or fairness implications. For one thing, they may refuse some applicants, although overt actions to discourage individuals are normally prohibited. More troublesome and difficult to monitor is that plans may distort the mix of the quality of health care they offer to discourage high-cost persons from joining the plan. As a number of reports have observed, decisions about what care is medically necessary are fundamentally outside the scope of direct regulation [4, 5]. The aim of this chapter is to consider how economic analysis can help to address the problem of inefficient quality of care caused by adverse selection. The policy context is a centrally financed, but competitively supplied, health insurance system. Most health economists' answers

Financing Health Care: New Ideas for a Changing Society. Edited by Mingshan Lu and Egon Jonsson
Copyright © 2008 WILEY-VCH Verlag GmbH & Co. KGaA, Weinheim
ISBN: 978-3-527-32027-1

to the question of how to address selection in this context center around the policy of risk adjustment of the premiums paid to insuring organizations. Whether risk adjustment is helpful and/or necessary, and what form of risk adjustment is most useful, depends on the nature of problem raised by adverse selection, and on the alternative tools that the regulator (or employer) has to deal with these problems. After briefly reviewing the quality problem caused by adverse selection, the discussion is organized around five cases, according to what the payer knows and can do about selection. In this respect, both contracting and information-based policies, as well as risk adjustment, will be considered.

9.2
The Basic Adverse Selection Problem

One aspect of selection is when enrollees with different costs are distributed unevenly across health plans or sickness funds. In Medicare in the United States (US), for example, there is plenty of evidence that lower-cost beneficiaries are more likely to enroll in managed-care plans paid by risk-adjusted capitation, and higher-cost beneficiaries remain in the fee-for-service (FFS) sector.[1] In private health insurance, managed-care plans also attract lower-cost enrollees.[2]

Selection of this form may, or may not, constitute a social efficiency problem. In any population, there will be diversity in tolerance for cost-control mechanisms, in the evaluation of different benefits, and in locational preferences. If any of these factors or other factors are correlated with expected health care costs, an efficient division of the market among plans (that is, one respecting diversity in tastes) will be characterized by the selection of higher risk individuals into some plans. As Feldman and Dowd [14] and Pauly [15] have effectively argued, evidence of risk segmentation of this form does not constitute a *per se* violation of conditions for economic efficiency in insurance markets. Nonetheless, selection of this type can be associated with unfairness in the sense of differential premiums or contribution rates. In the analyses referred to above, health plans are assumed to offer a fixed product, and the efficiency issue is sorting people among plans.

The analysis of adverse selection and efficiency of health insurance is incomplete, however, without recognizing that plans take actions to affect their membership.

---

1) Eggers and Prihoda [6] showed that people in Medicare health maintenance organizations (HMOs) had significantly lower costs than those in traditional fee-for-service sector. A survey by Rossiter and Wilensky [7] indicated that most of the studies during 1974 to 1986 supported the existence of selection behavior by HMOs. Brown et al. [8] found that the spending of Medicare enrollees in a managed-care

plan would be 10% lower than average if they had been in the FFS sector. Greenwald et al. [9] showed that there were significant differences between the actual cost of managed-care and FFS beneficiaries for inpatient services. Also see Hellinger [10].

2) Nicholson et al. [11]. See also Cutler and Zeckhauser [12] for a review.

Plans can do two main things:

- First, if a plan or fund knows the likely cost of an identifiable potential enrollee will be more (or less) than the revenue the plan receives for that person, the plan might take actions to discourage (or encourage) enrollment at the individual level. Suppose a government or employer pays a plan a fixed amount for each enrollee in the plan, disregarding observable factors, such as age, when paying the plan. Older workers cost more than younger workers. A plan has an obvious incentive to accept a young worker and deny enrollment to an older worker. Health plans are generally prohibited by regulation from denying enrollment to eligible applicants, but some covert actions to discourage costly applicants may be difficult to stop. This type of plan behavior is not associated with a quality distortion, and will not be the focus of this analysis.
- Plans can do a second thing, which does not require illegal actions directed against individuals. The plan can underprovide some services and overprovide others, attracting the low risks and deterring the high risks [5, 16].

Plan manipulation, in Cutler and Zeckhauser's [12] terminology, emerges in models of health insurance when plans compete on the basis of service quality [13, 17]. The basic idea draws on early analyses of insurance by Rothschild and Stiglitz [18]. Demand for treatment of chronic conditions, for example, may be much better anticipated, and more unevenly distributed in a population, than demand for acute care. In such a case, the health plan has a financial incentive to distort the mix of its care away from chronic care and towards acute illness, in order to deter/attract the high/low risks. Nearly all writers on the efficiency of health insurance markets with managed care acknowledge this effect, though they vary in the emphasis they put on it. It is in the foreground of the discussion in Cao, Frank et al., Glazer and McGuire, Luft and Miller, and Newhouse [13, 19–21], while being noted but given less prominence by Cutler and Zeckhauser, Feldman and Dowd, Pauly, and van de Ven and Ellis [12, 14–16, 22]. When a plan can set prices as well as quality, a version of this strategy is to provide low quality overall, and set a low price, to attract the low risks.

This quality distortion problem has received a good deal of attention in the literature in health economics. Here, we present the basic adverse selection model, as a point of reference, in order to highlight some of the key assumptions behind the model. Reconsidering these assumptions will structure our analysis of ways in which a regulator can address quality problems due to adverse selection.

Suppose that there are two types of individual, L and H, who can contract two illnesses, a and c. Illness a we call an acute illness and both types of people have the same probability of contracting this illness, $p_a > 0$. The two types are distinguished in their probability of contracting the chronic illness c. Let p_i, $i \in \{H, L\}$ denote the probability that a person of type i contracts illness c. Then, $p_H > p_L > 0$. The proportion of H types in the population is λ, $0 < \lambda < 1$. Let $p_c \equiv \lambda p_H + (1 - \lambda)p_L$ denote the (expected) probability that a randomly drawn person contracts the chronic illness. Throughout our analysis we assume that each individual knows their type.[3] It is also assumed that each individual must choose one plan.

If a person (of either type) has illness j, j ∈ {a, c}, their utility from treatment will be increased by $V_j(q_j)$, where $q_j > 0$ denotes the "quality" of the services devoted to treat illness j, with $V'_j > 0$ and $V''_j \leq 0$.[4] Thus, we make the simplifying assumption that the benefits from treatment are independent of one another and the same to all individuals. If a person has both illnesses, their utility, if treated, will simply be increased by $V_a(q_a) + V_c(q_c)$.

Treatment services are provided by health plans. A health plan is characterized by a quality pair (q_a, q_c), where q_j, j ∈ {a, c} is a summary indicator of the quality of services that the plan provides, devoted to treating illness j. Thus, if a person of type i, i ∈ {H, L} joins a plan with a quality pair (q_a, q_c), their expected utility will increase by:

$$U_i(q_a, q_c) = p_a V_a(q_a) + p_i V_c(q_c) \tag{9.1}$$

Throughout the analysis we assume that each plan gets to choose its quality pair, and that a plan can offer only one quality pair. All plans have the same cost function. A plan's cost of treating a person with illness j, j ∈ {a, c} at a quality level q_j is $C_j(q_j)$, where $C'_j > 0$, $C''_j > 0$. Thus, if a person of type i, i ∈ {H, L} joins a plan that offers a quality pair (q_a, q_c), the plan's costs are expected to increase by:

$$C_i(q_a, q_c) = p_a C_a(q_a) + p_i C_c(q_c) \tag{9.2}$$

The *socially efficient* quality pair (q_a^*, q_c^*) equalizes marginal benefit of treatment to marginal cost, thus solving the following pair of equations:

$$V'_a(q_a^*) = C'_a(q_a^*) \tag{9.3}$$

$$V'_c(q_c^*) = C'_c(q_c^*)$$

High- and low-risk types have different probabilities of becoming ill, but once ill, they receive the same utility from treatment. Thus, the efficient level of quality is independent of the probability of becoming ill, and is the same for both types.

We postulate the existence of a public regulator or payer whose objective is to implement the socially desired quality. The focus of this analysis will be on the tools that the regulator can use in order to achieve this goal, and on the conditions under which these tools can be applied. It is assumed that the regulator can enforce an open enrollment policy (thus, avoiding the first potential problem associated with selection noted above). Five key assumptions are behind the basic adverse

---

3) For further discussion of the assumptions in this section, see Glazer and McGuire [13].
4) The economic literature models quality in two ways: as a form of quantity rationing, as here and in Pauly and Ramsey [23], or as a shadow price as in Keeler et al. [24] or Frank, Glazer and McGuire [20]. When consumers are identical in their demands, given they are ill and differ only in the probability of having an illness, the two approaches are equivalent.

selection result:[5]

1. Quality is not contractible. The public regulator cannot condition payments to plans (either by the regulator or by the individuals) on the basis of their delivered quality.
2. Cost (per individual) is not contractible. The public regulator cannot condition payments to plans on the basis of costs (per person).
3. Plans can freely enter and exit the market. The public regulator cannot condition a plan's participation on the basis of its quality. However, once a plan participates, the regulator can require that it accepts every applicant (open enrollment).
4. Consumers can observe the quality of each plan and can freely choose a plan.
5. There is no risk adjustment. More specifically, it is assumed that the premium is set such that the plan is expected to break even if it offers the socially efficient quality pair (q_a^*, q_c^*) and attracts randomly drawn individuals from the entire population. Thus, the premium is set at r^*, where $r^* = p_a C_a(q_a^*) + p_c C_c(q_c^*)$.[6]

The order of moves in our model is as follows: first plans (simultaneously) choose their quality pair, (q_a, q_c), after which individuals choose plans and plans collect a revenue of r^* per enrollee; finally, each individual's health state (whether he or she has illness a and/or c) is realized and plans pay the costs of treatment. Our definition of a competitive equilibrium in this case is similar to that of Rothschild and Stiglitz [18]. A *competitive equilibrium* in this market is a set of quality pairs such that, when individuals choose a plan to maximize expected utility: (i) no quality pair in the equilibrium set makes negative expected profit; and (ii) there is no quality pair outside the equilibrium set that, if offered, will make a positive profit.

Following Rothschild and Stiglitz [18] and Glazer and McGuire [13], we know that if the proportion of the H types in the population is sufficiently large, then a competitive equilibrium exists and is characterized by two quality pairs.[7] H types choose the plan(s) that offer the quality pair:

$$
\begin{aligned}
(q_a^H, q_c^H) = \arg\max \quad & U_H(q_a, q_c) \\
\text{s.t.} \quad & C_H(q_a, q_c) = r^*
\end{aligned}
\tag{9.4}
$$

5) One could add another assumption – that the regulator can write only one insurance contract for the package of services. An insurer or other payer that can "carve out" one or more services from the main contract, has another policy instrument to work with. See Frank, Glazer and McGuire [20] for some discussion of this point.

6) The assumption that plans cannot compete on premium is not essential to the analysis. The starting point of our analysis is that when quality is multi-dimensional, adverse selection incentives induce plans to distort quality. If plans could also choose premium, then pre-mium would be just another instrument that plans could use to "select" patients. However, this instrument by itself would not generally be enough and plans would still have the incentives to distort quality in order to affect the mixture of enrollees. Even if we allowed for the possibility that plans choose copayments, the results would not change much, unless the plans could choose different levels of copayments for the different services they provide.

7) The exact condition is that λ should be sufficiently large so that $U_L(q_a^L, q_c^L) \geq U_L(q_a, q_c)$ for every (q_a, q_c) for which $p_a C_a(q_a) + p_c C_c(q_c) = r^*$.

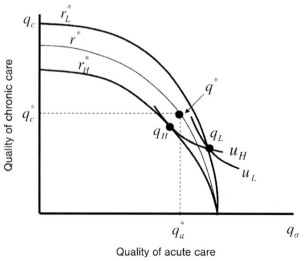

Fig. 9.1 The basic adverse selection result.

and L types choose the plan(s) that offer the quality pair:

$$\left(q_a^L, q_c^L\right) = \arg\max \quad U_L(q_a, q_c)$$
$$\text{s.t.} \quad C_L(q_a, q_c) = r^* \tag{9.5}$$
$$\text{and} \quad U_L(q_a, q_c) = U_L\left(q_a^H, q_c^H\right)$$

The equilibrium is described in Fig. 9.1. The curves r_i^*, $i = H, L$ represent all plans, i.e., pairs of (q_a, q_c), that break even if the plan attracts only individuals of type i, when the premium is r^*. The points denoted by q_i, $i = H$ or L, depict the plan chosen by type i in equilibrium, i.e., $q_i = (q_a^i, q_c^i)$. Curves u_i, $i = H, L$, represent type i's indifference curves that goes through the point q_i. The curve r^* represents all plans that break even if the plan attracts a random sample of the population, and the point q^* depicts the socially efficient levels of quality. We can see, therefore, that in a market where the five assumptions above hold, plans will not offer the socially efficient quality profile in equilibrium.

9.3
Dealing with Adverse Selection

The potential policy tools available to a regulator correspond to the five assumptions laid out above. Relaxing each assumption in turn can be used as a basis for a discussion of the different approaches to dealing with the basic adverse selection problem. The focus of this analysis will be the cases that correspond to the relaxation of the last two assumptions. For each of these cases, we will discuss the theoretical concepts and, where possible, make brief reference to policy settings that resemble the case. Initially, however, some implications of the relaxation of the first three assumptions will be briefly discussed.

9.3.1
Quality is Verifiable

If the quality of a plan is verifiable, then payments can be made on the basis of quality. The regulator can construct a contract by which a plan receives a premium per person that is a function of the plan's quality. If the premium function is such that when all plans offer the socially desired quality each plan makes zero expected profit and no plan wishes to deviate to another quality profile (possibly attracting only one of the two types), then the regulator's objective is achieved. One such premium function would be the one that pays plans nothing if their quality is different than the socially desired quality, and pays them exactly their expected costs if they do offer the socially desired quality.

It should be noted that in case discussed above, there is no need for competition in order to implement the desired quality. However, what the regulator needs to "know" exactly is the socially desired quality, in order for the premium to be dependent on any gap between the plan's actual quality and the desired one. One could assume a somewhat more realistic scenario where the quality is observable and verifiable, but the regulator does not have enough information (for example, about the plan's costs or the enrollee's health care needs) to be certain about the level of quality of each service that defines the socially desired quality bundle. In such a case. the regulator may enhance quality by having many plans and paying higher premiums to plans with higher quality.

Unfortunately, there are some major problems with paying on quality. First, it is very difficult to measure quality precisely, especially as a good quality measure needs to take into account the severity of illness for each patient. Adjusting for severity is rather complex and involves many of the issues related to risk adjustment (these are discussed later). Furthermore, even if a good quality measure can be developed for some services, it is practically impossible to develop a good measure for *all* services. However, paying on quality only for some services and not the other, may introduce a multi-tasking problem.

The number of health plans that have adopted pay-for-performance mechanisms is growing rapidly, especially in the US. However, most of these programs are in their early stages and at present very little evidence is available concerning their outcomes. Rosenthal and Frank [25] have surveyed the incentive issues and empirical results of pay-for-performance studies, with one conclusion being that, "Despite the assertions of its proponents, the empirical foundations of pay-for-performance in health care are rather weak." Rosenthal et al. [26] evaluated a natural experiment with pay-for-performance to a physicians groups in California, and concluded mainly that, in this instance, paying on quality transferred funds to the organizations with high performance at baseline and produced little improvement in quality for the money spent.

Overall, it seems that, whilst experimenting with pay-for-performance is becoming increasingly popular, it is likely to remain a small part of the contracts. At present, its effectiveness in contending with selection-related quality problems remains an open question, although this is beginning to be studied in empirical research.

9.3.2
Cost (Per Individual) is Verifiable

When the costs of a plan are verifiable, the regulator has the choice of several different payment schemes, conditioning payments to plans on their actual expenditures. One simple and commonly used strategy is that of cost-sharing. Under cost-sharing, the payer – in addition to paying the plan a fixed premium – covers a prespecified share of the plan's costs [5, 27]. One can easily see that in the model studied above, such a strategy would not fully solve the adverse selection problem. In Fig. 9.1, cost-sharing would simply produce a (parallel) shift in the zero profit curves, and the resulting equilibrium would still be a separating one. In a more general framework, however, cost-sharing could reduce the incentives of plans to select enrollees, as it makes the cost differential between a high-cost individual and a low-cost individual smaller. These weaker incentives to select enrollees might result in a more efficient equilibrium outcome, at least as far as adverse selection is concerned. It should be noted that, in order to implement the cost-sharing payment scheme, all the payer needs to verify is a plan's total costs, and not the cost per individual. Note also that plans must be efficient producers of care, which is ensured by assumptions 3 and 4.

If the regulator can verify a plan's cost per individual, then other payment schemes are feasible. The most commonly used and widely discussed scheme is that of outlier cost reimbursement, whereby the payer covers a share of the plan's expenditures on those individuals whose costs exceed a certain prespecified threshold level [16]. When public funds are limited, or incentives are an issue, then other – more general – approaches can be considered [28]. In our stylized model discussed above, it can be seen that under such a payment policy, if only a share of the plan's cost beyond the threshold level are covered, then the equilibrium will still be a separating inefficient one. But, if all of the plan's costs, beyond the threshold level, are covered, then multiple equilibria will emerge with only one of them being the efficient equilibrium.[8] In a more general setting, however, one should expect the outlier cost reimbursement scheme to lessen the plans' incentives to discourage high-risk enrollees as they are no longer very much more expensive to the plan than the low-risk enrollees.

Although cost-sharing mechanisms seem to be helpful in addressing adverse selection problems, they may also create some new problems. If plans costs are at least partially covered, the plans will have less of an incentive to save on costs and more of an incentive to over-provide some services [5]. It seems, however, that

---

8) This will not hold with a continuous distribution of risks.

while the trade-off between these two forces must certainly be taken into account when constructing a reimbursement mechanism, almost any optimal mechanism will contain some elements of cost-sharing, if costs are verifiable.

9.3.3
The Regulator Can Select Plans on the Basis of Quality

If it is assumed that the regulator can observe the quality of each plan, then subsequently they can decide whether or not it is eligible to offer the plan's services to the consumers. In such a case, the regulator can easily implement the socially desired contract by announcing a premium per person that exactly covers a plan's expected cost at the socially desired contract, and announcing that only the plans with the desired quality will be allowed to participate. It is easy to see that, in the model presented above, such a mechanism would implement an equilibrium in which all plans offered the desired quality. This approach requires only that the payer be able to observe quality, and be prepared to not contract with health plans that offer unsatisfactory quality.

While this is seemingly a very strong assumption about the knowledge and power of the regulator, this case corresponds to the private health insurance market in the US. Today, it is common in the US for workers and their families to obtain health insurance offered through their employer. Private health insurance is regulated in terms of pricing, coverage and who must be offered coverage in complex ways, by both the federal and state governments. As a general matter, however, there is no standard benefit, and no universal requirement that employers offer coverage. Nonetheless, because of favorable tax treatment of health insurance included as part of employee benefits, approximately 71% of workers in the US are covered through employer-based health insurance [29].

One crucial feature of the US private health insurance sector is that private employers do not contract with every plan in a market; in other words, employers choose who to contract with and pay on behalf of their employees. In fact, more than half of private employees have no choice of plans [30], and even when their employees are offered a choice of products [for example, a health maintenance organization (HMO), a preferred provider organization (PPO), or a point-of-service (POS) plan], the employers often contract with one carrier to provide all products. Because the entire risk pool of employees remains with the one carrier, there are no incentives at the plan level to influence risk selection among the various products (assuming that the plan itself obtains the same mark-up across products).

In the US, a private employer's authority to *not contract* with a plan or provider is regarded as the fundamental difference between Medicare and private buyers. This difference may be at the root of explanations for why Medicare and private buyers contract in very different ways. The employer's decision about which plan to offer to employees is made simultaneously with any negotiation about price. Employers decide to offer a plan based on the price they receive or can negotiate, and based on the characteristics of the plan.

It is the private employer – not the health plan – that decides how much of the price they pay to health plans will be contributed by workers. Numerous considerations come into play in an employer's decision about pricing. As employer contributions receive favorable tax treatment in comparison to wages, employers have a reason to maximize employer contribution. When more than one health plan is offered, an employer has an interest in making the sorting among plans efficient, and the pricing to the workers can help lead to sorting according to the workers' tastes for health insurance. One frequently advocated approach is for employers to pay the full cost of the lowest cost plan and to pass on any premium above this floor to the employers [31]. Although this may improve sorting, it is not fully efficient as the cost difference among plans itself differs by worker type.[9] "Risk-adjusting" the premium charged to workers (e.g., charging more to older workers) could, in principle, improve the efficiency of sorting, but this – or any other form of risk-adjusted charge – is infrequently observed in the US context. It may be that any incremental gains in efficiency over average cost pricing may not be worth the loss of fairness across the types of worker at any one firm. Miller [32] points out that employer profit maximization (as opposed to the criterion of compensation cost minimization) implies that, if an employer has some monopoly power in "selling" health insurance to its workers, then the price it charges for a more extensive coverage plan should also reflect a "mark-up" on the extra cost.

In summary, private employers address selection by structuring the choices facing their employees, both in terms of the plans that the employees may choose among, and in terms of the prices the employees pay to join a plan. While this mechanism – both in principle and in practice – appears to be quite successful in dealing with adverse selection, it may not be open to public regulators who are generally required to contract with all qualified plans. In these public environments (with versions of "any willing provider" governing contracting), the role of assumptions 4 and 5 come to the fore.

As mentioned previously, however, the focus of this analysis is the mechanisms available to the regulator when either assumption 4 or 5 above is relaxed. This will be discussed, in turn, in the following two sections.

9.4
The Regulator Can Observe Quality, But Consumers Cannot: Choosing What to Report

The basic adverse selection result presented above requires that consumers can observe the quality of all plans before choosing one. The fact that consumers are able to observe the quality of each service that each plan provides enables the plans

---

9) With information about the distribution of costs and tastes, a payer can choose a price differential with which to face consumers to sort the population between plans. (See Cutler and Zeckhauser [12] and Feldman and Dowd [14] for recent treatments.) In special cases, an efficient division of a population between plans can be achieved when the price to consumers for joining the more expensive plan is set so as to just ration the appropriate marginal consumer. As noted in the above reports, this price is not generally the difference in cost for the average consumer in plans. Normally, a payer cannot sort enrollees efficiently by using demand-side prices for plans, as these prices would need to be person-specific.

to distort quality in a way that will attract only one type of consumer, but not the other.

In reality, consumers cannot observe (many important aspects of) the plans' quality, and they often rely on information provided to them either by the plan itself or by some third party, before making their choice. In such a case, the general consensus among health policy makers is that by improving what consumers know, health care markets will function better. Better-informed consumers may choose providers more appropriately. Furthermore, consumers choosing on the basis of quality conveys incentives to providers to improve quality in the first place. These arguments are why public regulators and public groups such as business coalitions are making an effort to discover and reveal the characteristics of the providers' quality of care. The point to be made here, however, is that the revealing of more information is a double-edged sword for chronic and other illnesses in policy contexts in which forces of adverse selection are also affecting quality. From the standpoint of incentives to providers and plans, revealing more information about the quality of care for conditions such as mental illness can exacerbate incentives to reduce quality. Put bluntly, attracting consumers who value the quality of chronic and mental health care may be exactly what health plans may not want to do.

The following simple, but realistic, scenario illustrates the policy problem. Those eligible for Medicaid in the Boston area can choose among several managed-care plans.[10] If an eligible joins a plan, the plan receives a capitation payment. But, suppose the plans differ in the quality of mental health care they offer. For example, a better plan might have a larger network of more experienced therapists and/or wider coverage of drugs in its formulary. Suppose that this information is known imperfectly by those eligible. What are the effects of reporting more complete information about the relative qualities of mental health care of the plans? One effect – the good effect – is that Medicaid-eligible patients needing mental health treatment can join the plan with better coverage. However, there is a second effect: the plans' incentives change when the information is more accurately known. A higher quality mental health care now means that the plan is more likely to attract those who value mental health care. If attracting these eligible patients hurts the plan financially – and the evidence is clear that it does – then the plan has an incentive to *reduce* the quality of its mental health care, when more information about the quality of this service is reported to beneficiaries. A similar story can be told about Medicare beneficiaries and persons with employer-based coverage, all of which adds up to a market in which forcing plans to disclose the quality of their mental health departments might undermine the quality of care offered to enrollees.

The general point here is that the policy choices are not simply to report or not to report. The question that the regulator should ask itself is what is the best way to structure the reports to consumers to give them what they need to make choices, yet at the same time avoiding the danger of creating incentives to reduce the quality of care for chronic and other conditions. One such a direction is as follows: instead

---

10) Medicaid is a state-run program for low-income individuals.

of providing consumers with a separate rating of the quality of every service that the health plan provides, the regulator would group services together and provide consumers only with the average rating of the quality of the different services in the group. For example, instead of obtaining a separate rating for the network of mental health care from primary care, consumers would obtain one network rating that averaged the characteristics of both. While some information is obviously "lost" by averaging what is transmitted to the consumers, from the standpoint of incentives to the plan to maintain quality of mental health, there has been a gain. In the presence of an averaged report, if the plan were to reduce the quality of its mental health network, it would reduce the overall network rating, and the plan would lose enrollees who value primary care (the "winners") as well as enrollees who valued mental health care (the "losers"). Tying qualities for various services together in an averaged report forges a positive link between a plan's quality choice in a service subject to adverse selection to overall plan profitability.

The concept of averaged quality reporting can easily be demonstrated with the model discussed above. For a given quality pair (q_a, q_c), chosen by a plan, and $0 < \alpha < 1$, let

$$\bar{q}_\alpha = \alpha q_a + (1 - \alpha) q_c \tag{9.6}$$

be the (weighted) average quality of this plan.

Assume that individuals cannot observe (q_a, q_c). Assume that the regulator, who can observe (q_a, q_c), chooses to inform consumers only about the average quality, $\bar{q}_\alpha$, of each plan. That is, individuals cannot observe the quality of each of the services that a plan offers, but they can observe some summary indicator of the plan's quality profile, reported to them by the regulator.

The fact that individuals can only observe the "average" quality of each plan, and not the quality of each service that a plan offers, will affect the market equilibrium. The profitability of any quality pair (q_a, q_c), offered by a plan, depends on individuals' beliefs about the quality of each of the two services, given that they can only observe the average quality of the services. Therefore, in order to analyze competitive equilibrium in the market where individuals only observe average quality of each plan, one needs to incorporate individuals' beliefs about quality in the definition of equilibrium. Thus, we apply the following definition.

A *competitive equilibrium* is a set of quality pairs offered by plans and a set of individuals' belief functions that specify for each individual their beliefs about the quality pair of each plan, for every possible average quality $\bar{q}_\alpha$ of that plan,[11] such that: (i) each plan maximizes its profit given all the other pairs offered and given individuals' beliefs; (ii) each individual chooses a plan that offers them the highest

---

11) Formally, the assumption is that for each consumer, k, there is a belief function $B_k : R_+ \to R_+ \times R_+$, such that for every average quality $\bar{q}_\alpha$, the function specifies beliefs about a plan's quality profile (q_a, q_c) given that average quality. In order to simplify the analysis, it is assumed that a consumer's beliefs depend only on the plan's average quality, and not on the plan's identity or the average quality of the other plans. It can be shown that all our results will hold if we allow for more general belief functions.

expected utility given their information and given their beliefs; (iii) there is no quality pair outside the equilibrium set that, if offered, will make a positive profit; and (iv) in equilibrium, the individuals' beliefs are confirmed.

9.4.1
Optimal Quality Reporting

The following result (studied in Glazer and McGuire [33]) portrays the theoretical potential of averaged quality reporting.

Proposition 1

Suppose that all individuals can only observe the weighted average quality of each plan, and $\alpha = \alpha^*$, where α^* is given by

$$\frac{p_a C_a'(q_a^*)}{\alpha^*} = \frac{p_c C_c'(q_c^*)}{1 - \alpha^*} \tag{9.7}$$

then all plans offer the socially efficient quality pair (q_a^*, q_c^*) in the competitive equilibrium.

A detailed proof of this result can be found in Glazer and McGuire [33]. Here, a sketch is provided of the proof. The first observation to make is that for every α, $0 < \alpha < 1$, if individuals can only observe the average quality $\bar{q}_\alpha$ of each plan and if, in equilibrium, a plan offers the quality pair (q_a', q_c') and a share λ', $0 \le \lambda' \le 1$, of the individuals that join this plan are of type H, then it must be that

$$\frac{p_a C_a'(q_a')}{\alpha} = \frac{p_c' C_c'(q_c')}{1 - \alpha} \tag{9.8}$$

where

$$p_c' = \lambda' p_H + (1 - \lambda') p_L \tag{9.9}$$

The intuition for this first result is quite simple and very general. As individuals can only observe the average quality of all services that a plan offers, the plan has no incentive to provide a quality profile that yields the same average as another quality but costs more. The condition in Eq. (9.8) above (referred to as the incentive compatible (IC) condition) specifies the quality pair that minimizes the plan's costs, given a prespecified level of quality.

For a given α, $0 < \alpha < 1$, the curve $IC(\alpha, \lambda)$ in Fig. 9.2 represents all quality profiles that satisfy Eq. (9.8) above, for the (pooling) case where $\lambda' = \lambda$; that is, the case where the plan attracts a random sample of the population. The curve r^* in that figure depicts all quality profiles that satisfy the zero profit (pooling) condition:

$$p_a C_a(q_a) + p_c C_c(q_c) = r^* \tag{9.10}$$

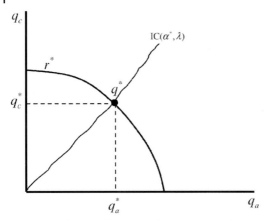

Fig. 9.2 Market equilibrium (pooling) with optimal averaged report.

The second part of the proof of this Proposition is to show that, for every α, the quality pair that is located at the intersection of these two curves, denoted by (q_a^α, q_c^α), is the unique quality pair offered by the plans in the competitive equilibrium in the case where individuals can only observe the average quality of each plan.

In order to show that (q_a^α, q_c^α) is indeed an equilibrium, assume that (all) individuals' beliefs are such that for every average quality $(\bar{q}_\alpha)$ they observe, and for every plan, individuals believe that the plan has chosen the quality profile that satisfies the IC condition, with $\lambda' = \lambda$, that yields $\bar{q}_\alpha$. Given these beliefs, one can see that if all plans offer the quality pair (q_a^α, q_c^α), the individuals' beliefs will be confirmed. Given the beliefs above, it can also be seen that if all plans offer the quality profile (q_a^α, q_c^α), then no plan has an incentive to deviate and, hence, it is an equilibrium.

In order to show that (q_a^α, q_c^α) is the unique equilibrium, it should be noted first that there cannot be any other (pooling) equilibrium in which each plan attracts a random sample of the population. Using the single crossing property, it can also be shown that in the case where consumers observe only an averaged quality, there cannot exist a separating equilibrium.

The final part of the proof is to show that when α is given by the condition in Eq. (9.7), the equilibrium quality is the socially desired one. This, however, is straightforward given the way that α^* is defined.

Returning to Eq. (9.7), it can be seen that the relative weights on quality of services a and c depend on the probabilities of the two illnesses and the marginal costs of quality at the efficient quality. The quality weights are like relative prices equal to marginal cost at the efficient level of production.

Casting quality reports as a policy instrument results in an important and simple conclusion – that an averaged quality report can remedy adverse selection incentives in markets for health plans. The reasoning behind this is straightforward: averaging quality across its many dimensions and reporting only the average enforces pooling in health insurance. Choosing the weights in the average to reflect relative marginal benefits at the efficient quality mix ensures health plans allocate resources to elements qualities in the right way.

The power of quality reporting to correct selection-related incentives seems not to have been appreciated previously. For purposes of comparison, as will be shown below, in the basic adverse selection model, an averaged quality report matches the performance of optimal risk adjustment.

9.5
Consumers Can Observe Quality and the Regulator Can Observe "Signals" About Consumers' Types: Risk Adjustment

When a plan is paid using risk adjustment, the premium paid to the plan (often referred to as "capitation") is conditioned on observable characteristics of the enrollee. The capitation payment might be based, for example, on the enrollee's age, with older enrollees having higher payments associated with them because they are expected to cost more. Methods of risk adjustment are concerned with how much more to pay the plan for an older enrollee than for a younger enrollee [12, 16].

In a competitive health insurance market, one of the main purposes of risk adjustment is to lessen plans' incentives for adverse selection. The question, of course, is what is the correct way to construct the premium paid to plans, so that their incentives to select enrollees are minimized? Two approaches to addressing this question have been taken in the economic literature.

Conventional risk adjustment sees the goal of risk adjustment as to pay plans as close as possible to the amount that the enrollee is expected to cost. If an older enrollee is expected to be twice as expensive as a younger enrollee, conventional risk adjustment would pay twice as much for the older enrollee. However, many factors other than age matter for expected costs. Research on conventional risk adjustment is statistical and data-oriented; researchers seek to find the correct combination of variables (referred to as risk adjustors) to include in regression models so that the explained variation in health care costs is high, without relying on risk adjustors that are difficult to collect in practice, or can be manipulated by providers seeking to increase revenue. The premise behind this research – sometimes regarded to be so obvious as to not require justification or analysis – is that the health care market in question will function better, the better job the regression model can do in predicting health care costs of enrollees.

Optimal risk adjustment methods also yield an answer of how much more to pay for an older enrollee, but by a different method. Optimal risk adjustment views risk adjustment as a set of incentives aimed at inducing providers to behave in accordance with some well-defined objective. Calculating the optimal risk adjustment begins with an explicit assumption about the functioning of price in the relevant market, and a model that relates the terms of that price (e.g., the payment for young and old) to the behavior of providers and patients. The economic objective (usually efficiency) is also stated explicitly. Then, by using principal-agent methods, the optimal risk adjustment is derived as the prices for young and old which maximize the efficiency of the health care market. Notice, therefore, that the term "optimal risk adjustment" does not refer to particular weights, but rather to a procedure by which the optimal weights are obtained. Whilst optimal risk adjustment also relies on data, the optimal weights are not in general regression coefficients, but rather a more complex function involving an economic maximization.

To illustrate how conventional and optimal risk adjustment are calculated, and how they might differ in their effectiveness, we can return to the model presented above. Suppose that the regulator receives a signal about each consumer's type – perhaps the consumer's age. The signal, s, which can take a value of 0 or 1 ("young" or "old"), contains information in the sense that a type H person is more likely than a type L person to receive the signal 1. Let y_i, $i = $ H or L be the probability that consumer of type i receives the signal 1. It is assumed that $y_H > y_L \geq 0$. (Note that if $y_H = 1$ and $y_L = 0$, the signal is perfect; that is, the regulator knows the individual's type.)

Let λ_s be the posterior probability that the consumer is of type H, given the signal s. Since the signal is informative, by using Bayes' theorem it can be shown that $1 \geq \lambda_1 \geq \lambda_0 \geq 0$ Thus, if a person received the signal 1, they would be more likely to be type H than a person who received the signal 0. Let,

$$P_s = P_H \lambda_s + P_L(1 - \lambda_s) \quad \text{for} \quad s = 0, 1 \tag{9.12}$$

and

$$r_s = C(q_a^*) + P_s C(q_c^*) \quad \text{for} \quad s = 0, 1 \tag{9.13}$$

P_s is the probability that a person with signal s will contract illness c, and r_s is the expected health care costs of such a person at the efficient quality of care. Clearly, $P_1 > P_0$ and $r_1 > r_0$. It can be readily confirmed that if plans are paid r_s for each person who received signal s, and consumers are randomly distributed across plans, the plans would break even when providing the optimal level of care.

The capitation payment r_s is what is meant by "conventional" risk adjustment. It can be shown, however, that conventional risk adjustment does not implement the socially desired outcome; that is, at the competitive equilibrium, plans do not provide the socially efficient quality. The same forces that break the efficient pooling equilibrium when premiums are not risk-adjusted will also break such equilibrium when the premiums are conventionally risk-adjusted. Market equilibrium under conventional risk adjustment will still be a separating one, where the H- and L-types choose different plans with a different quality profile. This separating equilibrium is more efficient (i.e., it induces a higher expected utility) than the one without risk adjustment, but it is not the best that the regulator can do. As shown below, an optimal risk adjustment can be constructed to implement precisely the socially desired quality.

Let

$$r_H^* = C(q_a^*) + P_H C(q_c^*) \tag{9.14}$$

and

$$r_L^* = C(q_a^*) + P_L C(q_c^*) \tag{9.15}$$

r_i^* is the expected costs of an individual of type i at the efficient quality profile.

We are now ready to discuss the conditions under which risk adjustors implement the socially desired contract.

Proposition 2

Let r_s^*, $s = 0,1$ be solution to the following system of equations:

$$\gamma_H r_1^* + (1 - \gamma_H) r_0^* = r_H^* \tag{9.16}$$

$$\gamma_L r_1^* + (1 - \gamma_L) r_0^* = r_L^* \tag{9.17}$$

Then, if plans are paid a premium r_s^* $s = 0,1$ for each individual who received the signal s, all plans will offer the socially desired quality in equilibrium.

The left-hand side of Eq. (9.16) is the expected premium that a plan receives for each enrollee of type H, under the risk-adjustment scheme r_s^*. The right-hand side of Eq. (9.16) is the plan's expected cost of an enrollee of type H, under the socially desired quality bundle. Equation (9.16) states the condition for the expected premium for a type H individual to be equal to the individual's expected cost. Equation (9.17) achieves the same for a type L individual.

Conventional risk adjustment redistributes some (but not enough) resources from the low-cost to the high-cost types. In Fig. 9.1, this redistribution would appear as a shift in the zero-profit curves relative to the curves in the no risk adjustment case. As the proposition above shows, the regulator may shift the zero-profit curves even further than is implied by conventional risk adjustment, by "overpaying" for a consumer who received signal 1, compensated by "underpaying" for consumers who received signal 0; by so doing, this brings the market closer to the socially desired outcomes. "Overpaying" and "underpaying" are in comparison to the conventional risk adjustment premiums. The equilibrium under optimal risk adjustment is illustrated in Fig. 9.3.

Intuitively, this result can be understood as follows. If the signal is not very precise, the difference in premium that conventional risk adjustment pays for a consumer who received the signal 1 and one who received signal 0 will be small. Furthermore, the proportion of consumers with signal 0 among the L types is not much larger than the proportion that received this signal in the entire population. Thus, by offering a quality profile that attracts only the L-type consumers, a plan

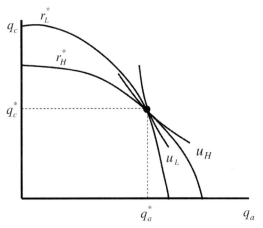

Fig. 9.3 Market equilibrium under optimal risk adjustment.

can reduce its cost by a significant amount relative to the reduction in premium it is expected to receive. If, on the other hand, the premium for an individual with the signal 0 is significantly lower than the premium for an individual with a signal 1, the plan is severely punished for attracting only individuals of type L.

The example studied above is, of course, very simple and presented simply in order to demonstrate the main idea of optimal risk adjustment. Glazer and McGuire [34] characterize optimal risk adjustment in a more general framework, and show that it depends on the first and second moments of the distribution of health care utilization patterns by service in the population. In order to equalize incentives to ration all services, the covariance of the risk-adjusted payment with the use of every service must track the covariance of the total predicted costs associated with the increase in use of the service. Intuitively, the optimal risk-adjustment formula must have the property that, by spending on a service, the cost consequences to a plan relate to the revenue consequences in the same way for all services. It is important to stress that the result for optimal risk adjustment states how a given average payment should be risk-adjusted, but does not answer the question of how high or low on average the payment should be.

The optimal risk adjustment emerges as a set of linear equations, one for each service, with unknowns equal to the variables available for risk adjustment. An interesting feature of this optimal risk-adjustment scheme is that the number of parameters available for risk adjustment could be greater or less than the number of services about which a plan is deciding (for example, some risk-adjustment systems have scores of weights.) If the number of available risk-adjustment parameters is larger than the number of services whose quality the plan decides on, there may be many risk adjustors that achieve optimality in the sense of incentive balance across services. Glazer and McGuire [34] label and characterize "minimum variance" optimal risk adjustment as the solution to the optimal risk-adjustment formula that minimizes the symmetric loss function in the square of deviations between payments and actual costs. The "second-best" optimal risk adjustment, when the number of risk-adjustment parameters is less than the number of services, has not yet been described in the literature. Others have studied optimal risk adjustment in a variety of contexts (see Refs. [35, 36]).

In closing this section, it should be emphasized that, while the theoretical basis of optimal risk adjustment is established, its practical application is yet to be developed. The challenge for proponents of the idea of optimal risk adjustment is to translate ideas from economic theory into concrete improvements, in the way risk adjustment is conducted in practice.

9.6
Concluding Remarks

Inefficient quality at the plan and provider levels stems from a number of sources, including poor-quality information about what should be done, general problems of inefficiency in organizations, and from incentives due to adverse selection – both, plans and providers wish to attract the profitable and discourage the unprofitable enrollees or patients. Economic analysis has been concerned with incentives due to selection, and has identified a number of strategies to deal with these problems. In theory, a number of approaches – including risk adjustment, quality reporting, cost sharing, paying for performance and selection of plans and providers – can lessen, if not solve, quality problems. The contexts in which these tools are applied, however, can deviate quite widely from the theoretical frameworks in which characteristics of optimal payment or reporting are derived.

The most basic implication of economic theory is this: when considering the design of any mechanism to deal with problems of adverse selection, the nature of the underlying inefficiency and an anticipation of how plans and providers react to the policy should provide the foundation for the analysis. In this chapter, attention has been focused on two such mechanisms: risk adjustment; and quality reporting. This observation implies that "conventional" approaches to both risk adjustment and quality reporting are not in general optimal, and encourages both researchers and policy makers to consider alternatives. In order to design an efficient quality report, it is necessary to know how plans/providers/patients will react to it. This also points to important research targets. Although theory can clarify what to expect from providers and patients, ultimately it is an empirical question as to how people use a quality report or how a plan reacts to payment incentives.

This chapter has also called attention to the use of a very simple mechanism that buyers have for inducing quality, namely choosing the plan/provider on the basis of observed quality. This strategy, which is common in private markets in the US, may actually dominate others, including formal risk adjustment, when all are available. However, the favoring of some plans and/or providers, which means treating others with less favor, is problematic for governments, who often are bound by procedural concerns with regards to fairness and openness in contracting with providers and plans. Governments do perform some selective contracting, but the application of lessons and strategies learned from the private sector appears to be a fruitful source of ideas for improving public sector purchasing in health care.

Acknowledgments

This chapter was presented at the conference on Health Care Finance, Calgary Alberta, September 14–15, 2006. Financial support for these studies was provided by the Agency for Healthcare Research and Quality (P01 HS10803) and the National Institute for Mental Health (R34 MH071242). The authors are grateful to Åke Blomqvist, Mingshan Lu, Joseph Newhouse, Anna Sinaiko and participants in the Calgary workshop for their helpful comments on an earlier draft.

References

1 Rice, N., Smith, P. (2001). Capitation and risk adjustment in health care financing: An international progress report. *The Milbank Quarterly*, **79**(1), 81–113.

2 Enthoven, A.C. (1993). The history and principles of managed competition. *Health Affairs*, **12**(Suppl.), 24–48.

3 van de Ven, W.P.M.M., Beck, K., Buchner, F., et al. (2003). Risk adjustment and risk selection on the sickness fund insurance market in five European countries. *Health Policy*, **65**, 75–98.

4 Miller, R.H., Luft, H.S. (1997). Does managed care lead to better or worse quality of care? *Health Affairs*, **16**(5), 7–25.

5 Newhouse, J.P. (1996). Reimbursing health plans and health providers: Efficiency in production versus selection. *Journal of Economic Literature*, **34**, 1236–1263.

6 Eggers, P.W., Prihoda, R. (1982). Pre-enrollment reimbursement patterns of Medicare beneficiaries enrolled in 'at-risk' HMOs. *Health Care Finance Review*, **4**(1), 55–73.

7 Rossiter, L., Wilensky, G. (1986). Patient self-selection in HMOs. *Health Affairs*, **6**, 66–80.

8 Brown, R.S., Clement, D.G., Hill, J.W., Retchin, S.M., Bergeron, J.W. (1993). Do Health Maintenance Organizations work for Medicare? *Health Care Financing Review*, **15**(1), 7–23.

9 Greenwald, L.M., Levy, J.M., Ingber, M.J. (2000). Favorable selection in the Medicare + Choice Program: New evidence. *Health Care Financing Review*, **21**(3), 127–134.

10 Hellinger, F. (1995). Selection bias in HMOs and PPOs. *Inquiry*, **32**, 135–142.

11 Nicholson, S., Polsky, D., Bundorf, K., Stein, R. (2004). The magnitude and nature of risk selection in employer-sponsored health plans. *Health Services Research*, **39**(6)Part 1, 1817–1838.

12 Cutler, D., Zeckhauser, R. (2000). *The Anatomy of Health Insurance*. North-Holland, Amsterdam.

13 Glazer, J., McGuire, T.G. (2000). Optimal risk adjustment of health insurance premiums: An application to managed care. *American Economic Review*, **90**(4), 1055–1071.

14 Feldman, R., Dowd, B. (2000). Risk segmentation: Goal or problem? *Journal of Health Economics*, **19**(4), 499–512.

15 Pauly, M.V. (1985). *What Is Adverse About Adverse Selection?* JAI Press.

16 van de Ven, W.P.M.M., Ellis, R.P. (2000). Risk adjustment in competitive health plan markets. In: *Handbook of Health Economics, Volume 1*, Culyer, A.J., Newhouse, J.P. (Eds.), Elsevier Science, Amsterdam.

17 Nuscheler, R., Knaus, T. (2005). Risk selection in the German public health insurance system. *Health Economics*, **14**(12), 1253–1271.

18 Rothschild, M., Stiglitz, J. (1976). Equilibrium in competitive insurance markets: An essay in the economics of imperfect information. *Quarterly Journal of Economics*, **90**, 629–649.

19 Cao, Z. (2002). Comparing the pre-HMO enrollment costs between switchers and stayers: Evidence from Medicare. In: *Service-Level Risk Selection by HMOs in Medicare*, PhD Dissertation, Boston University, Boston (Chapter 2).

20 Frank, R.G., Glazer, J., McGuire, T.G. (2000). Adverse selection in managed health care. *Journal of Health Economics*, **19**(6), 829–854.

21 Luft, H.S., Miller, R.H. (1988). Patient selection and competitive health system. *Health Affairs*, **7**(3), 97–112.

22 Pauly, M.V. (2000). The Medicare mix: Efficient and inefficient combinations of social and private health insurance for US elderly. *Journal of Health Care Finance*, **26**(3), 26–37.

23 Pauly, M.V., Ramsey, S.D. (1999). Would you like suspenders to go with that belt? An analysis of optimal combinations of cost sharing and managed care. *Journal of Health Economics*, **18**(4), 443–458.

24 Keeler, E.B., Carter, G., Newhouse, J.P. (1998). A model of the impact of reimbursement schemes on health plan choice. *Journal of Health Economics*, **17**(3), 297–320.

25 Rosenthal, M., Frank, R. (2006). What is the empirical basis for paying for quality in health care? *Medical Care Research and Review*, **63**(2), 135–157

26 Rosenthal, M., Frank, R.G., Zhonghe, L., Epstein, A.M. (2005). Early experience with pay-for-performance: From concept to practice. *Journal of the American Medical Association*, **294**(14), 1788–1793.

27 Ellis, R.P., McGuire, T.G. (1986). Provider behavior under prospective reimbursement: Cost sharing and supply. *Journal of Health Economics*, **5**, 129–151.

28 Kifmann, M., Lorenz, N. (2005). Optimal cost reimbursement of health insurers to reduce risk selection. URL: http://www.ub.uni-konstanz.de/kops/volltexte/2005/1430/.

29 Gruber, J., McKnight, R. (2002). *Why did employee health insurance contributions rise?* National Bureau of Economic Research, Working Paper #8878.

30 Marquis, M.S., Long, S.H. (1999). Trends in managed care and managed competition. *Health Affairs*, **18**(6), 75–88.

31 Feldman, R., Dowd, B., Coulam, R. (1999). The Federal Employees Health Benefits Plan: Implications for Medicare. *Inquiry*, **36**(2), 188–199.

32 Miller, N. (2005). Pricing health benefits: A cost minimization approach. *Journal of Health Economics*, **24**(55), 931–949.

33 Glazer, J., McGuire, T.G. (2006). Optimal quality reports for health plans. *Journal of Health Economics*, **25**(2), 295–310.

34 Glazer, J., McGuire, T.G. (2002). Setting health plan premiums to ensure efficient quality in health care: Minimum variance optimal risk adjustment. *Journal of Public Economics*, **84**, 153–173.

35 Jack, W. (2004). Optimal risk adjustment in a model with adverse selection and spatial competition. *Journal of Health Economics*, **25**(5), 908–926.

36 Shen, Y., Ellis, R.P. (2002). Cost minimizing risk adjustment. *Journal of Health Economics*, **21**(3), 515–530.

10
Equity in Health and Health Care in Canada in International Perspective
Eddy van Doorslaer

10.1
Overview

This chapter reviews some of the evidence reported to date on inequalities in health and health care by income in Canada, and which is comparable to similar evidence generated for other OECD countries. The results of various studies, when combined, provide a fairly coherent picture showing that, as in other countries – and despite more than 20 years of universal coverage of medical services – health and health care access are not equally distributed and favor higher-income groups. It is also seen that, in comparison to most other OECD countries, and despite the incomprehensiveness of the public coverage and provincial autonomy in the organization and delivery of services, the observed inequalities and inequities are relatively minor, but not innocuous. Some evidence shows that certain access inequalities appear to translate into outcome inequalities and as such, perpetuate societal inequalities. Although income-related inequalities in health in Canada are certainly not smaller than in other OECD countries, it seems that the influence and distribution of health determinants other than the use of medical care play a more important role in their generation and persistence.

10.2
Introduction: Canada's Health Care System and Equity

In Canada, as in many other Organisation for Economic Co-operation and Development (OECD) countries, equity in access to health care has always been – and still is – is a prominent goal of public policy. The recent Romanow Report [1] of the Commission on the Future of Health Care in Canada, which reviewed Medicare, engaged Canadians in a national dialogue on its future, and made recommendations to enhance the system's quality and sustainability. In his message to Canadians, Romanow emphasized that:

Financing Health Care: New Ideas for a Changing Society. Edited by Mingshan Lu and Egon Jonsson
Copyright © 2008 WILEY-VCH Verlag GmbH & Co. KGaA, Weinheim
ISBN: 978-3-527-32027-1

> "In their discussions with me, Canadians have been clear that they still strongly
> support the core values on which our health care system is premised – equity, fairness
> and solidarity. These values are tied to their understanding of citizenship. Canadians
> consider equal and timely access to medically necessary health care services on the
> basis of need as a right of citizenship, not a privilege of status or wealth."

The Romanow Report concluded that:

> "Medicare has consistently delivered affordable, timely, accessible and high qual-
> ity care to the overwhelming majority of Canadians on the basis of need, not
> income."

In order to provide reasonable access to health care, regardless of ability to pay,
the 1984 Canada Health Act established *de facto* the government as the sole payer
for medically necessary physician and hospital services: provincial regulations created in response to the CHA prohibit user charges for these services, and either
ban private insurance for publicly insured services outright, or make it economically unattractive for a physician to establish a practice providing such services for
private payment outside the public system [2]. In part because the value of equity
is deeply embedded in the Canadian health care system, most Canadian citizens
strongly believe that access to care should not depend on a person's ability to
pay [3].

Empirical studies using harmonized and comparable data and measures to look
into the degree of progressivity and/or redistribution of health care finance have,
until now, not included Canada. Some attempts have been made to examine the
incidence of health care payments by income, but these were either confined to
just one province (e.g., Alberta [4]) or to only the tax-funded payments (e.g., for
British Columbia [5]), and are therefore not directly comparable to comparative
OECD evidence as presented in Refs. [6, 7]. By contrast, many Canadian studies
have examined the question of whether factors other than need still affect the use
of health care in Canada (e.g., Ref. [8]), and have interpreted this as evidence of
inequity in utilization. A recent review of this literature can be found in Allin
[9]. These studies will not be reviewed again in this chapter; rather, attention will
focus on departures from an equitable distribution by income only, and on the
internationally comparable evidence to date on the distribution of medical care and
health by income.

10.3
Income-Related Inequity in Access to, and Delivery of, Care

Most OECD member states have chosen not to let willingness to pay for care, but
need for care to be the most relevant criterion for access to treatment. As such, the
egalitarian principle that those in equal need should be treated equally, irrespective
of other characteristics, such as income and place of residence, has received a

very important role in assessment of horizontal equity [6]. It may therefore be somewhat surprising nonetheless that in most countries – despite decades of fairly comprehensive and universal coverage – poorer individuals do not receive the same treatments as richer individuals. Simply removing the financial access barrier by making health care free of charge at the point of use, does not appear sufficient to ensure that, given needs, utilization patterns do not differ by income. The extent to which Canadian health care is, or is not, distributed according to need and the extent to which this principle is systematically violated by income, has been the subject of a number of international comparative studies. Van Doorslaer et al. [10] have measured horizontal inequity in the degree of physician visits in Canada and in 12 European countries and the United States. By analyzing data for adults taken from the 1996 National Population Health Survey (NPHS), these authors found no inequity in general practitioner (GP) visits, a significant degree of pro-rich use of specialists, and no significant inequity in overall physician visits after controlling for needs. Further control for regional differences and the degree of private insurance coverage for prescription medicines does not alter these findings, indicating that it is unlikely that these results are driven by provincial differences or inequalities in insurance cover. As in the United States (US), the mean physician visit rate is lower than in many European countries but, unlike the US, it appears to be fairly equitably distributed.

Recently, these results were updated and extended in a comparative study analyzing survey data from 21 OECD countries [11, 12]. By using the Canadian Community Health Survey (CCHS) 2001, not only physician visits but also hospital admissions and dental visits were analyzed, while a decomposition method allowed for a more detailed breakdown of the factors contributing to observed income-related inequality in use. In addition, the probability of use and subsequent use conditional on at least one contact were analyzed separately. Given the large size of the CCHS 2001 (n = 107 613 adults), the results for Canada are estimated with far greater precision (that is, narrower confidence intervals) than those for most other countries. There is some variation across types of care but, on the whole, the picture suggests that Canada's performance in terms of achieving equal treatment for equal need, irrespective of income, is at least as good as that of most other countries in the study.

Some selected results of the analysis were as follows. First, the quintile distributions before and after need standardization are presented, in order to provide some impression of the absolute disparities in utilization between richer and poorer Canadians. Second, the horizontal inequity indices (with confidence intervals) are presented graphically, in comparison to other OECD countries for which these summary statistics were computed in a similar manner. Finally, (a few) examples are presented of the detailed decomposition of the indices, the aim being to highlight the most important sources of unequal use by income for selected types of care use.

10.3.1
The Distribution of Care by Income

A selection of data reproduced from Ref. [11] is summarized in Table 10.1. The table presents distributions of mean use after standardization for need differences across quintiles. Need has been proxied by reported morbidity in terms of self-assessed health and the presence of limiting chronic conditions, as well as by age and gender of the individual. The concentration index (CI) in the penultimate column indicates the degree of inequality in observed, unstandardized use. It can be seen that this is negative for GP and total physician visits and even more so for hospital use, signaling the use to be more concentrated among the lower income groups. Exceptions are the probability of a physician visit (both specialist and GP) and especially the use of dental care visits, which are all more prevalent among the wealthier Canadians. The final column presents the horizontal inequity index (HI), which measures the degree of HI as the remaining degree of inequality in use by income quintile, after appropriate statistical standardization for need differences. In effect, it represents the difference between the actually observed distribution and the distribution that would be obtained if all individuals were treated equally on the basis of their (self-reported) morbidity characteristics. The procedure is explained in greater detail in Appendix 10.1.

Need standardization generally reduces the degree of pro-poor inequality in use, or increases the degree of pro-rich use. Only in the case of total specialist visits is the CI of unstandardized use significantly negative, while the HI is significantly positive. This means that the use of specialist visits is pro-poor but not sufficiently so to accommodate for the much greater needs of lower-income groups. Hence, the finding of pro-rich inequity. In all other cases, the signs of HI and CI are the same, but usually the HI is more positive or less negative. It needs to be

Table 10.1 Quintile distributions (after need standardisation), inequality and inequity indices for total physician utilisation

Country		Poorest	2	3	4	Richest	Total	CI	HI
All physician visits	Total	4.342	4.470	4.252	4.342	4.417	4.355	−0.064	*0.005*
	Prob	0.834	0.835	0.841	0.864	0.897	0.866	0.004	0.015
General practitioner visits	Total	3.469	3.605	3.304	3.237	3.162	3.265	−0.089	−0.016
	Prob	0.738	0.757	0.764	0.786	0.813	0.786	0.001	0.016
Specialist visits	Total	1.098	1.088	1.160	1.309	1.450	1.295	−0.015	0.054
	Prob	0.494	0.474	0.494	0.541	0.598	0.541	0.013	0.044
Hospital nights	Total	0.704	0.740	0.603	0.475	0.480	0.533	−0.256	−0.078
	Prob	0.100	0.101	0.087	0.080	0.075	0.082	−0.150	−0.051
Dental visits	Total	0.820	0.756	0.912	1.214	1.540	1.200	0.131	0.126
	Prob	0.434	0.386	0.467	0.612	0.746	0.598	0.119	0.113

Notes: Significant CI and HI indices in bold ($P<0.05$). Total = mean number in last 12 months. Prob = proportion with positive use in last 12 months.

stressed that because of the large sample, even very small indices (indicating very small inequities) are still found to be significantly different from zero. Statistical significance here may not coincide with societal significance. For example, how worrisome is it that, for example, the annual probability of seeing a doctor is about 0.03 higher in the highest than in the lowest income quintile? It seems safe therefore to say that, for GP and physician visits, generally the significant pro-rich inequity still found in contact probabilities is not really evidence of worrisome horizontal inequity. For specialist care visits, which are free of charge as no public copayments apply, the degree of pro-rich inequity is larger: for example, the need-standardized probability of a visit is 10% higher in the top than in the bottom quintile. For dental care visits, the unequal use (after age standardization only) is startling: the visit probability in the top quintiles is almost twice the probability in the bottom quintiles. For hospital care, on the other hand, significant and substantial inequity favoring the poor is found: even after need standardization, the lowest quintile's use of the hospital, both in terms of admissions and in terms of number of inpatient days, is higher than that of the higher quintiles. This is likely to reflect several data problems. First, the impossibility to appropriately standardize for severity of needs using the very general morbidity measures used here. It has often been shown (e.g., see Ref. [13]) that the inclusion of more detailed health information tends to reduce the degree of pro-poor inequity. Second, the measurement of hospital nights excludes day-case admissions which have been found to exhibit a more pro-rich distribution than overnight admissions [14].

10.3.2
How Does Canada Compare to Other OECD Countries?

One way of providing a better interpretation of the achievements of Canada's health care system in terms of equalizing treatment of equal needs is to compare these with those of other OECD countries which have similarly strived to equalize access irrespective of income. Again, this is illustrated with (selected) results taken from the recent OECD comparative study [11] and reproduced in Figs 10.1 to 10.10. Figure 10.1 presents HI indices along with 95% confidence intervals for 10 OECD member states. This serves to illustrate the close to perfectly horizontally equitable distribution of doctor visits in Canada, with a tiny HI index of 0.005; this is not significantly different from zero, despite the fact that the estimated confidence interval is very narrow. It is clear from the comparative picture that Canada's doctor visit distribution is about as close as one can get to a distribution according to need.[1] However, it is only when the GP and specialist data are analyzed separately that it becomes clear that treatment is not entirely equal at varying levels of income. The distribution of GP visits generally shows up as pro-poor, albeit to a slightly lesser extent in Canada than elsewhere. This is the case despite the pro-rich distribution of the probability of a visit, and therefore necessarily must mean that

1) The HI index for the probability of a visit is significantly different from zero, but is also
   very small (0.015), and indicates little reason for equity concern.

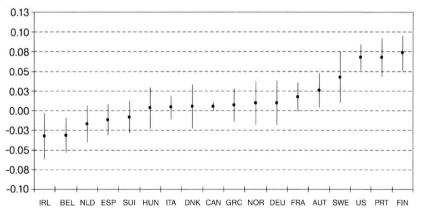

Fig. 10.1 HI indices for number of doctor visits, by country (with 95% confidence interval) [11].

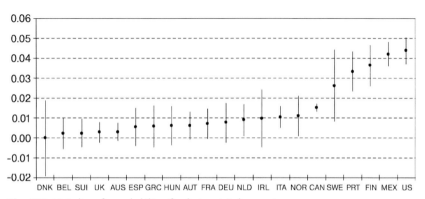

Fig. 10.2 HI indices for probability of a doctor visit, by country (with 95% confidence interval) [11].

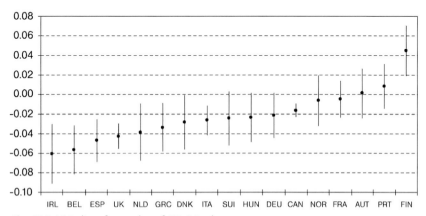

Fig. 10.3 HI indices for number of GP visits, by country (with 95% conf interval) [11].

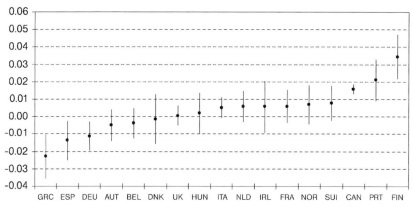

Fig. 10.4 HI indices for probability of a GP visit, by country
(with 95% confidence interval) [11].

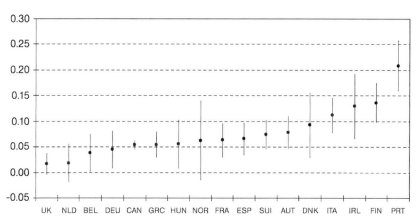

Fig. 10.5 HI indices for number of specialist visits, by country
(with 95% confidence interval) [11].

especially the subsequent use (i.e., conditional on at least one visit) is distributed pro-poor. If it is accepted that this distribution is more likely to be influenced by the GP advice/decision, then it may tentatively be concluded that, on average, Canadian GPs make sure that the less wealthy obtain their fair share of GP consultations, despite their slightly lower initial propensity to contact. That the picture is very different for both the probability and the number of specialist visits was already clear from Section 10.2.1, but the international comparisons presented in Figs. 10.5 and 10.6 demonstrate that the Canadian situation is certainly not extreme. It is significantly pro-rich, but below the OECD average and substantially lower than in a number of European countries (e.g., Portugal, Ireland, Finland, Italy), which have deliberately created options for parallel private insurance or delivery alongside their essentially publicly funded systems. The question of to what extent this is to be regarded as worrisome for outcome differentials will be revisited below.

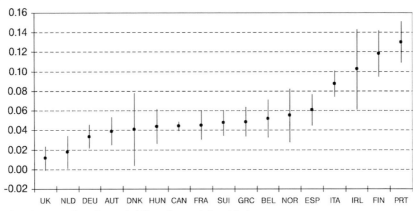

Fig. 10.6 HI indices for probability of a specialist visit, by country
(with 95% confidence interval) [11].

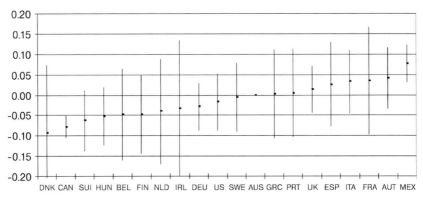

Fig. 10.7 HI indices for number of hospital nights, by country
(with 95% confidence interval) [11].

Canada does seem to take a somewhat more extreme position in terms of in-patient utilization, showing significantly negative HI indices for both the admission probability and the number of hospital nights in Figs 10.7 and 10.8. It was indicated above that the degree of pro-poor distribution might be somewhat overstated because of the limited inclusion of need proxies in the common core analyses, and the greater test power increases the likelihood of rejecting the null hypothesis of no inequity. Nonetheless, the results are remarkable and suggest that there appear to be no financial or other barriers to hospital access for lower-income adults in Canada. Literally, with all else equal, low-income Canadians are somewhat more likely to be admitted and to have longer stays in the hospital than higher-income Canadians.

Finally, the findings for dental care visits in Figs. 10.9 and 10.10 demonstrate that (after age–gender standardization only) in all countries, without exception, dental visits are distributed very much pro-rich. Canada's position here is slightly above

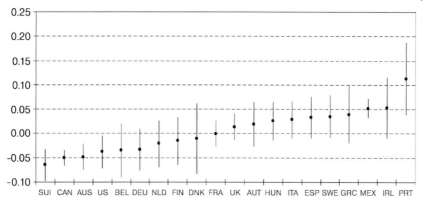

Fig. 10.8 HI indices for probability of a hospital admission, by country
(with 95% confidence interval) [11].

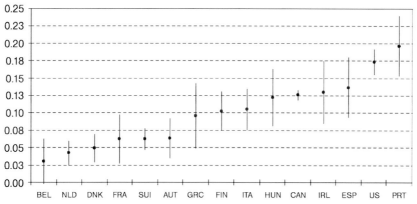

Fig. 10.9 HI indices for number of dentist visits, by country
(with 95% confidence interval) [11].

the OECD average, which is likely to be related to the lack of inclusion of dental care services in the public insurance package and the pro-rich uptake of private insurance cover for such care because of its relatedness to employment.

The above findings based on general population health survey data collected by Statistics Canada are to some extent confirmed and complemented by those from at least two comparative telephone interview surveys. The 2001 Commonwealth Fund International Health Policy Survey examined inequities in access to medical care and quality of care experiences associated with income, in five countries: Australia, Canada, New Zealand, United Kingdom, and United States [15]. They also sought to examine whether these inequities persisted after controlling for the effect of confounders such as health status, insurance coverage, age, education, minority and immigration status, and location of residence. A multivariate analysis of the telephone responses of about 1400 adults in each of these countries showed that wide and significant disparities exist in access and care experience between US

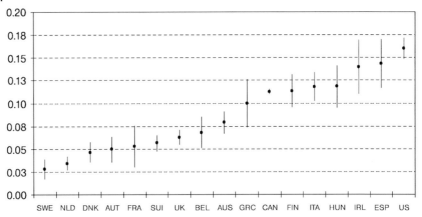

Fig. 10.10 HI indices for probability of a dentist visit, by country (with 95% conf interval) [11].

adults with above and below-average incomes, and persist after controlling for the above-listed confounding factors. In contrast, differences in the United Kingdom (UK) by income were rare, and there were also few significant access differences by income in Australia. Canada's results, like those of New Zealand's, fell in the mid-range of the five nations, with income gaps most pronounced on services less well covered by the public system, such as prescription medicines and dental care. In the four countries with universal coverage, adults with above-average income were more likely to have private supplemental insurance. Having private insurance in Australia, Canada, and New Zealand was found to protect adults from cost-related access problems. It was concluded that:

> "…reliance on private coverage to supplement public coverage can result in access inequities even within health systems that provide basic health coverage for all. If private insurance can circumvent queues or waiting times, low income adults may also be at higher risks for non-financial barriers since they are less likely to have supplemental coverage. Furthermore, greater inequality in care experiences by income is associated with more divided public views of the need for system reform. This finding was particularly striking in Canada where an increased incidence of disparities by income in 2001 compared to a 1998 survey was associated with diverging views in 2001." (p. 309, from Ref. [15])

More recently, the Joint Canada/US Survey of Health (JCUSH) conducted jointly by Statistics Canada and the US National Center for Health Statistics was administered by telephone between November 2002 and March 2003 among a random sample of non-institutionalized adults (3505 Canadian and 5183 US residents) [16]. Lasser, Himmelstein and Woolhandler [17] used it to compare access to care, health status and health in both countries, and found that disparities on the basis of race, income and immigrant status were present in both countries but were more extreme in the US. Like Katz et al. [18], Lasser and colleagues found that, in particular, the lower-income Canadians had better access to medical care than did low-income

US residents. The same authors found evidence that a similar mechanism is at play for hospital utilization: at each level of health status, poor Canadians received one-quarter to one-third more admissions than their counterparts in the US. However, higher-income sick persons received less hospital care in Ontario than in the US [19]. It was concluded that this represents, in part, a redistribution of in-patient care to those most vulnerable to illness, such as the poor, who receive substantially more hospital care in Ontario. All of this evidence suggests strongly that Canada's universal coverage has definitely reduced inequities in health care utilization by income, but it is not sufficient to eliminate health disparities by income, an issue which is discussed in Section 10.3.

10.3.3
What Explains Unequal Treatment of Those in Equal Need?

One way of shedding further light on which factors contribute to more or less inequality or inequity in use by income is to make use of a decomposition method proposed by Wagstaff et al. [20] and applied to the utilization of health care by Van Doorslaer et al. [21]. This approach was also used extensively in the OECD comparative study [11], and is explained in further detail in Appendix 10.1. Basically, it allows for a quantitative assessment of the extent to which the observed inequality can be attributed to various determinants of utilization. If the utilization of care can be explained through a (linear) regression equation, then the inequality in (or concentration index of) the dependent variable can be written as a weighted sum of the concentration indices of each of the determinants, weighted by their use elasticity [cf. Appendix 10.1, Eq. (8)]. In other words, a determinant can only have a substantial contribution to the measured degree of inequality in use if two conditions are met: (i) it is itself unequally distributed by income (i.e., it has a non-zero CI); and (ii) it has a substantial effect on use (i.e., a non-zero regression coefficient).[2] In this way, it is possible to determine, for instance, to what extent certain use inequalities are due to policy-relevant variables influencing the supply and demand for care such as insurance status or region of residence.

A summary of (some of) the decompositions obtained for the Canadian results is provided in Table 10.2. Unfortunately, in the CCHS 2001, no information on (private) health insurance status was collected, and only limited information on the province of residence. As a result, the main gain obtained from the decomposition analyses for Canada is a quantification of the extent to which inter-provincial differences in income and health care utilization do, or do not, contribute to greater national inequality. Interestingly, it can be seen that the contribution of the factor "region" (11 province dummies) shows only a small pro-rich contribution on GP and dental visits (indicating that richer provinces tend to have higher utilization rates), but that the opposite is true for specialist and hospital care (with higher

---

2) For dummy or 0/1 variables, an additional requirement is that its mean is not close to zero, as this could make even a substantial effect result in a very small elasticity, defined as the partial effect multiplied by the ratio of the mean of the explanatory over the dependent variable.

Table 10.2 Contributions to inequality in health care utilization by income

	Physician		GP		Specialist		Hospital		Dental	
	Tot	Prob	Tot	Prob	Tot	Prob	Tot	Prob	Tot	Prob
CI_M (Use)	−0.0636	0.0044	−0.0895	0.0011	−0.0150	0.0134	−0.2563	−0.1502	0.1314	0.1188
CI_N (Need)	−0.0685	−0.0108	−0.0732	−0.0148	−0.0687	−0.0307	−0.1784	−0.0997	0.0057	0.0061
$HI = CI_M - CI_N$	0.0049	0.0151	−0.0162	0.0159	0.0537	0.0441	−0.0779	−0.0506	0.1256	0.1127
Income	0.0044	0.0190	−0.0161	0.0133	0.0528	0.0427	−0.0341	−0.0216	0.1083	0.0929
Education	0.0048	0.0018	0.0009	0.0017	0.0157	0.0062	0.0024	0.0034	−0.0044	−0.0033
Activity status	−0.0092	−0.0009	−0.0083	−0.0016	−0.0145	−0.0029	−0.0326	−0.0233	0.0081	0.0129
Region	0.0044	0.0000	0.0063	0.0020	0.0003	−0.0018	−0.0107	−0.0076	0.0041	0.0041

provinces showing lower rates of use). It is a shame that the role of private health insurance coverage could not be examined with the CCHS 2001, given the findings of Stabile [22] on the NPHS 1996 data that higher-income Canadians are more likely to have supplemental drug insurance coverage (mainly because it is mostly employer-related) which induces them in turn to demand more physician services. The indirect approach adopted by Van Doorslaer et al. [10], using also the NPHS 1996, went some way towards answering this question. These authors assessed the impact on the measured degree of HI of controlling, in addition to need, also for supplemental drug coverage and region of residence.[3] Interestingly, the results for Canada (see Table 10.3) show that the unequal distribution of such private cover does indeed contribute to some of the observed patterns in physician use by income. Standardizing for insurance coverage makes the pro-rich inequity index for total physician visits non-significant, makes the index for GP visits significantly non-negative and reduces the pro-rich index for specialist services. This implies that its contribution to the use of physician services is clearly pro-rich. Or, in other words, it is likely that in the absence of such private insurance, physician visits would be distributed somewhat more pro-poor or less pro-rich.[4] Interestingly, using the same indirect method, it was also found that the contribution of region (again proxied by province) in general also has a pro-rich contribution, which is not entirely consistent with the findings in Ref. [11]. As the latter method is preferable because of its fuller model specification, the 1996 findings remain tentative and deserve further examination.

10.4
Inequalities in Health and Health Outcomes

Arguably, a more appealing notion of health care equity is the extent to which the distribution of health care (by income or other characteristics) helps to narrow down any systematic differentials in health outcomes [24]. However, this definition of health care equity is more difficult to implement empirically because of the problems with measuring changes in self-reported overall health questions using general cross-sectional and panel data surveys. In this context, disease-specific approaches are likely to prove more informative of the extent to which health care systems do, or do not, contribute to reductions in health outcome inequalities. Fortunately, this is precisely an area in which Canadian research efforts appear more advanced than in other countries. Here, the evidence on income-related health inequalities in Canada will first be reviewed, before moving on to the question of to what extent these health inequalities may be related to inequalities in health care assessment and utilization.

---

3) This is not entirely equivalent to the decomposition method, as no variables other than need, region and insurance were included in the equations used in the standardization process.

4) This was the finding in four European countries where supplementary private insurance seems to fuel the pro-rich distribution of the specialist visit probability [23].

Table 10.3 HI_{wv} indices for medical care use, Canada, 1996 [10]

				HI$_{wv}$ index adjusted for							
				(1) Need only		(2) Need + province		(3) Need + priv insurance		(4) Need + both	
Code	Type of visits	CM	t (5)	HI$_{wv}$	t (5)	HI$_{wv}$	t (5)	HI$_{wv}$	t (5)	HI$_{wv}$	t (5)
GP	GP visits	−0.0795	−11.07	−0.0063	−1.00	−0.0141	−2.27	−0.0149	−2.37	−0.0201	−3.24
Spec	Specialist visits	0.0009	0.08	0.0631	6.45	0.0608	6.23	0.0514	5.26	0.0500	5.12
Tot	All physician visits	−0.0595	−9.09	0.0107	1.87	0.0044	0.77	0.0013	0.23	−0.0029	−0.51

Notes:
(1) Need only = indirectly standardised for 15 need dummies (age, sex, self-assessed health and (hampered by) chronic condition)
(2) Need + region = ind stand includes need plus provincial dummies
(3) Need + private insurance = ind stand includes need plus private insurance dummy
(4) Need + both = ind stand includes need, province and private insurance dummies
(5) t-statistics based on robust standard errors

10.4.1
Income-Related Health Inequality

In Canada, as in most other countries, health is not equally distributed across groups and individuals with unequal incomes. This is true for measures of both morbidity and mortality.[5] For the sake of comparability, attention here will be focused on some of the empirical evidence that is directly comparable with that of other countries. Humphries and van Doorslaer [26] used data from the 1994 National Population Health Survey to compute concentration indices of the degree of income-related inequality in self-reported ill health using the standard question, and found that it was significantly higher than that reported by Van Doorslaer et al. [27] for seven European countries, but not significantly different from the health inequality measured for the UK and the US. All of these measurements used the self-assessed health (SAH) question, and scaled it using an approach proposed by Wagstaff and Van Doorslaer [28] and based on the assumption that the discrete relative distribution of adults across SAH categories derives from an underlying standard-lognormal distribution. These authors also observed that its income-related health inequality appeared to be higher than might be expected on the basis of the regression analysis of health inequality on income inequality [27], and concluded that:

> "It remains a question for further research why Canada and the UK – with income inequality only slightly higher than most European countries and universal access of their population to health care – show a degree of income-related health inequality that is closer to that found for the US than to that found for other European countries." (p. 670, from Ref. [26])

In the Canadian context, there is, however, no need to rely only on such a crude and simple measure as the five-point scale of the SAH question, as most national health surveys have – for over a decade now – also included more extensive and generic health indicators. In particular, the inclusion of a fairly comprehensive measure such as the McMaster Health Utility Index in the National Population Health Survey and the Community Health Surveys is a major advantage over most other countries. Using multi-attribute utility functions, the eight self-reported health attributes (vision, hearing, speech, ambulation, dexterity, emotion, cognition and pain) can be converted into health utility scores between zero and one [29]. Humphries and van Doorslaer [26] computed the CI for the utility loss (as (1 − HUI) score) for 1994, and found it to be equal to −0.0990 (s.e. = 0.0163), which was lower but not significantly different from the CI = −0.1214 (s.e. = 0.0182) obtained using the standard-lognormal scoring procedure for ill-health based on SAH. Of course, it is well known that the CI differs depending on whether good or bad health is being measured, and it is therefore no surprise that Van Doorslaer

---

5) For a recent review on health disparities in Canada in general, see for example Ref. [25].

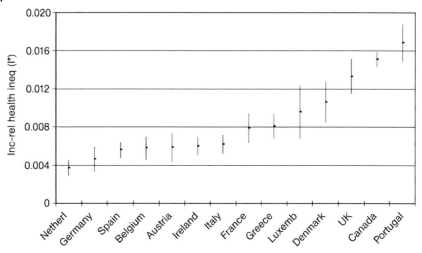

Fig. 10.11 Concentration indices for predicted HUI, standardized for age and gender (with 95% confidence interval). (Sources: for Canada [30]; all others [31]).

and Jones [30], using the same dataset, obtained a CI equal to 0.0141 (s.e. = 0.0009) for the health utility index (HUI).

The measured degree of income-related inequality in self-reported health, and its dependence on the underlying issue of health measurement, was revisited in Ref. [30]. Here, the aim was to exploit the simultaneous inclusion of the HUI and SAH in the NPHS 1994, in order to obtain a better estimate of health inequality for other countries/surveys which only have SAH observations. The authors avoided the arbitrary assumption associated with the use of a standard-lognormal distribution to determine the thresholds of ill-health; rather, they assessed the internal validity of several alternative approaches to scaling the SAH responses, and concluded that an interval regression approach that assigns interval thresholds on the basis of the a mapping of the empirical distribution function of HUI into SAH came closest to approximating the use of directly observed HUI values, with an estimated CI of 0.0151.

This estimate (for 1994) is directly comparable to estimates obtained for 13 European countries by Van Doorslaer and Koolman [31], using data from the 1996 wave of the European Community Household Panel (ECHP).[6] These CIs, standardized for age and gender, and with 95% confidence intervals, are reproduced in Fig. 10.11. It can be seen that the degree of income-related health inequality, as measured by the CI of HUI, is significantly higher in Canada than in all European countries, except for the UK and Portugal.

6) There are some minor differences. The NPHS 5 SAH response categories range from Excellent to Poor, whereas the ECHP categories range form Very good to Very poor.

These findings can also be compared to results for the US presented by Xu [32], who replicated these methods to examine state variations in income-related health inequality in the US with the 2001 Current Population Survey. Xu identified a CI of 0.0166 for the US as a whole, which was somewhat higher still, but ranging from a value of 0.0072 (for Utah) to 0.0259 (for Tennessee). These data were not included in Fig. 10.11 because they were not age–gender standardized, and no 95% confidence intervals were provided. Recent findings from the Joint Canada/United States Survey of Health 2002-03 confirmed that self-reported health is slightly better and less unequally distributed in Canada than in the US:

> "While in both countries, those in the poorest income quintile reported poorer health, more low income Americans did so compared with low income Canadians (31% vs. 23%). The same pattern prevailed regarding the distribution of severe mobility limitation, obesity and unmet health care needs. There were no systematic differences in the reporting of fair or poor health or mobility impairment among the most affluent households on either side of the border." [16].

The decomposition method described in Appendix 10.1 can also be used to ascertain the relative contributions of various explanatory variables to the observed patterns of health. As with utilization, any variable can only contribute to greater inequality in health by income if: (i) it is itself unequally distributed by income; and (ii) it has an effect on health. However, the Canadian results are very similar to the patterns observed for the average European country: the partial income effect itself contributes 43% to the measured degree of income-related health inequality; activity status (in particular disability and retirement status) accounts for about 31% of the total; and education contributes 20%. These results must be interpreted with care: whilst they are partial effects (i.e., holding all other variables constant), they are not necessarily causal influences as the underlying explanatory model does not represent causal relationships. They also only refer to inequalities in a measure of self-reported general health (SAH) which is known to have strong relationships with expected income-related inequalities in subsequent mortality [33], but nonetheless only presents a very partial and global picture on inequalities in health by income. In the next section, some disease-specific attempts at unraveling the contribution of income and other factors are described, including the use of medical care, to measured degrees of health outcomes by income.

10.4.2
Does Inequality in Use Lead to Inequalities in Outcome?

One obvious question that arises after having established that individuals with equal needs but unequal incomes do not receive equal medical treatment or utilization, is whether such horizontal inequity affects inequalities in health outcomes. As this question is far more difficult to answer with the general health survey questions, most investigators have adopted a disease-specific approach to try to shed light on the issue. The obvious advantage is that such an approach allows for a focus on more homogeneous groups of patients in a more similar broad diagnostic category, for whom it is more straightforward to identify appropriate treatment patterns and to compare relevant outcomes. By restricting attention to more homogeneous groups, treatment needs can be assumed to be more equal, or are at least much more similar. An obvious drawback of the disease-specific studies is, of course, that findings cannot be generalized to the overall system or population level. It is not because one observes unequal treatment by income of AMI patients that necessarily also rheumatoid arthritis or cancer patients are treated in similarly unequal fashion.

A number of Canadian studies have been at the forefront of the development of this approach. A classic example is the study of Alter et al. [34], which examined differences in access to invasive cardiac procedures after acute myocardial infarction (AMI) based on neighborhood income in the province of Ontario. Whereas the rates of coronary angiography and revascularization were found to be significantly positively associated with income, waiting times and one-year mortality rates were significantly negatively related to income. Each $10 000 increase in the neighborhood median income was associated with a 10% reduction in the risk of death within one year. Clearly, this does not indicate to what extent it is the differential treatment that is responsible for the income-related inequalities in outcomes. However, the authors concluded at the time that:

> "The causes of these socioeconomic disparities in access and outcome remain obscure, but their persistence poses a clear challenge to the egalitarian principles of Canada's publicly funded health care system." (p. 1366, from Ref. [34])

In a similar study for Quebec, Pilote et al. [35] found that in patients with a first AMI, socioeconomic status (SES) (measured by variables related to income level, educational attainment, poverty rate, and level of urbanization) had an influence on access to cardiac catheterization; however, once catheterization had been performed the SES had little effect on access to revascularization. These findings suggest that treatment is not identical across SES and that also outcomes vary, although the extent to which the differential outcomes are due to the access inequalities is less clear.

Several more recent investigations have also aimed at exploring the mediating factors in the observed gradient. Clearly, poorer patients are also more likely to smoke or to have diabetes and hypertension, all of which lead to accelerated atherosclerosis and higher subsequent mortality rates. A recent cross-country comparative study of male mortality [36], for instance, identified a two-fold difference between the highest and the lowest social strata in overall risks of dying among men aged 35 to 69 years (England and Wales 21% vs. 43%, USA 20% vs. 37%, Canada 21% vs. 34%, Poland 26% vs. 50%: four-country mean 22% vs. 41%, four-country mean absolute difference 19%; see Fig. 10.12). These authors estimated that more than half of this difference in mortality between the top and bottom social strata involved differences in risks of being killed at age 35 to 69 years by smoking (England and Wales 4% vs. 19%, USA 4% vs. 15%, Canada 6% vs. 13%, Poland 5% vs. 22%: four-country mean 5% vs. 17%, four-country mean absolute difference 12%). They

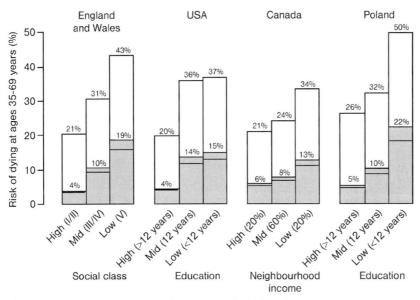

Fig. 10.12 Socioeconomic inequality in male mortality in 1996 from smoking and from any cause [36].

also argued that smoking-attributed mortality accounted for as much as almost half of total male mortality in the lowest social stratum of each country.[7] In other words, life style may matter more than access to medical care. Interestingly, among these four countries the lowest SES stratum (as proxied by the 20% with the lowest neighborhood income versus education used for other countries) has the lowest mortality rate in Canada.

The AMI income–outcome gradient also appears to persist even after adjustment for cardiovascular events and traditional cardiac risk factors. Alter et al. [39] have further explored the links in the Socio-Economic and Acute Myocardial Infarction (SESAMI) study, a prospective observational study of patients who were hospitalized because of AMI throughout Ontario, Canada. Income was strongly and inversely correlated with the 2-year mortality rate: 7.1% of patients in the high-income group died within 2 years, compared to 15.3% of those in the low-income group. Adjustment for age, pre-existing cardiovascular disease, and risk factors greatly attenuated the relationship between mortality rates and income. While this observation suggests that it may not be the differential treatment that causes the "wealth–health gradient" in cardiovascular mortality, the authors suggested that it does imply that the gradient may be partially ameliorated by more rigorous management of known risk factors among less affluent persons. Or in other words, positive discrimination in the treatment of the poor may be called for.

7) This estimate is substantially higher than the results obtained in a similar exercise by Mackenbach et al. [37] for 10 European countries (cf. Ref. [38]).

10.5
Conclusion and Discussion

In this chapter, some of the empirical evidence on health disparities and inequities in access to medical care by income in Canada have been reviewed. In doing so, particular attention has been paid to the evidence that was comparable to that obtained for other OECD countries, with a view to deriving some conclusion on the relative extent to which Canada's health care system has been more or less successful in reaching its goal of delivering "...affordable, timely, accessible and high quality care to all Canadians on the basis of need, not income". By drawing on the findings of a large number of existing studies, the following conclusions were reached.

First, it is clear that Canada's system of universal coverage of the greater part of essential medical services has, beyond any doubt, managed to get much closer to meeting the horizontal equity principle of equal treatment for equal need. It is clear from the comparative picture that Canada's current doctor visit distribution is fairly close to the estimated distribution of need by income.

Second, restricting attention solely to the overall distribution of doctor visits conceals quite a different picture with respect to GP and specialist care. While the probability of seeing a GP is still marginally pro-rich (after need standardization), this is more than compensated by the pro-poor distribution of (conditional) subsequent GP visits, making the overall GP visit distribution also significantly pro-poor, but the degree is small.

Third, the situation is very different for specialist visits. After standardizing for greater needs among the poor, both the access probability and total number of specialist visits show as being significantly pro-rich, though admittedly to a (much) smaller extent than in many other OECD countries, including a large number with universal and comprehensive coverage. In the absence of an international comparative picture, there might have been more reason for serious concern. Now, it appears as though Canada has already managed to keep the pro-rich bias in specialist use within very reasonable limits by international standards.

Fourth, Canada stands out internationally by showing a pro-poor pattern for hospital in-patient care: for equal needs (as measured in these surveys), low-income Canadians are more likely to be admitted to a hospital and more likely to stay there longer than higher-income Canadian residents. This may be related to the fact that the need measures used in the standardization process are too crude for in-patient care decisions, or to the inability to observe utilization patterns of (less time-costly) day case services, but it is unlikely that such refinements would tilt the balance in the opposite direction – that is, into significant inequity favoring the rich. In other words, the current evidence certainly does not reflect any inequities due to hospital access barriers for lower-income groups. On the contrary, when literally interpreted, it indicates an over-consumption of the worse-off.

Fifth, when turning attention to services not included in the public system's coverage, we could not report any comparative evidence of inequity in the use of prescription drugs (which is a major omission), although for dental care it is clear that in Canada – as in most other OECD countries, and largely irrespective of the degree of public coverage – dental visits are distributed strongly pro-rich. Given the complete lack of public coverage and the highly income-related uptake of private dental insurance, it is not surprising that Canada ranks fairly high in terms of its degree of pro-rich dental care inequity.

In summary, Canada's overall equity achievement for the distribution of publicly insured services compares favorably not only to countries without universal coverage (such as the US or Mexico) but also to many OECD and European countries which have relied on various types of financial barriers (such as public service co-payments) to combat moral hazard or on private options (insurance or delivery) to complement or supplement their public insurance systems. Specific US–Canada comparisons confirm that utilization disparities by income are smaller in Canada, and that this is mainly due to better access of the lower-income groups.

Sixth, a low degree of income-related inequity for access to physician and hospital care does not yet imply that health inequalities by income are small. In contrast, international comparisons of CIs of the predicted scores of the HUI suggest that Canada's income-related inequality – while definitely smaller than that in the US – seems to be greater than in the majority of European countries.

Seventh, a growing body of research, in particular on the treatment of AMI patients, has sought to address the pressing question of to what extent these outcome differentials can be attributed to different treatment patterns. The most recent additions to that literature suggest that it may not be so much the differential treatment that causes the "wealth–health gradient" in cardiovascular mortality, but that the existing gradient may be partially ameliorated by more rigorous management of known risk factors among less-affluent persons. Among the other important determinants, lifestyle factors such as smoking may play a much greater role, with one study suggesting that "…widespread cessation of smoking could eventually halve the absolute differences between social strata in adult male mortality ([36], p. 370).

Evidently, the review also detected some holes in the evidence to date. One question is whether the equity situation is similarly satisfactory for the types of care excluded from public coverage. The problems with income-related inequality in dental care access were illustrated above, but far less is known on prescription drugs. The Commonwealth International Health Policy Survey 2001 asked whether some prescriptions for drugs were not filled for reasons of cost. Unsurprisingly, below-average income individuals (22% said "yes") were threefold more likely to say "yes" to this question than above-average income individuals (7% said "yes"). While these percentages were larger in the US for both groups (and smaller in the UK), the interesting finding here is that the relative income-related difference is largest in Canada, and remained significant and of the same magnitude after controlling for health status, health insurance coverage, age, education, minority or immigration status and residential location.[8] In addition, those with private insurance were 40% less likely to report access problems because of cost. This suggests that income-related inequity in access to prescription drugs may be a result of the lack

8) Interestingly, the difference also remained statistically significant in New Zealand and the US, but was only a twofold, not a threefold, difference.

of universal coverage and unequal distribution of private insurance coverage across income groups in Canada, and seems to be one of the areas that deserves further investigation [40].

Inequity in the types of care currently not covered under the Canada Health Act (such as dental and prescription drugs), of the effects of recent and planned future reforms to the system, along with further well-controlled disease-specific efforts to unravel the contributions of unequal treatment to unequal health outcomes, appear to be some of the most important items on a future Canadian research agenda on equity in health and health care.

Acknowledgments

The author gratefully acknowledges the useful comments of Jerry Hurley, Ming-shan Lu and other participants at the workshop organized by the University of Calgary at the Banff Conference Centre September 2006.

References

1 Romanow, R.J. (2002) *Building on Values: The Future of Health Care in Canada*, Health Canada, Ottawa, 2002.

2 Flood, C., Archibald, T. (2001) The illegality of private health care in Canada. *Canadian Medical Association Journal*, 164 (6): 825–830.

3 Marmor, T.R., Okma, K.G.H., Latham, S.R. (2002) *National Values, Institutions and Health Policies: What Do They Imply for Medicare Reform?* Commission on the Future of Health Care in Canada Discussion Paper 5, Health Canada, Ottawa.

4 Smythe, J.G. (2002) *The redistributive effect of health care finance in Alberta.* Institute of Health Economics Working Paper 02–07, University of Alberta, Edmonton.

5 McGrail, K. (2006) *Equity in health, health care services use and health care financing in British Columbia, 1992 and 2002.* PhD Thesis, University of British Columbia, Vancouver.

6 Van Doorslaer, E., Wagstaff, A., Rutten, F. (Eds.) (1993) *Equity in the finance and delivery of health care: an international perspective*, Oxford University Press, Oxford.

7 Wagstaff, A., van Doorslaer, E., Van Der Burg, H., Calonge, S., Christiansen, T., Citoni, G., Gerdtham, U.G., Gerfin, M., Gross, L., Hakinnen, U., Johnson, P., John, J., Klavus, J., Lachaud, C., Lauritsen, J., Leu, R., Nolan, B., Peran, E., Pereira, J., Propper, C., Puffer, F., Rochaix, L., Rodriguez, M., Schellhorn, M., Winkelhake, O. (1999) Equity in the finance of health care: some further international comparisons. *Journal of Health Economics*, 18(3): 263–290.

8 Birch, S., Eyles, J., Newbold, K.B. (1993) Equitable access to health care: methodological extensions to the analysis of physician utilization in Canada. *Health Economics*, 2: 87–101.

9 Allin, S. (2006) *Equity in the use of health services in Canada and its provinces.* LSE Health Working Paper 3/2006, London.

10 Van Doorslaer, E., Koolman, X., Puffer, F. (2002) Equity in the use of physician visits in OECD countries: has equal treatment for equal need been achieved? In: *Measuring Up: Improving Health Systems Performance in OECD Countries.* OECD, Paris, pp. 225–248.

11 Van Doorslaer, C., Masseria, X., and the OECD Health Equity Research Group. (2004) Income-related inequality in the use of medical care in 21 OECD countries. In: *Towards High-Performing*

Health Systems: Policy Studies. Paris, OECD, pp. 109–166.

12 Van Doorslaer, C., Masseria, X., Koolman, X. and the OECD Health Equity Research Group (2006) Inequalities in access to medical care by income in developed countries. *Canadian Medical Association Journal*, **174**(2): 177–183.

13 Van Doorslaer, E., Wagstaff, A., van der Burg, H., Christiansen, T., De Graeve, D., Duchesne, I., Gerdtham, U.-G., Gerfin, M., Geurts, J., Gross, L., Häkkinen, U., John, J., Klavus, J., Leu, R.E., Nolan, B., O'Donnell, O., Propper, C., Puffer, F., Schellhorn, M., Sundberg, G., Winkelhake, O. (2000) Equity in the delivery of health care in Europe and the US. *Journal of Health Economics*, **19**(5): 553–583.

14 Morris, S., Sutton, M., Gravelle, H. (2005) Inequity and inequality in the use of health care in England: an empirical investigation. *Social Science Medicine*, **60**(6): 1251–1266.

15 Schoen, C., Doty, M.M. (2004) Inequities in access to medical care in five countries: findings from the 2001 Commonwealth Fund International Health Policy Survey. *Health Policy*, **67**(3): 309–322.

16 Sanmartin, C., Ng, E., Blackwell, D., Gentleman, J., Martinez, M., Simile, C. (2006) *Joint Canada/United States Survey of Health, 2002-03*. Statistics Canada, Ottawa and CDC, NCHS, Website http://www.cdc.gov/nchs/data/nhis/jcush_analyticalreport.pdf.

17 Lasser, K.E., Himmelstein, D.U., Woolhandler, S. (2006) Access to care, health status, and health disparities in the United States and Canada: results of a cross-national population-based survey. *American Journal of Public Health*, **96**(7): 1300–1307.

18 Katz, S.J., Hofer, T.P., Manning, W.G. (1996) Physician use in Ontario and the United States: The impact of socioeconomic status and health status. *American Journal of Public Health*, **86**: 520–524.

19 Katz, S.J., Hofer, T.P., Manning, W.G. (1996) Hospital utilization in Ontario and the United States: the impact of socioeconomic status and health status. *Canadian Journal of Public Health*, **87**(4): 253–256.

20 Wagstaff, A., Van Doorslaer, E., Watanabe, N. (2003) On decomposing the causes of health sector inequalities, with an application to malnutrition inequalities in Vietnam. *Journal of Econometrics*, **112**(1): 219–227.

21 Van Doorslaer, E., Koolman, X., Jones, A.M. (2004). Explaining income-related inequalities in doctor utilisation in Europe. *Health Economics*, **13**(7): 629–647.

22 Stabile, M. (2001) Private insurance subsidies and public health care markets: Evidence from Canada. *Canadian Journal of Economics*, **34**(4): 921–942.

23 Jones, A.M., Koolman, X., van Doorslaer, E. (2007) The impact of supplementary private health insurance on the use of specialists in selected European countries. *Annals of Economics and Statistics*, **83-84**.

24 Culyer, A.J., Wagstaff, A. (1993), Equity and equality in health and health care. *Journal of Health Economics* **12**(4): 431–457.

25 Frohlich, K.L., Ross, N., Richmond, C. (2006) Health disparities in Canada today: Some evidence and a theoretical framework. *Health Policy*, **79**(2): 132–143.

26 Humphries, K., van Doorslaer, E. (2000) Income-related inequalities in health in Canada. *Social Science Medicine*, **50**: 663–671.

27 Van Doorslaer, E., Wagstaff, A., Bleichrodt, H., Calonge, S., Gerdtham, U.-G., Gerfin, M., Geurts, J., Gross, L., Häkkinen, U., Leu, R., O'Donnell, O., Propper, C., Puffer, F., Rodriguez, M., Sundberg, G., Winkelhake, O. (1997) Socioeconomic inequalities in health: some international comparisons. *Journal of Health Economics*, **16**(1): 93–112.

28 Wagstaff, A., van Doorslaer, E. (1994) Measurement of health inequalities in the presence of multiple-category morbidity indicators. *Health Economics*, **3**, 281–291.

29 Feeny, D., Furlong, W., Torrance, G.W., Goldsmith, C.H., Zhu, Z., Depauw, S., Denton, M., Boyle, M. (2002) Multi-attribute and single-attribute utility functions for the Health Utilities Index Mark 3 system. *Medical Care*, **40**(2): 113–128.

30 Van Doorslaer, E., Jones, A.M. (2003) Inequalities in self-reported health: validation of a new approach to measurement. *Journal of Health Economics*, **22**: 61–87.

31 Van Doorslaer, E., Koolman, X. (2004), Explaining the differences in income-related health inequalities across European countries. *Health Economics*, **13**(7): 609–628.

32 Xu, K.T. (2006) State-level variations in income-related inequality in health and health achievement in the US. *Social Science Medicine*, **63**(2): 457–464.

33 Van Doorslaer, E. , Gerdtham, U.-G. (2003) Does inequality in self-assessed health predict inequality in survival by income? Evidence from Swedish data. *Social Science Medicine*, **57**(9): 1621–1629.

34 Alter, D.A., Naylor, C.D., Austin, P., Tu, J.V. (1999) Effects of socioeconomic status on access to invasive cardiac procedures and on mortality after acute myocardial infarction. *New England Journal of Medicine*, **341**: 1359–1367.

35 Pilote, L., Joseph, L., Belisle, P., Penrod, J. (2003) Universal health insurance coverage does not eliminate inequities in access to cardiac procedures after acute myocardial infarction. *American Heart Journal*, **146**(6): 1030–1037.

36 Jha, P., Peto, R., Zatonski, W., Boreham, J., Jarvis, M.J., Lopez, A.D. (2006) Social inequalities in male mortality, and in male mortality from smoking: indirect estimation from national death rates in England and Wales, Poland, and North America. *Lancet*, **368**: 367–370.

37 Mackenbach, J.P., Huisman, M., Andersen, O., Bopp, M., Borgan, J.K., Borrell, C., Costa, G., Deboosere, P., Donkin, A., Gadeyne, S., Minder, C., Regidor, E., Spadea, T., Valkonen, T., Kunst, A.E. (2004) Inequalities in lung cancer mortality by the educational level in 10 European populations. *European Journal of Cancer*, **40**: 126–135.

38 Marmot, M. (2006) Smoking and inequalities: comment. *Lancet*, **368**: 341–342.

39 Alter, D.A., Chong, A., Austin, P.C., Mustard, C., Iron, K., Williams, J.I., Morgan, C.D., Tu, J.V., Irvine, J., Naylor, C.D. (2006) SESAMI Study Group. Socioeconomic status and mortality after acute myocardial infarction. *Annals of Internal Medicine*, **144**(2): 82–93.

40 Hurley, J., Grignon, M. (2006) Income and equity of access to physician services. *Canadian Medical Association Journal*, **174**(2): 187–188.

41 Wagstaff, A., van Doorslaer, E. (2000) Equity in health care financing and delivery, In: Culyer, A.J., Newhouse, J.P. (Eds.), *Handbook of Health Economics*. North Holland, Elsevier, Amsterdam, pp. 1803–1862.

42 Jones, A.M. (2000) *Health econometrics*. In: Culyer, A.J., Newhouse, J.P. (Eds.), *Handbook of Health Economics*. North Holland, Elsevier, Amsterdam, pp. 265–344.

Appendix

Measurement and decomposition of income-related inequality in health and health care (cf. Ref. [11])

Measurement of Inequality and Inequity

Quintile distributions are difficult to compare across types of care, or across countries. The degree of inequality in a health indicator (or in the use of health care) can be measured using the (rank-based) concept of a *concentration curve* as shown in Fig. A10.1. This plots the cumulative distribution of use as a function of the cumulative distribution of the population ranked by income. A distribution is equal if the cumulative distribution coincides with the diagonal. If the curve lies above (below) the diagonal this indicates that use is more concentrated among the poor (rich). A *concentration index* (CI) measures the degree of inequality in use. When it is positive, it indicates pro-rich inequality, and when it is negative, it indicates pro-poor inequality.

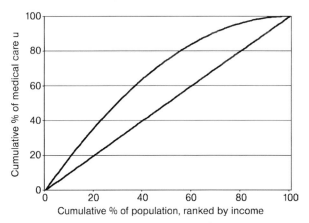

Fig. A10.1 A (stylized) concentration curve of medical care use.

The CI can be computed using a simple covariance formula, as shown below for weighted data:

$$C = \frac{2}{y^m} \sum_{i=1}^{n} w_i (y_i - y^m)(R_i - R^m) = \frac{2}{\mu} \text{cov}_w (y_i, R_i) \tag{A10.1}$$

where y^m is the weighted sample mean of y, cov_w denotes the weighted covariance and R_i is the (representatively positioned) relative fractional rank of the *i*th individual, defined as:

$$R_i = \frac{1}{n} \sum_{j=1}^{i-1} w_j + \frac{1}{2} w_i \tag{A10.2}$$

where w_i denotes the sampling weight of the ith individual and the sum of w_i equals the sample size (n).

Testing for differences between concentration indices requires confidence intervals. Robust estimates for C and its standard error can be obtained by running the following convenient (weighted least squares) regression of (transformed) y on relative rank:

$$\frac{2\sigma_R^2}{y^m} y_i = \alpha_1 + \beta_1 R_i + \varepsilon_{1,i} \tag{A10.3}$$

where σ_R^2 is the variance of R_i and $\hat{\beta}_1$ is equal to C, and the estimated standard error of $\hat{\beta}_1$ provides the estimated standard error of C.

The CI of the actual medical care use measures the degree of inequality and the CI of the need-standardized use (which is our horizontal inequity index, HI) measures the degree of needs-adjusted inequality. It is worth emphasizing that coinciding concentration curves for need and actual use provide a sufficient – but not a necessary – condition for horizontal equity. Even with crossing curves, one could have zero inequity if, for example, inequity favoring the poor in one part of the distribution exactly offsets inequity favoring the rich in another.

We would expect overall health to be pro-rich or health care use to be pro-poor, because lower income groups generally have poorer health status and therefore higher needs for care. A more appropriate measure of inequality would adjust use for differences in need. In this chapter we estimate the degree of inequality in need-standardized use.

The method used to describe and measure the degree of horizontal inequity in health care delivery is conceptually identical to that used in Refs. [41] and [10–13]. It compares the observed distribution of medical care by income with the distribution of need. In order to statistically adjust needs for groups or individuals, the average relationship between need and use estimated for the population as a whole is used as the "norm" of what treatment is needed. We investigate the extent to which there are any systematic deviations from this norm by income level. The approach is to model health care use employing ordinary least squares (OLS) regression techniques.

Health care utilization data such as physician visits are known to have skewed distributions, with typically a large majority of survey respondents reporting zero or very few visits and only a very small proportion reporting frequent use. Because these features cause violations of the standard OLS model, various specifications of non-linear, two-part models have been proposed in the literature, distinguishing between the probability of positive usage and the amount of usage conditional on use in the reference period (for a review, see Ref. [42]). While these models have certain advantages over OLS specifications, their intrinsic non-linearity makes the (linear) decomposition method described above impossible. In order to restore the mechanics of the decomposition, one has to revert to a re-linearization of the models using approximations (see Ref. [21] for an example). However, both Refs. [13] and [11] have shown that the measurement of horizontal inequity is not sensitive to the choice of specification. We are confident that our results are not conditional on the choice of the linear standardization model.

This study describes distributions of actual and need-adjusted use of health care by income quintile, each representing 20% of the total population ranked by household equivalent income from poorest to richest. "Need-expected" health care use is computed by regressing medical care use, y_i, (e.g., doctor visits or hospital nights) on a set of explanatory variables.

$$y_i = \alpha + \beta \ln inc_i + \sum_k \gamma_k x_{k,i} + \sum_p \delta_p z_{p,i} + \varepsilon_i \qquad \text{(A10.4)}$$

We distinguish between three types of explanatory variable: the (logarithm of) the household income of individual i ($\ln inc_i$), a set of k need indicator variables (x_k) including demographic and morbidity variables, and p non-need variables (z_p). α, β, γ_k and δ_p are parameters and ε_i is an error term.

Equation (1) is used to generate need-predicted values of use, $\hat{y}_i^X$; that is, the expected use of medical care of individual i on the basis of her/his need characteristics. It indicates the amount of medical care s/he would received if s/he had been treated as others with the same need characteristics (e.g., age), on average. By combining estimates of the coefficients in Eq. (1) with *actual* values of the x_k variables and *sample mean* values of the $\ln inc_i$ and z_p variables, we can obtain the need-predicted, or "x-expected" values of utilization, $\hat{y}_i^X$ as:

$$\hat{y}_i^X = \hat{\alpha} + \hat{\beta} \ln inc^m + \sum_k \hat{\gamma}_k x_{k,i} + \sum_p \hat{\delta}_p z_p^m \qquad \text{(A10.5)}$$

Estimates of the (indirectly) need-standardized utilization, $\hat{y}_i^{IS}$, are then obtained as the difference between actual and x-expected utilization, plus the sample mean (y^m)

$$\hat{y}_i^{IS} = y_i - \hat{y}_i^X + y^m \qquad \text{(A10.6)}$$

The quintile means of these indirectly standardized values provide our need-standardized distributions of medical care. They are interpreted as the expected distributions *if need were equally distributed across quintiles*.

Use of Decomposition to Explain Inequality

It is possible to estimate the "contributions" of the various determinants and their relative importance. Using the regression coefficients γ_k, (partial) elasticities of medical care use with respect to each determinant k can then be defined as:

$$\eta_k = \gamma_k x_k^m / y^m \qquad (A10.7)$$

where y^m is the (population weighted mean) of y and x_k^m is the (population weighted) mean of x_k. These elasticities denote the percentage change in y result from a percentage change in x_k.

It has been shown [20] that the total CI can then be written as:

$$C = \eta_r C_{\ln \, inc} + \sum_k \eta_k C_{x,k} + \sum_p \eta_p C_{z,p} + GC_\varepsilon \qquad (A10.8)$$

where the first term denotes the partial contribution of income inequality, the second term the (partial) contribution of the need variables, and the third term the (partial) contribution of the other variables. The last term is the generalized CI of the error term, ε. In other words, estimated inequality in predicted medical care use is a weighted sum of the inequality in each of its determinants, with the weights equal to the medical care use elasticities. The decomposition also makes clear how each determinant k's separate contribution to total income-related inequality in health care demand can be decomposed into two meaningful parts: (i) its impact on use, as measured by the use elasticity (η_k); and (ii) its degree of unequal distribution across income, as measured by the (income) CI (C_k). This decomposition method allows us to separate the contributions of the various determinants, and also to identify the importance of each of these two components within each factor's total contribution.

Index

a

access to health care   246
– inequities   253
ACG, *see* adjusted clinical group
actuarially fair   26, 42
adjusted average per capita cost (AAPCC)
   210
adjusted clinical group (ACG)   196f,
   209f
administrative costs   21, 30, 38
adverse selection   8, 13, 18, 21, 26, 29f, 35,
   39, 46, 223ff, 226ff, 241
AIDS   185
Alberta Blue Cross   206, 208
altruistic motives   161, 165f
asymmetric information   4, 7, 10

b

basic medical insurance   130
barriers to hospital access   252
biased selection   211

c

Canada   31, 177, 193, 201f, 206f, 213
– price control   31
– waiting lists   31
Canada health act   14, 86, 88, 246
– national standards   88
Canadian health care system   85
– provinces   85
– territories   85
– universal public health insurance   85
capitated health plans   190
capitation   8, 11, 24, 31, 37, 160, 162, 164,
   168
capitation payment   160, 163f, 179f, 187
case identification   178

case mix adjustment   178
CDHC (consumer directed health care)
   107, 113, 119, 105, 107
– high-deductible insurance plans   105
– incentive constraints   9, 107, 113
– income effect   107
CDHC studies, data collection   119
CDHC plans   3, 8, 118, 126
– health reimbursement accounts   118
– patient cost sharing   8
– premium-tiered models   118
– selection and cross subsidization   111
– tiered-benefit   118
Chaoulli   15, 36
Charleson Index   196f
Chile   184
China   127, 131, 133, 136, 140, 142f
chronic and disability payment system
   196
chronic disease score   196
clinical related group   196
clinical risk groups (CRGs)   197, 201
clinically detailed risk indication   196
Clinton plan   10, 18, 34
co-insurance   22
commune-based cooperative medical
   scheme (CMMS)   129
competitive equilibrium   227f, 234f
concentration index (CI)   248, 259
consumer cost-sharing   10
consumer-directed health care, *see* CDHC
contracting agents   180
conventional insurance plan   107
– adverse selection   8
conventional risk adjustment   183ff, 188f,
   217, 237f
co-payment systems   74

Financing Health Care: New Ideas for a Changing Society. Edited by Mingshan Lu and Egon Jonsson
Copyright © 2008 WILEY-VCH Verlag GmbH & Co. KGaA, Weinheim
ISBN: 978-3-527-32027-1

correlation between waiting lists and
  private health care   53
cost control, single payer   30
cost savings   55
cost sharing   139, 230
– co-payment   149, 154
– demand side   149
– per individual   227
– supply side   149
cost-sharing mechanisms   149
costs   230
– cost-related non-compliance   97
– out-of-pocket charges   97
coverage   7
cream-skimming   18, 25, 27, 29, 35,
  163
CRG, *see* clinical risk groups
cross-country comparisons   74
cross-subsidization   111

d
diabetes   185
DCG, *see* diagnostic cost group
DCG/HCC   202, 204, 211
death spiral   27
decentralization of funding and decision
  making   3, 37
decomposition method   255
deductible   8, 22
Dekker-Simmons plan   10, 18, 34
de-listing   59f, 64ff, 75
– accessibility problems   65
– by province   62
– price deregulation   65
– publicly funded services in Canada
  59
– services   60
– utilization   64
demand-side   10
– cost-sharing   149, 154
– incentives   9
derived demand   88
diagnoses   185, 198
diagnosis-related group (DRG)   164, 187,
  211, 215
diagnostic ability   164f
diagnostic cost group (DCG)   196f, 215
disease management   179
disease-specific studies   262
disparities   253
DRG, *see* diagnosis-related group

DRG-creep   164
drug   90, 91, 198
– adverse drug reactions   90
– budget   8
– information costs   91
– performance   91
– pre-market safety regulation   90
– scientific trials   91
drug expenditure   81
drug financing   81f
– Canadians   81
– North America   82
dumping   25, 27, 29, 35, 184, 188
duplicate coverage   6
dynamic model of demand   116
– increase consumption   116
– quantity accumulation   116

e
efficient consumption level   151
efficient provision of medical services
  166
egalitarian principle   246
end-stage renal disease (ESRD)
episode risk group (ERG)   196f, 201
equal treatment for equal need   14
equity in health care   13
ERG, *see* episode risk group
ethics constraint   170
expected utility   11
expenditure control   98f
– monopsony buyer   98
– preferred provider   99
– third-party payers   98
ex-post moral-hazard problem   153
external benefits   19
external effects   17
externalities in consumption   95f

f
fee for service (FFS)   10, 22, 155f, 162f,
  170, 187
– capitation   171
– monopolistic power   155
preventive measures   159
fee-for-service insurance   54
FFS, *see* fee for service
financial risk   92ff
– actuarial risk   94
– conditions   93
– cost of drugs   93

– health status   92
– high-cost treatments   93
– insurance   94
– predictability and persistence   94
financing structures   51
– economic theory and evidence   51
– private   51
– public   51
formal risk adjustment   213
fund holding   11, 40
funding of health services
– asymmetric information   4
– mixed systems   5, 29ff, 168,
– private/social insurance   4f, 17ff, 94f, 126f, 216
– risk pooling   7
funding system   29

g
gains from insurance   21
gate-keepers   158
GDP (gross domestic product)   86
– per capita   86
general care   159
general practitioner (GP)   11, 31, 182
– diagnostic ability   159
– gate-keeping   31f, 37
– single player   5
generalized linear model (GLM)   200
Germany   177, 181, 193, 202, 207, 215ff
global risk assessment model   196
government funding of health care   28
– models   28
government insurance scheme (GIS)   129
group insurance   24, 27
– employment-related   27
group-based private and public systems   74

h
HCC, *see* hierarchical condition categories
health care demand   114
– model   116
– non-linear prices   114
health care financing   74
– co-payment systems   74
– group-based private and public systems   74
– parallel private and public systems   74

– sectoral-based private and public systems   74
health care financing system   71
– government funded   28
– system type   71
health care services   50, 77
– quality   223ff
health care spending   83
health inequalities   259, 264ff
health insurance   4, 151, 231, 265
– private insurance   4
– social insurance   4
health maintenance organization (HMO)   24, 34, 119, 161, 204, 210, 213
health outcome inequalities   257
health plan   183f, 187f, 191
health reimbursement accounts (HRAs)   131
health savings accounts (HSAs)   126, 131, 142
health utility index (HUI)   259f
health-based payment   178
hierarchical condition categories (HCC)   196, 212
high-cost conditions   192
high-risk consumers   184
HMO, *see* health maintenance organization
horizontal equity   30, 247
horizontal inequity index (HI)   248
hospital utilization   255
hospitalization   164
HSAs, *see* health saving accounts

i
imperfect information   156
income inequality   245, 259, 261, 265
income-outcome gradient   263
India   184
individual rationality constraints   45
induced demand   157
inequities in access   145, 264
– inter provincial differences   255
– to medical care   253
information asymmetry   7, 10, 22, 26
– patient provider   18
information manipulation   157
insurance   29, 45
– among competing plans   29
– consumer choice   18, 29
– non-linear contract   45

insurance coverage 60
– decrease 60
insurance protection 19
interactions 55
– private 55
– public 55

j
Japan 31
– user fees 31
job lock 27

k
Kassenärztliche Vereinigungen (KV)
  216
Kirby Commission 58f

l
labor insurance scheme (LIS) 129
limits to the public offering 77
limits to the under-provision of care 161

m
managed care option in US Medicare
  3, 8f, 23, 32, 34, 37, 54, 185, 213
managed-care plans 105
– consumer-directed 105
– deductible threshold 105
marginal reimbursement 165
market failure 28
– private insurance 28
Medicaid 120
Medicaid plans 37
medical ethics 161
medical malpractice 161
– litigation 162
medical necessity 89f
– pharmaceuticals 89
medical savings accounts (MSAs) 3, 8f,
  126
– choice and access 140
– efficiency 138
– equity 141
– expenditure control 135
– financing and system performance 133
– publicly financed 137
– Singapore and China 9, 126
Medicare 41, 120, 132, 185f, 191f, 210ff,
  223
– advantage 34
– system 49
Medigap plans 5

Medisave 128, 141
Medishield 128
mixed financing 77
mixed public/private system 56
mixed public/private financing 5
mixed payment system 165, 168, 170
mixed payments 171
monopolistic power 155
moral hazard 18, 21, 23, 30, 43, 126, 139,
  149, 200
mortality 261
MSA, *see* medical saving accounts
multi-attribute utility functions 259
multiple sclerosis 185

n
national forum on health 7
national health service (NHS), UK 1, 31
national population health survey 61
need for care 246
– standardization 248
needs-based payment 178
Netherlands 177, 181, 192f, 207f, 214,
  217
non-linear insurance 45
non-linear prices 114

o
OECD, *see* organisation for economic
  co-operation and development
OLS, *see* ordinary least squares
open enrolment 25
optimal insurance contract 153
optimal risk adjustment 182, 190ff, 237ff
optimal quality reporting 235
opting out 6, 33, 35
ordinary least squares (OLS) 198, 200
organisation for economic co-operation
  and development (OECD) 49, 82, 65, 73
– analysis 69
– Canada 82
– health database 68
– USA 82
outcome inequalities 245
outliers 198

p
parallel private and public systems 74
patient cost sharing 8, 22
– co-insurance 22
– deductibles 22
patient selection 163

patient turnover 170
patient-provider information asymmetry 18
pay for performance 181, 213, 229f, 241
perfect information 184
perfect risk adjustment 185
pharmacare 7
pharmaceutical coverage 7, 85
– capitaion 7
– drug budget 7
– third-party payment 7
pharmaceutical financing reform 85, 96
– access to care 96
– efficiency 96, 99
– equity 96
– expenditure control 96
– national strategy 96
– risk-reduction 96
pharmaceuticals 89, 91
– credence goods 91
– medical necessity 89
– prescription-only drug 89
pharmacy-based cost groups (PCGs) 215
physicians 89, 92
– agency role 39, 89
– altruism and medical ethics 157, 161, 165f
– decision on medical services 167f
– effort 165f
– funding methodology 209
– monitoring 161f
– prescription only drugs 89, 92
physician payment mechanism 149
– capitation 11
– demand/supply side 10, 154
– induced demand 10
– supplier information assymmetry 10
plan manipulation 225
point-of-service (POS) 204, 213
policy-making process 60
population-based models 178
POS, *see* point-of-service
PPOs, *see* preferred provider organizations
practice-based commissioning 11
predictive modelling 178
preferred provider organizations (PPOs) 119, 205, 213
premium 227f, 230, 237ff
prescription 108
– drug financing 7
preventive care decisions 106
– competitive insurance market 106
– moral hazard 106
– risk attitude 106
preventive measures 159
price control 31
principal inpatient diagnostic cost group (PIPDCG) 187, 211
private employer 231
private funded health system 52
private health care 50
– financing in Canada 49, 50, 65
private health insurance 54, 257
– Australia 54
– Canada 54
– promotion 54
private information 186
private insurance 33, 53, 246, 254
– as a supplement to 33, 254
– complementary to 33
– duplicate 33
private insurance markets 86
– voluntary private drug coverage 86
pro-rich inequity index 257
prospective payment systems 160, 180
providers 180
– different types 164
– preferred providers 24
public coverage 85
– co-payments 85
– cost-sharing 85
public drug programs 86
– deductibles 86
– drug subsidies 86
– pharmacare 86
public financing 73, 98
– co-payment structure 73
– group-based system 73
– personal income tax 98
– progressivity 98
– social insurance 98
public goods 18
public health spending 70, 72
– effects of private health financing 70, 72
public regulator, *see* regulator
public services 120
– US Medicaid 120
– US Medicare 120
publicly funded health care 52, 57
– supplemental 52
public-private finance 66
purchaser-provider split 12

q

quadriplegia 185
quality of services, *see* service quality
  192, 226ff, 241

r

RAND corporation 211
RAND experiment 118
– fee-for-service plans 118
– price effect 118
– randomized experiment 118
RAND HIE, *see also* RAND experiment
  139
rationing, *see also* waiting lists 2
referral decisions 158
regional health authorities (RHAs) 12,
  208
regulator 226f, 229, 231f
– private employer 231
retrospective 168
– payment system 168
RHA, *see* regional health authorities
risk adjustment 12, 41, 177, 224, 227, 237
– adverse selection 12
– conventional 178, 188, 217, 237
– cost minimizing 195
– in the UK system 41
– optimal 190f, 237ff
– purchaser-provider split 12
– serious chronic diseases 185
risk adjustment model 178, 197
– quality 179
– US claims-based 196
risk aversion 28
risk fragmentation 120
– prior claims 120
– prior utilization 120
risk pooling 4, 7, 17, 19f, 20, 42
– implicit 20
– through private insurance 20
risk selection 195
risk sharing 106, 211
– cross-subsidization 106
rostering 37
RxGroups 196
RxGroups-IPHCC 201
RxRisk 196

s

Scandinavia 193
sectoral-based private and public systems
  74

select patients 214ff, 163
selective contracting 193, 211
self-reported health 259
separating equilibrium 47, 206, 236
service distortion 211
severity adjustment 178
short form 36 (SF-36) 197
sickness funds 30, 214f
SID, *see* supplier induced demand
Singapore 127, 133, 135, 143
– Medisave 141
single-payer 26, 29f
– payer systems 5, 40
South Africa 127, 132f
specialists (SP) 182, 189
– risk adjustment 183
specialty care 159
spillover benefits 17
square-root model 199f
standardization for need 248
state-contingent payouts 42
supplier-induced demand (SID) 10, 23,
  30, 156, 158
– empirical evidence 158
– present in a publicly funded system 30
supply-side 10
– cost-sharing 149
– side incentives 9
switching costs 170
Switzerland 207

t

technological change 54
– efficient consumption level of medical
  services 151
– private sectors 54
– public sectors 54
– rate of technological change 54
two-part models 198ff

u

uncertainty in the treatment-outcome
  relationship 170
uncertainty of demand 38
underwriting 25
United Kingdom 181, 207
United States 125ff, 133ff, 140, 177, 217
units of health care 114
– deadweight loss 115
universal coverage 247, 254, 264, 266
universality 18
user fees 5, 29

v

voucher   9

w

waiting lists   1, 6, 31f, 40, 52
– in the UK   32
waiting lists for public patients   56

– supply of medical services   56
waiting times   53, 55
– private insurance   53
– reduction   55
wait-time guarantee   77
wealth-health gradient   263, 265
weighted least squares   200